Jones, Ellen.

Modernization,
value change, and
fertility in the
Soviet Union

$44.50

DATE			

MODERNIZATION, VALUE CHANGE AND FERTILITY IN THE SOVIET UNION

SOVIET AND EAST EUROPEAN STUDIES

Editorial Board

The National Association for Soviet and East European Studies exists for the purpose of promoting study and research on the social sciences as they relate to the Soviet Union and the countries of Eastern Europe. The Monograph Series is intended to promote the publication of works presenting substantial and original research in the economics, politics, sociology and modern history of the USSR and Eastern Europe.

SOVIET AND EAST EUROPEAN STUDIES

MODERNIZATION, VALUE CHANGE AND FERTILITY IN THE SOVIET UNION

ELLEN JONES

DEFENSE INTELLIGENCE AGENCY

FRED W. GRUPP

CENTRAL INTELLIGENCE AGENCY

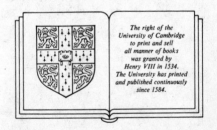

The right of the
University of Cambridge
to print and sell
all manner of books
was granted by
Henry VIII in 1534.
The University has printed
and published continuously
since 1584.

CAMBRIDGE UNIVERSITY PRESS

CAMBRIDGE

LONDON   NEW YORK   NEW ROCHELLE

MELBOURNE   SYDNEY

Published by the Press Syndicate of the University of Cambridge
The Pitt Building, Trumpington Street, Cambridge, CB2 1RP
32 East 57th Street, New York, NY 10022, USA
10 Stamford Road, Oakleigh, Melbourne 3166, Australia

First published 1987

Printed in Great Britain at the University Press, Cambridge

British Library cataloguing in publication data
Jones, Ellen
Modernization, value change and fertility
in the Soviet Union. – (Soviet and East
european studies)
1. Fertility, human – Soviet Union –
History – 19th century. 2. Fertility,
human – Soviet Union – History – 20th
century. 3. Soviet Union – Social conditions
I. Title. II. Grupp, Fred W. III. Series
304.6'32'0947   HB1017

Library of Congress cataloguing in publication data
Jones, Ellen.
Modernization, value change and fertility in
the Soviet Union.
(Soviet and East European studies)
1. Fertility, Human – Soviet Union. 2. Soviet Union –
Population. 3. Soviet Union – Social conditions –
1917– . 4. Soviet Union – Population policy.
I. Grupp, Fred W. II. Title. III. Series.
HB1017.J66 1987   304.6'32'0947   86-17633

ISBN 0 521 32034 8

Contents

Figures

ix

Tables

Introduction

This book is about social change in a multi-ethnic, socialist state. It explores the way in which the social, economic, and political transformations encompassed by modernization affect values and behaviors. Its analytical focus is the family and the system of norms and values governing sex roles and familial relations. This focus was chosen for several reasons. First, the way people feel about home and family – the relationships between husbands and wives and parents and children, authority patterns within the household, and approved gender roles – are among those values most resistant to change.[1] Examination of value change affecting the family thus provides a promising test of the extent to which structural or institutional modernization (that is, urbanization, industrialization, mass education) affects values. Second, change affecting the family is closely connected with fertility and represents a crucial component of social change in any national setting. Third, the family provides an intriguing focal point for the study of public policy. How effective is government at producing desired social change?

This monograph is part of a continuing effort to unravel the complex linkages between modernization, value change, demographic change, and public policy. It has two objectives. First, it explores the relationship between value change and fertility. Second, it examines the impact of public policies, both intended and unintended, on family values and fertility trends.

The geographical focus of our inquiry is the Soviet Union. There are several reasons why the USSR is a particularly instructive case. First, it is a multi-ethnic state, containing over 100 nationalities, with 28 per cent of the populace comprised of non-Slavic minorities. As in many other ethnically diverse societies, there are significant regional and ethnic differentials in the level and pace of modernization. The process of modernization began in the European north and west. Modernization came to the Islamic* southern tier regions and ethnic groups much later, and these areas still lag behind the European regions in urbanization and industrialization. There are also wide variations in family values, with traditional, patriarchal family systems more predominant in the Islamic south and east. These factors have affected the timing of demographic trends for different regions and ethnic groups. Analysis of the differential patterns of fertility change on minorities at different stages in the modernization process has much to tell us about the broader issue of demographic change in multi-ethnic societies. The Soviet experience, particularly as it relates to social change and continuity in the Muslim southern tier, is of particular relevance to the Muslim countries of the Third World.

Second, examination of the links between policy, social process, and fertility in the USSR provides a case study of these relationships within a socialist political system. Focus on the USSR should help to isolate the relationships that are specific to Soviet-style socialism and those that are shared with Western capitalist states. Although the focus is on the USSR, an effort will be made to place the Soviet findings within the broader context of analogous materials from both the Western world and developing nations. Another aspect of the Soviet political system of special relevance for an analysis of demographic and societal change is its high level of government involvement in areas of the economy and society that are not open to direct government intervention in many Western states. The Soviet experience in attempting to shape population resources and modify familial relations thus provides valuable insight into the potential for, and the potential limits of, public policy manipulation in these areas.

Perhaps the major reason for focusing on social and demographic processes in the Soviet Union is its importance in world affairs. Quite simply, what happens to familial relations and the associated population system in the USSR is important because of the sheer size of the Soviet population. The USSR is, after China and India, the third most populous country in the world. It is one of the two leading world

---

*Here and elsewhere the term "Islamic" and "Muslim" will be used in the Soviet context to refer to minorities whose religious affiliation before the Bolshevik revolution was Islam, and to the regions where these groups predominated. The percentage of religious believers among these groups is not known.

military powers; together, the Soviet Union and the United States, its chief military adversary, account for half of world spending on military capability. These factors mean that the economic, social, and political consequences of demographic change in the Soviet Union have an intrinsic importance in world affairs that goes well beyond the applicability of Soviet findings to other nations.

Among the most obvious consequences of Soviet fertility dynamics is the impact on the economic system. As will be detailed in Chapters 2 and 3, the timing and speed of the fertility transition in the USSR has differed by ethnic group. This is due in part to the fact that certain minorities occupied an earlier stage in socioeconomic development and in part to differing receptivity to the "modern" familial system associated with fertility decline. As a consequence, the Soviet Union's ethnic composition has not been stable and will continue to shift in favor of the fast-growing, less-modernized minorities for the next several decades. The large proportion of "Muslim" minorities, who have retained a relatively high fertility pattern at a time when the fertility decline has all but been completed in the European USSR, will serve to cushion the decline in young labor force entrants. The delay in the timing of the fertility transition in the Soviet southern tier also means a delay in the usual consequence of fertility decline (at least as experienced by Western Europe): a relatively stable or even declining population.

The social consequences of Soviet fertility dynamics are less obvious. As demonstrated below, fertility decline and the emergence of modern familial relations are interactive processes. The erosion of traditional patterns of family life and of traditional gender roles is closely associated with declines in expected and desired family size. Smaller families, in turn, produce greater opportunity for expansion of female roles outside the home, further accelerating the transition to modern familial roles. Both trends are well underway in the European portions of the USSR and have produced an increasingly common pattern of the "double burden:" women who combine the roles of wife and mother, *and* worker. While such a development has been welcomed by Soviet leaders (not surprisingly, given the ideological commitment to sexual equality and the practical need for high labor force participation rates), there are associated social problems as well. These include increasing pressure for family-oriented services and labor-saving consumer goods, a loosening of the strict social controls characteristic of the more traditional, patriarchal families, and a rise in juvenile delinquency. If the "European" familial pattern spreads to the Soviet southern tier, so too will the associated advantages and disadvantages; and the rate at which these changes take place will roughly parallel the timing of changes in family systems.

An analysis of Soviet fertility dynamics is also important for what it reveals of the probable political consequences of the USSR's population dynamics. The most obvious of these is the impact on military manpower. Because the USSR relies on a system of short-term draftees to procure much of its military personnel, the size of the draft-age pool (18 to 26-year-olds), is an important aspect of military capability. The delayed entry of the USSR's less developed minorities into the fertility transition means that supplies of draft-age males will be substantially larger than they would have been had a more uniform pattern of fertility decline taken place. It also means that the ethnic composition of the draft pool is undergoing a major shift in favor of non-Slavs. The duration and significance of both of these trends is, in turn, dependent on the timing of the fertility transition among the late-modernizing non-Slavic minorities.

Perhaps most important of the political consequences of Soviet fertility dynamics, and the associated societal processes, is the significance of such changes for Soviet political stability. Thanks to differential ethnic fertility, the proportion of non-Slavic minorities is projected to grow from 27.8 in 1979 to 33.4 in the year 2000; the less-modernized Muslims will increase from 16.4 per cent in 1979 to 22.9 per cent in the year 2000. Future Soviet cohesion depends, at least to some degree, on the leadership's ability to integrate its non-Slavic citizens into modern Soviet society. The Soviet strategy to deal with this challenge (a series of programs collectively referred to in the Soviet press as "nationality policy") involves measures to promote rapid modernization of the less developed minorities on the Soviet periphery. This strategy is based on the belief that removal of the socioeconomic differences between nationalities will strengthen Soviet cohesion by promoting a common value system.[2] Both history and social science theory provide some justification for this approach.[3] National or cultural identity has proven to be a more potent rallying point for political opposition when members of an ethnic group are united by common economic interests and common value systems. In other words, ethnic differences present a greater threat to political stability when ethnic, social, and economic cleavages coincide, when members of an ethnic group share similar life styles, occupations, and attitudes. There is a fair amount of evidence to suggest that the Soviets have been relatively successful in accelerating the modernization process among the more traditional minorities.[4]

Less clear is the extent to which these changes have in turn produced the intended convergence in value systems. Valid measurement of value change among these groups requires appropriate indicators of traditionality. The lack of appropriate statistical data precludes an assessment of more sensitive values, such as religious belief. As detailed in Chapter 1, change and continuity in the area of gender roles, familial relations, and fertility, however, provides an excellent alternative measure of traditionality. Because the way people feel about their home and family is much more resistant to change and much less responsive to direct policy manipulation than, for example, education, increased minority modernization may not lead to immediate shifts in family values. Change in the highly personal values relating to family life and sex roles can be expected, then, to lag well behind other kinds of value change. The degree to which Soviet nationality policy has produced an erosion of traditional family values among the late-modernizing groups provides an important measure of the breakdown of traditional value systems and the acceptance of values more compatible with modern Soviet society. Analysis of social change involving family formation among the less-modernized Soviet nationalities is thus an informative way to measure value convergence and the potential for political discord stemming from value conflict.

The book focuses first on the modernization–value change–fertility relationship and then on the impact of public policy on this process. Part 1 examines the effect of modernization and value change on fertility. Chapter 1 presents a theoretical framework for analysis of the fertility transition in the USSR. The specific hypotheses to be tested with Soviet data are then elaborated. Next, previous work by other scholars on the course of the demographic transition in Russia and the Soviet Union is surveyed. An extended discussion of data sources follows, noting data problems common in many studies that involve use of demographic and socioeconomic data as well as those specific to the Soviet case. In Chapters 2 and 3, data relevant to the hypotheses presented in the first chapter are analyzed. Chapter 2 explores patterns of social and demographic modernization since the turn of the century. Hypotheses involving linkages between modernization, the erosion of traditional family values, and natality are tested for the European areas of the USSR. In Chapter 3, the focus is on explaining current fertility differentials between nationality groups and regions.

Part 2 is a discussion of how public policy has affected family values and fertility in the USSR. Chapter 4 examines the impact of Soviet social programs. Its major focus is on the effects of socioeconomic development programs in the Soviet southern tier on the traditional family values once predominant in this region. Chapter 5 surveys the consequences of Soviet demographic policy. A predictive model of Soviet fertility trends, based on the empirical findings of the study, is presented in Chapter 6.

NOTES

1 J. B. Stephenson, "Is Everyone Going Modern? A Critique and a Suggestion for Measuring Modernization," *American Journal of Sociology*, No. 74, 1968, pp. 265–75.

2 CPSU nationality policy is summarized in "Natsionalnaya politika KPSS," in *Kratkiy slovar' spravochnik agitator i politinformatora* (Moscow: Politizdat, 1977), p. 50. See also "Rastsvet i sblizheniye sotsialisticheskikh natsiy," *ibid.*, pp. 73–75. A recent and authoritative analysis of goals, accomplishments, and problems of CPSU nationality policy is Brezhnev's 26th Party Congress speech. L. I. Brezhnev, "Report of the CPSU/CC to the 26th Communist Party Congress," in *Materialy XXV s"yezda KPSS* (Moscow: Politizdat, 1981), pp. 55–77.

3 The pluralist theory of reduction in the intensity of conflict through overlapping group membership and cross-cutting cleavages has a long standing. It received particular attention among political scientists in the 1950s with the reissuance of Georg Simmel, *Conflict and the Web of Group Affiliations*, translated by Kurt Wolff (The Free Press, 1955). The theory was further popularized by David B. Truman, *The Governmental Process* (Alfred A. Knopf, 1951); Lewis A. Coser, *The Functions of Social Conflict* (The Free Press, 1956); and Robert Kornhauser, *The Politics of Mass Society* (The Free Press, 1959).

For a theoretical discussion of the importance of cumulative ethnic and socioeconomic cleavages for the development of ethnic solidarity, see Michael Hechter, "Towards a Theory of Ethnic Change," *Politics and Society*, Vol. 2, No. 1, Fall 1971, pp. 21–45.

For more recent attempts to systematize the measurement of these concepts, see Douglas Rae and Michael Taylor, *The Analysis of Political*

Cleavages (Yale University Press, 1970); and Peter M. Blau and Joseph E. Schwartz, *Crosscutting Social Circles* (New York: Academic Press, 1984).

4 See also Ellen Jones and Fred Grupp, "Modernisation and Ethnic Equalisation in the USSR," *Soviet Studies*, Vol. 36, No. 2, April 1984, pp. 159–84; and Ellen Jones and Fred Grupp, "Modernization and Traditionality in a Multiethnic Society: The Soviet Case," *American Political Science Review*, Vol. 79, June 1985, pp. 474–90.

Part 1

The impact of modernization and value change on fertility

I

Social change and fertility transition

Political events in Russia have to a large degree shaped the pace and nature of socioeconomic change. Political revolution intervened in the early stages of industrialization. The political leadership that emerged victorious from the 1917 Bolshevik Revolution and subsequent Civil War espoused a series of social and economic transformations that radically altered how people lived their lives, earned their keep, related to their political leaders, and interrelated with each other. The rapid industrialization begun in the late 1920s and early 1930s, coupled with the ambitious social policies of the Stalinist leadership, were to leave a lasting imprint on the social fabric of the USSR. Some social change was the deliberate result of Party policy. Other change, however, was an unintended (though not always unwelcome) result of forced pace modernization. As in non-socialist settings, economic modernization in the USSR has been accompanied by a major transformation of familial relations and values. It has also been accompanied by demographic modernization: a long-term decline in fertility, albeit at different rates throughout the country.

In general terms, then, the USSR's socioeconomic-demographic experience conforms with that of many non-socialist states – social change has been accompanied by fertility transition. This portion of the book examines the interrelationships between modernization, value change, and fertility, utilizing fertility transition theory as it has been developed by demographers working in non-socialist settings. How applicable to the USSR are models of fertility transition developed from the socioeconomic-demographic experiences of non-socialist countries?

THEORIES OF FERTILITY TRANSITION

Social scientists examining fertility dynamics in many different national settings have noted several basic regularities in population patterns. In most premodern societies, both fertility and mortality are relatively high and fluctuating, producing relatively slow and irregular patterns of population growth. In most modern societies, by contrast, both fertility and mortality are relatively low, producing either moderate population increases or population stability.

To explain the process by which the patterns characteristic of modern society emerged, scholars developed a theory of demographic modernization, usually known as demographic transition; it laid major stress on macro-developmental variables, such as levels of socioeconomic development, to explain demographic change.[1] The theory, in simplified form, can be stated as follows: the immediate impact of modernization on premodern societies is to increase food supplies, improve nutrition and health, and thus lower mortality. The impact of modernization on natality lags; that is, natality remains at high levels while mortality is declining. This produces the rapid population growth rates characteristic of the earliest stages of the transition. Eventually, however, the socioeconomic changes encompassed by modernization undermine the economic and social underpinnings of large families and birth rates follow death rates in a declining pattern, eventually producing the configuration of low fertility and mortality, which result in the declining population growth rates characteristic of most modern societies.

The demographic transition theory also yields hypotheses specifying relationships between socioeconomic variables and natality. If modernization is presumed to be the engine propelling demographic change, then in a given society undergoing transition, those groups most affected by modernization (i.e., the educated, urbanized elite) can be expected to be the first to exhibit those factors associated with modernization (i.e., low mortality and fertility).

Both the pattern of change specified by the theory and the hypothesized relationships between variables have enjoyed a fair amount of empirical support.[2] The transition theory, however, has been considerably modified to account for empirical findings in conflict with the original theory.[3] For example, studies of the transition experience in Europe have shown that natality was relatively low in the pre-transition period. Moreover, the fertility decline in Europe did not begin in those areas most advanced in terms of socioeconomic development, as predicted by the theory. Early natality declines occurred in relatively rural and underdeveloped areas like Portugal, Spain, Hungary, and France, while in England and the Netherlands – two early industrializing countries – the natality decline began relatively late. Other studies have shown that pre-transition fertility levels, while relatively high, are not necessarily at or near the natural upper limits. The experience of developing countries seems to indicate that the immediate effect of modernization on fertility may be to produce an increase, rather than the steady, downward trend suggested by the theory as originally stated.

One series of revisions to demographic transition theory has been offered by economic theorists. Perhaps the best known among economic theories of fertility are those associated with Becker.[4] In Becker-type explanations, families make fertility decisions in the same way that they make decisions about whether or not to purchase a consumer durable. Fertility choices are thus viewed as arising from the interaction between preferences and income and price constraints. Subsequent modifications of the economic theory of fertility have introduced additional concepts.[5] One is that of a set of intervening variables: supply, demand, and regulation costs. According to this expanded model, modernization lowers the demand for children (by reducing their economic value), raises the potential supply (by increasing infant and child survival rates), and reduces the costs of fertility regulation (by increasing the effectiveness and availability of contraception). The major shortcoming of all of these theories is that the role of values in fertility dynamics was relegated to (at best) a secondary consideration.

Value change receives more attention in sociological studies of fertility transition, principally because sociologists place changed natality behavior within a larger process of social change. As such, the sociologist brings a tool kit to population studies that includes the major concepts of the discipline: attitudes and values, status, norms, and roles. Important, then, to the study of fertility transition is the complex of values and norms favoring the large family and attitudes and beliefs about the status of women, both in the home as wife and mother, and in public roles. In developing the modified theory of fertility transition that serves as the focus of this analysis of Soviet social and demographic modernization, we draw heavily on the concepts of social demography.[6]

An interesting variation of demographic transition theory – one that defies easy categorization as either economic or sociological – has been offered by John Caldwell, who argues that fertility decline may be traced to a change in the direction of intergenerational wealth flows.[7] In pre-transition societies, where familial production predominated and where families were structured hierarchically according to age and sex, the flow of wealth (which Caldwell defines as including both material and non-material benefits) was from the younger generation to the older generation. Once this arrangement changes (due, Caldwell maintains, to a number of complex economic and social factors), high fertility becomes uneconomical to the reproductive decision-makers and fertility decline begins.

Soviet demographers have adopted demographic transition theory to their own Marxist framework.[8] Much of the conceptual and methodological work in Soviet demography draws heavily from the writings of non-socialist demographers.[9] Not surprisingly, in incorporating these concepts into their own work, Soviet demographers stress the importance of productive relationships on demographic developments. The demographic revolution embodies the transition from the "traditional" to the "contemporary" type of population reproduction. The traditional type predominated in precapitalist, agrarian societies and in the early stages of capitalism. The level of economic development was low. Childbearing activity was not the result of rational choice by parents, but was governed by custom, tradition, and religious norms. The contemporary type of population reproduction is connected with economic development (the transition from an agrarian to an industrialized economy). The contemporary or "rational" type of fertility is characterized by widespread use of family planning methods and the emergence of reproductive decisionmaking by the couple themselves who decide if and when to have a child. In explaining the transition from the "traditional" to the "contemporary" type of natality, most Soviet demographers lay heavy stress on the importance of changes in mortality, but they also note the importance of sociological factors, especially the role of women. They have not, however, developed a comprehensive model of fertility decline that incorporates these assumptions into causal diagrams that yield explicit hypotheses about the relationships between socioeconomic and demographic variables. Indeed, one of the chief weaknesses of Soviet demography is the gap between theory and empirical research.

A modified fertility transition model

For this reason, although our geographic focus is the Soviet Union, in adopting a fertility transition model for our analysis of social change and natality, we have drawn primarily from the theoretical work of non-socialist demographers. Our model is based on the assumption, following the work of Allman and others, that different stages in demographic development are characterized by different sets of causal relationships.[10] Moreover, our model of fertility change applies only to the impact of modernization on those premodern societies that are characterized by patriarchal family systems. We have adopted the term "traditional patriarchal family values" (awkward though it may be) to avoid the implication that all premodern societies are necessarily patriarchal. Clearly, they are not. There is wide variation in premodern cultures and economic systems, and important differences in family values, the social position of women, and the distribution of authority.[11] In those premodern societies where women have "traditionally" enjoyed both economic independence and relatively high status, modernization may actually erode family autonomy. The impact of modernization on family values, then, depends on the type of value system that prevails in the premodern society. Therefore, we concentrate on one category of premodern society that has special relevance for the Soviet case – traditional patriarchal society.

The basic assumption undergirding the theory of fertility transition presented here is that modernized societies will have lower fertility than traditional patriarchal ones. Traditional patriarchal societies are generally characterized by a high degree of reliance on familial patterns of production. The family is not merely a social unit and a source of emotional comfort and security for its members, but an economic unit as well.[12] The family and local community are the major social arenas of everyday life and may be relatively independent of large political and economic units. The system of family values and gender roles generally is complimentary to the familial mode of production. Within such families, economic and social roles tend to be rather rigidly defined by age and sex. Hierarchical patterns of family authority, in which the young are required to defer to the old and the female to the male, are quite common. Women are traditionally assigned a subordinate status; and in some societies are secluded and segregated. They are often excluded from social, economic and political organizations or relegated to a marginal role in them.

In such societies, the traditional decisionmakers are the family patriarchs; and they place a high value on large families, for both economic and status reasons.[13] In an economic system where the family is the major unit of production, children are valued for both their productive activity within the household economy and for their potential as a source of old-age security to their families or insurance against future adversity.[14] Children are a particularly important economic asset among farmers, and especially among those whose landholdings are large enough to require large labor inputs. The highest natality in a 1974 study of rural southern Iran, for example, was found among farmers and among families with large landholdings.[15]

More importantly, perhaps, children and large families in traditional societies are also viewed as a source of respect and prestige, quite apart from their economic value. For example, in a 1974 study of a rural Eastern Nigerian clan, many of the sampled wives noted that, in their community, the power and influence of the household was dependent on the number of males in it.[16] Such perceptions reinforce preferences for large families. Caldwell, in his study of the Yoruba in Nigeria, found that most respondents placed a high value on building up a large network of relatives by reproduction and marriage, partly because these ties represent a source of security and potential aid during hard times and partly because they saw their own power and prestige as determined by the number of adult supporters.[17] Sons of peasant farmers who are successful in the city are seen by their fathers as an important source of status and pleasure.[18] These factors mean that males in patriarchal households, particularly the heads of household, place a high value on large families.

Women in patriarchal societies are also likely to favor large families. A large number of children may offer economic rewards, in the form of assistance in domestic tasks and security in old age. The maternal role is also associated with social rewards. Many cultures grant mothers, particularly those with sons, a higher status than childless women. Mothering also has vital (if less investigated) psychic rewards.[19] It is important to note, however, that many women in traditional cultures accept their maternal role and the high value on large families because they have no choice. Alternative roles

– i.e., through wage-earning occupations or community offices – are not open to them. Moreover, within the family and tightly-knit rural community, there are strong social controls promoting acceptances of the large-family norm and associated sanctions against those who deviate from it. A wife with few children is pressured by her immediate family, relatives, and community to have additional children. Women with few children frequently become the objects of pity or scorn. In some societies, childlessness may be justification for repudiation by the husband.[20] For economic, social, and psychological reasons, then, women in patriarchal societies are likely to favor large families.

Undergirding the familial and social relationships in patriarchal society are a network of beliefs, traditions, values and norms that operate to reinforce patriarchal behavior patterns and hence high fertility.[21] These supporting traditions and norms are necessary because members of the society are not equally advantaged by these relationships. Maintenance of the power of the family patriarch requires a subordinate status for women and children. This status, and the behavior associated with it, are often embodied in customs, traditions, and norms designed to reinforce patriarchal authority patterns. In some cases, these authority patterns are codified (and thereby reinforced) by the state in the form of legal codes that discriminate against women, especially with regard to marriage, divorce, and inheritance.[22]

In spite of the high value placed on large numbers of children during this period, natality may be only moderately high. Many studies of areas prior to the onset of the modern fertility transition have shown that natural fertility varies widely.[23] One factor in many non-contracepting societies that keeps natality below the theoretical maximum is poor health care. Nutritional deficiencies may delay the onset of menstruation or impair fecundity among fertile-age women. In some pre-modern societies, fertility is inhibited by fecundity-impairing disease; syphilitic infection, for example, is a common cause of sterility in Central Africa.[24] Prolonged breastfeeding also operates to keep fertility lower than the maximum.[25] In some societies, the natality-inhibiting effects of prolonged breastfeeding are accentuated by taboos on sexual activity for the duration of breastfeeding. Prolonged breastfeeding and postpartum sexual absti-nence operate to increase the interval between births and thus reduce natality. In some cultures, these practices are part of a conscious strategy to increase birth intervals. One study of rural women in North Yemen (one of the least-developed countries in the world) found that most women understood the connection between breast-feeding and delayed postpartum menses; and that many welcomed the longer intervals between birth associated with prolonged breast-feeding, because they felt it was healthier for both the mother and the baby. Similar findings have also been reported for rural Java.[26]

These considerations mean that traditional societies may exhibit a rather large range in natality levels depending on customs governing feeding and postpartum sexual abstinence, as well as overall morbidity. Reported levels of fertility, as detailed in the section on data sources that follows, will often be understated due to high levels of infant mortality and/or birth underregistration. Real fertility is assumed to vary from levels that are moderately high to very high. Within such societies, fertility differentials between various social, regional, and ethnic groups would be minimal, reflecting differing access to food supply, differences in adherence to customs affecting fertility (such as abstinence and breastfeeding), and differences in exposure to fecundity-impairing disease.

The onset of modernization sets in motion a process that eventually produces sustained fertility decline. The immediate impact of modernization, however, is on mortality and morbidity. Improved agricultural methods result in more stable food supplies. Improvements in health care technology and availability produce almost immediate declines in fecundity-impairing disease and fetal wastage, thus increasing natality. Modernization frequently leads to decline in observance of natality-inhibiting customs, such as prolonged breast-feeding and postpartum sexual abstinence. These trends may also lead to natality increases, as they have in Syria, Jordan, and Kenya.[27] These natality increases would likely to be more dramatic in societies that previously had strong customs of sexual abstinence after birth. A causal diagram embodying these relationships is provided in Figure 1.1.

In the early stages of the fertility transition, rather substantial fertility differentials between socioeconomic, ethnic, and regional groups may be expected, with those groups most affected by changes in health care trends and natality-inhibiting customs displaying early natality increases. For this reason, urban natality is likely to be higher than rural natality during this period; and natality is expected to vary directly with socioeconomic status. Indeed, some studies of

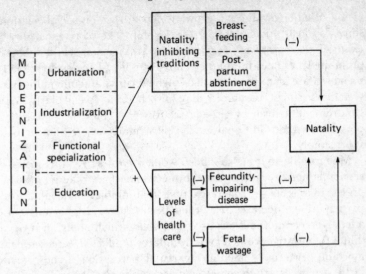

Figure 1.1 Causal diagram of the influences on natality at earliest stages of the fertility transition

fertility differentials in the earliest stages of fertility transition in developing countries have revealed precisely these patterns. Studies of rural Bangladesh, for example, reveal a positive correlation between indicators measuring socioeconomic status (education and landholding) and natality.[28] Analysis of rural Nigerian fertility differentials has shown that primary education tends to have a positive influence on fertility level.[29] A community study in rural Java found that middle-class women have higher fertility than lower-class women; this pattern was due mainly to longer breastfeeding and postpartum abstinence, more frequent marital disruptions, and a higher level of fecundity impairment among lower-class women.[30] Urban fertility rates in Pakistan are estimated to be slightly higher than rural rates.[31] These findings lend at least tentative support to the relationships hypothesized for the earliest stages of the fertility transition.

The value system underpinning traditional family relations and sex roles may take longer to change. Modernization, however, ultimately undercuts both the economic incentives supporting large families and the associated value system. Modernization involves an eventual shift away from a familial production system.[32] Specialization of labor produces a growing dependence on social relationships and institutions not based on kinship. The economic utility of children decreases (at least in those areas where child labor is prohibited), as does the status of large families. The development of social welfare institutions, such as social security and unemployment systems, reduces parental value on children (particularly male children) as a form of old-age security.[33] Urban life places new pressure on the traditional family, particularly where housing is in short supply.

Modern life-styles also affect women's roles. As the focus of economic activity moves outside the home, there may be growing pressures to relax sex role restrictions that inhibit female labor force participation. Increased use of females in the paid labor force also offers women alternative sources of status, which tends, in turn, to dilute the prestige women gain from large families. Decreased child mortality eventually modifies parental perception of how many births are necessary to achieve a given family size.[34]

These interrelated processes converge to erode the traditional family values that underpinned patriarchal society. It is this erosion of traditional values (*not* the modernization process, *per se*) that produces lowered family size and expectations, which in turn inhibit natality. Fertility decline can take one of several patterns. In many Asian countries where early and universal marriage was the primary component of high fertility, the first stage of fertility transition involved a delay in family formation, and hence significant fertility declines in the youngest age categories. An alternative pattern of demographic transition is the classic model of fertility decline in nineteenth-century Europe, where the major mechanism of declining fertility was the reduction of births in the middle and later years of the childbearing period.[35] The pace at which the fertility decline proceeds, particularly in this latter case, may be affected significantly by the availability, effectiveness, and public acceptance of family planning techniques. The theoretical relationships implied by these assumptions are depicted in Figure 1.2

The logic of the theory suggests that fertility differentials would continue in the intermediate stages of the fertility transition. Again, what is operating here is a tendency for some groups to be affected first by change, which only later diffuses to other parts of society. The relationships we are likely to observe in the early stages of the transition (i.e., a direct relationship between natality and status

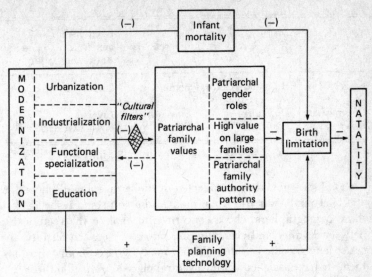

Figure 1.2 Causal diagram of the influences on natality at intermediate stages of the fertility transition

indicators) now reverse. In the intermediate stages, those groups most affected by the modernization process and the associated erosion of traditional family life styles and sex roles tend to exhibit the lowest fertility.

As the norms associated with smaller families and more flexible social roles for women spread throughout society, many of the relationships characteristic of the intermediate stages can be expected to become muted.[36] Once such norms have become fully accepted, fertility is expected to stabilize at relatively low levels and the wide fertility differentials will decline. Under those circumstances, urban/rural differences in fertility will be minimal. In the later stages of fertility transition, the relationships between social indicators and fertility may even reverse once more, with most women exhibiting relatively low levels of parity and higher-status women exhibiting marginally higher natality (Figure 1.3).

A word is needed here about how our fertility transition model differs from others. In elaborating the theory laid out here, we have drawn heavily on previous theoretical and empirical work. We make no claim of originality; we are merely clarifying existing transition theory to account for previous findings. However, because our focus

Stage	Fertility	Fertility differentials	Relationship between modernization and status and fertility
Early	High and possibly increasing	Some	Direct
Intermediate	Declining	Substantial	Inverse
Later	Low	Slight	Possibly direct

Figure 1.3 Stages in the fertility transition

is on values – how they are affected by modernization and how they affect fertility – our transition model differs in some respects from those demographers whose concern is to explore the relationship between fertility and economic indicators or between fertility and other demographic variables. Unlike many of the economic theorists, then, we have assigned values a central place in transition theory. In some cases, however, the difference is more one of terminology than substance. For example, we have drawn heavily on the work of Caldwell, despite the fact that his "wealth flows theory of fertility decline" might suggest a pre-occupation with economic indicators.[37] Caldwell's own findings, however, attest to the importance of non-economic factors, in particular to the importance of the nonmaterial benefits of high fertility, in the form of prestige, status, and honor. Caldwell's choice of terminology is unfortunate, because it obscures the significance he attaches to the noneconomic (political, social, and psychic) benefits of children that help maintain high fertility in patriarchal cultures. It makes more sense to us, particularly in light of our focus on the persistence and change in values, to speak of a patriarchal family value system that supports high fertility and to ask how, when, and under what conditions does that value system begin to break down.

Our model also differs from some of the other sociological theories of fertility decline in that it is intended to apply only to the impact of social change on societies where traditional patriarchal family values predominated in the premodern era. We adopted this approach because it seems reasonable to assume that modernization will affect different societies in different ways: and that fertility transition theory should recognize these differences. Moreover, our model explicitly incorporates stages of fertility transition and posits causal relationships between social and demographic variables that differ for the different stages. Finally, our model focuses on those linkages between modernization, value change, and natality that help explain fertility differentials between groups in one society at one point in time, rather than on explaining change over time.

Hypotheses linking modernization level, family values and fertility

The focus of this book is the relationship between modernization, values, and fertility at the intermediate stages of the fertility transition. The transition theory summarized above generated the following hypotheses concerning relationships between variables in the intermediate stages of the fertility transition:

Hypothesis 1. During the intermediate stages of fertility transition, the greater the level of modernization, the lower the fertility.

Hypothesis 2. During the intermediate stages of fertility transition, the greater the erosion of traditional familial relations and sex roles, the lower the fertility.

Each of the hypotheses will be tested empirically using the data described below.

Hypothesis 1 states that modernization has an inhibiting effect on natality. Demographic research in non-socialist countries provides some support for the hypothesized link between modernization measures and natality at the intermediate stages of the transition. For example, an examination of modern and traditional patterns of desired family size and contraceptive use in Kenya revealed a strong relationship between urban residence and modernity in demographic and contraceptive behavior; socioeconomic status was also positively related to demographic modernity.[38] Analogous findings are reported from Nigeria, where the highest level of demographic modernity (as measured by a series of questions tapping attitudes toward ideal family size and female roles) was associated with education (occupation), age, and size of residence.[39] Similarly, results of the Value of Children surveys reveal that in many countries the norms supporting high fertility are strongest in the countryside.[40] Data on twenty-two countries derived from the World Fertility Survey found urban residence associated with lower fertility (sometimes dramatically lower fertility).[41] Cross-national studies also provide some support for the modernization hypothesis. Cutright and Kelly, for example, found that the level of structural modernization is the most important influence on cross-national differences in fertility.[42]

Hypothesis 2 states that traditionality in family values has a direct impact on natality. The 1970 US National Fertility Survey found that traditonal role attitudes were associated with higher desired fertility among white respondents. Both Catholic and non-Catholic women who subscribed to more traditional positions concerning approval of working mothers and the appropriate distribution of roles by gender were more likely to want larger families.[43] Scanzoni found that several role dimensions tapping attitudes toward gender roles were good predictors of birth intentions for young blacks and non-Catholic whites.[44] Wrigley and Stokes, in their study of Atlanta high school girls, found that conceptions of the feminine role were strongly correlated with desired number of children.[45] Patricia Tobin's analyses of conjugal roles revealed a moderate correlation between traditionality in conjugal role definitions and value of children; this relationship was strongest among women with post-secondary education.[46] Susan de Vos' 1978 analysis of fertility among white, once-married women in the Detroit area revealed that women's orientations toward the wife and mother roles have a significant effect on fertility expectations.[47] Rosen and La Raia's study of the attitudes toward sex roles and family authority uncovered an inverse correlation between modernity in women and preferred and actual family size.[48] A similar link between sex-role values and natality was found in Taiwan; women who scored highly in family and gender role values had a lower preferred number of children and a lower number of live births.[49]

Note that, although the causal model (Figure 1.2) depicts an interactive relationship between "modernization" and "patriarchal familial relations," it is the latter that is assumed to operate directly on birth limitation. In other words, to the extent that modernization promotes fertility decline, it does so by promoting a change in values. This is an important distinction because one can conceive of scenarios where value change is largely independent of modernization (through deliberate socialization efforts, for example) and other scenarios where modernization does not produce much value change (perhaps, because of strong cultural resistance to such change). Therefore, we should expect a higher correlation between variables measuring erosion of traditional familial relations and fertility indicators than between modernization variables and fertility. Moreover, given the assumed lag between modernization and value change, and between the latter and natality, we should be able to observe a lag in our own data.

Note also that the focus of our inquiry is natality, not marital fertility. Our interest is in explaining the influence of socioeconomic factors on natality. One mechanism for influencing fertility is marital pattern. Aside from a severe imbalance of the sexes, the primary determinant of marital patterns is the social value system. Socially-defined standards as to what constitutes the appropriate age for marriage, interact with economic considerations (e.g., availability of land) to influence the average age of marriage and the degree to which marriage is a virtually universal state among fertile-age women. Societies may achieve relatively low fertility through social patterns that encourage relatively late marriage. Focusing exclusively on natality among married women, then, would lead us to overlook cases in which fertility decline is achieved through marital patterns. It would also lead us to overlook or underestimate the effects on fertility of factors that operate primarily through age at marriage. This point is documented by data from the twenty-two country World Fertility Survey. Those data demonstrate that education acts to inhibit fertility largely through age at first marriage. Thus, surveys that rely on married women alone will seriously underestimate the impact of schooling on fertility.[50]

Our model of fertility transition, then, assumes that values influencing marital patterns are part and parcel of a larger configuration of attitudes that determine whether and to what degree married couples practice family planning. Because we are interested in the interaction between social norms affecting the family and natality, our investigation extends to all areas of the family values/fertility relationship, including values relating to marriage patterns.

Two factors have been neglected in our discussion thus far. One is the relationship between socioeconomic development and patriarchal family values. The model outlined above indicates a link between modernization and the erosion of patriarchal gender roles and family authority patterns:

Hypothesis 3. The greater the level of modernization, the greater the erosion of patriarchal family values.

However, the "cultural filter" depicted in Figure 1.2 suggests that this relationship is mediated by cultural heritage. We assume that most societies will resist social change that threatens personal aspects of life-style. Changes involving family life and gender roles are among those most likely to generate resistance. It is also likely that differences in cultural heritage will produce differing levels of resistance to such changes. So, while almost every society exposed to socioeconomic development can expect to experience some erosion of patriarchal familial patterns, the level and nature of that process varies, depending on the importance that different cultures ascribe to traditional family patterns and sex roles. In some cultures, maintenance of traditional gender roles may be seen as absolutely critical to the maintenance of the culture itself. Such cultures are apt to be much more resistant to any erosion of traditional values affecting the home and the division of authority within it. There is, in fact, some empirical support for this assumption. For example, Youssef's analysis of Latin American and Middle Eastern nations at similar levels of socioeconomic development has revealed different levels of sex role stereotyping, with the traditional values opposing female participation in the non-agricultural labor force much more persistent in Muslim societies of the Middle East.[51] Similar factors may indeed be operating in the Muslim areas of the Soviet Union, acting to insulate at least some aspects of the traditional familial patterns of Muslim minorities from the expected inroads of modernization and to preserve large families and high natality. We will have an opportunity to test this hypothesis, using data drawn from the Soviet Union.

The implications of the cultural factor for patterns of natality are potentially of major importance. Demographic studies in a variety of cultures have demonstrated that the statistical relationship between socioeconomic development and the timing of the fertility transition is not nearly as strong as the original demographic transition theory would have led us to expect. In other words, measures of modernization at the start of the fertility transition vary widely.[52] A possible explanation for these findings is suggested by the theory of fertility transition presented here. If, as we suggest, the strongest correlation is between natality and erosion of traditional family patterns (rather than between measures of modernization and natality), then the real key to natality dynamics is not the modernization process itself, but the erosion of family values. Because cultural heritage may act as a filter, facilitating acceptance of new family life styles and gender roles in some cases and inhibiting it in others, the best predictors of natality may in fact be those measures which come closest to capturing directly the breakdown of patriarchal sex roles and authority patterns.

A second factor (which has not been incorporated in the causal diagram, but which will bulk very large in our analysis) is public policy. Government policy can be directed at any portion of the causal relationships depicted in Figure 1.2. Government can, for example, undertake programs designed to speed up or inhibit the changes associated with modernization: urbanization, industrialization, specialization of labor, and so on. In some cases, the state can act as a champion of the traditional patriarchal family, as it has in Khomeini's Iran, for example, inhibiting female labor-force participation through legal actions. In other cases, the state can adopt programs designed explicitly to promote more egalitarian attitudes toward sex roles, as it has in the USSR. Government policy can promote or constrain availability of effective birth limitation measures. All of these activities will have at least a marginal impact on the operation of the process sketched in Figure 1.2.

It is, however, impossible to generate reasonable assumptions governing the relationship between natality and policy. Some governments, faced with the dramatic natality and population increase associated with the immediate impact of modernization, have instituted vigorous anti-natalist programs. Others have not. Similarly, governments react differently to the slowdown in population growth associated with the later stages of fertility decline. For example, faced with what appeared then to be an imminent prospect of population stability, some European governments in the 1930s began exploring ways to stimulate the birth rate through a variety of pronatalist proposals. Many West European governments are now faced with a revived possibility of population stability or even decline; but the response now is very different and most governments appear unlikely to undertake the radical pronatalist measures seriously considered in the 1930s. In part, this response is due to changing perceptions about the desirability of unchecked population growth produced by the tremendous upsurge in world population in the 1960s and 1970s. In other words, the perception of policymakers of the desirability or undesirability of various population trends differs from country to country and over time within one country. Moreover, government ability, as well as willingness, to intervene directly in demographic trends, also differs from society to society. Finally, public policy can have very different effects than those

intended. Policies focused, for example, on child labor have unintended, but significant, implications for family limitation. These
considerations mean that an examination of the impact of public
policy on the causal relationships sketched in Figure 1.2 must figure
in the policy goals and levers specific to the time and place under
consideration.

The data analyses that follow in Chapters 2 and 3 are directed only
at testing the relationships hypothesized for the intermediate stages
of the fertility transition. Our decision to focus on the intermediate
stages of the transition was based partly on the particular pattern of
fertility change suggested by the Soviet data and partly by data
limitations that preclude fuller testing of the relationships posited in
either the early or later stages of the transition. It is to this latter
consideration – the strengths and weaknesses of the data base – that
we now turn.

TESTING THE THEORY IN THE SOVIET CASE

In order to test the hypotheses described above, the concepts had to
be defined and operationalized. This section addresses the methods
used to develop quantitative indicators for both the dependent and
independent variables. The major difficulty in analyzing Soviet
fertility is that of measuring it. In our own search for valid measures
of Soviet natality, we have drawn heavily on the experience of a
research team headed by Ansley Coale. Their book, *Human Fertility in
Russia Since the Nineteenth Century*, was the sixth in a series of country
studies produced by the European Fertility Project at Princeton's
Office of Population Research.[53] To analyze demographic trends in
Russia since the nineteenth century, the Coale team applied a series
of demographic measures based on the Hutterite fertility schedule.
We were able to adapt the Coale methodology (or, in some cases, a
modification of it) to calculate our own fertility measures. Specifically, we relied heavily on the index of total fertility, one of the
measures used by Coale for the Princeton project, as one of our
measures of natality.

Despite this similarity, our analysis differs in several key ways from
that of the Coale team. First, our primary concern was not description of demographic trends; something the Coale team has already
accomplished admirably, but rather the analysis of social change and
the exploration of the relationship between that social change and

fertility. In short, we are trying to take the Coale analysis one step forward by placing the demographic developments in a social framework.

Our analysis also differs from the Princeton study in its focus on fertility, rather than marital fertility – the major fertility indicator in the Coale research. In part, our rejection of marital fertility is due to our interest, noted above, in examining the influence of socioeconomic factors, including values that affect marital patterns, on natality. There is also an important data constraint involved: the Soviets do not publish marital fertility rates on a routine basis. Computation of the index of marital fertility requires, in addition to birth data, two other pieces of information: female marital rates by age group and non-marital fertility. Although the Soviets have published female marital rates by age group for 1959 and 1970 with separate breakdowns by nationality and by republic, the proportion of women married by age was not supplied for oblast-level units in either census. Moreover, there are no consistent series of data on non-marital fertility after 1913 for any unit of analysis. The Coale team devised a method for estimating the missing data for oblast level units in 1959 and 1970. Their estimates of oblast marital fertility for 1959 and 1970 rest on two assumptions: first, that oblast marital fertility rates can be estimated indirectly from republic rates and, second, that all reported births are legitimate. The first assumption, for reasons detailed in Appendix 2, is of questionable validity. The second assumption is fallacious. Fragmentary data on non-marital fertility (surveyed in Appendix 2) indicate that illegitimacy in some regions is significant, and that the level varies from region to region, as well as over time. Thus, the assumption that non-marital fertility is negligible introduces serious error into the Coale team's marital fertility estimates – a point earlier noted by David Heer.[54] For these reasons, we decided not to employ these estimates in our own analysis of the relationship between social change and natality.

We have also rejected – again for technical reasons – the correction techniques used by the Coale team to adjust the reported fertility data for the Soviet southern tier republics. Coale, *et al.*, devised the correction procedures as a way of adjusting for serious birth underregistration in those republics. This correction process, however, raises a host of unpleasant problems, which are detailed at some length in Appendix 1. Put briefly, virtually all methods to correct birth data for underregistration involve some form of reverse survival of 0–4-year-olds or 0–10-year-olds from census enumeration. This procedure, in turn, requires data on either child mortality or (in the case of procedures that use model life tables) expectation of life at birth; in neither case are reliable figures available by republic or oblast. In fact, the registration problems that result in birth underreporting have an even more detrimental impact on infant and child mortality records! For these reasons, we have chosen to use neither the Coale team's correction procedure nor the pre-1970 fertility measures that were based on it.

Our own analysis rests on two major types of data: a series of data sets derived from Soviet census material and other statistical sources, and published results of surveys conducted by Soviet researchers. The two types of data supplement one another. The data sets provide an opportunity to test hypothesized relationships and interactions between variables that Soviet researchers have been unable or unwilling to perform. The survey findings, which detail the responses of individuals, provide support that our aggregate findings were not marred by the ecological fallacy.

For this analysis, we constructed five separate data sets: one covering the 50 gubernias of European Russia in 1897 and four providing coverage of the 1959–80 time period. These latter data sets include data for both regions and nationalities. One covers 45 nationalities, another the 15 republics, a third the 15 republics provided separately for urban and rural components (i.e., 30 cases), and a fourth, 194 oblast-level units. Another body of data used in this analysis involved a series of 1959 and 1979 census tables providing the average number of children with separate tabulations for mother's education, residence, occupation, and social class. Specific steps used to adjust the available data are detailed in the appendix.

The major focus of this analysis was the relationship between natality and modernization/value change. Therefore, each data set involves material of two different types: variables measuring fertility and variables capturing various aspects of modernization and value change. Both types of variables raise measurement issues: some common to most studies that use data of this nature and some unique to the Soviet case. Because data limitations effectively closed off certain lines of research and opened others, the strengths and weaknesses of the data base are explored here at some length.

The dependent variable: natality

In examining the modernization/value–change/natality nexus, we have made use of multiple measures of natality:

    Crude birth rate (CBR)
    Number of children ever born
    General fertility rate (GFR)
    Age-specific fertility rates
    Total fertility rate (TFR)
    Child-to-woman ratio (CWR)
    Index of total fertility (If)
    Expected number of children
    Ideal number of children
    Desired number of children

These natality measures rely on three very different types of data collection systems: annual birth registry, census enumeration, and sample surveys. Each measure has strengths and weaknesses, some associated with the measure itself; others with the availability of data in the Soviet case.

Perhaps the most readily available and frequently used measure of natality is the *crude birth rate* (CBR), the number of births per 1,000 population. In the USSR, crude birth rates are computed from the annual birth registry; and their validity rests on the comprehensiveness of the registry. As an index of fertility, CBR suffers from a major weakness; it is greatly affected by the age structure of the population. For example, the CBR for a population with a stable level of fertility may increase if the proportion of fertile-age women (15 to 49-year-olds) increases. Nonetheless, CBR provides a relatively good indicator of fertility in a given population.[55] Moreover, CBR data is often the only available fertility indicator for many populations. In the Soviet case, CBR data is available on an annual basis for the 15 republics since at least 1950, and for selected dates for most of the 194 smaller (oblast-level) geographical units.

Another fertility indicator used in this study is the *number of children ever born*. The major weakness of this measure is that it, like CBR, is greatly affected by the age structure of the population. High-natality groups with a large proportion of women just entering the child-bearing years are likely to have a lower number of children ever born than a group with identical natality but a much larger proportion of women at later stages of their childbearing years. For this reason, these data are more useful when presented by cohort; that is, when separate data are provided for women born or married in the same year, or when the data are standardized by length of marriage. There are two major sources of data on number of children ever born: census data and data from Soviet surveys, which are usually regional in scope.

General fertility rates (GFR) – births per 1,000 women aged 15 to 49 – are another measure of natality. Like crude birth rates, general fertility rates are based on the annual birth registry. However, general fertility rates provide a more accurate picture of trends in real natality, because births are standardized to women of reproductive age. In the USSR, general fertility rates have been published by republic on an annual basis since about the mid-1960s. However, except for fragmentary data in the demographic and medical press, GFRs have not been published by oblast. However, estimates of general fertility rate by oblast can be estimated using age structure data from the Soviet census.

The GFR, however, is not wholly free from the effects of differing age structure. The key fertile ages, in most societies, are the twenties and early thirties. This means that, given stable reproductive behavior, an increase or decrease in the general fertility rate can occur due solely to changes in the proportion of women in the most active childbearing ages. Significant decreases in general fertility rates can occur with no change in reproductive behavior due to declines in the proportion of women in the key childbearing years. Similarly, a stable general fertility rate can mask important changes in actual natality behavior if the proportion of women in the most fertile ages increases while their family size preferences are declining. These problems also arise when trying to compare natality between two groups with different age structures.

To minimize this problem, demographers frequently turn to *age-specific fertility rates*, the number of births during the year to women of a given age per 1,000 women of that age. Age-specific fertility rates allow comparison between groups with different age structures, or between a single group or region at two or more points in time. Analysis of age-specific fertility rates is of particular importance for groups just entering the transition to lower fertility, since family limitation often begins among women in the latter stages of their childbearing period. Sharp declines in fertility among women over age thirty-five, then, may signal the beginning of long-term fertility decline.[56] Age-specific fertility rates are available by republic on an annual basis since the mid-1960s.

Age-specific fertility rates are also used to compute *total fertility rates* (TFR), which is a summary measure of period fertility allowing for age structure. The total fertility rate is computed by summing age-specific fertility rates, allowing for the period of exposure to childbearing. This measure provides the number of births a woman would have over the course of her reproductive life, if she bore children in a pattern characteristic of each age group in a specific calendar year. The chief advantage of this measure is that it avoids the effects of changing age structure. The data needed to compute TFR are available by republic on an annual basis since the mid-1960s.

Another measure of fertility used in this analysis is the *child-to-woman ratio* (CWR) – the ratio of children to women of childbearing ages. The data needed to construct the CWR consists of age and sex-specific census enumerations for each population. The major shortcoming of CWR as a measure of fertility is that the ratio is based not on births *per se*, but on survivors of previous births. The indicator is therefore affected by infant and child mortality. Increases in CWR for a given population may reflect variations in mortality rather than fertility. Thus far, we have found no satisfactory method to adjust the child-to-woman ratios for differential infant and child mortality. The primary advantage of this indicator is its availability. In the Soviet case, census data can be used to compute CWR for 1959 and 1970 for republics, oblasts, and ethnic groups. CWR is thus one of the few available measures of fertility for the nationality group – a major focus of interest to our inquiry.

Another major shortcoming of CWR as applied to ethnic data is the problem of children and mothers registered under separate nationalities. This is particularly problematical where rates of inter-marriage are high. For example, there is good fragmentary evidence that the children of some minority-Russian intermarriages adopt Russian as an official nationality. To the degree this occurs sys-tematically throughout the USSR, child-to-woman ratios of the affected minority will be systematically understated. It was necessary to purge our fertility data of those nationalities where this factor would bias the data. In making this selection, we considered both intermarriage rates and linguistic assimilation (the proportion declaring another language to be their "native" tongue). The specific methods and standards used in making this determination are detailed in the appendix. This process led us to delete six nationalities from our original nationality data set of forty-five nationalities, when analyzing fertility behavior. To minimize the problem of differential infant and child mortality, we restricted our analysis to 1970 natality data. (This, of course, means that we are unable to do trend analysis using fertility ratios derived from earlier censuses.)

Another measure of fertility used in this study is the *index of total fertility* (If), developed by Ansley Coale. The If is a ratio between reported number of births in a given population and the number of births that would have occurred had this population of women experienced a maximum rate of childbearing, defined here as the rate of childbearing of Hutterite women. The hypothetical maximum number of births for a given population varies considerably with the age distribution of the population. A population with a large proportion of women in their twenties (a period of relatively high fertility) will have a much larger hypothetical maximum number of births than one with a large proportion of women in the low-fertility forties. Thus, the index of overall fertility, in effect, adjusts for age structure and is a more precise measure of "real" natality levels than the measures discussed above.

Computation of If requires data on births (from the birth registry), plus data on the number of women aged 15 through 49, by five-year age groups. These data were available (or could be estimated directly from published materials) for both republics and oblasts. For the 1897 period (discussed in Chapter 2), we were able to make use of the indexes of overall fertility by oblast calculated by Coale, Anderson, and Harm. The Coale team also produced If estimates for the contemporary period, the period from 1959 to the present. However, we opted to compute independent estimates for this index for both European and non-European oblasts and republics. The main reason for the independent calculations is that the Coale team's focus of attention was European Russia. They did not provide indexes of overall fertility for the non-European oblasts. Because one of our primary interests was non-European fertility, it was necessary to compute indexes for the non-European oblasts for 1970. Since our calculations are based on a slightly different series of computations, incorporating what we believe to be a more precise methodology, our 1959 and 1970 oblast estimates of the index of overall fertility vary slightly from those used by the Coale team. In the interests of consistency, therefore, we have used our own independently-generated estimates for both European and non-European areas.

One of the disadvantages of the index of total fertility is that it requires birth data. Since birth data are not available by ethnic group, we developed a variation on If, an index of fertility computed from children under age ten, in order to produce If estimates for Soviet nationality groups. We used the same strategy to compute If estimates (based on children under ten) for the republic, republic urban/rural and oblast data sets. These estimates, of course, share the problems of the CWR, since they are both based on survivors, not on births. Our estimates have not been adjusted to account for this defect, since there are no reliable series of regional infant and child mortality data that would allow us to make this judgement. Another series of If estimates were computed using a similar estimating method but based on data from the 1979 Soviet census on the number of children ever born. These estimates are available by republic.

The final measures of fertility used in this analysis were *expected*, *ideal*, and *desired family size* as reported in Soviet sample surveys. Most such surveys are reported in the demographic and medical press. They ask large samples of married women how many children they expected to have altogether (expected family size), how many they considered "ideal" (ideal family size), how many they desired (desired family size), and how many they actually had had at the time of the survey. Several dozen such studies have been conducted since 1974.[57] Most are regional in scope, but three, sponsored by the Demographic Section of the Central Statistical Administration's Scientific Research Institute, were national in coverage. The first of these, conducted in 1969, was limited to workers and employees. The second and third, conducted in 1972 and 1978 respectively, cover all three "social groups:" workers, employees, and *kolkhozniks*.

All such surveys share the weaknesses of similar studies conducted in the West. For example, the Soviet data make clear that, in the USSR as in other countries, a woman's notion of the "desired" family size varies throughout her lifetime, as well as her idea of how many children she expects to her personally. One study that surveyed newly-married women and then resurveyed them four years later noted a significant decline in the desired number of children.[58] The results of such a survey cannot, therefore, be used to predict total completed fertility. Family size expectations are also modified by experience. A woman may begin married life "expecting" to have six children; by the time she is fifty she has only three. Most respondents in that situation report an "expected" family size of three; they may still want more children but common sense suggests that this is not a realistic expectation. So, comparing family size expectations of women in different stages of reproductive life is not valid. This is particularly true for women whose reproductive lives have been interrupted by catastrophic events like World War II.

Moreover, most such surveys select out large segments of women that cumulatively may have a significant impact on natality: unmarried women, women who have divorced or separated, and women married more than once. A research design that selects only married women has a particularly strong effect on the results concerning younger women. The 1972 Soviet survey, for example, included married women 18 to 59; single women in their late teens and early twenties were excluded – a significant group since only 19 per cent of the 18–19-year-old women and 56 per cent of the 20–24-year-old women were married.[59] Because women who marry early have a substantially higher pattern of natality, the exclusion of single women naturally distorts the findings. These distortions are magnified in Soviet surveys that are limited to specific categories of women. For example, one survey of high-parity women in Tashkent, the capital of Islamic Uzbekistan, examined family size desires of women who had four or more children.[60] This research design has an especially problematic effect on findings related to younger women, because the vast majority of women under 25 do not yet have four children and are therefore excluded from the sample.

Another weakness of family size desires, ideals and expectations as a measure of fertility is that some respondents, believing that their family size is determined by God or fate, are unable or unwilling to give a numerical response. In one 1971 Nigerian study, for example, almost half of the rural women, when asked about their family size desires, replied that it was up to God.[61] Findings from Soviet surveys indicate that nonnumerical answers are most prevalent among older, more traditional, women. For example, a 1976–77 study of family size ideals among married women in rural Uzbekistan found that only 22 per cent of the oldest women (born 1895–99) gave a numerical answer to the question on the ideal number of children in the family; 44.5 per cent said, "the more, the better"; and 33.5 per cent gave other answers (e.g., "however many God gives"). Among the youngest women surveyed (born 1955–59), only seven per cent responded, "the more, the better" and only an additional six per cent gave other nonumerical answers.[62] Similar results were found in an Azeri study; 36 per cent of the older women were unable to give a numerical answer to questions on ideal and desired family size, compared to only 20 per cent of the women in their twenties.[63] This means that the average family size desires/ideals/expectations are likely to be artificially depressed for older, more traditional women, since these are the women apt to have and value the largest families, yet their nonumerical responses cannot be calculated into the average reported by researchers. Older women are also prone to forgetting or misstating number of births.[64]

Soviet researchers have also found that results on expected family size differ, depending on how the question is asked. Most of the surveys simply ask: "How many children do you expect to have altogether?" Other surveys ask the woman how many children she has had, then how many more children she expects to have in the future, summing up the two answers to yield expected family size. One group of researchers discovered that expected family size obtained using the former method was smaller than that obtained using the two-question approach, because some women misinterpreted the question.[65] It should also be noted that these surveys do not specifically ask for number of births; and some women are apt to interpret the questions in terms of surviving children, rather than children ever born.

Despite all of these problems, the material from attitudinal surveys provides a valuable supplement to the fertility measures derived from census enumerations and birth registries.[66] Data on ideal and expected number of children are available for selected years for republics, for the urban and rural components of republics, and for ethnic groups.

The inherent strengths and weaknesses of each of the fertility measures were summarized above. The reliability and validity of each measure is also affected by the collection procedures that produce the basic data from which each of the fertility indicators is computed. The two major sources of data are the annual birth registry (based on the Soviet vital registration system) and the census enumeration. The reliability of these two data collection systems, which significantly affects the quality of the data base, is discussed below.

The Soviet vital registration system

The chief disadvantage of measures based on birth registration (including crude birth rate, general fertility rate, age-specific fertility rate, total fertility rate, and index of total fertility) is that all are dependent on birth registration procedures. Incomplete birth registration is a problem in many countries.[67] In the Soviet Union, the problem is exacerbated by the sheer size and diversity of the country, producing a pattern of differential levels of registration. Prior to the Bolshevik Revolution in 1917, records of births and deaths were based primarily on church records of baptisms and funerals. After the Revolution, this function, along with the existing registration books themselves, was transferred from the church to local government agencies.[68] Soviet sources claim that by 1923 a network of offices for civil registration, *Zapis Akkov Grazhdanskogo Sostoyaniya* (Record of Acts of Civil Status) (ZAGS) had been set up in most areas, with the exception of the Central Asian republics and other outlying areas. At first, registry officials were required to fill out special statistical cards for each birth and death; but this procedure proved burdensome (many of the cards were lost or simply never filled out), and, starting in 1926, the Soviets adopted a system of making two identical copies of civil status forms, one of which was forwarded to higher level registries for statistical processing.

Registration was still quite incomplete, however, in areas where there was no pre-revolutionary system of registration. For example, when statistical workers in the former area of Turkestan (now the republics of Uzbekistan, Tadzhikistan, Kirgizia, and Turkmenistan) tried to collect data on vital events in the early 1920s, they found that the existing registration books contained information on the European populace only. One area in Uzbekistan with a population of 130,000 recorded only five births in the first half of 1924! In 1927, civilian registry offices were set up in every city in the republic, with registration points in the rural governments; but underregistration continued. The result was an artificially low birth and death rate; eight *okrugs* in the republic reported an average birth rate of only 3.8 in 1927. To correct the incomplete reporting, census takers for the 1926 census also collected information about births and deaths; but methodological defects invalidated the results.[69] The problems facing statistical officials in Uzbekistan were probably symptomatic of the large problem of achieving an accurate population count in the southern tier areas. Soviet statistical sources for 1926 acknowledged incomplete registration for these areas, noting that the nonregistered populace constituted an estimated 14 per cent of the overall Soviet population.[70]

Efforts continued in the 1930s to improve the registration system. Registration offices were gradually set up in the rural areas of Central Asia; by 1934, the rural registry system in those areas was more or less complete. In 1935, nationwide standards for reporting births and deaths were established. On the eve of World War II, registration was fairly complete in the RSFSR, Ukraine, Belorussia, and the Baltic states. Incomplete registration remained a problem in some areas of Central Asia and the Caucasus.[71] The war disrupted statistical accounting work; and registry officials in newly-liberated areas had, in effect, to set up operations all over again. Beginning in 1948, Soviet officials began a series of systematic checks on birth and death records. The checks make use of birth and death records from individual farms, rural governments, and compilations maintained by medical institutions. This system probably resulted in at least marginal improvements in registration.

The current registration system represents several decades of effort to improve what the Soviet officials admit was a faulty system.[72] It involves three separate government bureaucracies: the hierarchy of registration (ZAGS) offices legally subordinate to the local government; the statistical hierarchy; and the health care hierarchy. The primary purpose of the registry is not to compile a statistical record for demographic purposes, but to establish legal certification for Soviet citizens.[73] For example, the receipt of pension benefits is contingent upon achieving a certain age; premilitary draft procedures require systematic information about the ages of young males. The legal benefits and responsibilities of parenthood depend upon proper registration of the child's birth. This basic mission of the civilian registry is reflected in the fact that the ZAGS (registration offices), although legally subordinate to the local government at each level, come under the general guidance of the Ministry of Justice, not the Central Statistical Administration.[74]

The current system still depends primarily on citizen initiative for the registration of vital events.[75] Parents (or, in the absence of a parent, a relative, friend, neighbor, or medical official) of newborn infants are required to apply for registration of the birth of their child – i.e., declare the birth. The time deadline for registration varies from republic to republic. In the Ukraine, Latvia, Armenia, Azerbaydzhan, Tadzhikistan, and Lithuania, parents have three months to register the birth; in the other republics, a one-month deadline is in effect.[76] Parents in rural areas go to the rural or village executive committee offices (rural/village *ispolkom*); at this level, there is no specialized registry office and the job of maintaining the registry usually falls to the executive committee secretary. In cities parents or relatives will report to a special registry bureau, subordinate to the rayon or city executive committee.[77] These same offices accept death registrations as well, although the time deadlines are generally much shorter. Parents declaring a birth must present documents testifying to their identity, as well as documents certifying that the birth itself took place. These latter documents are provided by the medical institution; in cases of home births without medical assistance, two witnesses must attest to the birth. There are two important exceptions to these rules. First, stillbirths that take place under medical supervision must be declared by the hospital or division physician. Second, the births and deaths of babies who die before the mother leaves the hospital must be declared by the hospital administration.[78]

Vital events recorded at this "primary" level must now be cumulated and records transmitted up the ZAGS hierarchies.[79] The lowest level registry agencies forward duplicate records of vital events on a monthly basis to the second-level offices (the rayon or city ZAGS). Here a monthly listing of births, deaths, and marriages is completed in three copies. One is retained; one is forwarded to the rayon statistical inspector; and the third, together with the duplicate record of each event, is forwarded to the next higher level ZAGS – usually the oblast ZAGS. The rayon statistical inspector checks the monthly listings received from the rayon ZAGS and forwards a copy to the oblast statistical office, which compiles a monthly account of vital events. Each year an audit of the birth and death registry is done by the rayon statistical office in cooperation with ZAGS officials. The audit uses information from maternity homes and hospital obstetrics departments on births, plus information from medical facilities on deaths. For rural areas, entries in the rural council account books are also used. A list of births and deaths is compiled from these sources and compared with the list derived from ZAGS entries. This latter step constitutes the major audit of the "primary registry".

In evaluating the comprehensiveness of the Soviet registry system, two sources of potential error in the records must be examined: (1)

errors that stem from omissions in reporting records between ZAGS officials and statistical agencies and from records lost in the transmission of material from lower level offices to the higher level offices that compile the data; and (2) those that stem from parental unwillingness to declare the birth. Effectiveness in communicating recorded births apparently varies from region to region with the overall efficiency of the local government system. Urban areas, by virtue of a specialized office to handle registration, apparently have done a better job in record-keeping than most rural areas.[80] Those parts of the country with relatively small rural and village administrative systems, such as the Baltic, have done a much better job at registering births and deaths in rural areas. Completeness in birth and death registration also appears to be inversely related to the proportion of home births.[81] Births that take place in a maternity home or hospital (i.e., in an institutionalized setting) are recorded in the institution's medical records and these records provide the primary check on the citizen-initiated registry. This means that comprehensiveness in birth recording is apt to be lowest in areas with a high proportion of home births. Comprehensiveness of infant death records is also tied to levels of pediatric care. The larger the proportion of infants under regular medical observation, the more likely that infant deaths will be recorded by the health care hierarchy. These records, again, provide a cross-check on the ZAGS registry; and even those deaths not declared by parents are more likely to be discovered in the annual audit and included in the statistical calculation of infant mortality.

Another key factor in evaluating registration comprehensiveness is the mix of incentives and disincentives affecting parental willingness to register their infants. There are some cases when certifying birth year can be disadvantageous. For example, in the early decades of Soviet rule in the Muslim southern tier, opponents of the Soviet system urged parents not to register their female children; this made it easier to evade laws requiring school attendance and laws stipulating a certain minimum age of marriage.[82] As may be seen, great obstacles faced Soviet authorities in the early decades of Soviet rule. They help to explain the chaotic conditions that hampered registration in those early days.

In more recent years, the major source of error in birth registration has probably been the difficulty in achieving an accurate count of births in those cases where the infant dies soon after birth.[83] Most infant deaths, in the Soviet Union as in many other countries at analogous stages of development, occur in the first hours and days after birth. In the USSR, parents are required to report both the birth and the subsequent death within one to three days; and they must also submit medical affidavits certifying the time and nature of death. Particularly in those cases where the birth took place outside a medical institution (and infant mortality is particularly high in such cases), many parents decide to skip the whole procedure. In the case of infants who survive, the registry is quite likely to be corrected when the child is entered in a day care institution or primary school; but there is no similar check for babies that fail to survive to this age.[84] So, levels of birth underregistration are quite likely to be closely related to real levels of infant mortality.

Soviet officials are aware of the problems in registration and have taken steps to achieve fuller registration. They have instituted programs to drill local officials in the importance of better registration and to make citizens more fully aware of their responsibilities for initiating registration. The expansion of programs, such as maternity payments for birth, has probably increased the incentive to register births, at least in cases where the baby survives. Probably the greatest aid in improving birth registration is the decrease in the proportion of home and non-medically assisted births; comparison of birth lists from medical institutions with those obtained from the civil registry is potentially the best check on the citizen-initiated system of reporting. This is particularly true in the case of infant deaths. Soviet officials are also moving to coordinate reporting from medical and educational institutions with the registry agencies. In 1964, for example, Kirgizia tightened up reporting procedures for medical officials. Health facilities were legally obligated to forward monthly lists of births, stillbirths, and deaths (including infant deaths) to local registration officials.[85]

These considerations have the following implications for use of Soviet birth and fertility rates. First, while registration systems throughout the USSR were probably somewhat haphazard in the first decade or so of Soviet rule, registration was more complete at a relatively early date in those regions that (1) came under continuous Bolshevik authority the soonest, and (2) had a strong, pre-revolutionary registration system for the Bolshevik officials to build on. This means that the European areas of the USSR had the most complete registration system.

Second, registration comprehensiveness remained low for many decades in those areas with a high proportion of home births and high (real) infant mortality. This was particularly true for the Muslim southern tier. In the immediate post-war period, for example, only half of the births in the southern tier republic of Tadzhikistan took place with medical assistance;[86] as late as 1970, nearly 20 per cent of the births were without medical assistance. By 1960, nearly all of the urban births in Islamic Azerbaydzhan took place in maternity homes or hospitals, but less than a quarter of the rural births occurred in these settings.[87] Hospital births accounted for 97 per cent of the urban births in Islamic Uzbekistan in 1957, but only 54 per cent of the rural births; births at home without medical assistance of any kind remained "a not uncommon occurrence."[88] The Uzbekistan Minister of Health reported in 1957 that 24 per cent of the births in rural areas occurred without medical assistance; this was traced to an inadequate distribution of health facilities.[89] In the Issyk-Kulsk area of Kirgizia (another southern tier republic), only 63 per cent of the births in 1956 took place in institutional medical facilities; and in some areas, institutional births accounted for only a quarter of the births.[90] As late as 1965, 25 per cent of the births in Islamic Turkmenistan took place at home (but with medical assistance), an additional 5 per cent involved no medical assistance whatever.[91] Data for rural Muslim areas of southern RSFSR presents a similar picture. In rural Chechen-Ingush ASSR, for example, 22.5 per cent of the births in 1959 occurred at home, without medical assistance of any kind. By 1963, nearly all births involved some medical assistance, but 25 per cent still occurred at home.[92] Another study, this time of infant mortality among Muslim women in Dagestan (another late-modernizing area in southern RSFSR), queried women on their birth histories between 1955 and 1964; 15 per cent had no medical assistance at birth whatsoever and many of those who did were attended in their homes by mid-level medical personnel, not physicians.[93]

This high proportion of home births means that incomplete registration remained a problem in most of the late-developing areas in the east and southern tier even in the 1950s and 1960s. Exacerbating this factor was a breakdown in administrative communication whereby even those births that were recorded at some level of the system (i.e., in farm records, medical records, or rural registration offices) were not always properly forwarded to higher-level ZAGS or

statistical officials. For example, a 1969 study of registration procedures in Islamic Uzbekistan revealed that 4.9 per cent of the births
and 9.3 per cent of the deaths were not registered; the corresponding
figures for Karakalpak ASSR (an oblast-level component of Uzbekistan), were 12.8 per cent and 28 per cent. These findings were
attributed to the relatively high workload of the officials (rural
executive committee secretaries) responsible for maintaining the
registry.[94] Since 1959, registration comprehensiveness has improved
greatly throughout the USSR, with the most improvements in those
areas, like the southern tier, where the problems were concentrated.

These trends mean that pre-1970 data for Central Asia, Kazakhstan, the Caucasus, and the late-modernizing areas of the RSFSR
should be approached with great caution.[95] It is not possible to make
valid comparisons between areas with substantially different levels of
registration comprehensiveness. We have experimented with a
number of "correction" techniques for reported southern tier data,
using adjustment processes (see Appendix 1) which are based on
available historical data on regional infant and child mortality.
While these adjustments are useful as a way of highlighting differential levels of regional underregistration, they are not firmly based and
so have not been used in our empirical tests of the hypotheses
summarized above. In short, the seriousness of birth underregistration in the non-European areas precludes use of the pre-1970
natality data for our tests of the hypotheses for those regions.
Consequently, we make little use of non-European fertility measures
prior to 1970.

For the post-1970 period, we are on firmer ground. There is every
reason to believe that registration has improved significantly. In
part, this results from the medical establishment's reaction to the
increased levels of *reported* infant mortality in the USSR that began in
the early 1970s. While Soviet officials readily conceded that some of
this increase was real, much of it was due to improved registration in
the southern tier areas, particularly in the rural regions of the
Caucasus, Central Asia, and Moldavia.[96] Soviet officials were quite
clearly embarrassed by the rise in reported USSR rates (from a low of
22.9 in 1971 to 27.9 in 1974) and further publication of the data was
abruptly curtailed. The improved registration must surely have
made Soviet medical officials painfully aware of what they ought to
have suspected for decades – real infant mortality in the southern
tier, although masked by underregistration, was appallingly high.

That realization generated a spate of programs, focused particularly on the southern tier area, to remedy what clearly was an embarrassment to Soviet national pride. The programs have three goals – to improve levels of medical monitoring of pregnant women (thus alerting medical personnel to potential problem births); to increase the proportion of births that receive medical assistance (preferably, in a medical institution rather that at home – the desired goal is clearly 100 per cent), and to see that all infants receive regular systematic medical checkups.

Part of the medical establishment's effort to control infant mortality in the southern tier focuses on collecting adequate data. In Tadzhikistan, for example, gynecological and obstetric sections at the various levels of the health care hierarchy are required to cumulate data on infant mortality on a monthly basis.[97] Obviously, this emphasis on better data collection will only succeed to the degree that pregnancies, births, and newborn infants come under the aegis of institutionalized medical care; but it is clear that considerable progress has taken place, at least in the area of medically assisted births. By 1975, for example, medical officials in the southern tier republic of Turkmenistan were claiming that 88 per cent of the births occurred in institutional settings, up from 71 per cent 10 years previously.[98] Most of the problems, where they remain, seem to be connected with inadequacies in the distribution of medical facilities and personnel.[99]

These trends all point to improved birth reporting. Medical records are, in theory at least, a systematic check on citizen-initiated registrations; and it is quite likely that much of the improved reporting within the medical hierarchy will produce some improvement in the vital registry. This is not to say that the Soviets have solved all their problems in the registration of vital events in the southern tier area. Nonetheless, Soviet efforts to tighten up the vital registration system had produced, by the early 1970s, a fairly reliable series of fertility data.

Soviet census data

A second source of fertility measures is the census enumeration. The procedures used in recent Soviet censuses suggest that the census enumeration is probably much more complete than the ongoing birth and death registry.[100] Preparations for the enumerations begin several years prior to the census date and the procedures have been deliberately designed to maximize the accuracy of the count.[101] The procedures followed for the 1979 census will serve as an illustration. Unlike the birth and death registries, which are administered by civilian registry offices subordinate to the Ministry of Justice, the census is conducted by the Central Statistical Administration. At the national level, a five-department Directory of the Census and Population Research coordinated preparation for the 1979 census; corresponding departments were set up in the statistical offices at each level of the regional hierarchy (republic, oblast, and city).

The first step in the lengthy process of preparing the provinces for the census began between 1975 and 1977 with the drawing up of lists of union population points, including up-dated boundary lines, street names, and house and apartment building members. Maps of each town, large village, and region were also prepared during this period. Armed with this material, approximately 40,000 special registry officials (working under the supervision of local government statistical officials) compiled a list of residential buildings in urban areas and larger villages. Meanwhile, in rural areas, local government officials were updating and correcting their village farm registry books in order to draw up a list of rural populated points, noting the number of buildings, farms, and people in each.

This work was completed by spring 1978. The statistical material was used during the summer and fall of 1978 to divide the nation into census departments, which were further divided into instructor's districts. These were then sub-divided into enumeration districts.[102] These procedures were designed to ensure full coverage and to eliminate double counting. At the same time, statistical officials began recruiting and training the army of nearly one million census workers.[103] Special courses were set up for the workers involved in the census. Hundreds of thousands of temporary workers – enumerators, instructor-controllers, and heads of census departments – were also hired and trained. Forty-one per cent of those involved in the 1979 census had participated in either the 1959 or 1970 Soviet censuses. These temporary workers were released from their regular jobs for assignment to census work. In December, many of them participated in a massive check of the lists of residential houses and associated cartographic material for accuracy.

The housing lists and maps formed the basis for the actual population count on 17 January 1979. In the week prior to the 1979 census, for example, each enumerator was required to make a preliminary visit to each household within her assigned district, get acquainted with the residents, remind them about the upcoming census, and set up a time to fill in the forms during census week.[104] The actual enumeration began at 8 a.m. on 17 January and lasted eight days. Each enumerator, who was responsible for between 530 and 630 people, was required to visit every residence within his/her district; the unit of analysis was the family.[105] As a rule, heads of households were interviewed first and the material on other household members included information on their relationship to the head of household. The basic method of data collection for the 1979 census, as it had been for all Soviet censuses since 1926, was the personal interview by the census enumerator, who completed the census forms. Soviet demographers acknowledge that this method is more time-consuming than self-enumeration (where the respondent fills in the form), but they claim that it is also more accurate.[106] For this reason, census takers were instructed to avoid leaving census materials for absent family members to fill out on their own; and on those occasions when this was necessary, enumerators were instructed to check the completed form over carefully when they return to pick it up.[107] In the week following the census, spot checks by a "controller-instructor" (the enumerator's supervisor) were made to ensure the comprehensiveness of the count.[108]

The lengthy preparations and painstaking double checks and control systems reflect the great effort Soviet statistical officials apply to achieving a full and correct count. This is one reason why Soviet census enumerations are apt to be much more comprehensive than the birth and death registries. The other reason is that the census is conducted by interview and does not rely on citizen initiative. Although considerable socialization work is done prior to the census to encourage citizens to cooperate with the census takers, the enumeration procedures are deliberately designed to place the initiative with the enumerator, not the citizen. Clearly, not all of these procedures are followed by every enumerator; and it would indeed be surprising if the actual enumeration did not encounter many of the same problems found in censuses conducted by other industrialized states. Nonetheless, these considerations do suggest that the Soviet census enumerations, particularly those for the last two censuses (which took place after years of preliminary effort to correct and update basic data), are fairly reliable, certainly more so than the pre-1970 birth registries.

Other measures of fertility

Several measures of fertility were deliberately excluded from the analysis. One was household size, available from the 1959, 1970, and 1979 Soviet censuses. This measure, which is a report of the average number of family members residing together, is useful in making general comparisons of family structure between regions or groups. Household size cannot, however, be used as a measure of fertility.[109] First, household size is affected by differential (and changing) patterns of infant and child mortality. It is also affected by both housing availability and custom. Regions with a higher proportion of extended (non-nuclear) families, for example, will have a larger household size, regardless of fertility behavior. Conversely, a decline in household size may simply mean an increase in the availability of separate dwellings for young married couples who previously were forced to double up with their parents. Frequently, household size trends result from a combination of fertility and socioeconomic factors. Declines in household size in Alma Ata over the last twenty years, for instance, are due to both an increase in family planning to limit families to one to two children *and* the desire of young couples after marriage to set up housekeeping separately from their families in their own homes.[110] Another problem with household size is that it is affected by educational and economic trends that are difficult to control for. For example, tekhnikum and university students, if they live at home, will be included with their family of procreation in the census enumeration. This means that the increasing duration of financial dependence associated with longer schooling will act to inflate household size.

Finally, household size is greatly affected by age structure. Even among high fertility regions, areas with a large proportion of young adults just starting their families may have a rather modest household size. Similarly, salient fertility declines may not be reflected in household size data because of age structure changes. Household size may hold steady or even increase under conditions of declining fertility if the populace contains a larger proportion of middle-aged couples who have completed their families. In Armenia, for example, republic general fertility rates declined precipitously from 159.2 per

1,000 in 1959 to 92.9 per 1,000 in 1970, yet average household size increased from 4.8 in 1959 to 5.0 in 1970. Similarly, in spite of the dramatic declines in republic fertility rates in Azerbaydzhan in the 1970s, household size did not change between the 1970 and 1979 censuses. For these reasons, household size is not used as a measure of fertility in our analysis.

A second measure often used by Soviet demographers as an indicator of fertility is the proportion of children born to women who have had at least two previous births.[111] While these data can provide a general indication of natality levels, its major weakness is that it, like household size, is substantially affected by age structure. Examination of trends in this indicator will often yield a very misleading impression of fertility trends. The proportion of third and higher order births can decline substantially under conditions of stable natality, simply because a larger proportion of women in the childbearing ages are young women just beginning their families.

The independent variables

The other series of indicators consists of material designed to measure modernization level and traditional familial patterns. "Modernization," as used here, refers to the process by which societies come to have high levels of structural differentiation. We follow other social scientists in using multiple economic and education indicators to measure it.[112] The economic indicators include:

High proportions of the population residing in urban areas

High proportions of the population employed in professional, technical and skilled occupations

High proportions of the population employed in industry, as opposed to agriculture.

The education indicators include:

High literacy rates

High proportions of the relevant age population enrolled in school

High proportions of the population with elementary schooling and above.

Translating each of these indicators into appropriate empirical measures involved considerations specific to the USSR and Soviet data. Nonetheless, measurement of modernization level in the Soviet Union proved to be relatively straightforward, because there is a fair amount of consensus among scholars about what modernization is and, at the aggregate or institutional level at least, how to measure it.

Far less attention has been paid to the key concept in the second hypothesis – patriarchal family values. A patriarchal family value system is defined as one in which an individual's economic and social role is determined by the individual's position in a fairly rigid hierarchy. Females are relegated to the lower ranges of this hierarchy. Their major mission is to fulfill the joint roles of wife and mother, with few alternative roles being available to them. Women are expected to subordinate their interests to those of their husband and children.

One aspect of the patriarchal value system – gender roles – has been investigated by Western social scientists. Most of these studies attempt to measure roles by examining the norms that structure them. One of the most detailed of these studies, conducted in 1971, was analyzed and reported by John Scanzoni. Based on a sample drawn from the east-north-central part of the United States, the study included a series of questions designed to measure norms regarding the social positions of wife, husband, and mother.[113] Scanzoni factor analyzed the responses and identified several role dimensions. One was the "traditional wife role." Respondents who scored highly on this dimension felt that the wife should subordinate her interests to other family members, that her primary responsibilities were caring for her husband and children, and that wives do not have equal authority with husbands in making decisions. Scanzoni's analysis also revealed a "traditional husband" role (respondents scoring high on this factor tended to agree with statements such as "the husband should be the head of the family") and a "traditional mother" role dimension. High scorers on this latter dimension believe that marriage without children is incomplete, that young children suffer when their mother is employed, and that nonworking mothers establish warmer relationships with their children than those employed outside the home. This approach – measuring the acceptance of norms governing sex roles – would be the most desirable way of operationalizing the concept "patriarchal family values." Because analogous data for the USSR are not available, we employ surrogate indicators; ones that have been found to be closely related to sex role ideology in the limited number of studies that explore this issue. These indicators include:

Age at marriage

Female educational attainment

Female labor force participation
Relative female to male educational attainment
Relative female to male access to high status occupations
The empirical support for these indicators is discussed below.

Most western research investigating socioeconomic correlates of sex role ideology has found a link between age at first marriage and patriarchal sex role norms. This is particularly true for younger age cohorts. For example, Scanzoni reported a moderately strong relationship between age at first marriage and the "traditional wife" dimension for young, non-Catholic, wives.[114] Bagozzi and Van Loo's analysis of the same data also found a positive correlation between acceptance of egalitarian sex roles and age at time of marriage.[115] A study of white, non-Catholic, high school girls in Atlanta revealed a moderately strong correlation between "contemporary" views of the feminine role and higher *expected* age at marriage.[116] These findings support the use of early marriage as a surrogate for patriarchal sex role values.

The most powerful social correlate of gender role norms, however, is female educational level. Scanzoni's analysis revealed that education and modern views of the "traditional wife" role were positively related for all groups except older Catholics. The correlation between attained level of education and rejection of the traditional wife role was 0.29 for the wives in the sample (N=1590). Similar findings were reported for the effect of education on the "traditional husband" role dimension, while education proved to be an even more powerful discriminator of differences in acceptance of traditional motherhood norms.[117] These conclusions were confirmed by Bagozzi and Van Loo's reanalysis of the data.[118] A 1970 US study of married women revealed a similar link between educational level and conjugal role definitions; less-educated women tended to score high on a five-item scale designed to measure concurrence with the traditional homemaker role for the wife.[119] Stolka and Barnett found a strong positive relationship between educational level and rejection of traditional female roles.[120] Similar results are reported from data on sex role attitudes collected in late 1970 from a national probability sample of ever married women under the age of 45; highly-educated women received more egalitarian scores on two scales tapping attitudes toward familial sex roles and labor market rights.[121]

Data from four other sample surveys involving attitudes toward gender roles provide confirming evidence of the strong link between a woman's education and her rejection of traditional sex roles.[122] A panel study examining changes in sex role attitudes between 1962 and 1977 found that the better educated women were more likely to adopt egalitarian sex role attitudes.[123] Similar findings emerged in an analysis of the values and attitudes of mothers with adolescent children in the Canadian province of Newfoundland.[124] Educational level was positively related to approval of wives earning money in business and industry among females in three separate NORC (National Opinion Research Center) General Social Surveys conducted between 1972 and 1978.[125]

Studies of fertility transition in other cultures reveal similar relationships between traditionality and education; in Taiwan, for example, women with higher educational attainments were most likely to choose "modern" answers to a six question measure of family values and gender role norms.[126] Researchers analysing the link between values and socioeconomic variables among fertile married women in five Brazilian communities found a strong direct relationship between the woman's educational level and scores on two indexes of modernity tapping attitudes toward sex roles and family authority patterns.[127] In another analysis of Brazilian data, Rosen and Simmons found a direct relationship between the wife's education and her role in family decisionmaking and between wife's education and non-traditional attitudes toward female roles.[128] In a later analysis of sex role attitudes in Brazil, Rosen concluded that "education combined with exposure to relatively higher status jobs in an industrial setting incline women toward modern sex role attitudes."[129] An examination of family attitudes in Ghana reported that well-educated respondents were much less likely to favor patriarchal patterns of marital authority; 33 per cent of the highly-educated respondents versus 10 per cent of the low-educated respondents favored an egalitarian distribution of family decisionmaking power.[130] These data provide persuasive evidence that the relationship between higher female education and acceptance of less traditional gender roles is one that transcends national boundaries.

Data from the study of Atlanta high school girls suggest the mechanism underlying this relationship – there was a strong correlation between espousal of contemporary sex roles and aspirations for higher education.[131] Zuckerman found similar relationships in her study of sex role attitudes among technical college and university students; among women, "feminist" attitudes were highly correlated with educational goals.[132] These studies suggest that there is an interactive relationship between education and the rejection of traditional gender roles.

These survey findings, which report the relationship between attitudes among individuals, indicate that female education or the lack of it serves to modify or maintain traditional sex roles. At the aggregate level, societies that espouse traditional family values tend to limit female access to education. The issue of expanded educational opportunities for women has often become the focal point for debate between supporters and opponents of traditional familial systems. This, too, indicates that female educational opportunity is a good surrogate measure of the acceptance or rejection of egalitarian sex roles.

There is less empirical support for the use of female labor force participation as a measure of patriarchal sex roles. Rosen and Simmons' analysis of family and sex role attitudes in Brazil revealed that the wife's exposure to higher status jobs was positively associated with nontraditional attitudes toward appropriate female roles.[133] An 18-year panel study of sex role attitudes of women and their children found that women with substantial work experience after marriage held more egalitarian views.[134] Scanzoni found that employed wives held more "modern" norms on the traditional wife and mother role dimensions than did unemployed wives.[135] These relationships, however, were not found for white Catholics or for blacks. Nor is involvement of females in production necessarily associated with a high social status for women in all societies. Sanday devised a method to measure female status through levels of participation and control within selected areas of life. She found that women were most apt to be subordinate in societies where women make a low contribution to subsistence and in those where they make a high contribution. Sex role egalitarianism was most likely in those societies where the female contribution was more nearly balanced by the male contribution. Sanday's findings suggest that there is no direct linear relationship between level of female labor force participation in a given society or region and support for egalitarianism in sex roles. For example, women are the main source of labor among the Azandi, a central African people, but their status is extremely low and they are treated much like slaves. Iroquois women, by contrast, participated in subsistence agriculture at about the same level as the males, while enjoying a fair amount of both political and economic power.[136]

These findings, although admittedly tentative, since they apply to very limited groups, suggest caution in automatically ascribing egalitarian sex roles to groups with high levels of female labor force participation.

For this reason, we turned to other measures of female labor force participation, i.e., those that tap female access to occupations in the modernized sector. Because our interest is in measuring the level of female access to public roles that confer status, we examined measures of female participation in those occupations that are well-remunerated and/or allocated high prestige. In the Soviet context, these occupations included non-agricultural jobs, industry and construction jobs, white-collar occupations, and "specialist" jobs (particularly those requiring a college degree). Since nations vary in the types of occupations that are well rewarded and prized, some of these indicators are clearly specific to the Soviet case. In the United States, where physicians are accorded both high status and high incomes, the proportion of female medical doctors within a given population may be a very good indicator of female status. In the USSR, although the occupation enjoys relatively high prestige, salary levels are not particularly high compared to other professional jobs or to skilled blue-collar work. Therefore, the proportion of MDs who are female is not as good an indicator of women's status. In the Soviet context we have sought to develop a series of indicators that measure the extent to which women have access to roles that are rewarded through high status and wages.

The major weakness of both the female educational data and the material on female participation in the modernized labor force is that both measures may be confounded by the changes in absolute level of modernization within a society or region. Suppose, for example, we are examining a region in which 15 per cent of the working-age females are employed in high status specialist occupations. The implications for female status and sex roles will be vastly different depending on what proportion of working-age males in that area are in similar occupations. If, on the one hand, 30 per cent of the males are so employed, this would suggest horizontal stratification of the labor markets that operates to discourage female access to specialist positions. If, on the other hand, we found that male participation is about the same as female, this would imply greater egalitarianism in occupational roles. Similar comments apply to educational measures. An area with a very low level of female attainment (say, the proportion with completed secondary and above) might not necessarily mean that females are excluded from modernized roles. In some cases, low female attainments are due, not so much to patriarchal gender roles that block female access to education, but to the low modernization level of that area or group as a whole.

Since we are concerned here with measuring traditionality in gender roles (and not modernization *per se*), we developed a series of indicators based on relative female-to-male participation. For each level of educational attainment for which data were available (literacy through completed college), we constructed female/male education ratios. For all of these ratios, a score of 100 indicates parity between the sexes, while a score less than 100 indicates that male participation exceeds that of females. There is support for this approach in Western research. Western sociologists have found, for example, that the relative husband/wife educational attainments are a better predictor of the husband's dominance within the family than is his education alone. Husbands married to women who are less well educated are more likely to exercise dominance in family decision-making than those married to wives with an equal or higher level of education.[137] These findings are very limited, but they do suggest that relative female-to-male educational attainments at the aggregate level might provide a better measure of traditionality in family relations than either overall education or female education. A similar strategy was used to compute female/male occupational roles.

None of the indicators we used to measure patriarchal familial values are ideal. Most are tainted to some degree by factors unrelated to the values. The female-to-male education and occupation indicators, which we term measures of "emancipation," come closest to measuring the concept and we expect those variables to be the better predictors of fertility differentials between groups.

Many of the indicators used as measures of modernization and traditionality were not available in usable form, but, as with the birth and census data, could be used as the basis for estimates. For example, the number of "specialists" are provided by the Soviets in raw numbers only. Data on students at various levels in the educational establishment are presented in a similar fashion. In order to make such material useful, the data had to be standardized to an appropriate comparison group. Both Western and Soviet scholars frequently use the most convenient reference point, the total population. For populations with very different age structures, such as characterize the USSR, this procedure leads to serious error.[138] For this reason, we chose a comparison group that was appropriate to each variable and computed relevant age groupings from the age data presented in the census, using procedures analogous to those used to calculate the fertility measures, as detailed in Appendix 2.

Survey data

The data sets described above were used to explore the modernization/value change/fertility nexus at the aggregate level. The danger with this approach is that relationships characteristic of aggregate data may not, in fact, reflect patterns at the individual level. The best-known example of this danger, usually referred to as the ecological fallacy, is the seminal article by W. S. Robinson, "Ecological Correlations and the Behavior of Individuals."[139] Using the American state as the unit of analysis, Robinson found a correlation between per cent foreign-born and per cent illiterate (1930) of −0.572; at the individual level, however, the correlation was 0.118. In other words, the state-level analysis suggested that foreign-born residents were more literate than the native-born. But this finding is spurious – an artifact of the concentration of foreign-born residents in states with high literacy. Examination of individual-level data revealed the real relationship between foreign birth and literacy: those of foreign birth were somewhat less likely to be literate. Robinson's work highlighted the pitfalls of ecological correlations (i.e., correlations produced by examining relationships at the aggregate level). Without individual-level data, then, we cannot be sure that the relationships we observe at an aggregated level – i.e., for republics, oblasts or nationality groups – are real or not. Fortunately, Soviet surveys of individuals provide a check on our results; none of our correlations produced a sign opposite to that of Soviet survey findings. Indeed, where our correlations were strongest, the Soviets reported their strongest relationships as well. We are in a much stronger position, therefore, to argue that our aggregated relationships reflect individual behavior in the Soviet Union.

The published results of Soviet surveys, therefore, proved to be an invaluable supplement to findings drawn from our aggregate data sets. The surveys are of two types: cohort analyses and attitudinal surveys. The cohort studies typically draw a sample based on year of birth or marriage, collect birth histories, and reconstruct fertility rates through the reported birth histories. A major weakness of these studies is the tendency of older women to forget or understate births. Moreover, a complete picture of the natality of a cohort can be obtained only after women have completed childbearing, so cohort analyses tend to deal with past trends. In the Soviet case, some cohorts have been affected disproportionately by catastrophic events in Soviet history – the Civil War and associated disruptions, forced collectivization, and World War II. Interpretation of the published results of cohort studies must factor in these considerations.

A second type of survey explores attitudes toward family size. These surveys provide data on expected, ideal, and actual number of children. Republic and ethnic-specific tabulations on expected family size were used in the data sets described above as an additional measure of fertility in the aggregate data analysis. The published results of these same surveys, moreover, also provide valuable individual-level data, since Soviet demographers generally provide the data broken out by age, age of marriage, urban–rural residence, education, occupation and/or social class.

These two approaches are supplemented by material on changes and continuity in the social role of women; the frequency of abortion and contraceptive use; surveys on attitudes toward child care, working mothers, and sharing of household tasks; and historical literature focusing on the development of ethnic life styles. The historical data provided valuable background material that helped to place the demographic trends of the last several decades in a broader historical perspective. The ethnographic literature provided a series of detailed case studies of the extent of social change among some of the late-modernizing minorities.

CONCLUSION

In exploring the hypotheses posed above, we examined the results of small-scale and nationwide Soviet surveys, then tested the relationships suggested in those studies with our own data sets, using all available measures of both natality (the dependent variable) and socioeconomic levels and values (the independent variables). The findings presented in the tables and discussed in the text are representative results of these multiple tests. This approach was partly dictated by a desire to explore the differences that result from using multiple measures of the same concept. It was also dictated by the problems inherent in Soviet data. None of the fertility measures available to us are ideal. Some are contaminated by reporting problems, others by errors necessarily introduced by estimation procedures, and still others (e.g., crude birth rate) by the nature of the measure itself. Similar comments apply to many of our independent variables. For instance, while our measures of family values represent the best and most comprehensive data available to Soviet specialists in the West, they are hopelessly crude by the standards of Western survey research. The most reasonable approach to dealing with these measurement problems is to limit the analyses to the most reasonable data and to perform multiple tests of the hypotheses, operationalizing the measures in several different ways. The conclusions of our analyses rest, then, not on the validity of a single measure or group of measures, but on a large body of data from many diverse sources.

NOTES

1 Ronald Freedman, "Theories of Fertility Decline: A Reappraisal," *Social Forces*, Vol. 58, No. 1, September 1979, pp. 1–17.
2 Steven E. Beaver, *Demographic Transition Theory Reinterpreted: An Application to Recent Natality Trends in Latin America* (Lexington, Massachussetts: Lexington Books, 1975), *passim*.
3 N. Krishnan Namboodiri, "A Look at Fertility Model-building from Different Perspectives," in Thomas K. Burch (ed.), *Demographic Behavior: Interdisciplinary Perspectives in Decision-making* (Boulder, Colorado: Westview Press, 1980), pp. 71–90. See also Barbara S. Janowitz, "An Empirical Study of the Effects of Socioeconomic Development on Fertility Rates," *Demography*, Vol. 8, No. 3, August 1971, pp. 319–30.
4 Gary J. Becker, "An Economic Analysis of Fertility," *Demographic and Economic Change in Developed Countries* (Princeton, NJ: Princeton University Press, 1960), pp. 209–31.
5 See, for example, Richard A. Easterlin, "Modernization and Fertility: A Critical Essay," in Rodolfo A. Bulatao and Ronald D. Lee (eds.), *Determinants of Fertility in Developing Countries*, Vol. 2 (New York: Academic Press, 1983), pp. 562–86; Rodolfo A. Bulatao and Ronald D. Lee, "The Demand for Children: A Critical Essay," in Bulatao and Lee, Vol. 1, 1983, pp. 233–87; John Bongaarts and Jane Menken, "The Supply of Children: A Critical Essay," Bulatao and Lee, Vol. 1, 1983, pp. 27–60; and Albert I. Hermalen, "Fertility Regulation and Its Costs: A Critical Essay," in Bulatao and Lee, Vol. 2, 1983, pp. 1–53. See also Harvey Leibenstein, "The Economic Theory of Fertility–Survey, Issues,

and Considerations," in *International Population Conference. Mexico 1977*, Vol. 2, pp. 49–64; and Richard A. Easterlin, "Fertility and Development." *Population Bulletin of U.N. Economic Commission for West Asia*, Vol. 18, No. 5, June 1980, pp. 5–40.

6 Two examples of social demography are: James Allman, "The Demographic Transition in the Middle East and North Africa," in James Allman (ed.), *Women's Status and Fertility in the Muslim World* (New York: Praeger Publishers, 1978), pp. 3–32 and Beaver, *Demographic Transition Theory Reinterpreted*, 1975, pp. 41–60.

    For a gentle chiding of sociologists to utilize the concepts of their discipline in population studies, see Charles B. Nam, "Sociology and Demography: Perspectives on Population," *Social Forces*, Vol. 61, No. 2, December 1982, pp. 359–73. On page 369, Nam lists a set of sociological concepts that he favors including in social demography.

7 John C. Caldwell, *Theory of Fertility Decline* (London: Academic Press, 1982), p. 35.

8 See, for example, A. G. Vishnevskiy and A. G. Volkov (eds.) *Vosproizvodstvo naseleniya SSSR* (Moscow: Finansy i Statistika, 1983), pp. 16–37, 127–8; A. G. Vishnevskiy, *Demograficheskaya revolyutsiya* (Moscow: Statistika, 1976), pp. 29–49, 189–99; and G. A. Slesarev, *Demograficheskiye protsessy i sotial'naya struktura sotsialisticheskogo obshchestva* (Moscow: Nauka, 1978), pp. 39–45.

9 See, for example, A. I. Antonov, *Sotsiologiya rozhdayemosti (Teoreticheskiye i metodologicheskiye problemy)* (Moscow: Statistika, 1980), *passim*.

10 Allman, "The Demographic Transition," 1978.

11 Mona Etienne and Eleanor Leacock (eds.), *Women and Colonization: Anthropological Perspectives* (New York: Praeger Publishers, 1980), *passim*.

12 Caldwell, 1982, *passim*.

13 Caldwell, 1982, pp. 171–2.

14 Lee and Bulatao, "The Demand for Children," pp. 233–87. One study of the link between old age security and high fertility calls into question the view that individuals who express a preference for large families are motivated by concern for filial support in their old age. M. Vlassoff and Carol Vlassoff, "Old Age Security and the Utility of Children in Rural India," *Population Studies*, Vol. 34, No. 3, November 1980, pp. 487–99.

15 Akbar Agharjanian, "Fertility and Family Economy in the Iranian Rural Communities," *Journal of Comparative Family Studies*, Vol. 9, No. 1, Spring 1978, pp. 119–27. See also John C. Caldwell, "Fertility and the Household Economy in Nigeria," *Journal of Comparative Family Studies*, Vol. 7, No. 2, Summer 1976, pp. 193–253.

16 Alfred O. Ukaegbu, "Socio-cultural Determination of Fertility: A Case Study of Rural Eastern Nigeria," *Journal of Comparative Family Studies*, Vol. 8, No. 1, Spring 1977, pp. 99–115.

17 Caldwell, 1982, p. 35.

18 *Ibid.*, p. 43.

19 Christine Oppong, "Women's Roles, Opportunity Costs, and Fertility," in Bulatao and Lee, Vol. 1, 1983, pp. 547–89.

20 Burton Benedict, "Social Regulation of Fertility," in G. A. Harrison and

A. J. Boyce (eds.), *The Structure of Human Population* (Oxford: Clarendon Press, 1972), pp. 73–89; and Malcolm Potts and Peter Selman, *Society and Fertility*, (Estover, Plymouth, GB: Macdonalds and Evans Ltd, 1979), pp. 89–90. See also Caldwell, 1982, pp. 171–2.

21 Norms, including those relating to family size, specify the way people ought to act in specific situations. "The purpose of norms in most views is to provide individuals with incentives for behaving in ways they would not otherwise behave." Karen Oppenheim Mason, "Norms Relating to the Desire for Children," in Bulatao and Lee, Vol. 1, 1983, pp. 388–428.

22 Halim Barakat, "The Arab Family and the Challenge of Social Transformation," in Elizabeth Warnock Fernea (ed.), *Women and the Family in the Middle East: New Voices of Change* (Austin, Texas: University of Texas Press, 1985), pp. 27–48.

23 C. Mosk, "Evolution of the Pre-modern in Japan," *Population Studies*, Vol. 35, No. 1, March 1981, pp. 30–52; and Peter T. Marcy, "Factors Affecting the Fecundity and Fertility of Historical Populations: A Factor," *Journal of Family History*, Vol. 6, No. 3, Fall 1981, pp. 309–26.

24 Rose E. Frisch, "Fatness, Puberty, and Fertility," *Natural History*, Vol. 89, No. 10, October 1980, pp. 16–27; Rose E. Frisch, "Nutrition, Fatness, Puberty, and Fertility," *Comprehensive Therapy*, Vol. 7, No. 7, July 1981, pp. 15–23; and A. Romaniuk, "Increase in Natural Fertility During the Early Stages of Modernization: Evidence from an African Case Study, Zaire," *Population Studies*, Vol. 34, No. 2, July 1980, pp. 293–310. See also Nicholas David and David Voas, "Societal Causes of Infertility and Population Decline Among the Settled Fulani of North Cameroon," *Man*, Vol. 16, No. 4, December 1981, pp. 644–64.

25 Sandra L. Huffman, A. K. M. Lanauddin Chowdhury and Zenas M. Sykes, "Lactation and Fertility in Rural Bangladesh," *Population Studies*, Vol. 34, No. 2, July 1980, pp. 337–47; Nancy Howell, "Demographic Behavior of Hunter-Gatherers: Evidence for Density-dependent Population Control," in Burch, *Demographic Behavior*, 1980, pp. 185–200; and N. A. Fisk, *et al.*, "Postpartum Amenorrhea in Turkey," *Studies in Family Planning*, Vol. 12, No. 1, January 1981, pp. 40–43; and Anrudh K. Jain and John Bongaarts, "Breastfeeding: Patterns, Correlates, and Fertility Effects," *Studies in Family Planning*, Vol. 12, No. 3, March 1981, pp. 79–99; John E. Anderson (*et al.*), "Determinants of Fertility in Guatemala," *Social Biology*, Vol. 27, No. 1, Spring 1980, pp. 20–35; and A. Romaniuk, "Increase in Natural Fertility During Early Stages of Modernization: Canadian Indians Case Study," *Demography*, Vol. 18, No. 2, May 1981, pp. 157–172.

26 Cynthia Myntti, "Population Processes in Rural Yemen: Temporary Emigration, Breastfeeding and Contraception," *Studies in Family Planning*, Vol. 10, No. 10, October 1979, pp. 282–9; and Valerie Hull, "Women, Doctors, and Family Health Care: Some Lessons From Rural Java," *Studies in Family Planning*, Vol. 10, No. 11/12, November/December 1979, pp. 315–17.

  Tabooes on sexual intercourse after the birth of a child are particularly prevalent among the cultures of Sub-saharan Africa. See Erika Bourguignon, *A World of Women: Anthropological Studies of Women in the Societies of the World* (Praeger, 1980), pp. 3–4. The use of fertility-limiting customs, along with abortion, withdrawal and infanticide, to achieve desired spacing of children is not necessarily incompatible with a desire for a large family. However, some small primitive societies, including some modern hunting and gathering groups, use such methods as part of a conscious strategy to reduce population growth. Potts and Selman, 1979, pp. 160–71.

27 Susheela Singh, J. B. Casterline, and J. G. Cleland, "The Proximate Determinants of Fertility: Sub-national Variations," *Population Studies*, Vol. 39, No. 1, March 1985, pp. 113–35. See also R. J. Lesthaeghe and H. J. Page, "The Post-partum Non-susceptible Period: Development and Application of Model Schedules," *Population Studies*, Vol. 34, No. 1, March 1980, pp. 143–69. See also David M. Heer, "Economic Development and Fertility," *Demography*, Vol. 3, 1966, pp. 423–41; and Eileen M. Crimmins, *et al.*, "New Perspectives on the Demographic Transition: A Theoretical and Empirical Analysis of an Indian State, 1951–1975." *Economic Development and Cultural Change*, Vol. 32, No. 2, January 1984, pp. 227–54.

28 John Stoeckel and A. K. M. Alauddin Chowdhury, "Fertility and Socioeconomic Status in Rural Bangladesh: Differentials and Linkages," *Population Studies*, Vol. 34, No. 3, November 1980, pp. 519–24. See also Mohammed Sohail, "Differentials in Cumulative Fertility and Child Survivorship in Rural Bangladesh," *Bangladesh Development Studies*, Vol. 7, No. 3, 1979, pp. 53–78. Other researchers have failed to uncover an inverse relationship between fertility and socioeconomic variables. Lee and Amin, for example, found no empirical link between cumulative fertility (as measured by the duration ratio) and socioeconomic indicators, such as urbanity or education. See Che-fu Lee and Ruhul Amin, "Economic Factors, Intermediate Variables and Fertility in Bangladesh," *Journal of Biosocial Science*, Vol. 13, No. 2, April 1981, pp. 179–88.

29 "More Education Leads to Higher Fertility for Rural Nigerian Women," *International Family Planning Perspectives*, Vol. 6, No. 4, December 1980, pp. 149–51. One researcher, focusing on data from southern Nigeria, has suggested that the observed lower rural fertility differences may be an artifact of differential under-reporting. A. O. Okore, "Rural-urban Differentials in Southern Nigeria: An Assessment of Some Available Evidence," *Population Studies*, Vol. 34, No. 1, March 1980, pp. 171–79.

30 Valerie J. Hull, "Intermediate Variables in the Explanation of Differential Fertility: Results of a Village Study in Rural Java," *Human Ecology*, Vol. 8, No. 3, 1980, pp. 213–43.

31 Farhat Yusief and Robert D. Retherford, "Urban–rural Fertility Differences in Pakistan," *Journal of Biosocial Science*, Vol. 13, No. 4, October 1981, pp. 491–99.

32 J. C. Caldwell, "The Mechanisms of Demographic Change in Historical Perspective," *Population Studies*, Vol. 35, 1981, pp. 5–27.

33 Cigdem Kagitcibasi, "Old-Age Security Value of Children: Cross-National Socioeconomic Evidence," *Journal of Cross-Cultural Psychology*,

Vol. 13, No. 1, March 1982, pp. 29–42.

34 Anne R. Pebley, "Fertility Desires and Child Mortality Experiences among Guatemalan Women," *Studies in Family Planning*, Vol. 10, No. 4, April 1979, pp. 129–36.

35 Charles Hirshman, "Premarital Socioeconomic Roles and the Timing of Family Formation: A Comparative Study of Five Asian Societies," *Demography*, Vol. 22, No. 1, February 1985, pp. 35–39.

36 Diane Vinokur-Kaplan, "Family Planning Decisionmaking: A Comparison and Analysis of Parents' Considerations," *Journal of Comparative Family Studies*, Vol. 8, No. 1, Spring 1977, pp. 79–98.

37 Caldwell, 1982, pp. 334–51.

38 Thomas E. Dow, Jr and Linda H. Warner, "Modern, Transitional, and Traditional Demographic and Contraceptive Patterns Among Kenyan Women," *Studies in Family Planning*, Vol. 13, No. 1, January 1982, pp. 12–23.

39 Caldwell, 1982, pp. 18–21.

40 Mason, 1983.

41 Susan H. Cochrane, "Effects of Education and Urbanization on Fertility," in Bulatao and Lee, Vol. 1, 1983, pp. 587–626.

42 Phillips Cutright and William R. Kelly, "Modernization and Other Determinants of National Birth, Death, and Growth Rates, 1958–1972," *Comparative Studies in Sociology*, Vol. 1, 1978, pp. 17–46.

43 Larry Bumpass, "Fertility Differences by Employment Patterns and Role Attitudes," in Charles F. Westoff and Norman B. Ryder, *The Contraceptive Revolution* (Princeton, New Jersey: Princeton University Press, 1977), pp. 311–31.

44 John H. Scanzoni, *Sex Roles, Life Styles, and Childbearing* (New York: The Free Press, 1975), pp. 215–19. See also John Scanzoni, "Gender Roles and the Process of Fertility Control," *Journal of Marriage and the Family*, Vol. 38, November 1976, pp. 677–91.

45 Alice P. Wrigley and C. Shannon Stokes, "Sex-Role Ideology, Selected Life Plans, and Family Size Preferences: Further Evidence," *Journal of Comparative Family Studies*, Vol. 8, No. 3, Autumn 1977, pp. 391–400.

46 Patricia L. Tobin, "Conjugal Role Definitions, Value of Children, and Contraceptive Practice," *The Sociological Quarterly*, Vol. 17, Summer 1976, pp. 314–22.

47 Susan de Vos, "Women's Role Orientation and Expected Fertility: Evidence from the Detroit Area, 1978," *Social Biology*, Vol. 27, No. 2, Summer 1980, pp. 130–37.

48 Bernard C. Rosen and Anita L. La Raia, "Modernity in Women: An Index of Social Change in Brazil," *Journal of Marriage and the Family*, No. 34, May 1972, pp. 353–60.

49 T. H. Sun and Y. L. Soong, "On its Way to Zero Population Growth: Fertility Transition in Taiwan, Republic of China," *Fertility Transition of the East Asian Populations* (Honolulu: The University Press of Hawaii, 1979), pp. 117–48.

50 Cochrane, 1983.

51 N. H. Youssef, "Social Structure and the Female Labor Force: the Case

of Women Workers in the Muslim Middle East Countries," *Demography*, Vol. 8, No. 4, November 1971, pp. 427–39. See also Elsa M. Chaney, "Women and Population: Some Key Policy, Research, and Action Issues," in Richard L. Clinton (ed.), *Population and Politics* (Lexington, Mass.: Lexington Books, 1973), pp. 233–46.

52 Robert D. Retherford, "A Theory of Rapid Fertility Decline in Homogeneous Populations," *Studies in Family Planning*, Vol. 10, No. 2, February 1979, pp. 61–7.

53 Ansley J. Coale, Barbara A. Anderson, and Erna Harm, *Human Fertility in Russia Since the Nineteenth Century* (Princeton, New Jersey: Princeton University Press, 1979), pp. 10–11.

54 David Heer, "The Decline of Fertility in Russia," *Contemporary Sociology*, Vol. 9, No. 5, 1980, pp. 653–57.

55 Mary Mederios Kent and Carl Haub, "In (Cautious) Defense of the Crude Birth Rate," *Population Today*, Vol. 12, No. 2, February 1984, pp. 6–7.

56 V. Kozlov, "On Several Aspects of Demographic Theory," in *Demograficheskaya politika v SSSR* (Moscow: Finansy i Statistika, 1983), pp. 82–92.

57 V. A. Belova, *Chislo detey v sem'ye* (Moscow: Statistika, 1975), pp. 44–8.

58 A. I. Salatich, "Study of the Birthrate in Rural Areas," *Zdravookhraneniye rossiyskoy federatsiy*, No. 4, 1971, pp. 18–23.

59 *Itogi vsesoyuznoy perepisi naseleniya 1970 goda*. Vol. 2 (Moscow: Statistika, 1972), p. 263.

60 I. I. Kashtanenkova, "Social-Demographic Analyses of High-Parity Women in Tashkent," *Regional'nyye demograficheskiye issledovaniya* (Tashkent: Tashkent State University, 1978), pp. 17–33.

61 Gary H. McClelland, "Family-Size Desires as Measures of Demand," in Bulatao and Lee, Vol. 1, 1983, pp. 288–343.

62 M. R. Buriyeva, "Opinion of Rural Women on the Number of Children in the Family," in *Demografiya sem'i* (Tashkent: Tashkent State University, 1980), pp. 69–81.

63 A. A. Akhmedov, "The Opinion of Women Living in Villages of Azerbaydzhan Concerning the Number of Children in the Family," *Azerbaydzhanskiy meditsinskiy zhurnal*, No. 6, 1975, pp. 76–80.

64 M. Buriyeva, "The Cohort Method of Studying Birthrate," in *Regional'nyye demograficheskiye issledovaniya*, pp. 34–38.

65 G. Ye. Tsuladze, *Sotsiologo-psikhologicheskoye izucheniye rozhdayemosti* (Tbilisi: Izdatel'stvo "Metsniyereba," 1982), pp. 31–4.

66 Use of data derived from attitudinal surveys as a predictor of fertility is discussed in Albert I. Hermaln, *et al.*, "Do Intentions Predict Fertility? The Experience in Taiwan, 1967–74," *Studies in Family Planning*, Vol. 10, No. 3, March 1979, pp. 75–95; Lolagene C. Coombs, "Underlying Family-size Preferences and Reproductive Behavior," *Studies in Family Planning*, Vol. 10, No. 1, January 1979, pp. 25–36; and Roger B. Trent, "Evidence Bearing on the Construct Validity of 'Ideal Family Size'," *Population and Environment*, Vol. 3, Fall/Winter 1980, pp. 309–27.

67 Potts and Selman, 1979, pp. 6–9. See also Patrick O. Ohadikes, "Data Collection Mechanisms and Methods of Analysing Fertility Data," in

International Population Conference. Mexico 1977, Vol. 2, pp. 269–89.

68 Information on the civilian registry is drawn from A. A. Isupov and R. M. Dmitriyeva, *Organizatsiya perepisey i tekushchevo ucheta naseleniya SSSR* (Moscow: Statistika, 1980), pp. 33–44; R. Dmitriyeva, "The Current Population Estimate," *Vestnik statistiki*, No. 4, 1980, pp. 54–63; V. A. Gracheva, *Grazhdanin obrashchayetsya v ZAGS* (Moscow: Yuridicheskaya Literatura, 1983), pp. 13–32; and A. M. Vostrikova and P. G. Pod'ya-chikh, "Population Statistics," in *Istoriya sovetskoy gosudarstvennoy statistiki* (Moscow: Statistika, 1969), pp. 360–80. For a brief English-language discussion of the tsarist and Soviet vital registration system, see David M. Heer, "The Demographic Transition in the Russian Empire and the Soviet Union," *Journal of Social History*, Spring 1968, pp. 193–240.

69 A. M. Khamitova, "To the Question of Birthrate and Fertility of the Urban Population of Uzbekistan," *Meditsinskiy zhurnal uzbekistana*, No. 5, 1963, pp. 59–64.

70 Vostrikova and Pod'yachikh, 1969.

71 A. Ya. Boyarskiy, *Kurs demografii* (Moscow: Finansy i Statistika, 1985), 3rd Edition, pp. 197–212.

72 R. I. Sifman, *Dinamika rozhdayemosti v SSSR (po materialam vyborochnykh obsledovaniy)* (Moscow: Statistika, 1974), pp. 64–6.

73 V. A. Gracheva, *Registratsiya aktov grazhdanskogo sostoyaniya ispolkomami poselkovykh, selskikh sovetov* (Moscow: Yuridicheskaya Literatura, 1980), pp. 3–36.

74 The juridical significance of citizen registration is evident in the administrative arrangements within the Justice Ministry, where citizen registration is managed through the Department of Notaries and ZAGS. See V. M. Manokhin (ed.), *Sovetskoye administrativnoye pravo* (Moscow: Yuridicheskaya Literatura, 1977), pp. 469–74. See also Yu.M. Kozlov *et al.* (eds.), *Upravleniye v oblasti administrativno-politicheskoy deyatel'nosti* (Moscow: Yuridicheskaya Literatura, 1979), pp. 259–61.

75 S. G. Stetsenko, "Several Questions of the Theory and Practice of Routine Observation of Natural Population Movement," in *Sotsial'no-ekonomicheskiye osobennosti vosproizvodstva naseleniya v usloviyakh razvitogo sotsializma*, Vol. 1 (Kiev: Institut Ekonomiki AN USSR, 1976), pp. 129–33.

76 "Akty grazhdanskogo sostoyaniya," in *Bol'shaya sovetskaya entsiklopediya*, Vol. 1, p. 361; and "Ob utverzhdenii kodeksa o brake i sem'ye ukrainksoy SSR," in *Sbornik zakonov ukrainskoy SSR i ukazov prezidiuma verkhovonogo soveta ukrainksoy SSR, 1938–1979*, Vol. 2 (Kiev: Izdatel'stvo Politicheskoy Literatury Ukrainy, 1980), pp. 245–82. The relevant portions of the code are articles 158 through 193. The Lithuanian code regulating citizen registration is available in *Kodeks o brake i sem'ye litovskoy sovetskoy sotsialisticheskoy respubliki* (Vilnius: Mintis, 1981), pp. 67–78. The relevant portions of the code are articles 173–203.

77 The civilian registry offices are subordinate to the local government executive committee and to the ZAGS at the next highest level of government. These arrangements are typical of Soviet management arrangements at this level. See "Polozheniye ob otdele (byuro) zapisi aktov grazhdanskogo sostoyaniya ispolnitel'nogo komiteta rayonnogo

soveta deputatov trudyashchikhsya," 19 July 1974, in *Sovety narodnykh deputatov: status, kompetentsiya, organizatsiya deyatel'nosti. Sbornik dokumentov* (Moscow: Yuridicheskaya Literatura, 1980), pp. 418–20.

78 S. Ya. Palastina, *Registratsiya aktov grazhdanskogo sostoyaniyu* (Moscow: Yuridicheskaya Literatura, 1978), p. 19.

79 This description of the procedures involved in compiling statistical records from ZAGS data is derived from Vostrikova and Pod'yachikh, 1969; *Posobiye po statistike dlya rayonnykh i gorodskikh inspektur gosudarstvennoy statistiki* (Moscow: Statistika, 1970), pp. 346–61; and *Uchebnoye posobiye po otdelnym otraslyam statistiki* (Moscow: Gosudarstvennoye Statisticheskoye Izdatel'stvo, 1958), pp. 32–43. See also *Sobraniye postanovleniye SSSR*, No. 16, 1969, pp. 450–5.

80 V. G. Vishnyakov, *Struktura i shtaty organov sovetskogo gosudarstvennogo upravleniya* (Moscow: Nauka, 1972), p. 183.

81 Dmitriyeva, 1980. Medical facilities are presumably required to maintain records of births and infant deaths that occur within hospitals and birthing homes as well as those in which medical personnel attend the woman in her home. Completeness of records, however, was (and apparently remains) much better for institutional, as opposed to medically-assisted, but non-institutional births. Thus, the value of an audit of ZAGS records by birth lists from the health care hierarchy is highest for births that occurred within a medical facility.

82 *Turkmenskaya iskra*, 7 April 1979, p. 2.

83 See, for example, *Posobiye po statistike*, 1970, p. 350; and R. M. Dmitriyeva's comments to the 1977 All-union Conference of Statisticians, excerpted in *Sovershenstvovaniye gosudarstvennoy statistiki na sovremennom etape* (Moscow: Statistika, 1979), pp. 149–51.

84 An ethnographic study in the Chechen Ingush ASSR (a Muslim area in southern RSFSR) noted that most rural births in the 1950s were not registered within the established time period; and the births were only recorded after the children had reached school age. A. S. Smirnova, "Family and Family Life," in G. K. Gardanov, *Kul'tura i byt narodov severnogo kavkaza* (Moscow: Nauka, 1968), p. 159.

85 "O registratsii aktov grazhdanskogo sostoyaniya v kirgizskoy SSR," 8 October 1964, in *Zakonodatel'stvo kirgizskoy SSR dlya mestnykh sovetov deputatov trudyashchisya* (Frunze: Kyrgyzstan, 1968), pp. 625–26.

86 Ya. T. Tadzhiyev, *Zdravookhraneniye tadzhikstana* (Dushanbe: Ifron, 1974), pp. 216–17. These and most other data on home vs. hospital births and medically vs. non-medically assisted births probably overstate the extent of medical care involvement. Except in those cases where data are based on birth histories, methodology is not specified. The most likely source of these data is, however, described in a Soviet text on demographic statistics. Birth records from the civilian registries are compared with recorded births from medical institutions. The civilian registry records are then corrected by including births recorded by the health hierarchy, but missing from the registry. Those registry births not found in medical records are then assumed to be "non-medically assisted." (Medical records apparently provide indicators of which medically assisted births

occurred within a hospital or maternity home and which did not.) This means, of course, that the only "non-medically assisted" births that will be included in the statistics are those that were registered at the local ZAGS. This method of estimating the extent of medical assistance will necessarily result in an overestimation of the number of medically assisted births. It should be recalled, however, that US official data on birth assistance are also limited to registered births. A. Ya. Boyarskiy, *et al.*, Kurs demografii (Moscow: Statistika, 1974), p. 253.

87 M. A. Ibragimov, *Zdravookhraneniye sovetskogo azerbaydzhana* (Moscow: Meditsina, 1967), p. 211.

88 Z. M. Dzhamalova, "The Status of Birth Assistance in Uzbekistan," *Meditsinskiy zhurnal uzbekistana*, No. 3, 1959, pp. 9–12.

89 K. D. Utegenova, "The 2nd Uzbekistan Republic Scientific Conference on Questions of Obstetrics and Gynecology," *Zdravookhraneniye kazakhstana*, No. 6, 1957, pp. 56–7.

90 N. Ye. Chernova, "Development of Birth Assistance in Issyk-Kulsk Valley of Kirgizia," *Sovetskaya zdravookhraneniye kirgizii*, No. 1, 1963, pp. 36–42.

91 T. R. Akhmedova, "Analyses of Contemporary Levels of Birth Assistance in TSSR," *Zdravookhraneniye turkmenistana*, No. 3, 1979, pp. 8–10.

92 Smirnova, 1968, p. 250.

93 F. A. Gamidov, "On Studying the Influence of Several Social Hygiene Factors on the Death of Nursing Children in Rural Localities of Dagestan ASSR," *Zdravookhraneniye rossiyskoy federatsii*, No. 8, 1967, pp. 15–19.

Most of the available data on the more modernized areas of RSFSR reveal considerably higher levels of hospital births at much earlier points in time. By the early 1960s, most areas were claiming virtually 100 per cent medical coverage, with 95–9 per cent of births occurring in institutional medical facilities. See A. I. Lagutyayeva, "Development of Obstetrics in Kalinin Oblast," in *Zdravookhraneniye kalininskoy oblasti za 50 let* (Moscow: Moskovskiy Rabochiy, 1967), pp. 66–72; M. A. Romanov and L. V. Zhabid, "Safeguarding the Health of Women," in *Ocherki po istorii stanovleniye i rosta sovetskogo zdravookhranneniy v gorode astrakhani i oblasti* (Astrakhan, 1968), p. 84; and V. V. Trofimov, *Zdravookhraneniye rossiyskoy federatsii na 50 let* (Moscow: Meditsina, 1967), p. 219.

94 Vishnyakov, 1972. For a discussion of more recent efforts to improve the rural population registry, see N. Okonishnikova, "Great Attention to the Registry of the Rural Populace," in *Vestnik Statistiki*, No. 7, 1977, pp. 49–52.

95 S. P. Ryspayev, "Birthrate and its Outlook in Kirgizia," in V. N. Yakimov (ed.), *Rayonnyye osobennosti vosproizvodstva naseleniya SSSR. Materialy vsesoyuznogo mezhvuzovskogo nauchnogo simpoziumu* (Cheboksary, 1972), pp. 86–8.

96 R. Ignat'yeva, "Infant Mortality: Status, Tendencies, Perspectives," *Nashe zdorov'ye* (Moscow: Finansy i Statistika, 1983), pp. 17–27. V. Kozlov, a leading Soviet ethnographer, has argued in print on at least three occasions that better registration, particularly for the younger age groups, contributed to an increase in the recorded crude death rate for the

four Central Asian republics during the 1970s: V. I. Kozlov, "Dynamics of the Ethnic Composition of the USSR Population," *Naseleniye SSSR segodnya* (Moscow: Finansy i Statistika, 1982), pp. 31–44; V. I. Kozlov, *National'nosti SSSR. Etnodemograficheskiy obzor* (Moscow: Finansy i Statistika, 1982), p. 206; and V. I. Kozlov, "Dynamics of the Ethnic Composition of the USSR Population and Demographic Policy Issues," *Istoriya SSSR*, No. 4, July–August 1983, pp. 20–30.

97 Ya. T. Tadzhiyev and M. M. Maksumova, "Practical Recommendations to Decrease Infant Mortality in Tadzhikstan," *Zdravookhraneniye tadzhikstana*, No. 4, 1979, pp. 47–51.

98 Akhmedova, 1979.

99 S. Dadabayeva, "Persistence, Aggressiveness, Planning," *Kommunist tadzhikistana*, 27 October 1981, p. 2. In 1980, Tadzhikistan medical officers claimed that 87.8 per cent of the births there occurred with medical assistance, 76 per cent in a medical facility; this accomplishment was associated with a decline in maternal deaths. See I. A. Sazhenin, "Several Results of the Activities of the Health Organs of the Republic in the 10th Five Year Plan," *Zdravookhraneniye tadzhikistana*, No. 2, 1981, pp. 6–11.

100 "Instructions on Procedures for Conducting the 1979 Census and Completing Residential Forms and Census Lists," in *Vestnik statistiki*, No. 5, 1978, pp. 28–46. See also *Materials on the Preparation and Conduct of the USSR All-Union Population Census of 1959* (Washington, DC: US Department of Commerce, 1959), *passim*. See also Boyarskiy, 1985, pp. 179–84.

101 This discussion of the preparations and conduct of the 1979 census was drawn from Isupov and Dmitriyeva, 1980, pp. 21–32; L. M. Eroshina, G. I. Kolosova and K. A. Orekhov, "Organization of Preparation and Conducting of the Census," in A. A. Isupov and N. Z. Shvartser (eds.), *Vsesoyuznaya perepis' naseleniya 1979 godu. Sbornik statey* (Moscow: Finansy i Statistika, 1984), pp. 26–51; A. Isupov, "On the Upcoming Population Census," *Vestnik statistiki*, No. 9, 1975, pp. 3–9; and V. Ivanova, "On Developing Organizational Plans for Conducting the 1979 Population Census," *Vestnik statistiki*, No. 4, 1978, pp. 64–72. See also, A. Isupov and T. Labutova, "The Experimental Population Census of 1976," *Vestnik statistiki*, No. 3, 1977, pp. 3–9; and I. Kazinyan, "A Matter of Great Importance," *Kommunist* (Yerevan), 27 January 1978, p. 2.

102 V. Ivanova, "In Preparation of Lists of Dwellings and Rural Populated Points in the RSFSR," *Vestnik statistiki*, No. 10, 1977, pp. 32–8. On the 1970 census, see K. A. Orekhov, "Organization of Preparations and Conducting of the Population Census," in G. M. Maksimov (ed.), *Vsesoyuznaya perepis' naseleniya 1970 goda. Sbornik statey* (Moscow: Statistika, 1976), pp. 48–81.

103 K. Orekhov, "Selection and Training of Cadres – an Important Condition for Successful Conducting of the Population Census," *Vestnik statistiki*, No. 8, 1978, pp. 42–6.

104 L. Volodarskiy, "Successfully Conduct the Population Census," *Vestnik statistiki*, No. 12, 1978, pp. 3–11.

105 Isupov and Dmitriyeva, 1980, p. 27.

106 A. Ya. Boyarskiy (ed.), *Kurs demografii*, 3rd Edition (Moscow: Finansy i Statistika, 1985), pp. 183–4.

107 P. G. Pod'yachikh, "The Program and Basic Methodological Questions of the 1970 Census," in Maksimov, 1976, pp. 9–48.

108 A. A. Isupov, "On Methodological and Organizational Questions of the 1979 All-union Census," *Sovershenstvovaniye gosudarstvennoy statistiki na sovremennom etape*, 1979, pp. 111–35.

109 A. Volkov, "Study of the Family – an Important Theme in the Census," *Vestnik statistiki*, No. 5, 1977, pp. 44–55.

110 *Alma Ata. Entsiklopediya* (Alma Ata: Glavnaya Redaktsiya Kazakhskoy Sovetskoy Entsiklopedii, 1983), p. 23.

111 See, for example, I. R. Mullyadzhanov, *Demograficheskoye razvitiye uzbekskoy SSR* (Tashkent: Uzbekistan, 1983), pp. 84–85; and V. Elizarov, "Changes in the Structures of Newborns and Dynamics in the Level of Natality," in *Naseleniye SSSR segodnya* (Moscow: Finansy i Statistika, 1982), pp. 83–88.

112 See, for example, Andrew J. Sofranko and Robert C. Bealer, *Unbalanced Modernization and Domestic Instability: A Comparative Analysis* (Beverly Hills, California: Sage Publications, 1972), pp. 19–35.

113 Scanzoni, 1975, pp. 19–62.

114 *Ibid.*, p. 214; and Scanzoni, 1976.

115 Richard P. Bagozzi and M. Frances Van Loo, "Decisionmaking and Fertility: A Theory of Exchange in the Family," in Burch, *Demographic Behavior*, 1980, pp. 91–124.

116 Wrigley and Stokes, 1977.

117 Scanzoni, 1975, pp. 34–35, 43–44, 54–55, 206, 208–9; and Scanzoni, 1976.

118 Bagozzi and Van Loo, 1980.

119 Tobin, 1976.

120 Susan M. Stolka and Larry D. Barnett, "Education and Religion in Women's Attitudes Motivating Childbearing," *Journal of Marriage and the Family*, No. 31, November 1969, pp. 740–50.

121 Karen Oppenheim Mason and Larry L. Bumpass, "US Women's Sex Role Ideology, 1970," *American Journal of Sociology*, Vol. 80, No. 5, 1975, pp. 1212–19.

122 Karen Oppenheim Mason, *et al.*, "Change in US Women's Sex Role Attitudes, 1964–1974," *American Sociological Review*, Vol. 41, No. 4, August 1976, pp. 573–96.

123 Arland Thornton and Deborah Freedman, "Change in the Sex Role Attitudes of Women, 1962–1977; Evidence from a Panel Study," *American Sociological Review*, Vol. 44, No. 5, 1979, pp. 831–42.

124 Pauline A. Jones, "Sociopsychological Correlates of Family Traditionalism," in E. James Anthony and Colette Chiland (eds.), *Preventive Child Psychology in an Age of Transitions* (New York: John Wiley and Sons, 1980), pp. 279–92.

125 Andrew Cherkin and Pamela Barnhouse Walters, "Trends in United States Men's and Women's Sex-Role Attitudes: 1972 to 1978," *American*

Sociological Review, Vol. 46, No. 4, August 1981, pp. 453–60.

126 Sun and Soong, 1979.

127 Rosen and La Raia, 1972.

128 Bernard C. Rosen and Alan B. Simmons, "Industrialization, Family and Fertility: A Structural–psychological Analysis of the Brazilian Case," *Demography*, Vol. 8, No. 1, February 1971, pp. 49–69.

129 Bernard Carl Rosen, *The Industrial Connection. Achievement and the Family in Developing Societies* (New York: Aldine Publishing Company, 1982), pp. 149–50.

130 Harold Feldman, *The Ghanian Family in Transition* (Cornell University Press, 1967), pp. 84–86.

131 Wrigley and Stokes, 1977.

132 Diana M. Zuckerman, "Family Background, Sex-Role Attitudes, and Life Goals of Technical College and University Students," *Sex Roles*, Vol. 7, No. 11, 1981, pp. 1109–26.

133 Rosen and Simmons, 1971.

134 Arland Thornton, *et al.*, "Causes and Consequences of Sex-role Attitudes and Attitude Change," *American Sociological Review*, Vol. 48, No. 2, April 1983, pp. 211–47.

135 Scanzoni, 1975, pp. 68, 81, 89, 212.

136 Peggy Sanday, "Female Status in the Public Domain," in Michelle Z. Rosaldo and Louise Lamphere (eds.), *Woman, Culture, and Society* (Stanford, California: Stanford University Press, 1974), pp. 189–206.

137 Stephen J. Bahr, "Comment on 'The Study of Family Power Structure: A Review 1960–1969'," *Journal of Marriage and the Family*, No. 34, May 1972, pp. 239–43.

138 For examples of the errors that can result from failure to adjust for age group structure, see Ellen Jones and Fred W. Grupp, "Measuring Nationality Trends in the Soviet Union," *Slavic Review*, Vol. 41, No. 1, Spring 1982, pp. 112–22.

139 W. S. Robinson, "Ecological Correlations and the Behavior of Individuals," *American Sociological Review*, Vol. 15, 1950, pp. 351–57.

2

Patterns of social and demographic modernization in the USSR

The tsarist empire of the late 1890s was characterized by wide differences in economic development, social system, religion, language, and culture. The major cities in the northwest had already experienced the beginning of a rapid industrialization process promoted by the state. In isolated rural areas of the southern borderlands, by contrast, Islamic tribal cultures eked out a meager living based on a primitive subsistence economy. As with many economically and culturally diverse states, demographic modernization in Russia and (later) the Soviet Union affected different parts of the country, at different times, and at different rates. These differences have persisted into the 1980s; and the major focus of this book is on exploring the link between the current natality differentials and the socioeconomic and value changes of the last several decades. In this chapter we are concerned with placing current social and fertility dynamics in the larger framework of long-term socioeconomic and natality change.

Some idea of long-term trends in Soviet fertility can be gleaned from the reported data, presented in Figures 2.1 and 2.2. As the data in Figure 2.1 make clear, the general trend for the USSR as a whole over the last half-century has been one of long-term fertility decline. As suggested by Figure 2.2, the long-term fertility decline has stabilized in most of the USSR's European regions (the Slavic republics of RSFSR, Ukraine, and Belorussia; the Baltic republics of Latvia, Lithuania, and Estonia; and the other European republics of Georgia, Armenia, and Moldavia). Regional trends in reported birth rates for the six Muslim republics of Uzbekistan, Kazakhstan, Azerbaydzhan, Tadzhikistan, Kirgizia, and Turkmenistan display a much different pattern and remain at very high levels relative to the

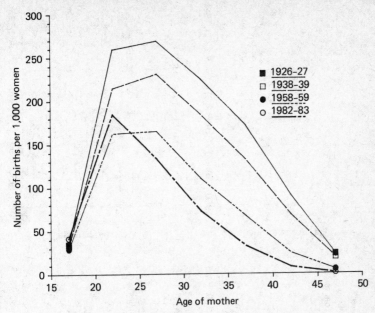

Figure 2.1 Age-specific fertility in the USSR, 1926–83

Source: Naseleniya SSSR 1973, p. 136; *Vestnik statistiki*, No. 11, 1984, p. 76

European north and west. However, the pre-1970 data for the non-European areas of the Soviet Union should be treated cautiously, because of the data problems described at some length in Chapter 1. Data for these areas must be supplemented by material from ethnographic and medical surveys that provide a more realistic picture of pre-1970 natality trends. Fortunately, data for the European areas is considerably more reliable, enabling us to chart fertility trends in these areas over a longer time span. It is to these areas that we turn first.

SOCIAL AND DEMOGRAPHIC TRENDS IN EUROPEAN RUSSIA TO 1970

European Russia on the eve of the twentieth century was still a predominantly agrarian country. To be sure, Russian industry had grown rapidly in the 1890s.[1] Large coal mines and metallurgical plants had been built in the Donets Basin and Krivoy Rog. By 1904,

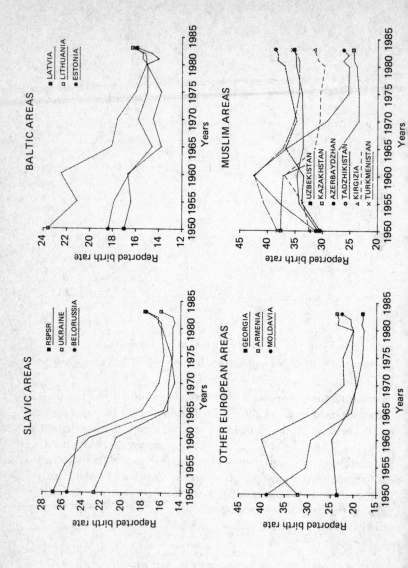

SLAVIC AREAS

■ RSPSR
□ UKRAINE
● BELORUSSIA

BALTIC AREAS

■ LATVIA
□ LITHUANIA
● ESTONIA

OTHER EUROPEAN AREAS

■ GEORGIA
□ ARMENIA
● MOLDAVIA

MUSLIM AREAS

■ UZBEKISTAN
□ KAZAKHSTAN
● AZERBAYDZHAN
○ TADZHIKISTAN
▲ KIRGIZIA
× TURKMENISTAN

72

there were an estimated half-million metallurgical workers in the tsarist empire. The textile industry, centered in Moscow, Vladimir, and St Petersburg, also had expanded rapidly in the last decade of the century. In 1904, tsarist Russia employed over 600,000 textile workers.

But if the industrial revolution had begun in earnest in Russia in the 1890s, much remained of traditional life styles. Even on the eve of the war, industrial and construction workers constituted only 9 per cent of the labor force.[2] Over three-fourths of the population then were peasants and 75 per cent of the labor force were agricultural workers.[3] The vast majority of the empire's subjects lived in the country; only 15 per cent of the populace in European Russia were classified as urban in 1897.[4] Literacy rates were relatively low for the empire as a whole (28.4 per cent of the 9 to 49-year-old populace), and only marginally higher for the three Slavic areas.[5]

The social system in the countryside conformed in many aspects with the patriarchal system described by the fertility transition model. Social and economic activities centered on the peasant household and the rural community.[6] The Russian peasant household was the focal point for economic and social relationships. Although the large extended family was no longer predominant by the turn of the century, the peasant family remained the major economic unit of production, as well as the basic unit of consumption. The earnings of household members belonged to the common fund, controlled by the head of the household.[7] The role of the household as an economic unit was reinforced by tsarist legal policy and peasant practices.[8] Land allotments were assigned, not to individuals, but to the household as a collective unit. The household was also subject to joint responsibility for both taxes and redemption payments on the landholdings. Household members could not leave the household without permission of the head; local authorities supported this practice by refusing to grant such individuals a passport against the wishes of the household head.[9]

The household, through its head (generally the eldest male), provided the primary intermediary between the individual household members and the second major social institution in peasant society – the commune. The pre-revolutionary commune served as the major unit of local government in the country; its administrative functions included law enforcement, tax collection, road maintenance, and social welfare. The commune was also an important economic institution; it was the legal owner of much of the peasant land. Individual households owned only the garden plot around their house. Most of the other land was not owned by the household, but by the commune, which allotted land to each household. These holdings were periodically re-allocated by the commune gathering (*skhod*). The commune also owned most collective-use property, primarily pasture and forest; and administered collective activities, such as workshops and mills. In short, the rural commune was, after the peasant household, the major social and economic institution.

The patriarchal authority patterns within the family/household unit were reflected in the social position of women. Women were not considered to be true household members and in most areas could not function as head of household or represent the family in the commune gathering. Since the commune fulfilled so many political and economic functions, the exclusion of women from it underlined their subordinate social status. This is not to deny that peasant women in pre-revolutionary Russia filled an important role within the household. In fact, much of the family labor was female labor. But this economic contribution was not reflected in equal social status either within the household or within the rural community. The subordinate status of women was also reflected in their much lower literacy rates, as shown in Figure 2.3. Only 15 per cent of the 9 to 49-year-old females in those areas of the Russian empire that later became the Russian republic were literate; compared to 44 per cent of the males.[10] The female/male literacy ratio for the region was 35 – one testimony to the differential access of the sexes to what schooling was available. Women derived much of their social prestige from their maternal role and early marriage was common.[11]

These social conditions were accompanied by relatively high fertility. The total fertility index for European Russia (according to the Coale, Anderson, and Harm figures) was 0.540.[12] The indexes for the 50 provinces ranged from a low of 0.290 for Livonia to 0.648 in Voronezh. Most of the provinces were clustered in the higher ranges; only 13 of the 50 provinces had a total fertility index below 0.500. This pattern – high natality with a moderate spread in fertility values – indicates that European Russia had only just begun the decline to lower fertility at the turn of the century (Figure 2.4). The lowest fertility was recorded in the three Baltic provinces. Fertility was also lower in the 5 gubernias of Belorussia; natality declines had already begun in those provinces in the 1860s.[13] The natality pattern

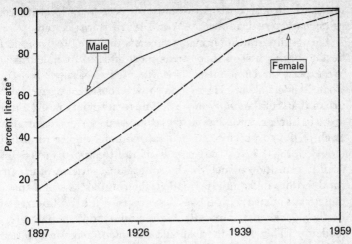

Figure 2.3 Literacy in the RSFSR, 1897–1959
*Ages 9–49

Source: *Narodnoye obrazovaniye, nauka i kultura*, Moscow: Statistika,
1971, p. 21

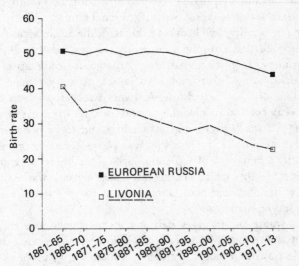

Figure 2.4 Birth rate trends in pre-revolutionary Russia

Source: *AG Rashin, Naseleniye rossii z 100 let:1811–1913*, Statisticheskiye
ocherki, Moscow, 1956, pp. 167–68

observed, then, is consistent with the socioeconomic level and gender roles characteristic of the pre-World War I tsarist empire.

The fertility transition model predicts that the process of fertility decline begins first in those areas most affected by modernization. We expect, therefore, lower urban than rural natality. Indeed, the Coale, Anderson, and Harm data show a consistent pattern of lower urban than rural natality in 1897. The total fertility index for urban areas in European Russia is 0.372, compared to 0.567 for rural areas. Each of the 50 provinces had a substantially higher rural fertility index in 1897. Also consistent with the trends suggested by the fertility transition model are the contrasting patterns of urban and rural fertility differentials. In 1897, the rural areas still displayed a pattern associated with the earliest stages of the fertility transition. Fertility is almost uniformly high; fertility differentials are only moderate. Therefore, there should be much more striking fertility differentials for the urban areas, since these regions were already advancing into the intermediate stages of the transition, which typically display pronounced fertility differentials. The Coale data show that this is indeed the case.

The fertility model also predicts that the relationships hypothesized for the intermediate stages of the transition (with measures of modernization and erosion of traditional family values negatively related to natality) will be most evident for the urban areas that have advanced furthest into the intermediate stages. Coale, *et al.*, provide the results of regression analyses of urban and rural marital fertility data using three socioeconomic variables: urbanity, female literacy, and socio-occupational status. As expected, their analysis revealed only weak correlations for the rural data. The strongest association ($r=0.373$) was between marital fertility and the proportion of the population in each province that was peasant. Socioeconomic variables did a better job of explaining urban natality – the relationship between natality and average city size (logged) was 0.623; that between natality and occupational status (proportion of workers in secondary industry) was -0.707.

To explore the linkages between social change and changes in natality more fully, we tested the relationships hypothesized by the fertility transition model in the fifty gubernias of European Russia. To minimize the disproportionate influence of outlying values, we logged both dependent and independent variables. Unlike the Coale team, we were interested in examining the impact of marital patterns,

Table 2.1. *Fertility relationships, 1897 (Zero Order Correlations)*

	(Index of Total Fertility)			
	Unlogged		Logged	
Measures	All 50 Gubernias	Excluding 3 Low-fertility Gubernias	All 50 Gubernias	Excluding 3 Low-fertility Gubernias
Modernization measures				
% Peasant	0.16	0.22	0.11	0.18
% Urban	−0.51[b]	−0.46[b]	−0.52[b]	−0.40[a]
Literacy	−0.82[b]	−0.66[b]	−0.83[b]	−0.65[b]
Measures of gender roles				
Early marriage	0.76[b]	0.75[b]	0.82[b]	0.76[b]
% Females over 15 married	0.87[b]	0.87[b]	0.86[b]	0.88[b]
Female literacy	−0.82[b]	−0.70[b]	−0.84[b]	−0.67[b]
Female literacy (over 10)	−0.82[b]	−0.68[b]	−0.83[b]	−0.66[b]
Female/male literacy ratio	−0.77[b]	−0.57[b]	−0.75[b]	−0.56[b]
Female/male literacy ratio (over 10)	−0.77[b]	−0.57[b]	−0.74[b]	−0.55[b]

[a] Significant at 0.005 level.
[b] Significant at 0.001 level.

as well as other aspects of family and gender role values, on natality. For this reason, we used the Coale team's total fertility index as the major dependent variable. We also examined two other measures of natality, the 1901–05 birthrate and the 1911–13 birthrate. Each of these measures – when correlated with various modernization and family values measures – yielded results similar to those when the Coale team's total fertility index was used. Pearson correlation coefficients between the index of total fertility and various measures of modernization and family roles are provided in Table 2.1. The Pearson correlation coefficient (r) is a measure of association between two variables that ranges from +1 to −1. Correlations near zero indicate the absence of a relationship between the two variables; those near +1 or −1 show very strong relationships.

Table 2.2. *Urban–rural fertility differentials in Belorussia, 1897*

| Gubernia | General fertility rate (Births per 1,000 women aged 15 to 49) | | |
	Total	in urban areas	in rural areas
Vilna	158.2	115.6	164.7
Vitebsk	168.2	131.0	174.9
Grodno	175.7	132.5	183.9
Minsk	193.5	143.3	199.8
Mogilev	194.9	136.8	200.7
Total for five gubernias	179.1	131.7	186.1

Source: L.P. Shakhot'ko, *Rozhdayemost' v Belorussii* (Minsk: Nauka i Tekhnika, 1975), p. 30.

The hypothesized relationship between modernization and natality receives limited support. We found no link between natality rates and social class (per cent peasant). The moderate correlation between per cent urban and natality (r=0.52 for the logged variables) declines substantially (r=0.40) when the three low fertility Baltic gubernias are excluded from the analysis. In part, these findings may be due to the inadequacy of those variables as measures of modernization. It is possible that administrative definitions of urban populations varied so widely from gubernia to gubernia that the impact of urbanization was obscured. A Soviet analysis of demographic developments in Belorussia revealed sharp urban–rural differentials in natality, with substantially lower general fertility rates among women residing in urban areas (Table 2.2). These findings confirm the pattern of lower urban fertility apparent in the Coale rural and urban fertility ratios.

Correlation analysis revealed a strong link between natality and another measure of modernization (literacy). Literacy was strongly linked with fertility (r=−0.82 for logged variables); and the relationship persisted (r=−0.65) even with the three Baltic provinces excluded from the analysis. This finding is in line with that reported by the Soviet demographer Shakhot'ko for the regions of Belorussia; he found an extremely strong relationship (−0.987) between literacy level and marital fertility.[14]

Somewhat stronger relationships are expected between measures of female participation and natality in modern society. Indeed, almost all measures of female participation – early marriage, female literacy, and female/male literacy ratios – proved to be strong predictors of fertility. Soviet analyses of the 1897 data also revealed strong statistical relationships between the proportion of brides below age 20 and natality. Urlanis found a 0.69 correlation for this variable and the birth rate for the 50 gubernias of European Russia; Shakhot'ko a correlation of 0.879 between this variable and marital fertility rates for the 50 gubernias.[15] Our measure of early marriage, derived from the 1897 census, was somewhat different; we computed the proportion of females aged 15 to 19 who were married. Like Urlanis and Shakhot'ko, we found a strong relationship between early marriage and fertility ($r=0.82$) for the logged variables. Two measures of female literacy (proportion literate and proportion of population aged 10 and above literate) were also strongly related to fertility ($r=-0.84$ and $r=-0.83$ respectively). We also computed a female/male literacy ratio for both total population and population aged 10 and over. Contrary to expectation, neither variable proved to be a better predictor of natality than female literacy. The correlation between total fertility and female/male literacy for total population was -0.75, between total fertility and female/male literacy for the population over ten, -0.74.

Another area of interest was the interrelationships between measures of family values. The relevant correlations are listed in Table 2.3. The six measures of female roles are moderately inter-correlated, although the strength of the relationships decrease in size when the three Baltic republics are excluded. These findings lend some support to the assumption, discussed in Chapter 1, that marital patterns are part of an interrelated set of behaviors and attitudes relating to the family and approved sex roles. In other words, those regions with traditional marital patterns (high levels of early marriage) also tend to be those with low levels of female literacy.

What does the 1897 data tell us about hypothesis 3, which states that those areas of greatest modernization should display the most erosion in patriarchal family values? This hypothesis receives only limited support (Table 2.4). Social class is unrelated to measures of gender roles; and the apparent relationship between the urban percentage and female literacy measures is radically decreased when the three Baltic republics are excluded. Only literacy levels reveal a strong relationship with female role measures.

Table 2.3. *Measures of patriarchal family values, 1897 (Pearson correlation coefficients, logged variables)*

	Early marriage	% Over 15 females married	Female literacy	Female literacy (over 10)	F/M literacy ratio	F/M literacy ratio (over 10)
Early marriage						
50 gubernias	1.00					
47 gubernias	1.00					
% Over-15 females married						
50 gubernias	0.832[b]	1.000				
47 gubernias	0.787[b]	1.000				
Female literacy						
50 gubernias	−0.599[b]	−0.671[b]	1.000			
47 gubernias	−0.388[a]	−0.571[b]	1.000			
Female literacy (over 10 population)						
50 gubernias	−0.613[b]	−0.660[b]	0.996[b]	1.000		
47 gubernias	−0.414[a]	−0.554[b]	0.993[b]	1.000		
Female/male literacy ratio						
50 gubernias	−0.584[b]	−0.537[b]	0.923[b]	0.933[b]	1.000	
47 gubernias	−0.397[a]	−0.381[a]	0.875[b]	0.892[b]	1.000	
Female/male literacy ratio (over 10 population)						
50 gubernias	−0.576[b]	−0.520[b]	0.915[b]	0.925[b]	0.999[b]	1.000
47 gubernias	−0.388[a]	−0.359	0.864[b]	0.882[b]	0.999[b]	1.000

[a] Significant at 0.005 level.
[b] Significant at 0.001 level.

Analysis of the 1897 data, then, reveals strong support only for that portion of our model that specifies a causal link between family values and natality. All six measures of female status proved to be moderate to strong predictors of natality. A scatterplot of rates of natality and female literacy is provided in Figure 2.5. Most of the gubernias in 1897 cluster in the high-natality, low literacy section of the plot. Fertility transition is most marked in the 10 or so gubernias that display reduced natality and higher levels of female literacy. While these findings are not definitive and our analysis of the 1897 data suffers from the lack of more valid measures of modernization, the relationships revealed here lend at least partial support to the hypothesized value system/natality relationship.

Three major events intervened between the census of 1897 and that of 1926, the next point for which we have natality data: World War I,

Table 2.4. *The link between modernization and family values, 1897*

Pearson correlation coefficients, measures of family values and gender roles
(Logged Values)

Modernization measures	Early marriage	% Over 15 females married	Female literacy	Female literacy (over 10)	F/M literacy	F/M literacy (over 10)
% Peasant						
50 gubernias	−0.041	−0.081	−0.226	−0.216	−0.278	−0.294
47 gubernias	−0.030	−0.074	−0.352	−0.335	−0.377[a]	−0.394[a]
% Urban						
50 gubernias	−0.199	−0.351	0.639[b]	0.638[b]	0.530[b]	0.536[b]
47 gubernias	−0.016	−0.230	0.591[b]	0.587[b]	0.425[b]	0.433[b]
Literacy						
50 gubernias	−0.588[b]	−0.701[b]	0.960[b]	0.956[b]	0.792[b]	0.780[b]
47 gubernias	−0.360	−0.621[b]	0.918[b]	0.912[b]	0.637[b]	0.621[b]

[a] Significant at 0.005 level.
[b] Significant at 0.001 level.

the Bolshevik Revolution in 1917, and the subsequent period of civil war and internal disorders. For the European areas of what became the USSR, urbanization increased only marginally during this period, from 15 per cent in 1897 to 18 per cent in 1926.[16] Literacy rates, however, rose dramatically – fuelled by Bolshevik ideological commitment to literacy and the overruling practical need for a literate labor force. The proportion literate among 9 to 49-year-olds in RSFSR increased from 28.6 per cent to 60.9 per cent.

Trends affecting traditional patriarchal familial systems and gender roles during this period present a picture of both change and continuity. On the one hand, the role of women in the family and peasant communities underwent a major change during World War I. With so many men called up for military service, the women began assuming a more influential role in commune affairs. Many war widows became the head of household.[17] After the war, the Bolshevik government instituted legal equality for women. Female access to educational and, to a lesser extent, occupational opportunity in the modernized labor force increased appreciably. Literacy rates for females tripled, up from 15.4 per cent in 1897 to 46.4 per cent in 1926.[18] The female/male literacy ratio, a rough measure of female access to social and occupational roles in the modernized sector, increased from 35 to 60. (A ratio of 100 would indicate female literacy

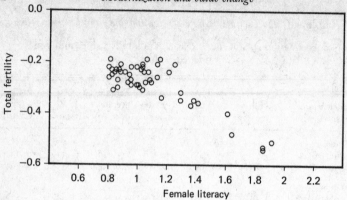

Figure 2.5 Total fertility and female literacy in 50 Russian gubernias (all values logged)

exactly even with that of males.) Female labor force participation rates were high, reflecting a long tradition of high rates of female participation in agricultural labor. In 1926, females in the Soviet Union as a whole constituted 47 per cent of the employed populace.[19] Female access to jobs in the modern sectors of the economy were considerably more restricted. Only 26 per cent of those engaged in mental labor were women;[20] and only 23 per cent of the non-agricultural labor force was female.[21] In 1928, women were 26 per cent of the industrial labor force.[22] These data suggest a wide range of social changes affecting traditional patriarchal familial systems and gender roles, at least for women in urban areas.

Rural life styles, however, were much less changed; and this was where the majority of people lived. Many peasant families in central Russia were still of the large, extended variety (three or more generations). Over a third of the inhabitants of Gadyshi, a small village studied by Soviet ethnographers in 1925, lived in families of this type.[23] Other Soviet studies of rural life from this period make it clear that arranged marriages were still fairly common. The family/ household unit still retained many of its traditional functions as an economic production unit. Nine-tenths of the households belonged to the peasant *mir* (commune) which met periodically as the village *skhod* to determine the allocation of land to each household (based on the number of members) and decide the timing of ploughing, sowing, and harvesting. The peasant household at this time was still to some degree a subsistence economy, with the family members consuming much of their own production. A growing number of peasants, however, were becoming increasingly dependent on the urban labor market, continuing a trend evident in the pre-revolutionary period of supplementing their agricultural livelihood with temporary jobs in lumbering, construction, and mining.[24] In addition, a large portion of peasant income was derived from sales of farm products on the market. Nonetheless, peasant life styles in central Russia still retained many aspects of pre-revolutionary values, a factor reflected in lower rural literacy rates (55 per cent of the 9 to 49-year-old cohort for RSFSR vs. 85 per cent in urban areas).

Approved roles for women were also more traditional in the countryside. This is reflected in relative female/male literacy ratios. In 1926, the female/male literacy ratio for rural areas of RSFSR was only 53, compared to 85 for the urban areas. In fact, the RSFSR female/male literacy ratio for rural areas was lower in 1926 than that for urban areas in 1897! Nonetheless, rural women in 1926 enjoyed much freer access to schooling than their counterparts in 1897; 39 per cent of the rural females aged 9 to 49 were literate in 1926, compared to only 11 per cent in 1897.[25] Socioeconomic and value changes associated with modernization were spreading, but at a slower pace, to the Russian countryside.

These social changes were accompanied by significant changes in natality levels. As the Coale data make clear, the process of fertility decline had, by 1926, affected almost every area in European Russia. The total fertility index declined from 0.540 in 1897 to 0.428 in 1926, ranging from 0.167 (in Latvia) to 0.537 (in the Bashkir ASSR). There were significant fertility differentials for both the urban and rural areas. Again, as one would expect in the intermediate stages of the fertility transition, urban natality (0.289) was significantly lower than rural natality (0.465). The urban/rural differentials were even more striking than those for 1897 and each of the 50 regions had significantly higher rural than urban fertility. Since both urban and rural areas were clearly well into the intermediate stages of the transition by this time, strong relationships should exist between modernization variables and natality in both the urban and rural fertility data. This expectation is only partly borne out by the regressions presented by Coale, *et al.* For the rural data, the best socioeconomic predictor is the proportion of peasants (1897); but the association is only moderately high ($r=0.555$). For the urban data, the best socioeconomic predictor is urban proportion in cities over 50,000; but again, the association is only a moderate one ($r=-0.450$).

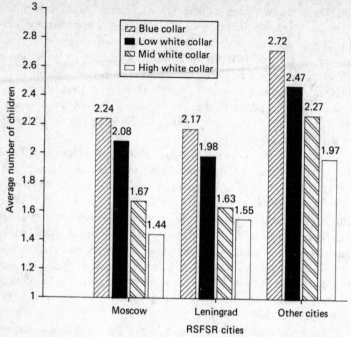

Figure 2.6 Family size and social class, 1926

Source: R. I. Sifman, "Fertility According to the Data of the 1926 Family Census", in A. G. Volkov (ed.), *Demograficheskoye razvitiye sem'i* (Moscow 1979), pp. 151–70

Stronger support for the hypothesized relationships is provided by an analysis of the 1926 census data provided by R. I. Sifman. She makes use of a special analysis of family size and composition in Moscow, Leningrad and 453 other RSFSR cities.[26] These data are used to construct measures of fertility (average number of children per family) for Moscow, Leningrad, and other urban areas, standardized by length of marriage. Sifman's analysis reveals higher blue-collar class natality for all three populations. Among white-collar families, those in higher status groups had correspondingly lower natality measures (Figure 2.6). Sifman also provides data showing the impact of early marriage on natality; an earlier age at marriage is associated with higher fertility, even when social group is controlled (Figure 2.7). In urban areas outside of Moscow and Leningrad, for example, women in the white-collar class who

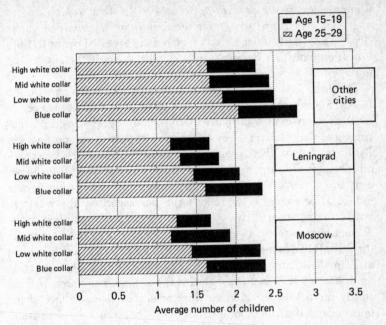

Figure 2.7 Family size in RSFSR cities, by social class and age at marriage, 1926

Source: as for Figure 2.6

married before age 20 averaged 2.42 children after 13 to 17 years of marriage; those who married between 25 and 29, averaged only 1.71. In other words, both variables – social class (a measure of modernization) and early marriage (a measure of traditionality in gender roles) – have an independent impact on natality.

Further insight into the role of social change in natality decline is provided by Strumilin's data, which detail the impact of migration to the city on natality. Nearly a third of his 1934 sample consisted of individuals who had migrated to the city after 1928. The natality of this group of migrants was substantially higher than that of long-term city residents – 212 births per 1,000 years of married life between 1929 and 1933 for migrants compared to 156 for long-term residents. Comparing the natality of migrant women before and after their arrival in the city, Strumilin found a strong pattern of diminished marital fertility for every age group; births per 1,000 rural women aged 16 to 44 averaged 280 for the four years prior to migration, compared to 216 for the four years after arrival in the city.[27] These data indicate that the patterns suggested by the fertility transition model for the intermediate stages were, in fact, occurring in the USSR in the mid-1920s.

The years following the 1926 census were tumultuous ones for the USSR. Stalin embarked on a program of enforced industrial development accompanied by a particularly bloody effort to seize firmer control of the countryside by collectivizing agricultural production. By the late 1930s, these programs had resulted in major socioeconomic changes. By 1937, agricultural workers had declined from 80 per cent to 56 per cent of the labor force, while the proportion of industrial personnel in the labor force increased from 8 per cent in 1926 to 24 per cent.[28] In 1939, 33 per cent of the population in the Slavic areas was urban (up from 18 per cent in 1926).[29] Literacy in the RSFSR had increased to 90 per cent of the 9 to 49-year-old cohort; and female literacy was 84 per cent. The female/male literacy ratio for this area was 87 in 1939.[30] During the 1930s, women were making steady inroads in the modern workforce. The female share of the blue-collar industrial labor force climbed from 29 per cent in 1928 to 40 per cent in 1935; female gains were particularly striking in the mining industry and in machine building/metal working – areas traditionally closed to women.[31] By 1939, the proportion of females in the overall labor force slipped slightly (down from 47 per cent in 1926 to 43 per cent in 1939), but they continued to make increases in the white-collar portion of the labor force involved in mental labor, which increased from 26 per cent in 1926 to 32 per cent female in 1939.[32] In 1940, 39 per cent of the non-collective farm labor force was female; the analogous figure for the RSFSR was 41 per cent.[33] Thirty-eight per cent of personnel in industry and nearly a quarter of those in construction were female.[34]

These trends continued after World War II. By 1955, 31 per cent of the labor force was employed in industry or construction.[35] By 1959, the urban share of the population in the Soviet Union's Slavic areas increased to 50 per cent.[36] The corresponding figure for all of European Russia was 52 per cent. For RSFSR alone, 43 per cent of the labor force was employed in industry, construction, transportation, and communication. Agricultural workers constituted only 30 per cent of RSFSR's labor force.[37] Literacy in the European areas was virtually universal for the 9 to 49-year-olds, and educational levels had also registered large increases. For example, in RSFSR, the percentage aged 10 and above with incomplete secondary education and above increased from 11 per cent in 1939 to 36 per cent in 1959.[38] Similar trends can be observed in other areas of European Russia.

Measures of the erosion of traditional sex roles also showed further change. Data on the sex breakdowns of various occupations in the RSFSR reveal continued increases in female participation in the "modern" blue-collar jobs between 1939 and 1959. The female share of chemical workers increased from 49 per cent in 1939 to 61 per cent in 1959. The most dramatic gains during this period, however, were in white-collar jobs. In 1939, only 13 per cent of the state and Party managers, six per cent of the economic managers – i.e., factory and farm directors, and 22 per cent of the engineer/technical employees in the RSFSR were women. By 1959, these percentages had increased to 27, 13, and 41 respectively.[39] The RSFSR female/male ratio for incomplete secondary education (for the working-age populace only) increased from 81 in 1939 to 100 in 1959 – a dramatic indicator of the extent to which women had been integrated in the modern sector.[40] The incidence of early marriage declined. In RSFSR, 14 per cent of the 18 to 19-year-old girls were married in 1959, down from 22 per cent in 1939.[41]

As in 1926, rural life styles in European Russia were affected less by the significant socioeconomic changes that had transformed the USSR into an industrialized power by 1959. Soviet ethnographic studies of life in central Russian collective farms reveal a great deal of continuity in peasant family life styles in the late 1940s and early 1950s. The rural family was still a powerful social and economic unit. Within European Russian collective farms, the right to cultivate a private plot and maintain private livestock was granted to the household unit, not the individual.[42] The more traditional patterns of family life are evident in 1959 data on early marriage; in the RSFSR, for example, 19 per cent of the 18 and 19-year-old girls from rural areas were married, compared to 11 per cent of their urban counterparts.[43]

Nonetheless, social changes had seriously undermined traditional familial patterns among the Russian peasantry in 1959. A diminishing proportion of the families were extended; and a growing proportion of families were headed by women, most of them widowed by World War II. Rural female heads of household represent an important break from pre-revolutionary Russian peasant practices, in which women were not allowed to represent the family in the village assembly.[44]

These social changes were accompanied by continuing natality declines. By 1959, as the Coale data demonstrate, fertility in the European areas had begun to stabilize at fairly low levels. Total fertility had declined to 0.207, ranging from 0.142 (Moscow and Poltava) to 0.375 (Kalmyk ASSR). By this time, the sharp fertility differentials observed in 1926 were evening out. This process is clearest in the urban areas. Rural–urban differentials in fertility levels are still apparent. Total urban fertility in 1959 was 0.171, while that for rural areas was 0.249. As these numbers demonstrate, the rural–urban differential had already become less sharp, suggesting that late-transitioning oblasts had begun to reach the lower natality levels of early transitioning areas. Contrary to expectations, Coale, Anderson and Harm found only weak correlations between rural marital fertility and the three socioeconomic measures that they tested. It is not clear, however, whether these findings reflect the real relationship, or whether they are the result of methodological weaknesses in the Coale measure.

To investigate the link between natality and socioeconomic development more fully, we examined 1959 fertility in 108 oblast-level units in the European areas of the USSR. The area covered includes all oblast-level territorial divisions in the Ukraine, Belorussia, Latvia, Estonia, Lithuania, Moldavia, and the RSFSR (excluding the six small Muslim autonomous republics in southern RSFSR). Our measures of natality were crude birth rate, child-to-woman ratio, general fertility rate, and two indexes of total fertility; one based on reported births, the other on the number of children under 10 years of age. Although the natality measures we used differ from those used by the Coale team, the general picture of fairly moderate natality differentials suggested by the Coale data was confirmed by our findings. The mean index of total fertility (based on reported births) ratio for the 92 cases for which data were available was 0.220, ranging from a low of 0.110 in Leningrad City to a high of 0.385 in Kalmyk ASSR. The coefficient of variation is a modest 0.209, indicating that most oblasts cluster fairly close to the mean. A similar pattern emerges from examination of differentials in general fertility rates. These findings are consistent with our theoretical model of fertility transition, which indicates that the later stages of

Table 2.5. *Modernization and fertility in European USSR, 1959 (Zero order correlations)*

				Index of total fertility	
Variable	Child-to-woman ratio (108 cases)	General fertility rate (92 cases)	Crude birth rate (92 cases)	(reported births) (92 cases)	(children under 10) (108 cases)
% Urban	−0.416[b]	−0.184	−0.112	−0.267[a]	−0.426[b]
White-collar employees as % of labor force	−0.321[b] (104)	0.023	0.026	−0.096	−0.332[b] (104)
% with higher educ. and above	−0.605[b]	−0.365[b]	−0.317[b]	−0.413[b]	−0.613[b]
% with complete secondary and above	−0.623[b]	−0.388[b]	−0.327[b]	−0.446[b]	−0.630[b]
% with incomplete secondary and above	−0.625[b]	−0.413[b]	−0.330[b]	−0.481[b]	−0.631[b]
Professionals per 1,000 25 to 59 year olds	−0.492[b] (101)	−0.256	−0.212	−0.300[a]	−0.501[b] (101)
Semi-professionals per 1,000 20 to 59 year olds	−0.125 (101)	0.053	0.098	−0.016	−0.137 (101)

[a] Significant at 0.005 level.
[b] Significant at 0.001 level.

the fertility transition are characterized by declining fertility differentials.

Our model also predicts that the strong relationship between modernization and value change, on the one hand, and natality on the other, will decline as late-modernizing groups and areas adopt the dominant family value system of the early-modernizing groups and regions. Consequently, we expect only moderate statistical relationships between socioeconomic variables and fertility measures. Tables 2.5 and 2.6 present representative results of our analysis. The strongest statistical associations are found using the child-to-woman ratio and the index of total fertility based on the number of children under age 10 as the dependent variable. This may be due to the nature of these measures, which capture ten years of natality behavior. Assuming, as suggested by the model, that socio-

Table 2.6. *Family values and fertility in European USSR, 1959 (Zero order correlations)*

				Index of total fertility	
Variable	Child-to-woman ratio (108 cases)	General fertility rate (92 cases)	Crude birth rate (92 cases)	(reported births) (92 cases)	(children under 10) (108 cases)
% Females with higher educ.	−0.556[b]	−0.298[a]	−0.238	−0.361[b]	−0.567[b]
% Females with complete sec. and above	−0.571[b]	−0.302[a]	−0.232	−0.374[b]	−0.582[b]
Female/male higher educ. ratio	0.340[b]	0.291[a]	0.350[b]	0.215	0.317[b]
Female/male complete sec. educ. ratio	0.342[b]	0.356[b]	0.406[b]	0.276[a]	0.311[b]
Dependency ratio	−0.024	0.130	0.183	0.059	−0.032
% Females of working age in labor force	−0.059	−0.160	−0.157	−0.156	−0.074
Female professionals	−0.583[b] (32)	−0.247 (31)	−0.174 (31)	−0.301[a] (31)	−0.594[b] (32)
Female semi-professionals	−0.056 (32)	0.147 (31)	0.196 (31)	0.105 (31)	−0.041 (32)
Female/male professionals	0.384 (32)	0.361 (31)	0.364 (31)	0.345 (31)	0.378 (32)
Female/male semi-professionals	0.572[b] (32)	0.603[b] (31)	0.615[b] (31)	0.584[b] (31)	0.555[b] (32)

[a] Significant at 0.005 level.
[b] Significant at 0.001 level.

economic correlates of natality decline in the late portions of the intermediate stages of the transition, we anticipate stronger results for these measures, which encompass 10 years of natality behavior, than for ones like general fertility rate and index of total fertility based on reported births that are based on only one year of natality behavior. The smaller correlations when crude birth rate is used are due to this same factor, plus the lower precision of the crude rates as a measure of fertility (unlike the other two measures, crude birth rate does not standardize for the proportion of women in the childbearing years). The crude birth rate results are provided to highlight the advantages of age-standardized measures of natality, particularly for analyses of areas in the later stages of fertility decline.

One pattern emerging from these findings is a declining role for measures of family values and an increasing role for modernization measures as predictors of natality. As suggested by the analysis of turn-of-the-century fertility relationships and confirmed by an examination of current fertility differentials within late-modernizing oblasts and minority groups (see Chapter 3), measures of female roles and, in particular, female-to-male education and occupation ratios, provide by far the most powerful predictors of fertility during the intermediate stages of the natality transition. As our investigation of the European oblasts as of 1959 makes clear, the strong negative relationship between female-to-male education ratios and fertility has disappeared. In fact, all four ratios have a weak positive association with natality. These findings suggest that as the values supporting egalitarian sex roles and small families are diffused throughout society, the relatively small remaining differences in fertility are better explained by measures of socioeconomic development.

We also examined the impact of labor force participation on natality. Our interest in this subject does not stem from the logic of our fertility transition model. Western studies, after all, indicate that female labor force activity *per se* is not a good indicator of the erosion of family values. However, other researchers who have examined the 1959 Soviet fertility data, particularly Peter Mazur and David Heer, have arrived at conflicting conclusions. Both the Mazur and Heer studies are based on separate urban and rural data for 157 oblast-level units using 1959 boundaries. (Our fertility analysis is based on the 1970 boundaries of those units). Mazur, who reported findings separately for European and southern tier oblasts, measured female labor force participation as the ratio of dependent women, "computed on the basis of information for women aged 16 to 54 (excluding students) who derive their sources of livelihood from persons other than their close relatives."[45] David Heer measured female labor force participation as the percentage of females who were not dependents.[46]

In our analysis, we used two measures of female labor force participation: a dependency ratio (the percentage of working-age women who were non-student dependents; that is, who were not in school, not in the labor force, and not involved in private plot agriculture) and the percentage of employed persons among the labor force age population. This latter measure rests on the assumption (untestable) that male labor force participation rates do not vary significantly from oblast to oblast. If this is true, overall labor force participation might be a useful proxy for female employment. It should be noted that these measures are very crude ones. Female *kolkhoz* members, for example, are included in the "employed" category by the Soviets, regardless of how many days they work on the collective farm. Indeed, a substantial minority of *kolkhoz* members (mostly women) are employed only a minimal number of days per year, yet are apparently enumerated as part of the labor force. Similarly, women involved in personal agriculture may in fact spend relatively small portions of their time on the private plot. Hence, our measure of labor force participation probably substantially overstates the level of female employment, particularly in rural, agricultural regions.

Neither of our measures revealed a link with natality in the European areas of the USSR. Mazur, likewise, found little support for a negative relationship between female labor force participation and natality. David Heer, although concurring that the "influence of variation in female labor force participation rates appears to be relatively minor," asserts nonetheless that "the relationship between the percentage of females in the work force and fertility is no less pronounced than that reported in studies concerning other nations." Our findings are difficult to reconcile with Heer's; he reported a negative 0.34 relationship between the percentage of female non-dependents and natality for the country as a whole. We found a correlation of only 0.12 for the nation and −0.24 for the European areas, indicating virtually no relationship between labor force participation and fertility. Our inability to replicate Heer's findings stems in part from differences in data; his work was based on 1959 boundaries, ours on 1970 boundaries. Despite the different approaches, none of these findings provide support for the hypothesis that female workforce participation, in and of itself, lowers fertility. However, when modernization is controlled, the dependency ratio shows a moderately strong relationship with fertility. For example, the partial correlation between dependency and the index of total fertility (based on children under 10) is 0.43, controlling for urbanization, and 0.34 controlling for completed secondary education and above.

Our analyses of the "European USSR" oblasts, then, indicates moderately strong statistical links between socioeconomic measures and natality. As predicted by the model, the continued erosion of patriarchal family values was accompanied by further fertility declines. The best predictors of natality were overall education (a measure of modernization) and female education (a measure of the erosion of patriarchal values). For other variables, the relationships have declined; and for measures of relative female-to-male education virtually disappeared or even reversed. This decline in the explanatory power of socioeconomic variables is in line with our expectations that fertility correlates are tied to specific stages of the fertility transition. As areas or groups converge at lower fertility levels, prior relationships change in a predictable way. We expect this trend to be even more pronounced for 1970 data about this region, since by 1970, the fertility transition had progressed even further in the European areas of the Soviet Union.

SOCIAL AND DEMOGRAPHIC TRENDS IN THE CAUCASUS AND CENTRAL ASIA TO 1960

Most of the non-European areas, particularly those on the southern tier, are still in a much earlier stage of the fertility transition. These areas were much less advanced in 1917 as reflected in the literacy data in Figure 2.8; and the traditional familial system characteristic of many conservative Muslim societies persisted there well into the twentieth century. Like many other conservative Muslim societies, the social system also tended to be traditional and patriarchal. Family and community life was strictly delineated by sex and approved roles for women were limited to those of wife, mother, and homemaker. This pattern was, in some cases, reinforced by physical segregation of women. Among some groups, women were not allowed to participate in community life at all.[47] Most families were patriarchal in authority patterns, as well as patrilocal (the young bride typically went to live with the family of her husband).[48]

As in many societies characterized by a traditional familial system, the family served as a production unit. Both females and children were an important source of labor in most families, but control of family resources and property was reserved for the oldest male, generally considered to be the head of the family. This system was reinforced through strictly-enforced patterns of authority; younger

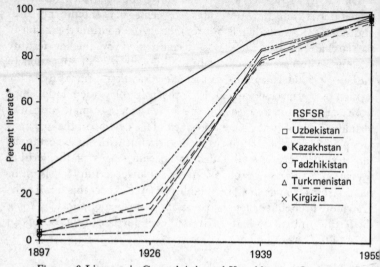

Figure 2.8 Literacy in Central Asia and Kazakhstan, 1897–1959
*Ages 9–49

Source: Narodnye obrazovaniye, nauka i kultura, Moscow: Statistika, 1971,
pp. 21–22

family members were required to defer to their elders, females to
males.[49] Females derived their social status from their position as
wives and mothers. The exclusively domestic role assigned to women
within this system reinforced the value placed on large families;
mothers of many children (particularly sons) were considered to be
particularly blessed. This stress on women's roles as wives and
mothers is reflected in both literacy and marriage data; women were
exposed to little schooling and married early. In the pre-
revolutionary southern tier areas virtually all women were totally
illiterate.

Muslim familial systems on the eve of the revolution were not,
however, homogeneous. There were important ethnic, regional, and
class differences in family patterns – differences that affected both
gender roles and family formation. In general, among the nomadic
and semi-nomadic Muslim peoples, such as the Kazakhs and the
Kirgiz, sex roles tended to be somewhat more egalitarian. Women in
these groups played an active role in economic life, working in the
fields and caring for livestock with men.[50] For example, Kazakh

women did not practice veiling; they could associate fairly freely with men and enjoyed some (albeit limited) authority within the social system.[51] Similarly, Kirgiz women were not required to cover their faces. They could socialize with men and had some independence in everyday life.[52]

In oasis cultures of Soviet Asia, including those of the Uzbeks and Tadzhiks, female roles were much more restrictive.[53] Veiling was common; and the physical segregation of the sexes was reflected in traditional architecture. Homes were divided into men's quarters and women's quarters to conform to Islamic law forbidding a woman to show her face to males other than the husband or close relatives. In pre-revolutionary Uzbekistan, for example, the birth of a daughter was greeted with sorrow. Daughters were generally married off at an early age, frequently without being consulted.[54] Within southern tier households, women occupied a subordinate status to men. Even among the women of the household there tended to be a strict hierarchy of status, with the wife of the head of the family exercising authority over the other women.[55] Among groups who resided in towns, females, like their rural counterparts in other parts of the southern tier, provided key domestic labor; but these activities were carried on inside the home and private courtyard. Much of this work, which included spinning, weaving, embroidery, and silkworm raising, was intended primarily for the family's personal needs. Some products, however, were produced for sale. But women were not allowed to go themselves to the bazaar to sell their surplus products and they had to depend on male relatives for that purpose. Women who ventured outside the confines of their home (usually to visit female relatives) covered themselves in a veil and long cloak.

Sexual segregation, even among the oasis cultures, tended to be followed less rigidly in the countryside, primarily because of the practical need for female labor. Women were not restricted to the home, but expected to work in the fields as part of their contribution to the family economy. Spinning and weaving, and other typical women's tasks, frequently took place in a common courtyard that permitted some interaction with male neighbors. Even in the rural areas, however, women were expected to avoid males and to turn their face aside if they met one. Conformity with the Islamic ideals of strict sexual segregation also tended to increase with status and income. While polygamy was a theoretical possibility for all males, in some areas, only rich men could afford to practice it. Similarly, wives of high status males tended to be more strictly segregated, in both a physical and social sense, than did lower status wives.

A key plank in Bolshevik domestic policy was the accelerated breakdown of the traditional familial system throughout what later became the USSR, as well as increased integration of women into the modernized workforce. This process necessitated in the non-European areas an enforced erosion of the traditional values limiting appropriate female roles to those of wife, homemaker, and mother. While this policy involved (as we have seen above) a modification of family life styles in the European areas as well, adjustment was most difficult in the southern tier where the traditional familial system and the low social and political status of women was reinforced by Islamic religious beliefs and traditions.[56] The Soviets did not gain control over much of these areas until 1922; and for nearly a decade thereafter, sporadic pockets of armed resistance to Bolshevik rule remained to complicate policy implementation in this area. There was also passive resistance. Many families refused to send their young girls to school;[57] and others objected to Bolshevik plans to integrate females in the collective farm workforce, because of an Islamic prohibition against women working alongside men.[58] Soviet efforts to recruit female Party members, political activists, and local government leaders were thwarted by customs that prohibited women from addressing meetings that included men.

Educational data from the 1926 census reveal that early progress was limited; virtually all women from the late-modernizing groups, especially the Muslims, were totally illiterate (Table 2.7). Even though male Muslim literacy rates trailed far behind those of more modernized European males, Muslim males in 1926 had far freer access to education than their female counterparts. It was males who virtually monopolized the educational opportunities of the early Bolshevik leadership. The literacy data provide persuasive empirical support for a point made repeatedly by Soviet ethnographic studies: traditional patriarchal family value systems in this area were extremely resistant to change.

Given what was a high value on childbearing at high parities which clearly persisted with only minor change throughout the 1920s, we would expect to see relatively high fertility in the 1920s and 1930s in the non-European areas. This expectation is not, however, borne out by the reported data, which indicate only moderate fertility in the 1920s, with steady increases (among most non-European

Table 2.7 *Female literacy, 1926*

Nationality	% Females who can read or write	F-M literacy ratio over-10 population
Slav		
Russian	42.8	56
Ukrainian	35.1	48
Belorussian	28.7	42
Muslim		
Uzbek	1.2	15
Kazakh	1.3	8
Azeri	2.9	16
Kirgiz	0.4	4
Tadzhik	0.5	9
Turkmen	0.1	2
Bashkir	18.9	40
Tatar	31.5	59
Chechen	0.2	3
Kumyk	5.3	22
Ingush	1.8	9
Karachayev	4.3	21
Karakalpak	0.1	4
Abkhazy	5.3	25
Other		
Georgian	41.9	25
Moldavian	13.3	24
Armenian	29.0	51
Buryat	11.2	25
Mari	12.9	22
Chuvash	22.2	34
Yakut	2.6	23
Jews	80.2	87
Mordva	10.2	20
Kalmyk	3.6	17
Karelian	41.6	60
Osetin	15.1	36
Khakh	6.6	25

Note: Data not available for the Balkar, Darginsty, Lezgins, Kabardinians, Avars, Adygirs, Cherkess, Komi, Udmurt, Tuvins, and Altay nationalities.
Source: Vsesoyuznaya perepis naseleniya 1926 goda. Vol. 17 (Moscow: Izdan'ye TsSU Soyuza SSR, 1929), pp. 93–96.

Table 2.8 *Ethnic fertility measures (reported data)*

Nationality	1927 Birth rates (within titular republic)			Child-to-woman ratios			Index of total fertility	
	Total	Urban	Rural	1926	1959	1970	1959	1970
Slav								
Russian	45.4	35.2	48.0	1.233	0.833	0.714	0.211	0.175
Ukrainian	42.7	36.4	43.4	1.354	0.714	0.667	0.176	0.166
Belorussian	42.3	37.2	42.7	1.486	0.836	0.742	0.202	0.182
Balt								
Latvian					0.612	0.672	0.149	0.165
Estonian					0.638	0.687	0.157	0.169
Lithuanian					0.823	0.847	0.197	0.208
Muslim								
Uzbek				1.134	1.877	2.493	0.441	0.590
Kazkah				1.261	1.896	2.178	0.456	0.541
Azeri	58.0[a]	37.1[a]	59.6[a]	1.794	1.711	2.127	0.409	0.502
Kirgiz				1.134	1.884	2.495	0.441	0.601
Tadzhik				1.257	1.782	2.561	0.421	0.607
Turkmen				1.384	1.809	2.548	0.430	0.603
Baskhir	39.7		40.0	1.441	1.431	1.527	0.345	0.359
Balkar					1.700	1.602	0.405	0.374
Tatar	53.1	49.6	53.3	1.432	1.105	0.993	0.267	0.240
Chechen				1.805	2.204	2.237	0.529	0.513
Dargins					1.427	2.229	0.344	0.521
Kumyk				1.590	1.505	1.832	0.364	0.434
Lezgin					1.722	2.194	0.414	0.515
Ingush				2.180	2.042	2.245	0.487	0.517
Kabardinian					1.537	1.570	0.363	0.371
Avar					1.334	1.950	0.322	0.460
Adygir						1.255		0.300
Karachayev				2.321		1.608		0.377
Cherkess						1.421		0.333
Karakalpak				1.230		2.219		0.532
Abkhazy				1.588		1.171		0.280
Other								
Georgian				1.483	0.905	0.925	0.217	0.223
Moldavian				1.377	1.190	1.037	0.288	0.252
Armenian	59.3	48.3	62.0	1.575	1.240	1.213	0.297	0.291
Buryat				1.043	1.460	1.558	0.356	0.367
Komi				1.266	1.052	1.034	0.257	0.244
Mari	53.5		53.7	1.202	1.146	1.299	0.277	0.302
Udmurt				1.248	1.131	1.095	0.276	0.256
Chuvash				1.339	1.037	1.144	0.253	0.270

Table 2.8 (*cont.*)

	1927 Birth rates (within titular republic)			Child-to-woman ratios			Index of total fertility	
Nationality	Total	Urban	Rural	1926	1959	1970	1959	1970
Yakut				1.410	1.494	1.606	0.359	0.382
Jews	22.6[b]	21.6[b]	26.7[b]			0.283		0.070
Mordva	48.3[b]		48.9[b]	1.432	0.933	0.831	0.230	0.200
Kalmyk	31.3		31.3	1.200	1.646	1.726	0.402	0.402
Karelian	42.6		42.5	1.335	0.702	0.477	0.174	0.115
Osetin				1.931	0.998	1.045	0.240	0.250
Tuvin					1.727	1.837	0.404	0.447
Altay						1.950		0.388
Khakhas				1.677		1.342		0.319
Komi-Permyak						1.133		0.273

[a] Within Armenian SSR.
[b] Within European areas of USSR.
Sources: 1927 birth rates based on civilian registration data reported in *National'nay politika VKP(b) v tsifrakh* (Moscow; Izdatel'stvo Kommunisticheskiy Akademii, 1930), p. 40. 1926 fertility ratios computed from *Vsesoyuznaya perepis naseleniya 1926 goda*, Vol. 17 (Moscow, 1929), Table 17. For 1959 and 1970 child-to-woman ratios and indexes of total fertility, see Appendix.

groups) to 1970 (Table 2.8). Fertility ratios among Muslim groups, as derived from reported data, were relatively low in 1926. The Uzbeks and Kirgiz had reported fertility ratios below all three of the Slavic groups and the fertility ratios of the other major Muslim groups (except the Azeri) were only marginally higher. Bear in mind that the Slavic groups had been most affected by the socioeconomic transformation begun before the Bolshevik Revolution. Fertility among these nationalities had been declining for at least three decades. The relatively low fertility ratios among many of the Muslim groups, which were characterized by much lower scores on a whole range of modernization measures, is indeed puzzling. There are several possible explanations. The first is that suggested by the survey of registration procedures in Chapter 1: underreporting of births through 1959 led to a serious understatement of real fertility in these areas.

A second explanation has been put forward by Coale, Anderson, and Harm in their survey of republic fertility trends from 1897 to

1970.[59] Although concurring that underregistration was a factor and introducing a series of corrections to adjust for it, they argue that real natality in the non-European areas, while somewhat higher than the reported figures, was well below the potential maximum. They cite series of factors which help explain the unexpectedly low rates. Lengthy breastfeeding inhibited natality, as did poor health care and low nutritional levels. The pattern of marriage characteristic of these areas – extremely early marriages of young girls, in many cases to spouses of middle-age or older – may also have served to keep natural fertility at a level well below the hypothetical maximum. The rather dramatic rise in fertility since 1926 can be attributed to a decline in average duration of lactation, an improvement in food supplies and medical care, and a shift in marriage patterns which led to a decline in the age difference between spouses. This explanation is not inconsistent with the model of fertility change presented in Chapter 1.

To evaluate the validity of the Coale analysis, we examined the published results of medical, ethnographic, and demographic studies conducted in the non-European southern tier. What these studies suggest is that there was, not surprisingly, a fair amount of variation in natality and family patterns within this area. Evidence pertaining to some localities is consistent with the relationships hypothesized for the earliest period of the fertility transition; that pertaining to others is not. These conclusions should be caveated with the comment that most of the studies we examined suffered from some serious methodological defects as a source of fertility information. Most simply focused on one or more small villages, collecting data on the birth histories of all wives present. In some cases, information on the timing of births was not collected, making it impossible to reconstruct fertility schedules. Many of the respondents were older women who had completed their fertile period, so the natality implied by their birth histories may not reflect the natality patterns at the time the survey was taken. Reliance on such an approach would naturally filter out those women who died in youth or middle age; and this again biases the survey results. Moreover, the older respondents were much more apt to forget or misstate their early birth histories. Infant and child mortality data were supplied by the mothers themselves, again introducing the possibility of misreporting of real mortality. Nonetheless, material provided by these studies provides important insight into the life styles of non-European women in the Soviet southern tier and an important corrective to impressions gleaned from the incompletely reported fertility data.

Two studies of villages in Kirgizia – both conducted during the 1920s – reveal conditions quite similar to those suggested by Coale, *et al*. The first study, reported by Pavel Kushner, focused on the mountainous areas of Kirgizia, in particular, the Talasskiy rayon, one of the poorest and least populated areas in Kirgizia at that time.[60] Kushner journeyed to the area in the summer of 1925. The socioeconomic system he describes is extremely primitive, based primarily on stock-raising.[61] Kushner contends, however, that the social system in the area he studied could no longer be termed a tribal system, although tribal traditions and relationships were still very strong. He describes the prevailing social system as *manapstvo* – a tribal genealogical social organization with an influential and sometimes well-off *manap* at the head of each village.

The basic unit of the economy was the family. Villages consisted of ten to twelve families apiece. Relatives resided together in a yurt (a felt-covered dwelling) and held property in common. Distribution of family resources was controlled by the head of the household, generally the oldest male. The social position of women was consistent with that characteristic of many traditional, patriarchal systems.[62] Girls married early (age fourteen), and a fair number of the families Kushner studied were polygamous. Kushner contended that only poor men were limited to one wife. The more powerful role among females in a family of plural wives was that of the senior wife, who distributed domestic responsibilities among the other women of the household. Kushner reports that most Kirgiz families of the time were small, due principally to the extremely large proportion of children who died before age three. Although he provides no empirical data, he explains the high mortality by noting that many deaths occurred when the child was weaned from the breast at about three years of age. He also reports that the incidence of infertility is high (again, no data are provided), due primarily to syphilis and gonorrhea.

Another ethnographic study of the Kirgiz, this time in southern Issyk-kulsk, confirms some of the Kushner findings. The field work for this study was conducted by Lev Oshanin in 1924, as part of a medical study.[63] Polygamy was quite rare among the groups Oshanin studied, a factor he attributes to the extremely impoverished state of the economy: few men could afford more than one wife.

Oshanin's retrospective survey of children ever born in monogamous families revealed an average of 4.9 births per family. He cautions against using this as a measure of fertility, since the husband in some of his families may have been widowed and remarried, so we are in some cases measuring the birth histories of more than one wife. Like Kushner, Oshanin observed an extraordinarily high level of infant and child mortality. About 40 per cent of the infants born had died before the survey took place, with the highest mortality among nursing infants and young children. Oshanin also cites comparable infant and child mortality from medical studies of Kazakhs – 41 to 47 per cent.[64] Oshanin, echoing Kushner, reports that syphilis was widespread among the Kirgiz.

While neither Oshanin nor Kushner provide natality data, material from population surveys in 1927 and 1928 provide some indication of fertility levels in Kirgizia in the mid to late 1920s. Both surveys were part of agricultural studies and sampled 10 per cent of the population. The surveys indicated an estimated birth rate of 52.0 (births per 1,000 population). Regional variation was substantial; birth rate estimates by rayon ranged from 46.8 to 60.9. These differences may be due to some degree to the comprehensiveness of the survey. Nonetheless, the Oshanin and Kushner studies suggest that real natality probably did vary widely from region to region, depending on the level of infertility. The demographic survey data indicate that some areas of Kirgizia, at least, were characterized by extraordinarily high natality in the mid and late 1920s.[65]

Data from Turkmenistan suggests a social system similar to that in rural Kirgizia, but a somewhat different pattern of natality. The data were derived from a 1927 expedition conducted to analyze health problems and the status of medical delivery systems in rural Turkmenistan. The expedition results, available in two medical surveys written by M. I. Rubin and I. A. Minkevich (physicians who participated in the field study), provide a graphic portrait of an extremely primitive economy and geographical isolation.[66] Most of the *auls* (villages) visited by the team did not have a market; and most products used by the family were produced by the individual families. The social role of women as depicted by the research team suggests fairly rigid gender roles. Females were expected to produce large families, while serving as an important source of labor. The majority of the workload fell on the women, who were responsible not only for housework and meal preparation, but also for fuel collection and construction of the primitive dwellings (yurts). Even very small girls were given domestic responsibilities; and the women were expected to maintain a heavy workload, even when they were pregnant or nursing – which was most of their adult lives.

The familial system described by Rubin and Minkevich was patriarchal, with strictly defined authority patterns subordinating the young to the old, and the women to the men. Most women married young; the average age of marriage in one village where the Rubin team made a detailed study of marital and fertility patterns was 14.2 years. The average age of menarche was 14.8 years. A quarter of the families were polygamous. Turkmen women nursed their children for two to three years; and among fertile women, those who had completed their reproductive lives at the time of the expedition had averaged one birth every 2.7 years.[67] This group of women averaged about eight pregnancies and about seven births. However, about a quarter of the menopausal women in the village studied had not given birth. Among all women who had passed menopause, the average number of previous births was 4.9. Among the younger women (those still in their fertile years), only about 10 per cent were childless. This group, which included many women still in relatively early stages of their reproductive lives, averaged a little over five pregnancies and nearly five live births per woman.

Minkevich provides data for another area in Turkmenistan. These data are not directly comparable to the Rubin material, but confirm in general the picture painted by Rubin of moderately high fertility and extraordinarily high infant and child mortality. In the villages of Kara-Dashli and Emreli, in Tashauz *okrug*, nearly a quarter of the married women aged 18 to 30 (with an average duration of married life of eight-and-a-half years) had not yet had a birth. The average number of births for all 18 to 30-year-old wives was 2.3, but 56 per cent of these infants had died by the time of the survey.[68] Among wives over thirty (average duration of marriage 22 years), the average number of births was 6.05; 53 per cent of these children had died by the time of the survey. Infertility in these villages among the over-thirty wives was much lower than that reported by the Rubin expedition; only 4.2 per cent of these older wives had failed to give birth at the time of the survey. Minkevich's comments make clear that the absence of births among some Turkmen women was not due to conscious family limitation practices; he attributes the high rate of infertility among the younger wives to the fertility-inhibiting effects of syphilis. Of the forty barren wives in the villages studied, thirty-six had syphilis, compared to 12 per cent of the wives with four or more children.

The data provided by Minkevich imply extraordinarily high rates of infant and child mortality. High rates were also observed in other parts of Turkmenistan. Rubin's data revealed that 60 per cent of the children ever born to women surveyed in 1926 died before age sixteen; 61 per cent of these deaths occurred, according to data provided by the mothers, in the first year of life, over three-quarters before the third birthday. Minkevich estimates that overall mortality in the first year of life was 36.5 per 100 infants ever born.[69] This material helps explain why the 1926 fertility ratios for both Turkmenistan and the Turkmen themselves are so low. The Rubin and Minkevich reports also suggest that natality patterns varied from village to village in rural Turkmenistan. Total completed fertility for Minkevich's older wives was clearly somewhat higher than that of Rubin's post-menopausal women. The major factor accounting for this variation was not conscious limitation of births but the incidence of infertility associated with disease and poor health.

While the Turkmen studies do not allow us to reconstruct fertility rates, these materials suggest natality levels somewhat below the theoretical "natural" limit. The conditions reported by the Rubin team are much more consistent with a pattern of moderately high fertility in the pre-transition period suggested by the model presented in Chapter 1. High levels of infertility were reported, particularly by those women who were post-menopausal at the time of the study; and lengthy lactation apparently also operated to lengthen the interval between births for these older women. These factors have also been found to inhibit natural fertility in more recent studies of fertility dynamics in developing countries; and are consistent with the arguments presented in Coale, Anderson, and Harm. The Minkevich findings suggest that not all Turkmen populations were equally affected by these factors; and some areas (particularly those with low rates of fecundity-impairing disease), had somewhat higher natality.

Other studies of natality in the non-European southern tier present a significantly different picture from that of Turkmenistan. These studies indicate that in some areas of the Caucasus, real fertility in the 1920s and 1930s was extremely high (near the theoretical maximum limit for natural fertility). These data were derived from a sample survey of fertility and infant mortality in rural areas of

Table 2.9. *Total fertility rates for rural Caucasian republics, 1910–41*

Year	Georgia	Azerbaydzhan	Armenia
1910–14	5.00	7.77	7.16
1915–18	4.89	6.96	6.88
1919–21	5.19	8.01	6.91
1922–26	5.71	7.51	8.41
1927–31	6.03	8.64	9.80
1932–36	5.62	8.56	8.95
1937–41	5.19	8.40	8.47

Source: R. I. Sifman, *Dinamika rozhdayemosti v SSSR* (Moscow: Statistika, 1974), p. 80.

Georgia, Azerbaydzhan, and Armenia. The survey, as reported by Roza Sifman, was conducted in 1947 by the Institute for the Organization of Health and Medical History of the Academy of Medical Sciences.[70] The study involved a questionnaire administered to women aged fifteen and over; it included questions on previous births, with dates and age of mother for each birth. Like many studies of this nature, which rely on retrospective data to reconstruct natality patterns, findings pertaining to the oldest women and to the earliest period are quite apt to be incomplete, as some women in the older groups are prone to forgetting, or misstating, their early birth history. Nonetheless, the survey results provide valuable insight into real natality levels in rural areas of the Caucasus for the first four decades of the twentieth century.

The survey yielded data presented in Table 2.9. Although fertility in rural areas of the Caucasus was quite high at the turn of the century, there were already significant regional differentials. The total fertility rate in rural Azerbaydzhan for 1910 to 1914 was over 50 per cent higher than that in rural Georgia. Sifman attributes this partly to differences in the landholding system. Agricultural land in Azerbaydzhan and Armenia was apparently redistributed much more frequently than in Georgia, with appropriate adjustments made for changes in family size. This system increased the economic incentive for large families because it meant that family holdings would increase with increasing family size.

The natality differentials can also be attributed to different patterns of urbanization and exposure to modern "European" life styles and value systems. In Azerbaydzhan, the rapid growth of industry in Baku had only a limited impact on the surrounding rural environment. Most of Baku's oil workers were not local to the area; and the dramatic growth of Baku did little to transform the traditional life styles and customs of rural Azeris. Many of the Armenian peasants who had been displaced from agricultural work migrated to large industrial centers outside of Armenia. This pattern of migration, again, minimized the impact of urban life styles on rural traditions. In Georgia, by contrast, particularly in western Georgia, a large-scale outflow of small landholders to neighboring towns had begun in earnest in the last half of the nineteenth century. Most of these urban migrants retained close contact with their home village, returning home when industrial jobs were not available. Many others became seasonal workers who migrated back and forth between city and the nearby countryside. This particular pattern of urbanization produced much greater contact between recent migrants to urban areas and their rural families. The result was a much higher level of impact of urban values on rural life – a factor reflected in republic literacy rates and child mortality data. In 1897, for example, less than 2 per cent of the rural females (aged 9–49) in Azerbaydzhan and Armenia were literate, compared to 11 per cent in Georgia.

World War I had only a marginal impact on fertility in the Caucasus. Fertility levels were low for the duration of the war, but much less so than in the European areas of Russia, which experienced a substantial drop in natality. During the period 1918 to 1921, when much of the Caucasus enjoyed a brief period of independence, natality increased slightly from the war years. In fact, natality was higher in rural Georgia and Azerbaydzhan during this period than it had been in the immediate pre-war period. However, the chaotic conditions of civil war produced an upsurge in infant and child mortality – one reason why reported child-to-women ratios in the 1926 census were at relatively moderate levels.

Fertility remained at extraordinarily high levels throughout the 1920s and 1930s. Sifman estimates that the average general fertility rate for rural areas in 1930–41 was 255.1 per 1,000 women aged 15–49 for Azerbaydzhan, 260.2 for Armenia, and 168.4 for Georgia. The corresponding estimates for rural birth rates (per 1,000 population) are: Azerbaydzhan, 59.2; Armenia, 59.3; Georgia, 39.2. These rates, which seem extraordinarily high, are in line with estimates for the rural areas of Georgia and Armenia derived from other surveys.

For example, the reported 1927 birth rate among Armenians in Armenia (compiled from citizen registries) was 59.3 overall; 62 in rural areas. For Azeris in Armenia, the corresponding figures were 58 and 59.6.[71] A similar picture emerges from survey data on births and deaths connected with the 1926 census; the estimated rural birth rate for Armenia was 56.2, while data from an agricultural survey yielded an estimate of 60.2.[72] Finally, 1927 birth rate data published by the Central Statistical Administration includes a rate of 56.1 for Armenia as a whole and 59 for rural Armenia.[73] Sifman's examination of birth histories of the 50 to 59-year-old women from Azerbaydzhan and Armenia (i.e., women whose reproductive lives spanned the years 1905–40) revealed that nearly a quarter of the women from rural Azerbaydzhan and Armenia had ten or more births! Total fertility in both areas appears to have peaked in the 1927–31 time period (although marital fertility did not reach its highest point until the late 1930s). Results from a second survey conducted in rural Azerbaydzhan in 1968 suggest that marital fertility took a sharp dip during the war years; recovered in the post-war period; then assumed a gradual decline during the 1950s.[74] Again, Sifman links this pattern to the persistence of traditions affecting the role of women, pointing to the relatively low educational levels of women from these areas on the eve of the war. Educational attainments among ethnic Azeri women in the countryside were particularly low.

The close congruence between rural natality in Armenia and Azerbaydzhan during the interwar period is consistent with the relationships posited by the fertility model. In pre-revolutionary Armenia and Azerbaydzhan, patriarchal family patterns prevailed in the countryside.[75] These patterns persisted in both republics well into the Soviet period. Although overall literacy was substantially higher in Armenia in the 1920s, most indicators of female roles (early marriage rates, female-to-male literacy and industrial employment ratios) were quite similar in the two areas. By 1959, considerable inroads in patriarchal roles are evident in the Armenian socio-economic data and those trends help explain why Armenia's fertility decline preceded that of Azerbaydzhan. In the interwar period, however, female roles in both rural Armenia and rural Azerbaydzhan conformed closely to the patriarchal model.

In Georgia, by contrast, considerable inroads in traditional family patterns were already evident in the 1930s. Women enjoyed freer access to education and early marriage was much less common than in the rest of the Caucasus. By the late 1930s, natality, although still moderately high here, was much lower than in the rest of the Caucasus. The pattern of marital fertility reveals that rural Georgian women at this time were sharply cutting back on childbearing over the age thirty. This was particularly true of the more Europeanized areas of western Georgia.

The pattern suggested by both Armenia and Azerbaydzhan is one of extraordinarily high rural fertility peaking in the late 1920s, and declining thereafter, but remaining at relatively high levels into the postwar years. There is fragmentary evidence from other non-European regions to suggest that this pattern was not unique to the eastern Caucasus. In 1976, Tashkent University did a sample survey of 867 rural Uzbek, Kirgiz, Tadzhik, and Turkmen families in two oblasts of Uzbekistan.[76] The sample was limited to women born between 1900 and 1944 who had been married at least ten years. The women born between 1900 and 1914 represent the cohort that entered their fertile period in the 1920s. For those women, the average age of marriage was 16. As in Kirgizia and Turkmenistan, infant mortality was extraordinarily high – approximately 300 (in some years reaching 500 to 600 per 1,000 live births). Over half of the women born between 1900 and 1924 (i.e., women whose reproductive lives spanned the period 1915 to the mid-1960s) had had between ten and fifteen births. These data imply a pattern of natality consistent with those of the Armenians and Azeris – that is, natality levels at or near the theoretical maximum in the interwar period.

There is also fragmentary data suggesting high natality levels in Kazakhstan. Demographic surveys from 1926, 1927, and 1928 indicate fertility somewhat lower than Azerbaydzhan and Armenia, but considerably higher than natality recorded in European Russia. Birth rate estimates for 1927 per 1,000 population, for example, were 48.4 for the Kazakh population and 55.4 for the non-Kazakh nationalities.[77] The estimated republic birth rate was 51.1. However, Soviet demographers caution that this figure represents a significant underestimation of natality due to known defects in the survey's birth and death data for ethnic Kazakhs. We are safe, therefore, in assuming that the real Kazakhstan birth rate was considerably higher than 51.1. Both the Uzbekistan and Kazakhstan data point to extremely high interwar natality, in at least some areas of the southern tier.

The findings from the regional studies presented above suggest that we should be cautious in generalizing data from local studies to other non-European areas in the USSR. There was obviously wide variation in the natality experience within the non-European southern tier. Some of the southern tier areas clearly experienced extraordinarily high natality in the early Soviet period; in other areas, poor nutrition, natality-inhibiting disease, and lengthy lactation kept fertility at a somewhat lower level, at least in the first decade of Soviet rule.

The immediate impact of the nutritional and health care improvements sponsored by the Soviet government appears to have been an increase in natality, at least in those areas where natural fertility was low due to disease and poor nutrition. As noted above, fertility increases peaking in the late 1920s were recorded in the trans-Caucasus study for all three Caucasian republics (Georgia, Armenia, and Azerbaydzhan). The timing and magnitude of the increase for the other southern tier republics is masked by the incomplete reporting of the earlier periods, coupled with reporting improvements, particularly after 1959.

These data limitations mean that it is impossible to pinpoint when fertility peaked in these areas. The results of Soviet surveys on expected and ideal family size and number of children ever born suggest that the fertility peak occurred considerably later in the four core Central Asian republics. Where these data are reported by age they generally reveal that for the major Muslim groups the highest natality and family size expectations and ideals are reported by women marrying in the late 1940s to late 1950s.[78] Such women typically report higher natality than women marrying in the 1930s, in part because the reproductive careers of many of these women were interrupted by World War II. This would imply a fertility peak occurring sometime in the early 1950s to early 1960s – the time when these high-fertility generations were in their primary childbearing years. This pattern does not seem to hold, however, for ethnic Azeris; their interwar marital generations report higher fertility than women who married after the war.

While this survey material is consistent with the hypothesis that real fertility peaked in Central Asia and in Kazakhstan (among ethnic Kazakhs) sometime between, say, 1955 and 1965, the evidence is not conclusive. Women marrying before and during World War II experienced a prolonged disruption of married life that must surely have decreased their real fertility. The extraordinarily high infant and child mortality of the late 1920s in these areas suggests that real infant mortality was probably still quite high in the 1930s. Both of these factors would bias self-reporting of expected number of children in a downward direction. We also cannot discount the probability that some of the women married in the 1930s (who would have been over fifty by the time the survey was taken) may well have misstated the number of births. As Soviet demographers associated with the surveys caution, such individuals are particularly prone to forget the births of children who died soon after birth.[79] For these reasons, the survey data, although consistent with the suggestion that fertility peaks in Central Asia may have occurred as late as the mid-1960s, do not provide conclusive evidence of that.

There are, moreover, conflicting data that suggest rather earlier fertility peaks in Central Asia. These data are drawn from a 1959 Central Statistical Administration study of 4,000 women (married and unmarried) reported by Roza Sifman.[80] Sifman presents average general fertility rates for 1920–41 and 1946–59 (see Figure 2.9). Her results reveal an 18 per cent decline in general fertility, from 188.3 in the interwar period to 166.4 in the 1946–59 period. Sifman cautions that these data may well understate real natality levels, particularly those of older women. Her data, while certainly not conclusive, indicate high interwar natality in Central Asia – reinforcing the impressions suggested by the birth rate estimates for Kirgizia and Kazakhstan that were derived from surveys. Further support for the hypothesis that Central Asian fertility peaked some time before World War II is provided by sample surveys conducted in the late 1970s in rural Uzbekistan. One survey conducted in 1979 by Tashkent State University's Population Laboratory found that women born between 1900 and 1910 had an average of 9.3 births.[81] Much of the reproductive activity of these women would have occurred in the interwar period, suggesting extremely high natality during this period.

These data are reported here to provide the reader with an appreciation for the problems and contradictions inherent in available data on southern tier fertility dynamics. In short, lack of reliable natality data in the southern tier area precludes any firm judgement on the timing and pace of the fertility transition in the pre-1970 period.

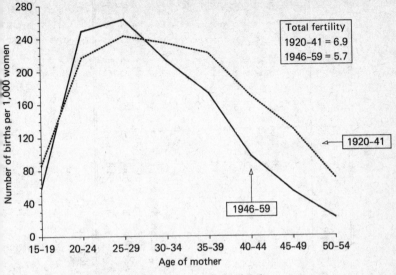

Figure 2.9 Fertility trends in Central Asia, 1920–59

Source: based on a 1959 survey. See R. I. Sifman, "Dynamics of Birth-Rate
in Central Asian Republics and Methods of its Study", in *Problemy
narodonaseleniye. Trudy vsesouznoy mezhvuzskoy nauchno konferentsii posvyashennoy
problemam narodonaseleniye sredney azii* (Tashkent, 1965; Moscow: Izdatel'stvo
Moskovskovo Universiteta, 1970), pp. 297–301

RECENT SOVIET FERTILITY TRENDS

In characterizing more recent natality trends, we are on firmer
ground, because the grossly incomplete registration of the early
decades in the non-European areas has improved significantly,
making reported natality trends a more reliable indicator of real
fertility. Table 2.10 presents reported general fertility rates for the
fifteen republics for the last decade and a half. Table 2.11 provides
total fertility for the corresponding years. The lowest natality levels
were recorded in the European areas; the fertility decline in Estonia,
Latvia, Lithuania, RSFSR, the Ukraine, and Belorussia appears to
have more or less stabilized at a total fertility of two children per
woman. The marginal increases in general fertility rates in several of
these republics from a low point in the mid-1960s appears to be
primarily the result of the changing age structure of the fertile-age
cohort.

Table 2.10. *General fertility rates by Union Republic (births per 1,000 women 15–49)*

Republic	1958 1959	1965 1966	1967 1968	1969 1970	1971 1972	1972 1973	1973 1974	1974 1975	1975 1976	1976 1977	1977 1978	1978 1979	1979 1980	1980 1981	1981 1982	1982 1983
RSFSR	82.9	59.0	53.3	53.4	55.2	54.9	55.3	56.6	57.7	57.7	58.1	59.0	59.6	60.6	62.4	65.8
Ukraine	70.7	57.1	55.3	55.3	57.1	56.2	55.7	56.4	56.8	56.5	56.1	57.5	57.9	58.2	58.2	61.1
Belorussia	91.0	67.1	62.0	61.3	61.1	59.7	58.9	58.9	58.9	59.2	59.6	60.9	61.4	62.8	63.3	66.6
Uzbekistan	158.8	165.3	161.9	158.5	159.5	156.0	156.8	156.8	157.1	154.0	150.6	149.6	148.9	149.6	151.7	152.7
Kazakhstan	143.0	107.9	98.1	96.1	95.7	93.6	94.1	94.8	94.7	94.1	93.4	94.5	93.8	94.4	95.2	95.5
Georgia	85.0	78.2	72.9	73.3	70.8	69.0	69.4	69.1	68.9	68.1	66.8	68.2	68.5	69.5	70.0	70.0
Azerbaydzhan	163.3	165.8	148.9	134.6	119.1	111.4	108.0	105.1	104.4	102.8	100.0	98.6	98.3	99.8	98.9	98.5
Lithuania	82.8	68.6	66.9	67.2	66.1	63.1	60.9	60.2	59.8	59.5	58.8	59.0	58.9	58.5	58.9	61.5
Moldavia	111.7	79.2	76.3	71.6	75.4	75.6	75.1	75.2	75.3	74.6	74.0	75.0	75.2	76.3	77.6	82.0
Latvia	59.2	51.9	52.6	53.5	54.8	53.8	53.4	53.8	53.4	52.8	52.5	53.2	54.1	55.1	56.5	60.2
Kirgizia	140.1	137.2	131.2	134.7	136.1	132.9	131.6	130.1	130.5	129.1	125.7	128.8	127.4	129.2	132.1	134.0
Tadzhikistan	123.5	166.2	170.5	166.4	171.9	168.0	170.6	172.3	173.2	170.0	167.1	168.9	167.3	168.1	170.5	170.3
Armenia	159.2	122.4	104.9	92.9	90.0	87.3	84.7	84.3	84.9	84.4	83.5	82.8	83.8	85.2	86.2	87.2
Turkmenistan	161.6	176.6	168.5	165.6	161.8	159.3	158.6	157.1	156.0	154.3	151.5	151.3	150.4	148.2	148.4	149.6
Estonia	59.5	55.3	55.6	59.3	59.8	58.5	57.9	58.1	58.5	59.2	59.2	58.6	59.0	60.3	61.3	62.8
USSR	88.7	70.8	66.3	65.7	67.2	66.4	66.8	67.8	68.5	68.7	68.8	69.9	70.5	71.6	73.1	76.0

Sources: 1958, 1965, 1969, 1972: *Naseleniye SSSR, 1973* (Moscow: Statistika, 1975), pp. 137–8.
1967 *Vestnik statistiki*, No. 12, 1971, p. 75.   1977 *Vestnik statistiki*, No. 11, 1979, p. 66.
1971 *Vestnik statistiki*, No. 12, 1973, p. 75.   1978 *Vestnik statistiki*, No. 11, 1980, p. 76.
1973 *Vestnik statistiki*, No. 12, 1975, p. 80.   1979 *Vestnik statistiki*, No. 11, 1981, p. 71.
1974 *Vestnik statistiki*, No. 11, 1976, p. 86.   1980 *Vestnik statistiki*, No. 11, 1982, p. 65.
1975 *Vestnik statistiki*, No. 12, 1977, p. 76.   1981 *Vestnik statistiki*, No. 12, 1983, p. 52.
1976 *Vestnik statistiki*, No. 11, 1978, p. 82.   1982 *Vestnik statistiki*, No. 11, 1984, p. 76.

Table 2.11. *Total fertility rates by Union Republic*

Republic	1958 1959	1965 1966	1967 1968	1969 1970	1971 1972	1972 1973	1973 1974	1974 1975	1975 1976	1976 1977	1977 1978	1978 1979	1979 1980	1980 1981	1981 1982	1982 1983
RSFSR	2.63	2.12	2.00	1.97	2.05	2.02	2.00	1.99	1.97	1.97	1.94	1.90	1.89	1.90	1.95	2.05
Ukraine	2.30	1.99	2.02	2.04	2.12	2.08	2.04	2.04	2.02	1.99	1.94	1.96	1.96	1.94	1.95	2.04
Belorussia	2.80	2.28	2.23	2.30	2.34	2.28	2.23	2.20	2.14	2.10	2.07	2.06	2.04	2.02	1.94	2.09
Uzbekistan	5.04	5.56	5.68	5.64	5.76	5.67	5.71	5.68	5.66	5.48	5.25	5.10	4.91	4.81	4.77	4.65
Kazakhstan	4.46	3.50	3.31	3.31	3.37	3.32	3.31	3.30	3.26	3.21	3.13	3.03	2.94	2.91	2.93	2.93
Georgia	2.59	2.60	2.54	2.62	2.61	2.57	2.58	2.54	2.52	2.45	2.35	2.29	2.25	2.25	2.26	2.25
Azerbaydzhan	5.01	5.27	4.93	4.63	4.30	4.13	4.03	3.95	3.92	3.82	3.64	3.48	3.33	3.23	3.11	3.01
Lithuania	2.63	2.23	2.24	2.35	2.38	2.29	2.23	2.20	2.13	2.16	2.11	2.07	2.01	1.98	1.97	2.03
Moldavia	3.57	2.68	2.73	2.56	2.63	2.63	2.59	2.56	2.52	2.46	2.39	2.38	2.38	2.40	2.45	2.57
Latvia	1.94	1.73	1.82	1.93	2.01	1.99	1.97	1.98	1.95	1.91	1.87	1.86	1.88	1.88	1.92	2.03
Kirgizia	4.32	4.71	4.67	4.85	4.97	4.89	4.81	4.75	4.85	4.78	4.56	4.41	4.13	4.09	4.09	4.09
Tadzhikistan	3.93	5.49	5.87	5.90	6.15	6.07	6.20	6.26	6.31	6.16	5.99	5.97	5.76	5.63	5.59	5.47
Armenia	4.73	3.91	3.55	3.20	3.17	3.07	2.91	2.82	2.79	2.72	2.60	2.46	2.38	2.34	2.34	2.35
Turkmenistan	5.12	6.04	6.00	5.93	5.90	5.87	5.85	5.77	5.71	5.67	5.50	5.27	5.13	4.92	4.80	4.75
Estonia	1.95	1.92	1.98	2.14	2.19	2.15	2.11	2.10	2.08	2.10	2.07	2.01	2.01	2.03	2.06	2.09

Sources: 1958, 1965, 1969, 1972: *Naseleniye SSSR, 1973* (Moscow: Statistika, 1975), pp. 137–8.
1967 *Vestnik statistiki*, No. 12, 1971, p. 75.   1977 *Vestnik statistiki*, No. 11, 1979, p. 66.
1971 *Vestnik statistiki*, No. 12, 1973, p. 75.   1978 *Vestnik statistiki*, No. 11, 1980, p. 76.
1973 *Vestnik statistiki*, No. 12, 1975, p. 80.   1979 *Vestnik statistiki*, No. 11, 1981, p. 71.
1974 *Vestnik statistiki*, No. 11, 1976, p. 86.   1980 *Vestnik statistiki*, No. 11, 1982, p. 65.
1975 *Vestnik statistiki*, No. 12, 1977, p. 76.   1981 *Vestnik statistiki*, No. 12, 1983, p. 52.
1976 *Vestnik statistiki*, No. 11, 1978, p. 82.   1982 *Vestnik statistiki*, No. 11, 1984, p. 76.

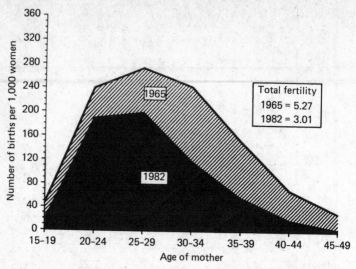

Figure 2.10 Age-specific fertility in Azerbaydzhan, 1965 and 1982

Two of the Caucasian republics, Georgia and Armenia, were already well into the fertility decline by the mid-1960s. Georgia had reached a relatively low natality level (total fertility rate of about 2.6 children) by 1965, with natality continuing to decline slowly over the next fifteen years.[82] Armenia's fertility was well above the Georgian level in the mid-1960s, but had declined significantly from the extraordinarily high levels recorded in rural areas in the 1930s and 1940s. Natality continued to decline rapidly over the last fifteen years, from 3.91 in 1965/66 to 2.35 in 1982/83.[83]

Even more striking are the natality declines registered in Azerbaydzhan over the last fifteen years. Total fertility declined from 5.3 children per woman in 1965/66 to 3.01 in 1982/83, or over 43 per cent (Figure 2.10). These trends cannot be accounted for by in-migration of low-fertility Europeans. Over the last two decades, the European proportion of the population in Azerbaydzhan declined from 27 per cent in 1959 to 17 per cent in 1979. The proportion of Azeris in the fertile-age cohort, by contrast, was increasing during this period. Nor can the natality declines be attributed to a smaller family size among the European population, since European family size preferences in this area appear to have stabilized by the mid-1960s at about two children.[84] One must conclude, therefore, that the dramatic downturn

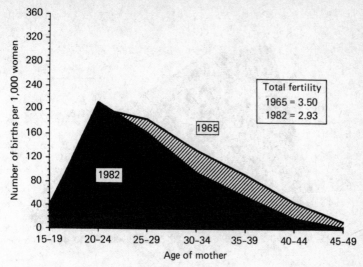

Figure 2.11 Age-specific fertility in Kazakhstan, 1965 and 1982

in natality rates is due primarily to real change in family size among ethnic Azeris.[85] Dramatic decreases in total fertility in the 1960s were reported for ethnic Azeris living in Georgia; Azeri fertility there declined by 32 per cent between 1959 and 1969.[86] These data are certainly consistent with the image of declining Azeri natality suggested by the republic fertility rates.

Significant declines in reported natality have also been recorded in Kazakhstan. Total fertility dropped from 3.5 in 1965/66 to 2.93 in 1982/83, or 16 per cent (Figure 2.11). Again, this downturn cannot be attributed to a greater proportion of low-fertility European nationalities, since the European share of the population has been declining over the last two decades. European nationalities accounted for 59 per cent of Kazakhstan's population in 1959, 58 per cent in 1970, and 54 per cent in 1979. Changes in the nationality breakdown of the fertile-age cohort were even more striking during this period, with the share of ethnic Kazakhs in the fertile-age cohort increasing and the share of Russians (by far the largest European nationality in Kazakhstan) decreasing.[87] As with Azerbaydzhan, European natality in these areas appears to have declined only marginally in the last decade, so the reductions in total fertility cannot be attributed to this factor. The primary cause of the

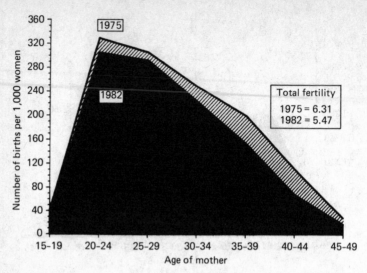

Figure 2.12 Age-specific fertility in Tadzhikistan, 1975 and 1982

sustained fertility decline in Kazakhstan is almost certainly declining family size preferences among the ethnic Kazakh population.

Decline in reported fertility is a much more recent phenomenon in the four core Central Asian republics, where data have been most seriously affected by underregistration. In Tadzhikistan, reported total fertility increased between 1965 and 1975. This trend was more likely due to increasingly complete birth reporting than to real fertility increases – a point also noted by Soviet demographers.[88] Reported total fertility hit a high point as recently as 1975/76 and had declined by only 13 per cent by 1982/83. Much of this decline, as shown in Figure 2.12, was due to a decreased rate of childbearing by women over age 35.

The downward trend is much clearer in Turkmenistan. Reported total fertility peaked at 6.00 in 1965/66, and has since declined by 21 per cent to 4.75 in 1982/83. As indicated in Figure 2.13, fertility has declined in all age groups, but is most pronounced for women over age 30. Again, it should be born in mind that the Turkmenistan data are affected by underregistration; and that the fertility decline is masked to some degree by increasingly complete reporting.

Similar comments apply to Uzbekistan. Here reported fertility fluctuated at high levels in the early 1970s, and began a convincing

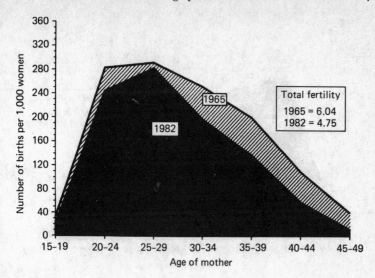

Figure 2.13 Age-specific fertility in Turkmenistan, 1965 and 1982

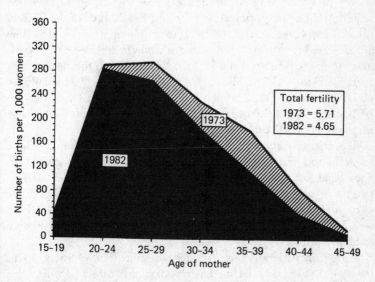

Figure 2.14 Age-specific fertility in Uzbekistan, 1973 and 1982

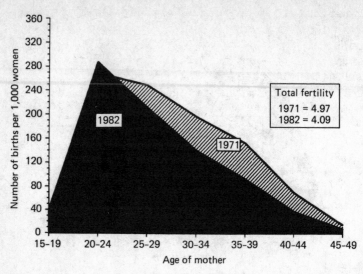

Figure 2.15 Age-specific fertility in Kirgizia, 1971 and 1982

decline only in 1974/75. Reported total fertility then declined 16 per cent in nine years, moving from 5.71 in 1973/74 to 4.65 in 1982/83. As shown in Figure 2.14, these declines may be traced to curtailed childbearing among women over the age of 30. Much of the fertility decline, moreover, apparently took place among urban women. The general fertility rate for the republic as a whole declined 14 per cent, from 173.6 in 1961 to 148.9 in 1980. In the cities, the decline was more striking: from 125.9 in 1961 to 100.4 in 1980.[89] It should be noted that the 1961 data probably understate real fertility, so that the real decline in fertility over the last two decades is probably greater than the reported data indicate.

Reported fertility rates in Kirgizia began at significantly lower levels in the mid to late 1960s. Reported total fertility peaked in 1971/72 at 4.97 and declined by about 8 per cent over the next decade to 4.09 in 1982/83. As with the other Central Asian republics, the pattern of fertility decline in Kirgizia (Figure 2.15) is one in which women begin limiting their families after age 30 and the birth of three or four children.

Trends in general, total, and age-specific fertility rates, then, indicate that natality decline has now begun in all six southern tier republics. The process is most advanced in Azerbaydzhan and

Kazakhstan. Data defects associated with birth underreporting have masked the timing and pace of the fertility transition in the four core Central Asian republics. Still, what is clear from the reported data is that the process of fertility decline has begun in earnest in all of these areas and could very well accelerate in the coming decades – a point noted by Soviet demographers as well.[90]

CONCLUSION

The patterns of social and demographic change over the last eight decades may be summarized as follows. At the turn of the century, most areas within the boundaries of what later became the Soviet Union were either in a premodern stage of socioeconomic development or, at most, in the early stages of the modernization. The social changes associated with industrialization were limited in large part to that very small proportion of the empire's subjects who resided in urban areas in European Russia. Here, the fertility decline was already well underway by 1897. But for the vast majority of Russians and other European nationalities, who lived in small villages scattered across the empire's hinterlands, many aspects of peasant life remained little changed. Traditional patriarchal family systems were still strong in the rural areas of European Russia; and natality levels remained high in 1897. Conscious family limitation practices were limited. Socioeconomic conditions for the societies on the empire's southern tier were still more primitive. The Islamic minorities here remained virtually untouched by modernization. Their social systems were hierarchical; and, as in rural areas of European Russia, traditional patriarchal family patterns held sway. The social position of these women, however, was even more restrictive than that of their counterparts in European Russia. Many of the Islamic cultures practised strict physical segregation of the sexes; and some adhered to customs, such as veiling, that severely limited female participation outside the home. These social characteristics were accompanied in some areas by extremely high fertility. In other areas, natality was lower, considerably lower than in rural European Russia, because of disease and poor health conditions.

The socioeconomic differences that existed in 1897 were to some degree perpetuated in the twentieth century. Early-industrializing areas were among the first beneficiaries of Stalin's forced modernization program. These areas were already well into the fertility decline by the 1926 census. The value changes associated with urban life styles and employment in the paid labor force diffused only slowly to the European Russian countryside; but by 1926 even these areas had begun to experience some fertility decline. Change was even slower coming to the predominantly rural peoples of the Soviet southern tier. Here, high natality areas continued to register extraordinarily high fertility rates; although some areas, like western Georgia, had begun to record striking fertility declines. Other groups, like the mountain Kirgiz, continued to be affected by high rates of infertility and infecundity, associated with poor health.

The three decades between the census of 1926 and that of 1959 were incredibly tumultuous ones. But, in spite of the disruptions caused by coerced collectivization, a major purge, and world war, it was during these years that a far-reaching transformation in economic base took place in European Russia. The paucity of reliable data does not permit us to track this process with precision, but by 1959 the USSR was a rapidly modernizing country. Urbanization rates tripled in the RSFSR; the proportion of the labor force employed in the modernized sectors quadrupled. The percentage of the labor force engaged in agriculture was halved. Women poured into the modernized sectors of the labor force at rates roughly double those of 1926. They achieved access to educational institutions that was roughly equal to that of males. Behind these statistics were salient changes in the way people lived their lives. Some aspects of traditional family systems remained relatively undisturbed in the countryside, but even there social change had already eroded many aspects of the patriarchal system. The fertility trends that accompanied these massive social changes were precisely those predicted by the fertility transition model: fertility continued its steady downward trend and rural natality followed urban natality into the fertility transition. By 1959, urban fertility rates had already begun to stabilize at a low level – a trend rural fertility rates for European Russia would follow in the 1959 to 1970 time frame. Total fertility in most of the European republics has declined only marginally since 1970; the fertility transition appears to be almost completed in most of these areas.

The years between 1926 and 1959 were also ones of massive social change for the Asian southern tier; but these areas began from a lower base; and the differentials that characterized these areas persisted during this period. Many of the changes observed in the

European areas occurred later here. In 1926, Muslim women were much more fully cemented in their exclusively domestic role than their European counterparts; traditional family systems and values persisted among Islamic groups much longer and much more strongly than among the central Russian peasantry.[91] As one would predict from the fertility transition model, natality remained high in these areas much longer. In some areas where poor health conditions had kept natality low, major increases in fertility occurred. Data limitations preclude a precise evaluation of where and when such increases took place. By the 1970s, however, most areas in the non-European southern tier were showing the first signs of a fertility decline. Armenia, whose natality levels in the 1920s and 1930s were almost unbelievably high, exceeding even those of neighboring Azerbaydzhan, has entered into a prolonged and rapid natality decline. Azerbaydzhan and Kazakhstan are now clearly well into the intermediate stages of transition. While the other four central Asian republics appear to have only recently entered this stage.

The trends we have charted in this chapter, then, are quite consistent with those hypothesized by the fertility transition model. This does not necessarily mean, however, that natality in the various areas of the USSR actually exhibited the relationships hypothesized by the model. To test the hypothesized relationships for 1897, we explored the statistical linkage between various measures of natality and measures of modernization and traditional familial systems. The strongest statistical relationships were found between measures of the role of women (early marriage, female literacy, female/male literacy ratios). By 1959, the predictive power of some measures had decreased, while those of others were still fairly strong in the European areas. Overall education and female education were the most highly correlated with measures of natality in this region. These findings provide some support for the hypothesized relationships. However, data limitations preclude a more rigorous test of these relationships for European Russia and preclude any test of the relationships for non-European Russia. For the contemporary period, however, we have both reliable measures of natality and data permitting us to construct multiple measures of modernization and the erosion of family values. These data are used in Chapter 3 to more fully analyze the link between socioeconomic change and fertility.

NOTES

1 P. A. Khromov, *Ekonomicheskoye razvitiye rossii v XIX and XX vekakh, 1800–1917* (Moscow: Gosudarstvennoye Izdatel'stvo Politicheskoy Literatury, 1950), pp. 456–59, 462; and R. S. Livshits, *Razmeshcheniye promyshlennosti v dorevolyutsionnoy rossii* (Moscow: Izdatel'stvo Akademii Nauk SSSR, 1955), p. 169.

2 *Narodnoye khozyaystvo SSSR v 1956 godu. Statisticheskiy Yezhegodnik* (Moscow: Gosudarstvennoye Statisticheskoye Izdatel'stvo, 1957), p. 201.

3 *Ibid.*

4 Data computed from *Naseleniye SSSR (Chislennost', sostav i dvizheniye naseleniya) 1973. Statisticheskiy sbornik* (Moscow: Statistika, 1975), pp. 10–13.

5 *Narodnoye obrazovaniye, nauka i kul'tura v SSSR. Statisticheskiy sbornik* (Moscow: Statistika, 1971), pp. 21–22.

6 On rural community and family life in the 1890s see *Narody yevropeyskoy chasti SSSR*, Vol. 1 (Moscow: Nauka, 1964), pp. 406–26, 462–78, 685–93, 702–14; and *Selo viryatino v proshlom i nastoyashchem. Opyt etnograficheskogo izucheniya russkoy kolkhoznoy derevni* (Moscow: Izdatel'stvo Akademii Nauk SSSR, 1958), pp. 75–84. Secondary analyses are available in Stephen P. Dunn and Ethel Dunn, *The Peasants of Central Russia* (New York: Holt, Rinehart and Winston, 1967), pp. 8–13; and Teodor Shanin, *The Awkward Class: The Political Sociology of Peasantry in a Developing Society: Russia 1910–1925* (Oxford: Clarendon Press, 1972), *passim*.

7 L. A. Anokhina and M. N. Shmeleva, *Kul'tura i byt kolkhoznikov kalininskoy oblasti* (Moscow: Nauka, 1964), pp. 169–83; and Geroid Tanquary Robinson, *Rural Russia Under the Old Regime. A History of the Landlord-Peasant World and a Prologue to the Peasant Revolution of 1917* (Berkeley: University of California Press, 1967), pp. 118–20.

8 A. Lisitsyn, "Dvor," in *Entsiklopediya gosudarstva i prava*, Vol. 1 (Moscow: Izdatel'stvo Kommunisticheskoye Akademii, 1925), pp. 561–66.

9 William T. Shinn, Jr, "The Law of the Russian Peasant Household," *Slavic Review*, Vol. 10, 1961, pp. 601–21.

10 *Narodnoye obrazovanniye, nauka i kul'tura v SSSR*, 1971, pp. 21-2.

11 Dunn and Dunn, 1967, pp. 8–13.

12 Ansley J. Coale, Barbara A. Anderson, and Erna Harm, *Human Fertility in Russia since the Nineteenth Century* (Princeton, NJ: Princeton University Press, 1979), pp. 15–84.

13 L. P. Shakhot'ko, *Rozhdayemost' v Belorussii* (Minsk: Nauka i Tekhnika, 1975), p. 33.

14 *Ibid.*, p. 32.

15 *Ibid.*, pp. 30–31.

16 *Naseleniye*, 1973, pp. 10–13.

17 Shanin, 1972, pp. 175–77.

18 *Narodnoye obrazovanniye, nauka i kul'tura v SSSR*, 1971, pp. 21–22.

19 *Zhenshchiny v SSSR. Statisticheskiy sbornik* (Moscow: Statistika, 1975), p. 27.

20 *Ibid.*

21 *Ibid.* Data refer to blue-collar workers and white-collar employees.

22 *Zhenshchiny v SSSR*, 1975, pp. 32–33.

23 Dunn and Dunn, 1967, pp. 20–26.

24 R. W. Davies, *The Collectivization of Soviet Agriculture, 1929–1930* (Cambridge, Massachusetts: Harvard University Press, 1980), pp. 6–18; and Moche Lewin, *Russian Peasants and Soviet Power: A Study of Collectivization*, translated by Irene Nove (London: George Allen and Unwin, 1968), *passim*.

25 *Naseleniye*, 1973, pp. 44–45.

26 R. I. Sifman, "Fertility According to the Data of the 1926 Family Census," in A. G. Volkov (ed.), *Demograficheskoye razvitiye sem'i* (Moscow: Statistika, 1979), pp. 151–70.

27 S. G. Strumilin, "To the Problem of Fertility in a Worker's Environment," in S. G. Strumilin, *Izbrannyye proizvedeniya v pyati tomakh. Problemy ekonomiki truda*, Vol. 3 (Moscow, Nauka, 1964), pp. 132–47.

28 *Narodnoye Khozyaystvo SSSR v 1956 godu*, 1956, p. 201.

29 *Naseleniye*, 1973, pp. 10–13.

30 *Narodnoye obrazovaniye, nauka i kul'tura v SSSR*, 1971, pp. 21–22.

31 *Zhenshchina v SSSR* (Moscow: Tsentral'noye Upravleniye Nar.-Khoz. Ucheta Gosplana SSSR, 1936), p. 48.

32 *Zhenshchiny v SSSR*, 1975, p. 27. The data refer to women "having employment," including collective farmers, but excluding those involved exclusively in personal subsidiary agriculture. See *Itogi vsesoyuznoy perepisi naseleniya 1959 goda. SSSR* (Moscow: Gosstatizdat, 1962), pp. 96, 167.

33 *Zhenshchiny v SSSR*, 1975, pp. 32, 35.

34 *Zhenshchiny v SSSR*, 1975, p. 32.

35 *Narodnoye khozyaystva SSSR v 1956 godu*, 1957, p. 201.

36 *Itogi vsesoyuznoy perepisi naseleniya 1959 goda. SSSR (Svodnyy tom)* (Moscow: Gosstatizdat, 1962), pp. 20–29.

37 *Itogi vsesoyuznoy perepisi naseleniya 1959 goda. RSFSR* (Moscow: Gosstatizdat, 1963), p. 180.

38 *Narodnoye khozyaystov SSSR v 1970 g. Statisticheskiy yezhegodnik.* (Moscow: Statistika, 1971), p. 25.

39 *Itogi 1959. RSFSR*, 1963, pp. 285–88.

40 *Itogi 1959. RSFSR*, 1963, p. 108.

41 *Itogi 1959. RSFSR*, 1963, p. 98.

42 Stephen P. Dunn, "Structure and Functions of the Soviet Rural Family," in James R. Millar (ed.), *The Soviet Rural Community* (Chicago: University of Illinois Press, 1971), pp. 327–28; and Dunn and Dunn, 1967, pp. 47–58.

43 *Itogi 1959. RSFSR*, 1963, p. 98.

44 Dunn and Dunn, 1967, pp. 70–74.

45 Peter Mazur, "Birth Control and Regional Differentials in the Soviet Union," *Population Studies*, November 1968, pp. 319–23.

46 Heer describes the variable as the percentage of females studying or working. More precisely, it is the total number of females aged 16–54 minus female (nonstudent) dependents divided by females aged 16–54. David Heer, "Fertility and Female Work Status in the USSR," in Helen Desfosses (ed.), *Soviet Population Policy: Conflicts and Constraints* (New York:

Pergamon Press, 1981), pp. 62–94.

47 Z. Z. Mukhina, "Changes in the Role of Tatar Women in the Years of Soviet Power," in *Voprosy etnografii srednogo povolzh'ya* (Kazan: Izdatel'stvo Kazanskogo Universiteta, 1980), pp. 69–81.

48 N. A. Kislyakov, *Ocherki po istorii semi'i i braka u narodov sredney azii i kazakhstana* (Leningrad: Nauka, 1969), pp. 12–38.

49 O. A. Sukhareva and M. A. Bikzhanova, *Proshloye i nastoyashcheye seleniya aykyran. Opyt etnograficheskogo izucheniya kolkhoza imeni stalina chartakskogo rayona namanganskoy oblasti* (Tashkent: Izdatel'stvo AN Uzbekskoy SSR, 1955), pp. 173–78.

50 M. V. Bagabov, *Islam i sem'ya* (Moscow: Nauka, 1980), pp. 44–45.

51 On family values among nomadic peoples, see S. M. Abramson, "To the Question of the Patriarchal Family among Central Asian Nomads," AN SSSR. Institut Etnografii, *Kratkiye soobshcheniya, XXVIII* (Moscow: AN SSSR, 1958), pp. 28–34.

   On female roles among Kazakhs, see *Kul'tura i byt kazakhskogo kolkhoz-nogo aula* (Alma Ata: Izdatel'stvo Nauka Kazakhskoy SSR, 1967), pp. 173–80, 196; Elizabeth Bacon, *Central Asians Under Russian Rule: A Study in Culture Change* (Cornell University Press, 1980), pp. 19–20, 35–41, 137–78; and A. Zhakipova, *Razvitiye semeyno-brachnykh otnosheniy v kazakhstane* (Alma Ata: Kazakhstan, 1971), pp. 22–65.

52 S. I. Karakeyeva, *Sovremennaya kirgizskaya gorodskaya sem'ya* (Frunze: Ilim, 1981), pp. 8–9.

53 On sex roles among oasis peoples, see Bacon, 1980, pp. 67–72, 85, 87–88. On the role of women among Uzbeks, see M. A. Bikzhanova, *Sem'ya v kolkhozakh uzbekistana* (Tashkent: Izdatel'stvo Akademii Nauk Uzbekskoy SSR, 1959), pp. 21–34; and N. P. Lobacheva, *Formirovaniye novoy obrayd-nosti uzbekov* (Moscow: Nauka, 1975), pp. 14–17. On Tadzhik women, see N. A. Kislyakov (ed.), *Kul'tura i byt tadzhikskogo kolkhoznogo krestyanstva* (Moscow: Izdatel'stvo AN SSSR, 1954), pp. 162–63; and N. A. Kislyakov, "Family and Marriage among Tadzhiks," (avtoreferaty dissertatsiy) in Institut Etnografii, *Kratkiye soobshcheniya*, XVII, (Moscow: AN SSSR, 1952), pp. 74–80. The role of women among the Pamir Tadzhiks was less constricted. Pamir women did not veil and were not isolated from male society. See L. F. Monogarova, *Preobrazovaniya v bytu i kul'ture pripamirskikh narodnostey* (Moscow: Nauka, 1972), pp. 103–36.

   The role of women among the semi-nomadic Turkmen appeared to occupy an intermediate position between the strictly subordinate role of oasis women and the higher status of Kazakh and Kirgiz women. See G. P. Vasil'yeva, *Preobrarzovaniye byta i etnicheskiye protsessy v severnom turkmenistane* (Moscow: Nauka, 1969), pp. 251–67. On the role of women among ethnic groups from the Caucasus areas, see S. Sh. Gadzhiyeva (ed.), *Sovremennaya kul'tura i byt narodov dagestana* (Moscow: Nauka, 1971), pp. 153–210; Ya. S. Smirnova, *Sem'ya i semeyni byt narodov severnogo kavkaza* (Moscow: Nauka, 1983), pp. 29–44; and Louis J. Luzbetak, *Marriage and the Family in Caucasia*, Studia Instituti Anthropos, Vol. 3 (Vienna: St Gabriells Mission Press, 1951), pp. 156–61.

54 M. Vasikova, *Pravovoye polozheniye zhenshchin sovetskogo uzbekistan* (Tash-

kent: Uzbekistan, 1981), pp. 16–31; and G. P. Vasil'yeva, "Women of the Republics of Central Asia and Their Role in Transforming Rural Life," *Sovetskaya etnografiya*, No. 6, 1975, pp. 17–27.

55 R. D. Artykbayev, "Past and Present Families in Uzbekistan," *Sovremennaya sem'ya* (Moscow: Finansy i Statistika, 1982), pp. 13–24.

56 Gregory J. Massel, *The Surrogate Proletariat: Moslem Women and Revolutionary Strategies in Soviet Central Asia, 1919–1929* (Princeton, NJ: Princeton University Press, 1974), *passim*.

57 M. V. Vagabov, *Islam i zhenshchina* (Moscow: Mysl, 1968), pp. 100–103. See also S. D. Begmatova, "Activities of the Communist Party of Uzbekistan to Solve the Women Question, 1925–1930," *Trud samarkandskogo gosudarstvennogo universiteta*, No. 308 (Samarkand: Ministerstvo Vyshchego i Srednogo Spetsialnogo Obrazovaniya Uzbekskoy SSR, 1976), pp. 33–50; and S. Abayev, "To the History of the Liberation of Women of Karakalpakia," *Obshchestvenniy nauki v uzbekistane*, No. 4, 1974, pp. 41–43.

58 A. Kh. Khashimov, *Formirovaniye novykh semeyno-bytovykh otnosheniy u narodov sredney azii* (Dushanbe: Irfon, 1972), p. 67.

59 Coale, Anderson, and Harm, 1979, pp. 106–108.

60 Pavel I. Kushner, *Gornaya kirgiziya. Sotsiologicheskaya razvedka*. Trudy Nauchno-issledovatelskoy Assotsiatsii pri Kommunisticheskom Universiteta Trudyashchisya Vostoka. Vyp. 2 (Moscow, 1929).

61 *Ibid.*, pp. 3–21.

62 *Ibid.*, pp. 68–76.

63 L. V. Oshanin, *Materialy po antropologii sredney azii. Kirgizy yuzhnogo pobezhiya issyk-kulya* (Tashkent, 1927).

64 *Ibid.*, pp. 5–6. Even these extraordinary figures represent an improvement over pre-revolutionary mortality patterns. In Chimkent oblast (Kazakhstan) the death rate for children up to one year of age was said to be 60 to 80 per cent. M. A. Altynbekov, "The Health Care of Chimkent Oblast in the Pre-revolutionary Period," *Sovetskoye zdravookhranenye*, No. 8, 1981, pp. 63–65.

65 A. Kumma, "Birth and Death Rates in RSFSR Borderland in 1927," *Statisticheskoye obozreniye*, No. 9, 1929, pp. 74–76.

66 M. I. Rubin, *Voprosy ozdorovleniya turkmenistana* (Ashkhabad, 1929); and I. A. Minkevich, *Sotsial'nyye bolezni turkmenii* (Ashkhabad: Turkmenskoye Gosudarstvennoye Izdatel'stvo, 1928). See also I. Der'yayev, "From the History of Maternity and Childhood in Turkmen SSR," *Zdravookhranenye turkmenistana* No. 6, 1980, pp. 33–35.

67 Rubin, 1929, pp. 127–32. The findings of this study accord closely with one done among Turkmen women at the turn of the century. This latter study found that most Turkmen women had their first child at age 18 or 19, and then experienced an average of one birth every 2.5 to 3 years over a 20–25-year span, yielding a total of 7–9 births for one healthy woman. Sh. Kadyrov, "From the History of Population Reproduction in Turkmenistan," *Izvestiya AN turkmenskoy SSR. Seriya obshchestvennykh nauk*, No. 5, 1981, pp. 24–28.

68 Minkevich, 1928, p. 61.

69 Minkevich, 1928, pp. 87–88.

70 R. I. Sifman, *Dinamika rozhdayemosti V SSSR* (Moscow: Statistika, 1974), pp. 79–84; and R. I. Sifman, "Rural Birthrate from the Beginning of the Twentieth Century to the Great Fatherland War," in A. G. Volkov (ed.), *Problemy demograficheskoy statistiki* (Moscow: Nauka, 1966), pp. 176–210; and R. I. Sifman, "From the Experience of an Anamnetic Demographic Study in the Caucasus," in *Problemy demograficheskoy statistiki* (Moscow: Gosstatizdat, 1959), pp. 211–23.

71 Kommunisticheskaya Akademiya. Komissiya po izucheniyu natsional'nogo voprosa, *Natsional'naya politika VKP(b) v tsifrakh* (Moscow: Izdatel'stvo Kommunisticheskoy Akademii, 1930), p. 40. The date on Azeri natality within Armenia, plus the Sifman data on rural Azeri natality, provide an important correction to the ZAGS-generated fertility data on Azerbaydzhan, which were artificially low due to underreporting. One source, for example, cites survey results showing a birth rate of 52 per 1,000 population for Armenia but only 34.2 per cent per 1,000 population for Azerbaydzhan. See D. M. Divnogortsev, "Natural Growth of the Population in Rural Areas," *Statisticheskiy obozreniya*, No. 9, 1927, pp. 87–89.

72 Sifman, 1966.

73 *Statisticheskiy spravochnik SSSR za 1928 g* (Moscow: Statisticheskoye Izdatel'stvo TsSU SSSR, 1929), pp. 76–79.

74 More detailed results of this survey are reported in A. A. Akhmedov, "General Fertility Rates of Women Living in Rural Localities of Azerbaydzhan," *Azerbaydzhanskiy meditsinskiy zhurnal*, No. 7, 1974, pp. 16–21; and A. A. Akhmedov, "Marital Fertility among Rural Women in Azerbaydzhan," *Sovetskiy zdravookhraneniye*, No. 3, 1974, pp. 43–49.

75 A. Ye. Ter-Sarkisyants, *Sovremennaya sem'ya u armyan. Po materialam sel'skikh rayonov armyanskoy SSR* (Moscow: Nauka, 1972), pp. 90–101. See also A. Ye. Ter-Sarkisyants, "Contemporary Family Among Armenians of Nagornogo Karabakha," *Kavkazskiy etnograficheskiy sbornik*, No. 6 (Moscow: Nauka, 1976), pp. 11–46.

76 M. Bariyeva, "Family Formation in Rural Areas of Uzbekistan," in D. I. Valentey (ed.), *Lyudi v gorode i na sele* (Moscow: Statistika, 1978), pp. 95–102.

77 Kumma, 1929.

78 V. A. Belova (ed.), *Skol'ko detey budet v sovetskoy sem'ye. Resultaty obsledovaniya* (Moscow: Statistika, 1977), pp. 36–39; 49–50; and G. A. Bondarskaya, *Rozhdayemost' v SSSR. Etnodemograficheskoy aspekty.* (Moscow: Statistika, 1977), pp. 65–66, 74, 78.

79 V. A. Belova and G. A. Bondarskaya, "Perspectives for Fertility Decline in Republics with a High Birthrate," in *Sotsial'no-ekonomicheskiye osobennosti vosproizvodstva naseleniya v usloviyakh razvitogo sotsializma*, Vol. 2 (Kiev: Institut Ekonomiki AN USSR, 1976), pp. 26–29.

80 R. I. Sifman, "Dynamics of Birth Rate in Central Asian Republics and Methods of Its Study," in *Problemy narodonaseleniye. Trudy vsesouznoy mezhvuzskoy nauchno konferentsii posvyashennoy problemam narodonaseleniye sredney azii* (Tashkent, 1965; Moscow: Izdatel'stvo Moskovskovo Univer-

siteta, 1970), pp. 297–301. Sifman's findings are consistent with those of a 1968 survey conducted in Uzbekistan, Tadzhikistan, and southern Kirgizia. See M. K. Karakhanov, *Nekapitalisticheskiy put' razvitiya i problemy narodonaseleniya* (Tashkent: Fan, 1983), p. 144.

81 M. Buriyeva, "Large Families in Uzbekistan," in *Naseleniye sredney azii* (Moscow: Finansy i Statistika, 1985), pp. 29–34.

82 G. V. Pirtskhalova, "On Tendencies in the Birthrate and Leveling of Ethnic Differences in Fertility in Georgia," in *Sotsialno' ekonomicheskiye osobennosti*, 1976, pp. 131–33.

83 R. A. Bardanyon and G. G. Gevorkyon, "Change in the Level of Birthrate in Armenia," in *Rozhdayemost': Izvestnoye i neizvestnoye* (Moscow: Finansy i Statistika, 1973), pp. 93–99.

84 Data on expected number of children by marital cohort for Russians within Azerbaydzhan is available in Belova, 1977, p. 49. The proportion of Azeris in the fertile-age cohort (ages 20–49) within Azerbaydzhan was estimated by use of reported age data for Azeris in Azerbaydzhan from the 1970 census. According to these estimates, the Azeri share of women in the fertile ages in Azerbaydzhan increased from about 76 per cent in 1960 to 78 per cent in 1970 to 84 per cent in 1980.

85 I. I. Fel', *et al.*, "Social Health and Its Social-Hygienic Significance," *Azerbaydzhanskiy meditsinskiy zhurnal*, No. 9, 1981, pp. 58–61.

86 Galena P. Kiseleva, "The Impact on Demographic Behavior of Historical Changes in the Forms of Family Organization and the Social Status of Women," *International Population Conference. Mexico 1977*, Vol. 2, International Union of the Scientific Study of Population, pp. 517–27.

87 The share of Kazakhs in the fertile-age group was estimated by using the reported number of Kazakhs in Kazakhstan by age group to generate estimates of the fertile-age population (20–49) in 1960, 1970, and 1980. Using this method, the estimated share of Kazakhs within the 20–49-year-old cohort in Kazakhstan increased from 23 per cent in 1960 to 25 per cent in 1970 to 29 per cent in 1980. Estimates for the Russians were made by applying the age structure of Russians residing outside of the RSFSR to the reported number of Russians in Kazakhstan. Using this method, the estimated share of Russians in the 20–49-year-old cohort in Kazakhstan decreased from 53 per cent in 1960 to 50 per cent in 1970 to 43 per cent in 1980.

88 R. Ubaydullayeva and R. Shadiyev, "Features of Population Reproduction in Central Asian Republics", in *Naseleniye sredney azii*, 1985, pp. 3–20.

89 M. R. Buriyeva and S. N. Kononenko, "Women in Uzbekistan," in *Nashi zhenshchiny* (Moscow: Finansy i Statistika, 1984), pp. 90–97.

90 A. Kvasha, "Theoretical Problems of Demographic Policy in the USSR," *Voprosy ekonomiki*, No. 11, 1983, pp. 72–80.

91 Findings from an anthropological field study conducted in 1954, for example, underline the extent to which traditional gender and family values persisted, even in the early 1950s. G. P. Snesarev, "Work of the Uzbek Ethnografic Detachment of the Khorezm Expedition in 1954," in Institut Etnografii, *Kratkiye soobshcheniya*, *XXVI* (Moscow: AN SSR, 1957), pp. 131–37.

3

The social correlates of fertility in the USSR

The current Soviet demographic situation is characterized by wide regional differences in natality (Table 3.1) This pattern of regional differentials is consistent with that suggested by the survey of recent trends in republic general and total fertility rates presented in Chapter 2. All measures of current fertility in the Slavic and Baltic republics indicate relatively low natality, with a family size of about two children. The highest indices of fertility are reported for the Muslim republics of Central Asia: Uzbekistan, Tadzhikistan, Turkmenistan, and Kirgizia. The Caucasian republics and Kazakhstan, on the Soviet southern tier, occupy intermediate stages; all are clearly embarked on a steady fertility decline, with the greatest decline in Georgia, followed by Armenia, Kazakhstan, and Azerbaydzhan. Fragmentary data from the 1979 census on the number of children ever born provides dramatic evidence of substantial regional differences in natality. As shown in Figure 3.1, even relatively young women in Islamic Tadzhikistan have strikingly larger families than their counterparts in the Ukraine; 58 per cent of the Tadzhikistan women in their early thirties, compared to only 3 per cent of the women in the Ukraine, had given birth to four or more children.

These regional fertility differentials, significant as they are, mask even greater disparities between nationality groups. In Central Asia, for example, high natality is moderated by the presence of low-fertility Europeans. In 1970 in Uzbekistan, birth rates for Uzbeks were 39.2 compared to 17.5 for Russians. The analogous figures for Kirgizia were 39.3 and 19; for Tadzhikistan, 39.5 and 19.9; for Turkmenistan, 40.9 and 19; and for Azerbaydzhan, 33 and 15.1.[1] In Uzbekistan in 1979, Uzbek birth rates were 38.5, compared to 16.5 for Russians; 35.8 for Tadzhiks; 37.7 for Turkmen; 33.6 for Kirgiz;

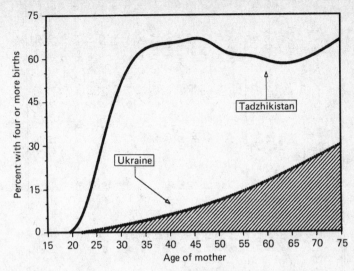

Figure 3.1 Women with four or more births, by region, 1979

and 42.7 for Karakalpaks.[2] The average number of children ever born for Uzbek women, according to the 1979 census, was 6.13 for women aged 35 to 39; 6.67 for those aged 40 to 44; 6.68 for those aged 45 to 49; and 6.11 for those aged 50 to 54.[3] Data from the mid-1970s, when reported total fertility peaked, reveal extremely high natality among Central Asian ethnic groups within their titular republics (see Figure 3.2). The total fertility rate for Turkmen women in Turkmenistan was an amazing 7.9 in 1974–75!

The most striking differentials, then, are between ethnic groups. Table 3.2 presents several measures of natality and family patterns for nineteen nationalities that allow us to make comparisons across ethnic groups. As these data illustrate, Slavs, Balts, and Jews fall into one group with natality measures at relatively low levels. Moldavians, Georgians, and one relatively urbanized Muslim minority, the Tatars, fall into an intermediate group, with expected family size between two-and-a-half and three children. The Abkhazians (another Muslim minority) and the Armenians fall into another intermediate group with family size expectations of around three-and-a-half to four children. Kazakhs and Azeris (both Muslim minorities) form yet another intermediate group with an expected family size of around five children. The highest natality indicators

Table 3.1. *Regional differences in fertility and family size*

Republic	Birth rate[a] 1983	General fertility rate[b] 1982/83	Child/woman ratio[c] 1970	Children living with mothers[d] 1970	Total family size[e] 1979	Fertility ratio[f] 1979	Expected no of Children[g] Blue & white collar 1969	Expected no of Children[g] All social classes 1978	Ideal no of Children Blue & white-collar 1969[g]	Index of total fertility 1980[c]	Total fertility 1982/83[h]
RSFSR	17.6	65.8	0.731	1.80	3.3	0.209	2.21	2.04	2.69	0.166	2.05
Ukraine	16.0	61.1	0.696	1.68	3.3	0.191	2.07	2.02	2.63	0.163	2.04
Belorussia	17.5	66.6	0.834	1.92	3.3	0.223	2.41	2.22	2.93	0.171	2.09
Uzbekistan	35.3	152.3	1.968	3.30	5.5	0.393	4.31	4.86	4.55	0.395	4.65
Kazakhstan	24.4	95.5	1.300	2.50	6.1	0.296	3.19	3.20	3.38	0.240	2.93
Georgia	18.0	70.0	0.940	2.18	4.0	0.228	2.88	2.77	3.95	0.186	2.25
Azer. SSR	26.2	98.5	1.764	3.27	5.1	0.346	4.25	4.23	4.52	0.266	2.93
Lithuania	16.3	61.5	0.803	1.84	3.3	0.199	2.20	2.17	2.75	0.169	2.03
Moldavia	22.5	82.0	0.944	2.23	3.4	0.252	2.25	2.41	2.74	0.200	2.57
Latvia	15.9	60.2	0.613	1.55	3.1	0.158	2.11	2.03	2.60	0.166	2.03
Kirgizia	31.5	134.0	1.630	2.85	4.6	0.356	3.72	3.94	3.94	0.322	4.09
Tadzhikistan	38.7	170.3	2.075	3.38	5.7	0.450	4.08	5.32	4.18	0.441	5.47
Armenia	23.6	87.2	1.436	2.90	4.7	0.314	3.42	3.50	4.10	0.233	2.35
Turk. SSR	35.6	149.6	1.953	3.29	5.5	0.396	3.79	5.11	4.10	0.398	4.75
Estonia	16.0	62.8	0.642	1.57	3.1	0.167	2.29	2.18	2.74	0.180	2.09
USSR	19.8	76.0	0.859	1.96	3.5	0.224	2.42	2.44	2.89	0.196	2.37

Sources: [a] *Narodnoye khozyaystvo SSSR v 1983g* (Moscow: Finansy i Statistika, 1984), pp. 32–33; and *Zhenshchiny i deti v SSSR. Statisticheskiy sbornik* (Moscow: Finansy i Statistika, 1985), p. 81.

[b] *Vestnik statistiki*, No. 11, 1984, p. 76.

[c] Computed from Soviet census and registration data, see Appendix 2.

[d] Number of children residing with mothers in families comprised of one married pair with children or a single mother with children. *Itogi vsesoyuznoy perepisi naseleniya 1970 goda*, Vol. 7, pp. 444–49.

[e] Average number of family members residing together. *Vestnik statistiki*, No. 12, 1980, p. 59.

[f] Ratio of children ever born per woman 15 years and older to children ever born in a hypothetical population with similar age structure and maximum fertility. Computed from average number of children ever born to women age 15 and above, reported in *Vestnik statistiki*, No. 1, 1982. See Appendix 2.

[g] V. Belova, "Differentiation of Opinion on Best and Expected Number of Children in the Family," *Vestnik statistiki*, No. 7, 1973, pp. 27–36; V. Belova, et al., *Skol'ko detey budet v sovetskoy sem'ye* (Moscow: Statistika, 1977), p. 75; and V. Belova, et al., "Dynamics and Differentiation of Birth Rate in the USSR," *Vestnik statistiki*, No. 12, 1983, pp. 14–24.

[h] Computed from age-specific fertility rates provided in *Vestnik statistiki*, No. 11, 1984, p. 76.

Table 3.2. *Ethnic differences in fertility and family size*

Nationality	Child/woman ratio 1970[a]	Index of total fertility 1970[a]	Family size 1979[b]	Estimated birth rate[c] 1959 1969	Estimated birth rate[c] 1970 1978	Expected number of children 1972[d]	Expected number of children 1978[e]
Slavs							
Russian	0.714	0.175	3.2	18.9	16.5	2.00	2.02
Ukrainian	0.667	0.166	3.2	15.8	14.0	2.08	2.09
Belorussian	0.742	0.182	3.2	19.2	13.1	2.31	2.27
Balt							
Latvian	0.672	0.165	3.0	12.3	12.4	1.99	2.07
Estonian	0.687	0.169	3.0	12.3	12.8	2.18	2.16
Lithuanian	0.847	0.208	3.3	20.5	16.8	2.23	2.21
Muslim							
Uzbek	2.493	0.590	6.2	45.1	40.8	6.26	5.42
Kazkah	2.178	0.541	5.5	41.2	30.6	5.01	4.85
Azeri	2.127	0.502	5.5	43.7	31.7	4.89	4.67
Tadzhik	2.561	0.607	6.5	45.2	41.9	5.97	6.09
Turkmen	2.548	0.603	6.3	45.6	39.5	5.93	5.86
Kirgiz	2.495	0.601	5.7	44.1	38.4	6.04	5.44
Tatar	0.993	0.240				2.86	
Karakalpak	2.219	0.532				5.98	
Abkhazian	1.171	0.280				3.83	
Other							
Georgian	0.925	0.223	4.4	24.0	18.4	2.83	2.65
Armenian	1.213	0.291	4.5	28.4	22.5	3.42	3.36
Moldavian	1.037	0.252	3.5	24.7	19.3	2.62	2.75
Jews		0.070				1.71	

[a] Computed from Soviet census data. See Appendix 2.
[b] This is a measure of the average number of family members residing together. It covers only families in which all members are of the same nationality. *Vestnik statistiki*, No.12, 1981, p. 57.
[c] V. A. Borisov, "Birthrate in the USSR: Tendencies and Problems," in *Rozhdayemost': izvestnoye i neizvestnoye* (Moscow: Finansy i Statistika, 1983), pp. 18–29.
[d] V. A. Belova, *et al.*, *Skol'ko detey budet v sovetskoy sem'ye* (Moscow: Statistika, 1977), p. 77.
[e] A. G. Volkov, *et al.*, *Vosproizvodstvo naseleniya SSSR* (Moscow: Finansy i Statistika, 1983), p. 187.

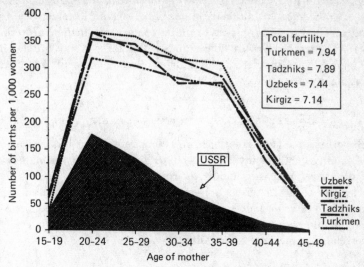

Figure 3.2 Age-specific fertility of Central Asian Muslims, 1974–75
(nationality within titular republic)

characterize the Uzbeks, Karakalpaks, Tadzhiks, Kirgiz, Turkmen –
all Muslim minorities with an expected family size of about six
children. The 1972 expected family size for the Uzbeks (6.26 children) is almost four times that of the Jews (1.71 children).

A major focus of this study is to examine the socioeconomic basis
and value systems that underlie these differences. Because the data
on natality trends indicates that most areas and nationalities of the
USSR are in some stage of fertility decline, hypotheses associated
with the intermediate stages were tested to determine how well the
hypothesized relationships fit the actual pattern of fertility. Each
hypothesis was examined by analyzing published results of Soviet
individual level studies, then tested against the four data sets
described in Chapter 1. As detailed above, both Soviet findings and
our own empirical tests provide some support for both hypotheses:
measures of both modernization level and erosion of traditional
familial systems are inversely related to natality. That is, the more
modernized minorities and those which have adopted more modern
family patterns display lower natality. There are also significant
differentials in fertility *within* ethnic groups; again, measures of
modernization and erosion of traditional family values were strongly

correlated with lowered fertility, with the more modernized segments of even the most "traditional" minorities displaying lowered natality rates. These relationships also pertain to several of the European nationalities, but fertility differentials within these groups are much narrower, as smaller families have become widely accepted throughout the group.

CORRELATES OF FERTILITY: MODERNIZATION

Hypothesis 1 suggests that measures of modernization and measures of natality should be inversely correlated; in other words, as modernization level increases, natality is expected to decrease. To test the relevance of the modernization–natality link in the Soviet Union, we examined three measures of modernization level: urbanization, education, and functional specialization. All were found to be inversely correlated to measures of natality.

Urbanization and fertility

Soviet studies linking urbanization and fertility are abundant, and almost all show that urban women have fewer children than their rural counterparts. Children in the city are no longer the economic resource they were on the farm, where even fairly young children can make an important economic contribution to the family's private plot. Limited housing in the city may provide a strong disincentive to bearing an additional child.[4] Moreover, the urban woman soon discovers that juggling a baby and a job in the city is far more complicated than combining motherhood and agricultural work in the country.[5] The impact of urban residence on fertility is reflected in substantially lower urban fertility indicators for the USSR as a whole (Figure 3.3) and for individual regions for which appropriate data are available (Figure 3.4).

Survey data reveal similar patterns. For example, in the 1960 study of children ever born, total fertility rate was 3.86 for rural areas, 2.76 for urban localities.[6] The urban–rural differential in natality was observed when age at marriage and duration of marriage were controlled.[7] The 1969 nation-wide study of desired and expected number of children among white and blue-collar social classes found that urban women desired and expected fewer children than rural women when age cohort, education, and income were held constant.[8]

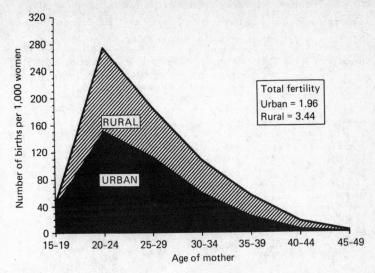

Figure 3.3 Urban–rural fertility differences in the USSR, 1982

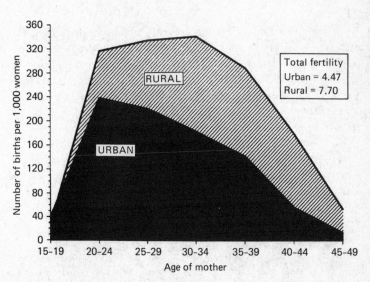

Figure 3.4 Urban–rural fertility differences in Turkmenistan, 1969

Table 3.3. *Effect of city size on family expectations, 1972*

Republic	Total pop.	Urban pop.	In cities with population of:				Rural pop.
			under 20,000	20,000– 100,000	100,000– 500,000	over 500,000	
RSFSR	2.08	1.86	2.14	1.96	1.85	1.63	2.69
Ukraine	2.02	1.86	2.07	1.93	1.80	1.73	2.36
Belorussia	2.33	2.06	2.31	2.12	1.94	1.91	2.84
Uzbekistan	5.32	3.61	4.74	4.02	3.69	2.76	6.60
Kazakhstan	3.11	2.44	3.08	2.55	2.33	2.13	4.06
Georgia	2.91	2.56	2.89	2.66	2.34	2.46	3.28
Azerbaydzhan	4.16	3.09	4.46	4.22	3.51	2.61	5.68
Lithuania	2.20	2.00	2.15	2.00	2.00		2.63
Moldavia	2.39	1.98	2.06	2.18	1.83		2.84
Latvia	1.93	1.75	1.93	1.73	1.71	1.64	2.30
Kirgizia	4.14	2.91	3.38	3.44	2.44		5.35
Tadzhikistan	4.84	3.81	4.17	4.50	3.15		6.11
Armenia	3.66	3.20	3.48	3.48	3.39	2.91	4.48
Turkmenistan	4.57	3.68	4.74	3.90	2.88		6.21
Estonia	2.10	1.92	2.10	1.85	1.83		2.46

Source: V. A. Belova, *et al.*, *Skol'ko detey budet v sovetskoy sem'ye* (Moscow: Statistika, 1977), p. 75.

More recent nation-wide studies reveal similar patterns; a September 1978 study of 310,000 families revealed that only 7 per cent of the worker and white-collar families living in urban areas had more than two children; this compares with 23 per cent of their rural counterparts.[9] These relationships were also found in studies confined to one region; they persist when age, equipment, social class, educational level, nationality, or income are held constant.[10]

Furthermore, Soviet surveys have also found that urban women who live in large cities have correspondingly smaller family size expectations than those in medium-sized or small cities (Table 3.3). For example, a 1967 national study of fertility among workers and employees revealed an average of 2.1 births for women with fifteen years of marriage (married between 1950 and 1954), while analogous women in Moscow, Leningrad and Kiev averaged only 1.5 births.[11] Similar findings were reported in the 1969 nationwide study of expected and ideal family size among workers and employees; expected family size was 4.3 children in Uzbekistan, but only 2.8 in

Tashkent (the republic capital). Similar patterns were observed for other republic capitals and for other measures of family size preferences, such as ideal number of children.[12] An inverse correlation was observed between urbanity and fertility measures for both ideal and expected number of children, even when age was held constant.[13] Similar findings, but with less striking differences, are reported for a survey of Latvian women marrying in 1959. The Latvian survey, which was conducted in 1966–67, is one of the most interesting of the USSR's many regional socio-demographic studies. The Latvian data reveal a modest but steady decrease in the number of children as the size of the city of residence increases. A similar pattern was observed when the measures of natality were ideal and desired number of children.[14]

Several Soviet studies of the effects of migration on expected family size suggest that moving from the country to the city leads to a gradual decline in family size preferences. A mid-1970s study of residents of Izhevsk who had migrated from rural areas revealed that 63 per cent of the migrants reduced their family size expectations after the move; average expected family size decreased from 3.0 children to 2.2 children.[15] An earlier study of the effects of migration on fertility in the Bashkir ASSR showed a similar shift; from 3.2 to 2.4 children.[16] A 1963 study of fertility in Yerevan (the capital of Armenia) found that the fertility rate of migrants was 44.5 per cent higher than that of long-term residents during the first five years of city residence; by the end of the next five years, however, the fertility levels of the migrants had declined to that of the "natives."[17] In all of these studies, respondents who had lived in the city longest changed the most – suggesting that the effects of an urban environment on family values and family size preferences are both gradual and cumulative.

The link between rural and urban social environments was explored further in a 1978 study of ideal, desired, and expected family size among women who had migrated to the Georgian city of Rustavi. This study found that those women who had migrated to Rustavi from rural settlements had higher ideal, desired, and expected family size than those women who had moved to Rustavi from other urban areas. This relationship persisted when educational level was held constant. The researchers also found higher family size expectations among women who had lived in Rustavi (after moving from the countryside) less than five years.[18]

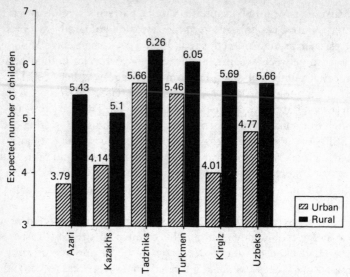

Figure 3.5 Urbanization and Muslim family size expectations, 1978

The link between urban residence and fertility affects all areas; but is particularly striking for the late-modernizing regions, such as the Soviet southern tier, where overall family size expectations are so large. For instance, one study of fertility and urban residence in Turkmenistan reported a strong negative correlation between urban residence and childbearing.[19] Another study indicated that 1965 fertility rates in Azerbaydzhan were 126 per 1,000 in urban areas, compared with 238 in the countryside.[20] It would be tempting to attribute these findings to the differing ethnic composition of rural and urban areas, since the Slavic populace in the Soviet southern tier is concentrated primarily in the cities. But the strong statistical relationship between urban residence and family size is evident within ethnic groups as well; and is particularly dramatic for Soviet Muslims. The results of the massive nationwide surveys of expected family size conducted in 1972 and 1978 reveal that urban residence is strongly associated with smaller families for relatively late-modernizing groups (Figure 3.5). Size of urban residence was shown to have an inverse relationship with family size for all ethnic groups surveyed in both studies, including Soviet Muslims (Figure 3.6).

These findings are consistent with other, more limited surveys of family size in predominantly Muslim regions. For example, a study of

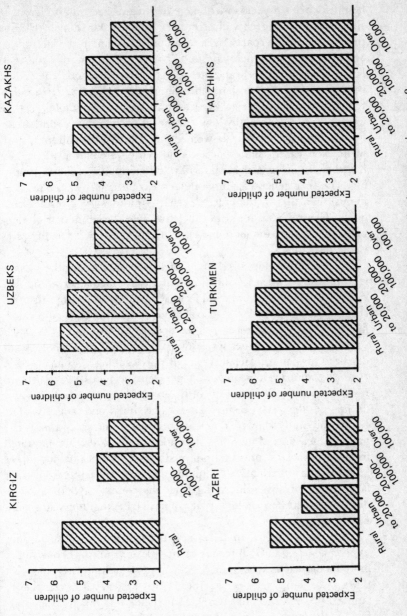

Figure 3.6 Effect of city size on Muslim family size expectations, 1978

139

families after ten years of marriage in Tselinograd oblast (Kazakhstan) reported larger family size for rural Kazakh women than for their urban counterparts, even when participation in the labor force and education were held constant.[21] An examination of natality in Kirgizia found that rural general fertility rates among the Kirgiz were 38 per cent higher than those among urban Kirgiz.[22] In another Kirgiz study, family size expectations and ideals among Islamic women were substantially lower in the cities than in the rural areas. For example, urban Kirgiz women considered 4.48 children ideal, while their rural counterparts considered 6.32 children ideal.[23] In Uzbekistan, the urban–rural fertility differential is even more striking. The 1980 general fertility rate in the countryside was 88 per cent higher than that in the cities.[24] What is more, survey results from Soviet Central Asia indicate that cities with large industrial components – that is, the more modern cities – have lower fertility rates than "old cities."[25]

In the more modernized areas of European Russia, the inverse relationship between urbanity and natality is much less striking. For example, standardized marital fertility rates in the rural parts of all six oblasts of Belorussia for 1969 are higher than the analogous urban figures. But the urban–rural differences in Belorussia had declined substantially from earlier levels. For the republic as a whole, standardized rural marital fertility was 38.7 per cent higher than urban in 1958/59, compared to only 22.3 per cent in 1969/70.[26] Reported results of a 1973 to 1977 study of Leningrad women reveal a similar decline in the relationship between urbanity and natality. The Leningrad study showed no clear-cut results from migration. The natality measures of migrants depended on the area they migrated from, with those migrating from medium-sized cities having larger families than either native Leningraders, those migrating from other large cities, or those migrating from the country. There were no differences between the family size of native Leningraders and those migrating from rural areas.[27]

These data suggest that, as indicated by the model of fertility trends presented in Chapter 1, natality patterns in rural areas in the more modernized areas of the USSR are gradually converging with those of urban localities, as the values associated with smaller families become accepted throughout society. Those analyses confined to the more modernized, European areas are expected to reveal only diminishing and perhaps disappearing relationships between indicators of modernization and natality. The Soviet sample surveys and ethnographic studies suggest, however, that nation-wide analyses or those confined to the less-modernized areas would reveal strong negative correlations between modernization and natality.

To test the Soviet findings, we examined both republic and nationality data. We also investigated fertility correlates at the oblast level. Since our hypotheses relate only to the intermediate stages of the fertility transition, we limited the analysis to those oblasts (N=61) in the southern tier where fertility differentials and the hypothesized relationships are expected to be the largest. Our non-European USSR sub-file includes oblast-level units from Central Asia, the Caucasus, and Kazakhstan, and six small oblast-level units from southern RSFSR – the Bashkir, Tatar, Dagestan, Kabardino-Balkar, Severo-Osetin, and Chechen-Ingush autonomous republics. In general, the Soviet survey results were confirmed by all four data sets. Urbanization rates, for example, have a negative correlation with various measures of fertility at all levels of aggregation (Table 3.4).* The 1970 correlation between the urban percentage and the index of total fertility (based on children under 10) is −0.55 for the 39 nationalities and −0.73 for the 61 non-European oblasts. Urban residence is also associated with lower indices of total fertility (−0.56) and expected number of children (−0.53) in the 15 Soviet republics.

The major weakness of the urban percentage as a measure of urbanization is that Soviet populations are divided into urban and rural on the basis of the administrative status of the area in which they live. The cut-off point dividing rural from urban areas varies from republic to republic. In the RSFSR, for example, a populated point must have 3,000 citizens; moreover, 85 per cent of the populace must be comprised of workers and white-collar employees, and members of their families. In Azerbaydzhan, by contrast, a village of only 500, with an absolute majority of workers and employees, is counted as "urban."[28] These differences in the definition of urban constitute a weakness in the urban proportion as a measure of real urbanization. Accordingly, we developed several alternate indicators by computing the proportion of the population residing in cities of 20,000 or more, 50,000 or more, and 100,000 or more. As expected, the correlations between these three alternate measures of urbanization and index of total fertility in the republics were uniformly negative (−0.62, −0.65, and −0.64 respectively), and reveal a

Table 3.4a. *Urbanization and fertility differentials in the USSR, 1970 (Pearson correlation coefficients)*

| | Nationalities | | Republics | | Non-European oblasts | |
	Index of total fertility (children under 10) 1970	Expected number of children 1972	Index of total fertility (reported births) 1970	Expected number of children 1972	Index of total fertility (Reported births) 1970	Index of total fertility (Children under 10) 1970
% Urban (administrative definition)	−0.55[b] (39)	−0.72[b] (17)	−0.56[a] (15)	−0.53[a] (15)	−0.71[b] (36)	−0.73[b] (61)
% In cities over 20,000			−0.62[b] (15)	−0.54[a] (15)		
% In cities over 50,000			−0.65[b] (15)	−0.58[a] (15)		
% In cities over 100,000			−0.64[b] (15)	−0.49[a] (15)		

[a] P < 0.05.
[b] P < 0.01.

Table 3.4b.

	Nationalities		Republics		Republics Urban/ rural
	Index of total fertility (children under 10)	Expected number of children 1972	Index of total fertility 1980	Expected number of children 1978	Expected number of children 1978
Share of population living in locale less than 2 yrs.	−0.68[b] (15)	−0.73[c] (15)			
Share of population living in locale since birth (1979)			0.69[b] (15)	0.78[c] (15)	0.77[c] (30)

[a] Significant at < 0.05.
[b] Significant at < 0.01.
[c] Significant at < 0.001.

stronger relationship with fertility than the original measure. These findings confirm those of Soviet studies that show that women in larger cities have fewer children than women in smaller cities. Thus, every indicator of urbanization, as applied to both the republic and nationality data sets, is negatively related to measures of fertility.

Correlation analysis also provided evidence that less mobile populations will have higher natality than those that are more mobile (Table 3.4b). For nationalities, the correlation between the index of total fertility and the share of the population that had changed place of residence within the preceding two years was −0.68. The 1979 census provided a different measure of geographic mobility: the share of the population that had lived in the same locale since birth. As expected, this measure is correlated positively with fertility for both the 15 republic and the 30 case urban–rural republic data. All of these data provide further support for Hypothesis 1: the higher the modernization level, the lower the fertility rate.

*The statistics presented in this section are Pearson correlation coefficients. They range in value from +1 to −1, with zero indicating no linear relationship between variables. The size of the coefficients expresses the strength of the relationship; the sign expresses the direction of the relationship. For example, a strong negative correlation between per cent urban and fertility for the republic data means that the more urbanized republics have lower fertility rates.

Education and fertility

Another measure of modernization is educational level. This indicator was found to be a fair predictor of fertility: the higher the educational level, the lower the natality (Table 3.5). This held true for all measures of attained education tested: percentage of population with complete higher education and above, incomplete higher education and above, complete secondary education and above, and incomplete secondary and above. The 1970 correlation between higher education and index of total fertility is -0.39 for the nationalities; -0.36 for republics; -0.51 for the urban–rural republic data; and -0.61 for the sixty-one non-European oblasts. The relationship between fertility and other measures of attained education were also uniformly negative. Educational level had the most explanatory power for the 61 non-European oblasts. Analogous relationships for the nationality file were weaker; and for the republics they were not significant, although all correlations were in the predicted direction. We will see below that the education of women is a much better predictor of fertility than the overall level of education in a republic or ethnic group. Enrollment data for specialized secondary students (but not for college students) also exhibited a moderate link with natality.

Functional specialization and fertility

A final indicator of modernization level is the extent to which the economy is characterized by functional specialization. To measure the extent of functional specialization, we used two indicators: social class, and proportion of the labor force employed in "modern" occupations. Given the conceptual problems with the Soviet category "social class," we would expect to observe weaker correlations between it and fertility. Soviet statistical sources and sociological studies use three broad terms to denote social class: *kolkhoznik* (collective farmer); *rabochiy* (blue-collar worker on a state farm or in a factory or construction site); and *sluzhashchiy* (white-collar employee). The major conceptual problem with this categorization is the broadness of the terms. For example, the blue-collar category includes agricultural workers on state farms whose conditions are not much different from collective farmers. This means that proportion blue collar has major weaknesses as a measure of modernization; a

Table 3.5. *Education and fertility in the USSR, 1970 (Pearson correlation coefficients)*

	Nationalities		Republics		Republic urban/rural	Oblasts (Non-European areas)	
	Index of total fertility (children under 10)	Expected number of children 1972	Index of total fertility (reported births)	Expected number of children 1972	Index of fertility (children under 10)	Index of total fertility (reported births)	(children under 10)
Educational level (% age 10+)							
Higher Educ.	−0.39[b] (39)	−0.38 (17)	−0.36 (15)	−0.21 (15)	−0.51[b] (30)	−0.64[c] (36)	−0.61[c] (61)
Inc. higher Educ. and above	−0.35[a] (39)	−0.37 (17)	−0.33 (15)	−0.17 (15)	−0.51[b] (30)	−0.66[c] (36)	−0.62[c] (61)
Complete sec. and above	−0.36[a] (39)	−0.31 (17)	−0.25 (15)	−0.09 (15)	−0.47[b] (30)	−0.65[c] (36)	−0.60[c] (61)
Inc. sec. and above	−0.48[c] (39)	−0.41[a] (17)	−0.23 (15)	−0.13 (15)	−0.45[b] (30)	−0.62[c] (36)	−0.63[c] (61)
Enrollment							
Specialized sec. students per 1,000 16–24	−0.44[b] (35)	−0.58[b] (17)					
College students per 1,000, 17–29	0.01 (35)	0.23 (17)					

[a] P < 0.05.
[b] P < 0.01.
[c] P < 0.001.

Table 3.6. *Social class and family size, 1978*[a]

All families having children 16 years of age and younger	Families of workers and white-collar employees		Families of collective farmers %
	Total (%)	Urban (%)	Rural (%)	
Families with 1 child	57.4	61.5	44.2	37.8
Families with 2 children	31.8	31.4	33.1	30.2
Families with 3 children	6.4	4.7	11.7	14.7
Families with 4 children	2.3	1.4	5.3	7.6
Families with 5 and more children	2.1	1.0	5.7	9.7

[a] Based on a sample of 310,000 families of workers, white-collar employees, and collective farmers conducted in September 1978.
Source: Deti v SSSR (Moscow: Statistika, 1979), p. 9.

largely agricultural region could have a high proportion of *rabochiy*, employed on state farms. The proportion of white-collar employees in the population is a better measure of modernization; but it should be recalled that this category includes employees such as clerks in stores and offices who are poorly paid relative to many blue-collar occupations, as well as highly qualified professionals (i.e., the specialists).

In spite of these problems, we expect to find at least a weak relationship between these social class indicators and family size. Indeed, Soviet studies have found that *kolkhoz* women generally have larger families than white-collar women (Table 3.6). This is true when age, education, rural–urban residence, and income are held constant. For example, the 1967 marital cohort study revealed larger marital fertility for women in the collective farm social class for all marital cohorts surveyed. This was true even when education was held constant.[29] The 1969 survey of expected and ideal family size among women from the blue and white-collar working classes revealed higher family size preferences and expectations among women in the blue-collar class, even holding constant for age, education, and income.[30] R. I. Sifman presents data from low natality republics gathered in 1972 as part of a nationwide sample of 347,000 women. These data are standardized by length of marriage and presented by social class with income held constant. At all levels of income, women in the white and blue-collar social classes (exclusive of state farm women) have a significantly lower number of births than women from the agricultural social classes (collective and state farm workers).[31]

Similar findings are reported in studies that focus on a single region.[32] For example, an analysis of number of children of Ukrainian mothers aged 35 to 39 found the lowest number of children (1.67) for white-collar women and the highest (2.38) for collective farm women.[33] Family size orientations are more dramatically differentiated by social class for Muslim women. In a study of the ideal number of children among Uzbek women, 28.8 per cent of the rural white-collar women indicated a preference for six or more children; 3.9 per cent responded, "the more, the better." The analogous figures among collective farm women were 34.8 per cent and 31.7 per cent.[34] In Islamic Dagestan, the general fertility rate for collective farm women (142.7) was 1.5 times higher than that of white-collar women (90.3).[35]

To test these Soviet findings, we examined the relationship between social class indicators and natality in republics (Table 3.7). We found weak to moderate correlations between the percentage of the population in blue-collar households and several indicators of fertility – the index of total fertility ratio; the general fertility rate; crude birth rate. While the relationships were not strong all were in the predicted direction. For example, the correlation between index of total fertility and percentage of blue collar for the republics was −0.47 and −0.60 for the republic urban/rural data. We got similar results with a variable that involved the proportion of the employed population that belonged to the blue-collar social class. Somewhat stronger relationships were found for the same variable in the non-European oblast areas. In these regions, the share of white-collar workers in the labor force also proved to be moderately good predictors. For example, the zero-order correlation between index of total fertility based on children under age 10 and the percentage of the labor force that are white-collar employees was −0.74 for the 61 non-European oblasts. In general, however, social class was a disappointing predictor of natality.

These findings were not unexpected, given the inadequacy of social class as a measure of modernization. Accordingly, we tested the hypothesis with several other measures that more directly capture the extent to which an area or group had been affected by the

Table 3.7. *Functional specialization and fertility in the USSR, 1970 (Pearson correlation coefficients)*

	Nationalities		Republics		Republic urban/rural		Oblasts (non-European areas)	
	Index of total fertility (children under 10)	Expected number of children 1972	Index of total fertility (reported births)	Expected number of children 1972	Index of total fertility (children under 10)	Expected number of children 1972	Index of total fertility (reported births)	Index of total fertility (children under 10)
Social class								
% Blue collar			-0.47[a] (15)	-0.41 (15)	-0.60[c] (15)	-0.58[c] (30)		
% of employed who are blue collar			-0.50[a] (15)	-0.46[a] (15)	-0.60[c] (30)	-0.60[c] (30)		-0.57[c] (30)
% White collar			-0.23 (15)	-0.17 (15)	-0.48[b] (30)	-0.43[b] (30)	-0.64[c]	
% of employed who are white collar			-0.28 (15)	-0.19 (15)	-0.52[b] (30)	-0.47[b] (30)		
Modern occupations								
% employed in mental labor			-0.30 (15)	-0.23 (15)	-0.54[c] (30)	-0.49[b] (30)	-0.71[c] (36)	
% employed in industry			-0.68[b] (15)	-0.67[b] (15)	-0.69[c] (30)	-0.65[c] (30)		-0.74[c] (61)

% employed in agriculture			0.54[a] (15)	0.53[a] (15)	0.61[t] (30)	−0.57[c] (30)	
Semi-professionals per 1,000, 20–59	−0.55[c] (35)	−0.72[c] (17)				−0.60[b] (30)	−0.61[c] (48)
Professionals per 1,000, 25–59	−0.12 (35)	−0.08 (17)				−0.56[c] (30)	−0.41[b] (48)
Scientific workers per 1,000, 25–59	−0.34[a] (35)	−0.43[a] (17)					

[a] P < 0.05.
[b] P < 0.01.
[c] P < 0.001.

increasing levels of functional specialization associated with economic modernization. As expected, the correlations using these indicators were marginally stronger. The correlation between index of total fertility and the percentage of the labor force employed in agricultural work was 0.54 in the 15 republics and 0.61 in the republic urban–rural file; that between the index of total fertility and the percentage of the labor force in industry was −0.68 for the republics and −0.69 for the 30 urban–rural republic cases. Another indicator of functional specialization is the percentage of the working-age population employed as white-collar specialists: scientists, teachers, lab technicians, and researchers. Again, this measure was associated with reduced fertility. For nationalities, the correlation between semi-professionals per 1,000 25–59-year-olds and index of total fertility is −0.55.

Thus, all the measures of modernization were correlated negatively with fertility; those groups with higher indicators of modernization have lower natality indicators. While not all of these results were statistically significant, the associations were strongest for those indicators of modernization that best measured the concept, such as urbanization level and employment in modern occupations; all available indicators of urbanization and functional specialization reveal strong negative relationships with fertility. While these relationships affect both the Europeanized and late-modernizing groups, they are most striking for late-modernizing minorities.

CORRELATES OF FERTILITY: FAMILY VALUES

The fertility transition model presented in Chapter 1 suggests that the link between indicators of modernization and fertility level is due, in large part, to the impact of a "modern" environment, particularly urban life styles, on norms and values regulating gender roles and familial patterns. In traditional, patriarchal family systems, women are limited to the domestic sphere (reproduction and homemaking); and, although they may represent an important source of labor within the family economy, are concomitantly blocked from access to the public sphere. Modernization facilitates a gradual breakdown in the patriarchal sex-based division of labor by undermining the economic basis for these values. With much of the focus of economic life moving away from the home, pressure grows to relax the social and legal strictures limiting women to a domestic role; this is particularly true in areas where females are needed in the paid labor force. Removing the barriers to female participation in the community at large (the public as opposed to the domestic role) acts eventually to depress fertility by providing an alternate source of social status and personal satisfaction.

These assumptions are embodied in Hypothesis 2, which states that fertility is inversely correlated with erosion of patriarchal familial systems and their supporting norms and values defining appropriate sex roles. In order to test this hypothesis, we needed measures of traditionality in family values and sex roles. As noted in Chapter 1, most desirable would be survey data on attitudes toward sex roles and family, but such data are not available for the USSR. We sought surrogate measures of traditional familial norms by examining behavioral indicators tapping the extent of educational and occupational opportunities for women outside the home. This strategy is based on Western family research that shows a strong statistical link between those behavioral indicators and attitudinal measures of gender role egalitarianism. The indicators we examined include: early marriage, employment in the paid labor force, female educational level, and an index of relative male/female educational attainments.

Marriage, family patterns, and fertility

Indicators of traditionality in gender roles include marriage and family patterns: the incidence of early marriage, frequency of divorce, and the proportion of extended families. The incidence of early marriage among females provides a good measure of relative emphasis on domestic roles. A higher proportion of teenage brides is suggestive of social pressures stressing a domestic role for women. All available data for the Soviet case show a strong correlation between early marriage and large families (Figure 3.7, Table 3.8). The direct association between early marriage and natality was noted in the 1960 study of children ever born.[36] Among rural women in the sample, total fertility was 6.1 for women marrying before age 20, but only 2.9 for women marrying between ages 25 and 29.[37] The 1967 marital cohort survey of blue and white-collar class women found that women in the European republics who married between the ages of 25 and 29 had a 20 per cent lower fertility than women who married before age 20.[38]

Table 3.8. *Effect of early marriage on family size*

Age at marriage	All marriages	Average number of children born in a first marriage over entire childbearing period							
		Urban areas				Rural areas			
		1	2	3	Total	1	2	3	Total
15–19	5.187	2.433	3.325	4.597	3.185	3.702	5.014	7.775	6.149
20–24	3.259	2.225	2.716	3.302	2.545	3.216	4.350	6.929	4.313
25–29	2.341	1.990	2.266	2.966	2.110	2.483	3.026	4.336	2.930
30–34	1.700								

Territory 1 Ukrainian SSR, Latvian SSR, Estonian SSR.
Territory 2 Belorussian SSR, Georgian SSR, Lithuanian SSR, Moldavian SSR, RSFSR (excluding autonomous republics).
Territory 3 Central Asian republics, Azerbaydzhan SSR, Armenian SSR, autonomous republics of RSFSR.
Source: "Indicators of Marriage and Fertility," *Vestnik statistiki*, No. 8, 1967, p. 94.

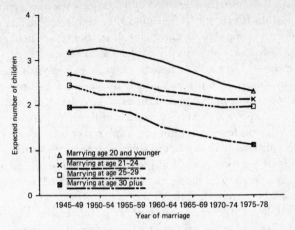

Figure 3.7 Effect of early marriage on family size expectations, 1978

Source: Data compiled from V. A. Belova, *et al.*, "Dynamics and Differentiation of Birth Rate in the USSR," *Vestnik statistiki*, No. 12, 1983, pp. 14–24

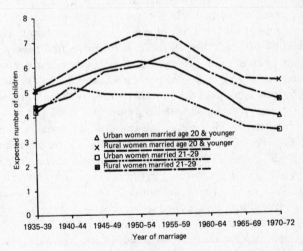

Figure 3.8 Effect of early marriage on Muslim family size expectations, 1972

Source: Data compiled from V. A. Belova *et al.*, *Skol'ko detey budet v sovetskoy sem'ye*, Moscow: Statistika, 1977, p. 51

The strong statistical relationship between early marriage and large families is evident for both Muslim and non-Muslim women, even when marital cohort and place of residence are held constant (Figure 3.8). These findings are confirmed by regional level surveys. One study of Uzbek women with four or more children in the Uzbekistan cities of Andizhan and Leninsk found a direct relationship between early marriage and the expressed desire to have another child.[39] Sifman's 1967 study of women in the Kirov region of Baku (Azerbaydzhan) found that low age at marriage was associated with higher fertility for both Azeri and Russian women.[40] Another Sifman study, this time using data from a 1959 budgetary survey, found a similar relationship. Among those women married in the 1920s, women who married when they were 15 to 17 years old averaged 7.53 births, while the average number of births for women who married aged 18 to 19 and those who married in their early twenties was 6.68 and 5.63 respectively.[41] Regional studies of more modernized areas show predictably less striking effects of early marriage on natality. The Latvian study, for example, revealed modest differences in the desired number of children by age at marriage. Women who married before age 20 had an average desired family size of 1.89; the analogous figure for those who married after age 20 was 1.66. Similar patterns were found when urban–rural residence was controlled.[42]

Soviet findings on the effect of early marriage on family size are confirmed by correlation analysis for both the republic and nationality data (Table 3.9a). The correlation between early marriage (percentage of 16 to 19-year-old women who are married) and index of total fertility is 0.71 for the 39 nationalities; 0.88 for 15 republics; and 0.91 for the 30 urban–rural republics.

Divorce rates provide another indicator of traditionality in family values. Those cultures that place strong emphasis on marriage and family life also have relatively low divorce rates. Frequency of divorce is closely linked with measures of fertility (Table 3.9b). For example, the correlation between expected number of children and the proportion of adult females who are divorced or separated is −0.74 for the 30 urban–rural republic cases. A related measure of traditionality – the percentage of families that are extended – is also related to natality. The correlation between the proportion of the population living in extended families in the 15 republics is 0.58 for the index of total fertility and 0.68 for expected number of children. The analogous figures for the 30 urban–rural units are 0.46 and 0.51.

Table 3.9a. *Early marriage and fertility in the USSR, 1970 (Pearson correlation coefficients)*

	Index of total fertility		Expected number of children 1972
	(reported births)	(children under 10)	
Nationalities		0.71[c] (39)	0.89[c] (17)
Republics	0.88[c] (15)		0.93[c] (15)
Republics urban/rural		0.91[c] (30)	0.92[c] (30)

([a] P < 0.05.)
([b] P < 0.01.)
 [c] P < 0.001.

Table 3.9b. *Divorce and fertility in the USSR (Pearson correleation coefficients)*

	Republics		Republics urban/rural
	Index of total fertility 1970	Expected number of children 1972	Expected number of children 1978
Number of divorces per 1,000 married couples 1969–70	−0.61[b] (15)	−0.69 (15)	
Proportion of females age 16 and over divorced or separated, 1979			−0.74[c] (30)

([a] Significant at < 0.05.)
 [b] Significant at < 0.01.
 [c] Significant at < 0.001.

Female employment and fertility

Another indicator of the extent of female participation in the public sphere is employment. Western investigations of the employment/natality nexus have produced conflicting results. Some studies in developed countries (and some in developing countries, as well) have found an inverse relation between employment and natality.[43] However, demographers have not yet produced an unambiguous answer to the question of causality: does employment reduce fertility or does fertility affect labor force participation?[44] In other cultures, moreover, participation in the labor force (paid and unpaid) is not necessarily incompatible with the maternal role; and in such cases, the expected negative correlation does not appear. In Africa, for example, both natality and female labor force participation rates are high.[45] In Upper Volta the female economic activity rate exceeds that of men and the birth rate is 50. Not even professional women curtail natality while employed, partly because childcare is readily available and partly because social norms are strongly supportive of working mothers, including professionals, with small children. A study of female employment in the Dominican Republic found only a minimal relationship, apparently because extended families and inexpensive domestic help provide acceptable sources of childcare.[46]

To explain these inconsistencies, demographers have suggested a theory of "maternal role incompatibility." The theory states that female employment will have an inhibiting impact on natality only when the two roles "woman as mother" and "woman as worker" are incompatible. Role incompatibility can derive from two sources – the way the labor force is organized and the unavailability of reliable childcare. In an agricultural setting, women are frequently able to bring their nursing children with them to the fields; much of the labor is household based; and there may be greater flexibility in work scheduling. Most formal work settings in modernized occupations do not provide these opportunities. Societies with a high proportion of extended families also tend to have greater access to female relatives who are able to provide childcare while the mother is at work.[47]

However, there is a growing body of evidence suggesting that "role incompatibility" is learned and the degree to which worker responsibilities are defined as incompatible with child rearing is due to the social expectations about what constitutes "good mothering." As Mason has pointed out, these social norms interact with the "real" spatial or temporal conflict to determine how much incompatibility a working mother feels.[48] In some rural communities in the Third World, children essentially provide their own care; and childcare arrangements that might be totally unacceptable to an American mother are common. To a large degree, then, perceived role incompatibility in some industrialized societies is due to socially-defined requirements for intensive and exclusive maternal care.[49] The American working mother who feels stress when her children are at the childcare center does so, at least in part, because there is still strong social disapproval of the worker role for women with young children. In other words, natality decline among employed women may be the result of a combination of internalized disapproval of mothers who work and the practical difficulties of trying to fulfill both roles. The key to understanding the fertility-inhibiting impact of working motherhood, then, is the extent to which the conditions of employment are *perceived* to conflict with child rearing responsibilities.

There is evidence that such perceived conflict exists in the Soviet Union, particularly for women in non-agricultural employment. In spite of a large network of pre-school childcare facilities, many women do not return to work immediately after their paid maternity leave ends. A late 1960s study in the Ukraine, conducted at a time when working Soviet women received only a three-month paid leave, revealed that almost all women opted to take an additional three-month unpaid leave after the birth of their child. Seventy per cent of the women in this study chose to remain at home with their baby for at least a year.[50] In part, this is due to the difficulty of placing a child under the age of three, particularly an infant, in an institutional childcare setting. Even those mothers who are lucky enough to find a place for their child in a conveniently-located day care center find that their work schedule is frequently interrupted by childhood illnesses. An absence of many of the labor-saving household devices that American mothers take for granted means that rearing a small child in the Soviet Union is an extraordinarily time-consuming task; and many Soviet women, particularly those not blessed with relatives willing to share the burden, find that job responsibilities and motherhood come into frequent conflict.[51] All of these factors help orient the working mother in the USSR to smaller families.[52]

Indeed, Soviet studies demonstrate that women employed outside the home have smaller families. This finding emerged from the 1960

Table 3.10. *Female labor force participation and parity, 1970 (Pearson correlation coefficients)*

	Republics		Republic urban/rural		Oblasts (non-European areas)
	Index of total fertility (reported births)	Expected number of children 1972	Index of total fertility (children under 10)	Expected number of children 1972	Index of total fertility (children under 10)
% Working-age women in paid labor force	−0.52[a] (15)	−0.61[b] (15)	−0.30 (30)	−0.32[a] (30)	
Dependency ratio (% working-age women who are dependents)[d]	−0.34 (15)	−0.33 (15)	−0.39[a] (30)	−0.34[a] (30)	−0.39[a] (33)
% Employed females in mental labor	−0.52[a] (15)	−0.47[a] (15)	−0.63[c] (30)	−0.59[c] (30)	
% Working-age women employed in non-agriculture	−0.71[b] (15)	−0.73[c] (15)	−0.72[c] (30)	−0.69[c] (30)	
% Working-age women employed in white- or blue-collar work	−0.74[c] (15)	−0.73[c] (15)			
% Working-age women employed in industry	−0.76[c] (15)	−0.78[c] (15)	−0.73[c] (30)	−0.69[c] (30)	
% Specialists per 1,000 women, 20–54	−0.79[c] (15)	−0.79[c] (15)			−0.65[c] (20)

% Semi-professionals per 1,000 women, 20–54	−0.69[c] (20)
% Professionals per 1,000 women, 25–54	−0.55[b] (20)

[a] P < 0.05.
[b] P < 0.01.
[c] P < 0.001.
[d] 1959 data.

marital cohort study, and has been replicated in other regional studies.[53] For example, in a 1963 study in Yerevan the fertility rate of employed women was 37 per cent lower than that of housewives.[54] The 1967 Latvian study found higher levels of natality among nonworking women, even when rural–urban residence was controlled. For the entire sample, the fertility of nonworking wives was 23 per cent higher than wives employed in the paid labor force.[55]

The relationship between female labor force participation and natality is particularly striking in studies confined to the late-modernizing regions, with Muslim housewives reporting significantly higher fertility than Muslim women employed outside the home. For example, a study of marital fertility in a rural and predominantly Azeri area revealed that total fertility for Azerbaydzhani housewives was 7.25 children; white-collar employees, 5.14 children.[56] Similar trends were noted in a study of desired family size among young unmarried women in Baku and rural areas of Azerbaydzhan.[57] In the Tselinograd study, young urban Kazakh wives who worked had 27 per cent fewer children after ten years of marriage than their nonworking counterparts; a similar pattern was observed for rural Kazakh women.[58] A Soviet analysis of the statistical link between fertility and female labor force participation (operationalized as the percentage of women who are white and blue-collar workers) at the oblast level revealed a very strong inverse relationship (-0.84).[59] The same relationship between labor force participation and lower natality was also noted in a 1970 study of a predominantly Muslim area in Dagestan.[60] A recent study of Islamic women in Central Asia found that the average number of children ever born, standardized by length of marriage, was consistently lower for employed women than for their housewife counterparts. This relationship was observed in both urban and rural areas.[61] Similarly, a 1962–63 study in the rural areas of Islamic Uzbekistan found that the average number of births, standardized by age of mother, was lower for employed women in every age group, even when nationality and level of education was held constant.[62] On the other hand, a 1978 study of children ever born among rural Uzbek women (standardized by length of marriage) found no consistent relationship between employment and natality.[63]

We tested the hypothesized relationship between female labor force participation rates and natality within republics (see Table 3.10). The correlation between percent of working-age women who are employed in the paid labor force (exclusive of those women who were self-employed in agricultural labor) and the index of total fertility is −0.52 for the 1970 data. Similar relationships were also found between female labor force participation and other measures of fertility.* Contradictory findings resulted from analysis of the link between natality and female dependency (share of working-age women who are non-working dependents). For republics, the correlation was contrary to the predicted direction, but not statistically significant. For both the republic urban–rural data and the non-European oblasts a weak, though statistically significant, inverse relationship was found between the dependency ratio and natality. This relationship is opposite that which was expected; that is, regions with higher levels of female dependents have lower fertility! We interpret this partly as a reflection of the inadequacy of the dependency ratio as a measure of labor force participation; the findings cannot be used to reject the hypothesized relationship between natality and female workforce participation. Nonetheless, our findings do not provide strong support for the hypothesis and we conclude, in the absence of other data, that female labor force participation is not a particularly powerful predictor of natality in the Soviet context.

More important than a job *per se* are the attitudinal changes that accompany employment in the paid labor force.[64] Participation in the formal labor force helps break down the feeling of dependency to which many women in traditional or transitional societies are socialized; and this, in turn, serves to erode traditional patriarchal authority systems that support large families.[65] It should be noted that this is not a process that happens overnight. In some rural areas of the Muslim southern tier, Soviet officials, who had succeeded in the early decades of Soviet rule in recruiting Muslim wives into the collective farm workforce, were chagrined to discover that many Muslim husbands felt that their wives' paychecks belonged to them; and some collective farm managers were colluding by delivering the women's pay envelopes to their husbands. Even when Soviet officials intervened to make sure that the female collective farm workers received their paychecks directly, in many families the working wife was expected to turn her pay envelope over immediately to her husband. It was some time before these women could be socialized to think of their paycheck as their own.[66] Eventually, however, as Soviet

* Data on labor force participation was not available by nationality.

studies have found, a job in the paid labor force provides most women with additional authority within the family.[67]

Professional employment, in particular, tends to modify the woman's attitudes toward motherhood. In effect, the opportunity costs – both economic and social – of an additional child are greater. The professionally employed woman has more interests outside the home and is less eager to commit all her energies to baby and housework.[68] Professional women have most to lose by a prolonged absence from the job. This interpretation is supported by studies showing that among women employed outside the home, fertility declines further as the skill and qualifications of the occupation increase.[69] Women engaged in mental work have fewer children than those in physical labor – a finding noted in the Latvian study, the 1967 study of the Naro-Fominsk rayon in Moscow oblast, and the 1965 Udmurt ASSR study.[70] Industrial workers have fewer children than agricultural workers.[71] In the Baku study, married Azeri women who were employed in white-collar occupations had smaller family size ideals than either blue-collar women or housewives. This pattern was also found when marital cohort was held constant.[72] A 1974 study in Kazan (Tatar ASSR) found a strong connection between the wife's upward social mobility to professional occupations, and family size. Standardizing for the age of the mother, the research team found that women who were upwardly mobile – i.e., attaining specialist positions after marriage – tended to have fewer children than either those who were stationary or downwardly mobile.[73] These findings are in line with Safilios-Rothschild's suggestion that the fertility-inhibiting impact of labor force participation hinges in part on the extent to which work provides an alternate identity to the mother role.[74]

As with other social indicators, the impact of labor force participation diminishes as one focuses attention exclusively on the more modernized groups. In the Ukrainian study, the average number of children was 19 per cent higher for rural women 35 to 39 years old involved in physical occupations versus intellectual occupations (2.32 vs. 1.95 children). The analogous urban differential was only 12 per cent (1.87 vs. 1.67 children).[75] In the 1970 Moscow study, the standardized index for average number of children is 1.13 for non-qualified blue-collar workers, compared to 0.91 for engineers and other college-educated specialists.[76] Another study in Moscow, this time using samples of birth registries from one rayon at five-year intervals from 1940 to 1965 revealed a similar pattern. The lowest natality measures were found, in all five time periods, for women employed as technicians and engineers. What is interesting about this study is that it demonstrates how rapidly socio-occupational status is declining as a predictor of natality patterns in the city of Moscow. The differences in natality patterns between low and high-status women were much more striking for the 1945 sample than for that of 1965.[77] Data from the 1973–77 study in Leningrad were consistent with this pattern of diminishing occupational differentials for the more modernized areas. The expected, ideal, desired, and actual family sizes of Leningrad housewives were only marginally higher than those of employed women; and the expected differences between women engaged in high and low status occupations were not evident at all. For example, non-qualified blue-collar workers had a lower planned family size than qualified workers, students, administrative employees, teachers, and doctors.[78]

We tested the hypothesized relationship between modern labor force participation and natality using all four data sets. Measures of female involvement in the modern labor force are fairly strong predictors of fertility in republics (Table 3.10). For example, the correlation between the percentage of working-age women (16 to 55 years of age) who are employed in non-agricultural work and the index of total fertility is -0.71 within republics. We also tested the relationship using other measures of female labor force participation. Because Western research has pointed to the importance of the degree of conflict between involvement in the paid labor force and motherhood, we looked for variables that would more directly capture female participation in the more modernized sectors of the economy. Two variables available for the republics (proportion of employed women in mental labor, and proportion in industrial and construction work) revealed moderate to strong relationships with natality (-0.52 and -0.76 respectively). The percentage of working-age women employed as specialists also proved to be a useful predictor of fertility; the 1970 correlation between this variable and index of total fertility for the nationalities was -0.67, for the republics, -0.79; and -0.65 for 20 non-European oblasts.

Female education and fertility

Another indicator of traditional gender roles is female educational level. Many cultures that restrict females to purely domestic roles also provide extremely limited female access to education. Hypothesis 2 indicates that as female educational attainments increase, fertility levels will decrease. Western demographic studies provide some empirical support for the hypothesis. Results of a 1963 national survey in India, for example, revealed that the total number of children born alive for less-educated women (illiterate or primary grade education only) was 6.6, compared with 2.0 for women with some university training.[79] Education is negatively related to fertility in Sierra Leone.[80] A study of fertility differentials in the Philippines revealed a strong negative relationship between female education levels and natality.[81] In Kenya, "modern" patterns of family size desires and contraceptive usage were more prevalent among better educated women.[82] In Costa Rica, female literacy was the single most powerful variable explaining regional fertility trends and differentials.[83] In the US, both census and survey results show a modest, but declining, inverse relationship between education and the number of children ever born, at least for cohorts born to the early 1950s.[84] Later studies have found that this relationship is due primarily to the impact of education on age at first birth.[85]

However, not all studies of the education/fertility relationship show consistent results. Some researchers have suggested that education and labor force participation interact to affect fertility.[86] Some of the confusion probably stems from the fact that some of the research involves developing countries at the earliest stages of the fertility transition (not surprisingly, some of these studies reveal a direct education fertility relationship); others have studied populations in the intermediate stage where fertility differentials are large and education *is* found to be a strong inverse correlate of fertility; while still others have examined populations whose values have coalesced about a small-family norm (here we would expect the inverse relationship to weaken or even reverse). These findings can be described as conflicting only if we begin with the assumption that female educational levels will exhibit a uniform influence on fertility at all stages of demographic development.[87]

Given the Soviet Union's current stage in the fertility transition, we expect a strong inverse relationship between natality and female educational levels for the country as a whole. This expectation is confirmed by Soviet surveys. The 1978 survey revealed that better educated women expected fewer children than their less educated counterparts; this finding was observed when rural–urban residence

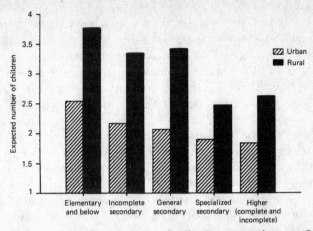

Figure 3.9 Effect of education on family size expectations, 1978

Source: V. A. Belova *et al.*, "Dynamics and Differentiation of Birth Rate in the USSR," *Vestnik statistiki*, No. 12, 1983, pp. 14–24

was held constant (Figure 3.9). Among rural women, however, there were few differences between the family size expectations of women with incomplete and complete general secondary education and between those with specialized secondary higher education. The 1969 study conducted among blue and white-collar women found, moreover, that as income or social class were controlled, there was very little difference in the family size expectations and desires of women in the two highest categories of education.[88] In the 1972 nationwide study of children ever born, fertility was found to be inversely related to educational level for every income level except the lowest. These data, which pertain only to the white and blue-collar workers (excluding state farm workers) in the low natality, European republics, reveal fairly strong educational differentials even among populations at a relatively advanced stage of fertility decline. For example, women with higher education in the highest income groups averaged 1.59 births, compared to 2.73 births for high income women with only primary education and below.[89]

Regional studies also reveal an inverse relationship between female educational levels and natality measures. In the Latvian study, for example, the negative relationship between fertility and education was strongest for women who married before age 25; for example, marital fertility among rural women who married before age 25 was 161 (per 1,000 married women aged 15–49) for those women with higher education, compared to 243 for those with only elementary education.[90] The strong negative association between fertility and educational level persists when place of residence, age, income, and/or social class are held constant. In the Ukrainian study, level of education was inversely correlated with family size for 30 to 35-year-old women, even when urban–rural residence was held constant.[91] In the Yerevan study cited above, for example, 18 to 29-year-old women with an income of 25 rubles or less per person reported a desired family size of 2.8 children if their educational level was completed secondary or below, compared with 2.4 children for women with higher and specialized secondary education.[92] The Georgian study found an inverse relationship between education and family size desires, ideals, and expectations, even when urban–rural residence, urban–rural origin, nationality, and number of children in parental family were controlled.[93]

The strong statistical relationship between education and fertility is especially striking for those late-modernizing groups in early stages of the fertility decline. The 1969 study of family size preferences for women from blue and white-collar social classes provides separate data for marital cohorts from 1950 to 1967. For Muslim women married between 1965 to 1967, the expected family size for college-educated women was 3.76, that for women with elementary education and below was 6.73. In other words, the lower educated women had an average expected family size that was three children, or 80 per cent higher, than their college-educated counterparts! The negative relationship between educational level and fertility measures was evident for all marital cohorts but the oldest (married 1945 to 1949); for this group, those women with incompleted secondary education both expected and had slightly more children than the women in the lowest educational category.[94] The inverse relationship between educational level and natality among Muslim women was also observed in the 1978 study of expected family size (Figure 3.10). For nearly all marital cohorts, however, the largest family size expectations were expressed by women with incomplete secondary education, rather than by those in the lowest educational category.

Regional studies of Islamic areas produce similar findings.[95] A study of marital fertility in a rural and predominantly ethnic Azeri

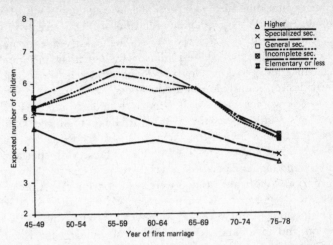

Figure 3.10 Effects of education on Muslim family size expectations by year of first marriage, 1978

Source: Data compiled from V. A. Belova *et al.*, "Dynamics and Differentiation of Birth Rate in the USSR," *Vestnik statistiki*, No. 12, 1983, pp. 14–24

area showed that women with seven years of education or less averaged 6.9 children; women with specialized secondary or higher education averaged only 4.5 children – almost two-and-a-half children less![96] A mid-1970s study in Tashkent of Muslim women with four or more children indicated that those with specialized secondary education and above averaged 4.9 children; those with secondary education or less, 5.8 children.[97] Similar findings were reported for Uzbek wives in the Uzbekistan cities of Andizhan and Leninsk.[98] The 1976–77 study of rural women in Islamic Uzbekistan also found an inverse relationship between education and fertility. Among women born between 1930 and 1959, for example, 17.9 per cent of those with higher education considered six or more children ideal and only 2.6 per cent said, "the more, the better." The average ideal family size for the higher educated was 4.7 children. Among women with incomplete secondary education, 55.2 per cent considered six or more children ideal and an additional 19.5 per cent responded, "the more, the better" or gave other non-numerical answers. The interviewers found that the women with lower education had spent their entire lives in a rural setting, while the more highly educated women had spent some time in the city, usually in conjunction with their schooling.[99] Sifman's 1967 survey of fertility in Baku revealed that standardized fertility of Azeri women with elementary education was over twice as high as that of Azeri women with higher and incomplete higher education.[100] Akhmedov also found an inverse relationship between desired family size and educational level in his study of young single women in Baku and the surrounding countryside.[101] Akhmedov's study of married women in Baku produced similar results. Azeri women with seven years or less of schooling expressed an average ideal family size of 4.1 children; those with specialized secondary and higher education, 2.9 children. This pattern persisted when marital cohort and/or age were held constant.[102] Analogous findings were reported for Kazakh women in Alma-Ata.[103] Similarly, the Tselinograd study revealed an inverse relationship between education and ideal and actual number of children for Kazakh women, even controlling for urban–rural residence.[104]

In the early-modernizing areas of the European northwest, the strength of the relationship between female educational levels and natality, while still present to some degree, has begun to decline, following a pattern observed with the urbanization and occupation measures. Sifman presents data derived from the 1967 study of blue and white-collar social classes. The data for low-natality republics reveal a steady decline in the differences in fertility for women at either end of the educational spectrum. For the group marrying between 1930 and 1934, the average number of births over twenty years of marriage was 68 per cent higher for women with primary education than for women with higher education.[105] The analogous figure for the group marrying between 1950 and 1954 was only 35 per cent. Sifman also found an interesting pattern when age of marriage was controlled. For women marrying before age 25, the inverse education/fertility relationship was present. For women marrying after age 25, the relationship becomes curvilinear, with college-educated women marrying after age 30 displaying slightly higher fertility levels than women with secondary education.[106] Sifman also presents data for the number of births for women to age 40 at the time of the survey; these data show that fertility differentials for women with various levels of education are lower for urban areas and lowest in the three major urban centers of Moscow, Leningrad, and Kiev.[107]

Belova presents data from the 1969 survey of expected and desired family size that reflect the diminishing importance of education as a predictor of expected and desired family size orientations among the more modernized groups. For the European ethnic groups, college-educated women have an ideal family size that is only 12 per cent higher than women with elementary education. For Muslim women, the analogous difference is 60 per cent. A similar pattern was found for expected number of children as well.[108]

Those regional studies that are confined to the most modernized portions of the USSR also reveal the diminishing importance of education as a correlate of fertility for those areas most advanced in the fertility transition. For example, the educational differentials observed in the 1970 study of Moscow city were much less striking than those for less-modernized areas of the same period.[109] A study of expected and ideal family size in Odessa oblast revealed an inverse relationship between educational level and both expected and ideal number of children, but the differences were only marginal.[110] A study conducted between 1973 and 1975 in Yakutia provides evidence of a similar trend. While educational level demonstrated the expected negative effect for the family size ideals and expectations of the Yakuts, for the Russians, educational level exerted no clear effect on ideal family size and only a slight negative effect on expected family size.[111] A Latvian study conducted in 1978–79 found only marginal differences in planned and desired number of children among women of various educational levels.[112] Similar findings emerged from a 1978 study of Kazakh and Russian women in Alma-Ata. Expected number of children was 1.84 for women with higher education and 1.9 for those with general secondary. The corresponding numbers were 2.6 and 2.7 for ideal number of children.[113]

Soviet surveys do provide strong support for the hypothesized relationship between female education and fertility. These studies suggest that variables, like female education, which relate more directly to the breakdown of traditional familial systems, are much better predictors of fertility than are measures of overall modernity. As predicted by the fertility transition model, the relationship between female educational level and natality was strongest for those areas and groups in the intermediate stages of natality decline – i.e., the Muslim southern tier, less strong within groups and regions like European Russia where the fertility decline had already begun to

Table 3.11. *Female education and fertility in the USSR, 1970 (Pearson correlation coefficients)*

	Nationalities		Republics		Republic urban/rural		Oblasts (non-European areas)	
	Index of total fertility (children under 10)	Expected number of children 1972	Index of total fertility (reported births)	Expected number of children 1972	Index of total fertility (children under 10)	Expected number of children 1972	Index of total fertility (reported births)	Index of total fertility (children under 10)
Educational level (% age 10+)								
Higher	−0.61[c] (39)	−0.61[a] (17)	−0.54[a] (15)	−0.39 (15)	−0.60[c] (30)	−0.54[c] (30)	−0.69[c] (36)	−0.69[c] (61)
Inc. higher+			−0.53[a] (15)	−0.38 (15)	−0.60[c] (30)	−0.54[c] (30)	−0.70[c] (36)	−0.70[c] (61)
Complete sec.+	−0.59[c] (39)	−0.59[b] (17)	−0.52[a] (15)	−0.37 (15)	−0.59[c] (30)	−0.53[c] (30)	−0.73[c] (36)	−0.74[c] (61)
Inc. sec.+	−0.59[c] (39)	−0.59[b] (17)	−0.38 (15)	−0.27 (15)	−0.51[b] (30)	−0.45[b] (30)	−0.65[c] (36)	−0.69[c] (61)
Specialized sec.	−0.80[c] (39)	−0.88[c] (17)					−0.85[c] (36)	−0.91[c] (61)
Enrollment								
Specialized sec. students per 1,000, 16–24	−0.53[c] (35)	−0.80[c] (17)						
College students per 1,000, 17–29	−0.29[a] (35)	−0.41 (17)						

[a] P < 0.05.
[b] P < 0.0...

170

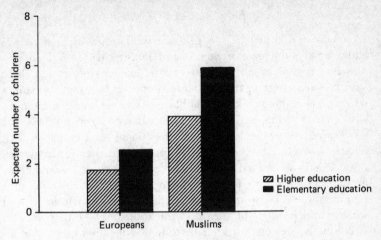

Figure 3.11 Effects of educational level on Muslim and European family size expectations, 1972

Source: V. A. Belova *et al.*, *Skol'ko detey budet v sovetskoy sem'ye*, Moscow: Statistika, 1977, pp. 63, 65, 69

stabilize (Figure 3.11). These findings suggest a strong statistical relationship between measures of female educational level and natality in nationwide data sets and data limited to the later-modernizing areas.

These expectations were borne out by correlation analysis of both the nationality and geographic data (Table 3.11). All data sets tested revealed fairly strong statistical relationships between most measures of female education and natality. Moreover, female educational levels – which provide a more direct measure of the breakdown of traditional patriarchal gender roles – are a better predictor of natality than analogous data for overall educational attainment. For example, whereas the 1970 correlation between the percentage with completed secondary education in the general population and the index of total fertility within nationalities was only -0.36, the correlation between the percentage of females with that level of education and the index of total fertility is -0.59. The comparable figures for the republics was -0.25 and -0.52; for the non-European oblasts, -0.60 and -0.70; and for the urban–rural republic file, -0.47 and -0.59.

Emancipation and fertility

As noted in Chapter 1, the primary weaknesses of both female educational and female occupational data as measures of the breakdown of traditional familial systems and gender roles is that these variables are an aggregate of two interconnected factors: the extent to which a given minority or region has modernized, and the extent to which the females within that society have participated in the modernized sector. A low female educational level could, in fact, reflect low overall levels of modernization, rather than restrictive sex roles. What was needed, therefore, were variables that would allow us to examine *relative* female-to-male rates of participation, thus tapping more directly the social position of women within a given society, independent of the modernization level of that society. Accordingly, we computed female-to-male education ratios by dividing the percentage of females with a given educational level by the percentage of males with the same educational level. This series of variables, which we call "emancipation," more accurately captures the extent of female participation in society, because it measures female access to education relative to males, regardless of the overall educational level of the society. We computed emancipation variables for each of the four major educational levels: complete higher, incomplete higher and above; complete secondary and above; and incomplete secondary and above. We also computed emancipation scores for labor force participation by calculating relative female/male involvement in the modernized workforce. Because these variables more accurately measure the erosion of traditional family values, we expect them to be better predictors of fertility than any of the socioeconomic variables.

In fact, all of the emancipation variables are strongly correlated with measures of fertility for all data sets. Table 3.12 provides simple correlations between the ratios of female-to-male education levels and fertility rates. For the republics, the correlation between index of total fertility and relative female/male levels of completed higher education is -0.91. For the urban–rural republic file (30 cases), the correlation between this variable and index of total fertility ratio (based on children under 10) is -0.92. For the nationalities (39 cases), the corresponding correlation is -0.80; for the non-European oblasts, -0.89 (61 cases). These extraordinarily strong associations were observed for all levels of education tested and for all measures of

Table 3.12. Women's emancipation and fertility in the USSR, 1970. Education (Pearson correlation coefficients)

	Nationalities		Republics		Republic urban/rural		Oblasts (non-European areas)	
	Index of total fertility (children under 10)	Expected number of children 1972	Index of total fertility (reported births)	Expected number of children 1972	Index of total fertility (children under 10)	Expected number of children 1972	Index of total fertility (reported births)	Index of total fertility (children under 10)
Educational level (female to male ratio)								
Higher	-0.80^c (39)	-0.92^c (17)	-0.91^c (15)	-0.87^c (15)	-0.92^c (30)	-0.90^c (30)	-0.91^c (36)	-0.89^c (61)
Inc. higher+	-0.80^c (39)	-0.92^c (17)	-0.88^c (15)	-0.84^c (15)	-0.90^c (30)	-0.89^c (30)	-0.90^c (36)	-0.88^c (61)
Complete sec.+	-0.76^c (39)	-0.91^c (17)	-0.89^c (15)	-0.87^c (15)	-0.87^c (30)	-0.87^c (30)	-0.92^c (36)	-0.87^c (61)
Inc. sec.+	-0.61^c (39)	-0.79^c (17)	-0.65^b (15)	-0.59^a (15)	-0.74^c (30)	-0.72^c (30)	-0.63^c (36)	-0.66^c (61)
Specialized sec.	-0.75^c (39)	-0.91^c (17)					-0.89^c (36)	-0.83^c (61)
Enrollment (female to male ratio)								
Specialized sec. students	-0.51^c (35)	-0.84^c (17)						
College students	-0.57^c (35)	-0.83^c (17)						

[a] P < 0.05.
[b] P < 0.01.
[c] P < 0.001.

173

Table 3.13. Women's emancipation and fertility in the USSR, 1970. Labor force participation (Pearson correlation coefficients)

	Nationalities		Republics		Republic urban/rural		Oblasts (non-European areas)
	Index of total fertility (children under 10)	Expected number of children 1972	Index of total fertility (reported births)	Expected number of children 1972	Index of total fertility (children under 10)	Expected number of children 1972	Index of total fertility (children under 10)
Female to male ratios							
Industry			−0.79[c] (15)	−0.80[c] (15)	−0.77[c] (30)	−0.75[c] (30)	
Specialist	−0.80[c] (35)	−0.95[c] (17)					−0.57[b] (20)
Semi-professional							−0.56[b] (20)
Professional							−0.68[c] (20)
Mental labor			−0.76[c] (15)	−0.79[c] (15)	−0.81[c] (30)	−0.81[c] (30)	

[a] P < 0.05.
[b] P < 0.01.
[c] P < 0.001.

fertility used. Female-to-male ratios for occupational data also proved to be consistently strong predictors of natality (Table 3.13). These findings provide persuasive evidence in support of Hypothesis 2.

SOCIAL CHANGE AND FERTILITY

The republic and nationality data also permitted us to test assumptions relating to the lag between social change and fertility behavior. The presence of a strong statistical relationship between two variables does not provide evidence of causality. In the case of women's emancipation and fertility, for example, one may conclude either that increasing levels of emancipation led to lower fertility, *or* that lower fertility opened greater opportunities for educational and/or occupational advancement. Our model of the fertility transition assumed that there is an important causal relationship between erosion of traditional familial patterns and sex roles, on the one hand, and family size orientations on the other. In other words, we assume that changes affecting socially-approved sex roles precede shifts in fertility. If this assumption is correct, one would expect stronger correlations between 1959 indicators of traditional sex roles and 1970 measures of fertility than between analogous variables for 1970.

The correlation analysis reveals that this is indeed the case (Table 3.14). In every case, the correlations are strongest when 1959 measures are used to predict 1970 fertility. For example, the correlation between the 1959 female/male ratio for completed secondary education and the 1970 index of total fertility ratio was −0.88 for the nationalities; −0.93 for the republics; and −0.90 for the rural–urban republic data. The analogous correlations between 1970 social data and 1970 fertility measures are −0.76; −0.89; and −0.87 respectively. By contrast, with measures of modernity, it is the 1970 variables that tend to be slightly better predictors of 1970 fertility than are the 1959 variables, although all the correlations tend to be weaker. We make extensive use of the strong relationships between measures of traditional sex roles and fertility in building our predictive model of Soviet natality presented in Chapter 6.

The correlation analysis provided an opportunity to examine the relationship between cultural variables and fertility. Western demographers analyzing fertility trends in Third World Muslim countries have suggested that the Islamic culture of these areas was the

Table 3.14. *Comparison of 1959 and 1970 measures with 1970 index of total fertility (Pearson correlation coefficients)*

	Nationalities		Republics		Republics urban/rural	
	1959	1970	1959	1970	1959	1970
Traditional Sex Roles						
Early marriage	0.83^c	0.71^c	0.92^c	0.88^c	0.96^c	0.91^c
	(34)	(34)	(15)	(15)	(30)	(30)
Completed sec. educ. (F-M ratio)	−0.88^c	−0.76^c	−0.93^c	−0.89^c	−0.90^c	−0.87^c
	(39)	(39)	(15)	(15)	(30)	(30)
Specialists (F-M ratio)	−0.90^c	−0.80^c				
	(27)	(35)				
Modernization						
Higher educ.	−0.40^b	−0.39^b	−0.20	−0.36	−0.48^b	−0.51^b
	(39)	(39)	(15)	(15)	(30)	(30)
% urban	−0.47^c	−0.55^c	−0.29	−0.56^a		
	(39)	(39)	(15)	(15)		
White collar as % of employed			−0.16	−0.28	−0.54^c	−0.52^b
			(15)	(15)	(30)	(30)
Scientific workers per 10,000	−0.33^a	−0.34^a				
	(28)	(35)				

^{a} P < 0.05.
^{b} P < 0.01.
^{c} P < 0.001.

primary factor responsible for the high fertility rates in these regions. This over-simplified view of fertility dynamics has since been challenged by more thorough analysis.[114] The nationality data set allowed us to explore the socioeconomic basis for high Muslim fertility in the Soviet Union. For the nationality data, a cultural designator for Muslimness was added by coding each Muslim nationality as one and each non-Muslim group as zero. Soviet ethnographic studies indicate that Muslim women appear to have deviated less from their traditional female roles, as mother and homemaker, than the women of the more modernized nationalities. Indeed, the cultural designator for Muslimness was correlated highly with the female emancipation variable (r=−0.74). This indicates that "Muslimness" provides a crude indicator of the social position of women.

Table 3.15. *Correlates of index of total fertility for Soviet oblasts (Pearson correlation coefficients)*

	USSR	European area		Muslim area
	1970	1959	1970	1970
Modernization				
Urbanization	−0.58[c]	−0.47[c]	−0.74[c]	−0.75[c]
	(169)	(108)	(108)	(54)
% employed as white collar	−0.40[c]	−0.38[c]	−0.61[c]	−0.77[c]
	(169)	(104)	(108)	(54)
Higher educ.	−0.34[c]	−0.65[c]	−0.64[c]	−0.60[c]
	(169)	(108)	(108)	(54)
Complete sec. and above	−0.33[c]	−0.67[c]	−0.68[c]	−0.53[c]
	(169)	(108)	(108)	(54)
Gender Roles				
Dependency ratio[d]	0.10	−0.08	−0.35[c]	−0.39[a]
	(148)	(108)	(108)	(33)
Female higher educ.	−0.44[c]	−0.61[c]	−0.65[c]	−0.71[c]
	(169)	(108)	(108)	(54)
Female complete sec. educ.	−0.48[c]	−0.62[c]	−0.67[c]	−0.74[c]
	(169)	(108)	(108)	(54)
Female specialized sec. educ.	−0.73[c]	−0.27[a]	−0.54[c]	−0.93[c]
	(169)	(108)	(108)	(54)
Female/male higher educ.	−0.79[c]	−0.27[a]	0.03	−0.90[c]
	(169)	(108)	(108)	(54)
Female/male complete sec. and above	−0.74[c]	−0.26[a]	0.05	−0.86[c]
	(169)	(108)	(108)	(54)

[a] $P < 0.05$.
[b] $P < 0.01$.
[c] $P < 0.001$.
[d] For this variable, 1959 values used to predict both 1959 and 1970 fertility measures.

The weakness of a cultural variable, however, is that it refers to a cultural heritage that remains fixed, while the complex of values relating to family and women's roles is dynamic. In other words, what is important about being a Muslim woman in the Soviet Union is not "Muslimness" *per se*, but rather the values associated with traditional familial systems. Because these values are being modified by changing socioeconomic conditions and life styles, one would expect that they would be more accurately measured by variables (such as our emancipation variable) that capture change in rates of female participation in society. This reasoning suggests that emancipation should be a better predictor of fertility than the Muslimness variable. As expected, the relative female/male levels of completed secondary education and above is a much better predictor of the 1970 index of total fertility ($r=-0.88$) than is the Muslim variable ($r=0.68$).

A related area of interest is the change in fertility relationships in early versus late-modernizing Muslim areas. To explore this issue further, we examined the linkage between socioeconomic measures and natality within the European oblasts and the Muslim oblasts. Representative results are provided in Table 3.15. The findings suggest several conclusions. First, by 1970, all measures of gender roles (with the exception of the dependency ratio) and most measures of modernization are still fair to strong predictors of natality for the USSR as a whole. Second, the expected decline in explained variance between 1959 and 1970 for the European areas does not emerge as strongly as our fertility transition model predicts; zero-order correlations decreased for about half of the measures and increased or stayed the same for the remainder. It is noteworthy, however, that several emancipation variables that proved to be such strong predictors of natality for the non-European oblasts, as well as for the USSR as a whole, have virtually disappeared as correlates of natality in the European areas of the Soviet Union by 1959. The most powerful predictors in those areas are percentage urban, education, and female education. This pattern is more pronounced in 1970 than in 1959.

A similar pattern was found by the Soviet demographer Zvidrins. He provides the results of correlation analysis between fertility measures and socioeconomic variables for thirty-three rayons and cities in Latvia (Table 3.16). These findings are interesting because they relate to fertility differentials in a European republic where overall fertility is low and the differentials have declined substantially.[115] Nonetheless, Zvidrins still found that socioeconomic variables explained a substantial portion of the remaining differences in fertility behavior. As with our analysis, Zvidrins found that female labor force participation had only limited explanatory power; urban residence and education level, however, proved to be strong pre-

Table 3.16. *Correlates of fertility in Latvia*

Socioeconomic measure	Marital fertility 1959–67[a]	Period gross reproduction rates	
		1969–70[a]	1973–74[b]
Urbanity	−0.838	−0.822	−0.442
% Women married 15–49	0.178		0.669
% Population of retirement age			0.392
% Women 16–49 economically active	−0.403	−0.321	
% White collar	−0.826	−0.823	−0.235
% Collective farmer	0.767	0.771	
% Persons employed in agriculture and forestry	0.815	0.851	
% 20–29-year-olds with sec. educ. and above	−0.804	−0.917	
Sex ratio	0.038	0.223	
Infant mortality rate			0.065
Ratio of divorces to marriages		−0.511	

[a] Data based on a sample of women married in 1959; data cover all 26 rayons and 7 cities (N = 33).
[b] Data covers only 26 rayons.
Source: Adapted from Peter Zvidrins, "The Dynamics of Fertility in Latvia," *Population Studies*, Vol. 33, No. 2, July 1979, pp. 277–82.

dictors of fertility within Latvia. These findings, together with the results of our regional analyses, indicate that although socio-economic-based fertility differentials had indeed declined by 1970 in the European areas of the USSR, the empirical relationships between certain socioeconomic measures and natality persisted. The early-modernizing areas of the USSR may indeed reach the point as predicted by our transition model when these relationships will no longer hold, but that had not occurred by 1970.

Nonetheless, our model predicts that an analysis limited to those areas that are in the intermediate stages of the fertility transition will produce stronger relationships than one involving the entire country. This expectation was confirmed by the data. Zero-order correlations for the Muslim portions of the country were extraordinarily high; for instance, a single variable (percentage of females with specialized secondary education) explains nearly 90 per cent of the variance in index of total fertility in the 54 oblasts (see Table 3.15). For virtually every variable, the relationship with natality was significantly stronger when the analysis was restricted to the Muslim subfile than when it was restricted to some other area or for the country as a whole.

Also confirmed were earlier findings on the virtual absence of a relationship between the dependency ratio (percentage of working-age females who are dependents) and natality. The only link between this variable and natality occurs for the non-European areas and that was in a direction opposite to that predicted by economists; that is, as dependency increases, natality decreases! As noted above, the dependency ratio is a weak measure of female labor force participation. However, only moderate relationships were found between the percentage of females in the labor force (exclusive of those in private agriculture) for the two republic data sets. In other words, while our data are not precise enough to reject, without qualification, the labor force participation hypothesis, our findings suggest that labor force participation, in and of itself, is not a very good predictor of fertility. This conclusion, however tentative, is consistent with Western studies that also question the existence of a direct relationship between female paid labor and egalitarian family values. Female access to modernized occupations and, within them, to high status positions are better predictors of natality because these measures are better indicators of the erosion of patriarchal values than is mere labor force participation.

The findings presented above provide persuasive evidence of how a woman's family size orientations are directly affected by her own social and economic status. However, attitudes affecting family formation are also influenced by what the woman's family, peers, and community see as an appropriate family size and life style. While education and urban residence may substantially modify a woman's perception of appropriate female roles, this perception is also influenced by the attitudes of others – spouse, relatives, friends, and community. Soviet studies have found that many Central Asian men pressure their wives to bear more children than they desire, because of the traditional link between male prestige and fathering many sons. The woman's in-laws, as well, often impose their own traditional view on the desirability of a very large family. Women who live with their in-laws in extended families are particularly susceptible to such pressures.[116]

Women's family size expectations are also influenced by their parental family, even when other socioeconomic variables are controlled. In other words, women from large families have larger family size expectations than similar women from small families. The Latvian study revealed that the strongest impact of the size of family of origin is on those women who marry before age 25. Among these women, those whose parents had only one child averaged 1.33 children; those women whose parents had six or more children averaged 1.53 births. The size of the husband's family also affected family size.[117] Similar results were noted in the 1974 study of Odessa oblast (Ukrainian SSR).[118] Similarly, a 1980 study of expected number of children in the Georgian capital of Tbilisi found that women whose parents had small families tended to have lower family size expectations than those who came from large families, even when education was controlled.[119]

Another influence on the woman's attitude toward family formation is her husband's educational level. The 1969 nationwide study of expected and ideal family size among blue-collar workers and white-collar employees revealed that highly educated women married to men with lower educational attainments have correspondingly larger family expectations than highly educated women married to similarly well-educated men. These findings were noted for both modernized and late-modernizing minorities.[120] The pattern of differentials revealed by this study was similar to that noted for other correlates of fertility; differences were moderate for the more modernized nationalities, more substantial for the non-European groups. For example, those European women with higher or secondary education who were married to similarly well-educated men had an average ideal family size of 2.53 children; those who were married to men with incomplete secondary education and below had an average ideal family size of 2.67, only marginally higher. The analogous figures for highly educated Muslim women were 4.85 and 5.26.[121] These findings suggest that overall social opinions interact with the woman's personal attributes (such as her education, occupation, and so forth) to affect her attitudes about family size.

The impact of social environment is perhaps best illustrated by data on the regional differences in family size expectations within each ethnic group. The 1972 nationwide survey on expected number of children provides data demonstrating the effects of republic of residence on family size. Muslim women who live outside Central Asia tend to have much smaller families than their counterparts

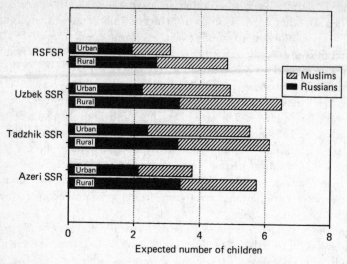

Figure 3.12 Republic of residence and family size expectations, 1972
Source: V. A. Belova, *et al.*, 1977, pp. 45–46

within Central Asia, even controlling for urban or rural residence.
The family size orientations of these women are probably affected by
the much lower natality of the European women. Similarly, Russian
women living outside the RSFSR, particularly those residing in
Central Asia, tend to have larger family size expectations than those
living within RSFSR (Figure 3.12).

SUMMARY

The data summarized above provide persuasive support for the
fertility transition model suggested in Chapter 1. Both hypotheses
were tested using multiple measures; and for each, the data provided
support for the hypothesized relationship. Natality is closely related
in a statistical sense both to a group's general level of socioeconomic
development (modernization) and to the erosion of traditional familial systems and sex roles in that society. As predicted, the breakdown
of traditional familial systems and restricted sex roles is a process that
is itself closely linked with measures of modernization. But all
societies that have reached a given level of socioeconomic development do not display identical familial systems. Different cultures

place differing levels of importance on the maintenance of patriarchal family systems and the associated limitations in women's public roles. The specific complex of cultural and economic factors within each society plays a role in determining how resistant these traditional familial relations are to the social change that accompanies modernization. For these reasons, measures of family and gender role values were expected to be better predictors of natality than were measures of modernization. The data analyzed in this chapter suggest strongly that this is indeed the case; the strongest statistical relationships were found between natality and indicators of the social position of women, particularly those that controlled for modernization level by measuring *relative* female-to-male participation rates.

The data analyzed above also provide insight into the differential stages of Soviet nationalities and regions in the fertility transition. Most of the European areas and ethnic groups began the fertility transition several decades before their counterparts on the Soviet southern tier. Groups in this latter area are now experiencing the onset of fertility decline similar to that experienced earlier by the more modernized nationalities to the north and west. The later onset of fertility decline in the Muslim areas of the USSR is due in part to the low stage of socioeconomic development in these regions on the eve of the Revolution. But this is only part of the explanation. An additional, and perhaps more crucial factor, is the persistence of traditional sex roles and family systems in these areas that reinforce cultural traditions assigning women to a maternal role. Muslim traditionality, however, has not meant that these minorities are immune to the effects of social and economic change, or to the impact of public policy. The family systems and natality patterns of both the European and late-modernizing minorities have been affected by a government-sponsored series of programs designed to promote rapid industrialization and development. An evaluation of the results of these programs – intended and unintended – on Soviet familial systems and population dynamics provides the focus for Part 2.

NOTES

1 N. M. Aliakberova, "Analysis of Contemporary Levels of Fertility in Central Asia," in O. B. Ata-Mirzayev, *et al.* (eds.), *Regional'nyye demografi-cheskiye issledovaniya* (Tashkentskiy Gosudarstvennyy Universitet. Sbornik

nauchnykh trudov No. 548; Tashkent, 1978), pp. 18–26; and Ch.A. Bakhyshov, "A Change in the Ethnic Composition of the Population of Azerbaydzhan," *Sovetskaya etnografiya*, No. 5, 1982, pp. 65–71. Abdullin provides slightly different ethnic birthrates for Kirgizia in 1970: Kirgiz, 39.0; Uzbeks, 38.7; Tadzhiks, 36.0; Kazakhs, 30.6; Belorussians, 30.2; Tatars, 22.7; Ukrainians, 17.1; and Russians, 16.9 per 1000. See K. D. Abdullin, "Birthrate of the Population Among Several Nationalities Living in Kirgizia," *Sovetskoye zdravookhraneniye kirgizii*, No. 2, 1973, pp. 41–43.

2 I. R. Mullyadzhanov, *Demograficheskoye razvitiye uzbekskoy SSR* (Tashkent: Uzbekistan, 1983), p. 81.

3 Mullyadzhanov, 1983, p. 228.

4 L. Ye. Darskiy, "Birthrate and the Reproductive Function of the Family," in A. G. Volkov (ed.), *Demograficheskoye razvitiye sem'i* (Moscow: Statistika, 1979), pp. 85–125. An example of Western research on the impact of urbanity on fertility during the intermediate stages of the fertility transition in Frank Travato and Carl F. Grindstoff, "Decomposing the Urban–Rural Fertility Differential: Canada, 1971," *Rural Sociology*, Vol. 45, No. 3, 1980, pp. 448–68.

5 R. I. Sifman, *Dinamika rozhdayemosti v SSSR* (Moscow: Statistika, 1974), p. 129. See also Ya. I. Golin, "Indicators of Population Production in Dagestan," *Zdravookhraneniye rossiyskoy federatsii*, No. 10, 1972, pp. 6–8; and O. M. Karryev and Ya. Aganiyazov, "Several Factors Influencing Birthrate Levels of the Population of Turkmenistan," *Zdravookhraneniye turkmenistana*, No. 3, 1975, pp. 45–7.

6 L. Ye. Darskiy, *Formirovaniye sem'i* (Moscow: Statistika, 1972), pp. 106–35; and L. Ye. Darskiy, "Marital Fertility in the USSR, 1949–1959," in A. G. Volkov (ed.), *Faktory rozhdayemosti* (Moscow: Statistika, 1971), pp. 5–12.

7 Darskiy, *Formirovaniye sem'i*, 1972, pp. 119–20; and L. Ye. Darskiy, "Analysis of Marital Fertility," in A. G. Volkov (ed.), *Voprosy demografii* (Moscow: Statistika, 1970), pp. 188–214.

8 V. Belova, "Differentiation of Opinions on the Most Desirable and Expected Number of Children in the Family," *Vestnik statistiki*, No. 7, 1973, pp. 27–36.

9 *Deti v SSSR* (Moscow: Statistika, 1979), p. 9. Similar findings were reported in a similar study for 1972, reported in *Zhenshchiny v SSSR. Statisticheskiy sbornik* (Moscow: Statistika, 1975), pp. 92–96.

10 Regional studies revealing an inverse relationship between urbanity and natality include a 1967 study of natality in Naro-Fominsk rayon (Moscow oblast): R. K. Zotina, "On Several Social-hygenic Factors Influencing Birthrate," *Zdravookhraneniye rossiyskoy federatsii*, No. 6, 1972, pp. 23–26; studies of Yakutia: N. S. Yagya, "Birthrate in Yakutia," *Zdravookhraneniye rossiyskoy federatsii*, No. 7, 1973, pp. 19–22; and I. Ye. Tomskiy, *Sotsial'no-ekonomicheskiye problemy zhenskogo truda (na materialakh yakutskoy ASSR)* (Novosibirsk: Nauka, 1979), pp. 123–9; Chuvash ASSR: K. Sidorov, "Dynamics of Birthrate and Fertility in Chuvash ASSR," *Vestnik statistiki*, No. 1, 1975, pp. 43–49; and K. K. Sidorov, "Dynamics of the Birthrate

in Chuvashia," in V. N. Yakimov, *et al.* (eds.), *Rayonnyye osobennosti vosproizvodstva naseleniya SSSR (Materialy vsesoyuznogo mezhvuzovskogo nauchnogo simpoziuma)* (Cheboksary, 1972), pp. 46–57; Mari and Mordva ASSR: M. Kh. Vakhitov and Ya. I Tarnopol'skii, "Some Comparative Data on Population Reproduction in the Volga Autonomous Republics," *ibid.*, pp. 57–62; and G. A. Bondarskaya and V. I. Volkov, "On Ethnic Aspects of the Birthrate in Several Volga Republics," *ibid.*, pp. 62–5; northwest RSFSR: N. V. Dogle, "Territorial Peculiarities of Birthrate in the Northwest Economic Region of RSFSR," in L. L. Rybakovskii (ed.), *Territorial'nyye osobennosti narodonaseleniya RSFSR* (Moscow: Statistika, 1976), pp. 245–67; Belorussia: L. P. Shakhot'ko, "Demographic Characteristics of the Family in Belorussia," in A. A. Rakov and Ya. I. Rubin (eds.), *Problemy narodonaseleniya i trudovykh resursov* (Minsk, 1976), No. 7, pp. 9–15; Estonia: A. I. Tamre, "Dynamics and Factors of Birthrate in Estonia," in A. G. Volkov (ed.), *Problemy demograficheskoy statistiki* (Moscow: Nauka, 1966), pp. 161–75; Moldavia: *Rost narodonaseleniya i formirovaniye trudovykh resursov moldavskoy SSR* (Kishinev: Kartya Moldovenyaski, 1974), pp. 25–27; and Georgia: G. Ye. Tsuladze, *Sotsiologo-psikhologicheskoye izucheniye rozhdayemosti* (Tbilisi: Izdatel'stvo Metsniyereba, 1982), pp. 73–78. The Georgian study examined ideal, desired, and expected family size.

11 Sifman, *Dinamika rozhdayemosti*, 1974, p. 60.

12 V. A. Belova, *Chislo detey v sem'ye* (Moscow: Statistika, 1975), pp. 93, 96, 103, 109.

13 Belova, *Chislo detey*, 1975, p. 127.

14 Sh. I. Shlindman and P. P. Zvidrin'sh, *Izucheniye rozhdayemosti* (Moscow: Statistika, 1973), pp. 55–56, 123–24. See also B. Mezhgailis, "The Demographic Situation in Latvia," in D. I. Valentey, *Vozobnovleniye pokoleniy nashey strany* (Moscow: Statistika, 1978), pp. 55–62. A study conducted in Udmurt ASSR also revealed that women in large cities have lower natality than their counterparts in small cities. See E. K. Vasil'yevna, *Sem'ya i yeye funktsii* (Moscow: Statistika, 1975), p. 72.

15 A. A. Petrakov, "Sociological Study of the Influence of Migration on Birthrate," in *Problemy formirovaniya i razvitiya naseleniya urala* (Sverdlovsk, 1977), pp. 124–31.

16 A. A. Petrakov, "On the Influence of Migration on Birthrate," in D. I. Valentey (ed.), *Lyudi v gorode i na sele* (Moscow: Statistika, 1978), pp. 52–58.

17 L. M. Davtyan, "The Influence of Socio-Economic Factors on Natality (As Exemplified in the Armenian Soviet Socialist Republic)," *Proceedings of the World Population Conference*, Vol. 2 (New York: United Nations, 1967), pp. 73–77.

18 Tsuladze, 1982, pp. 78–83.

19 Ya. Aganiyazov, "To Several Tendencies in Changes in the Birthrate in Turkmenistan," *Sovetskoye zdravookhraneniye*, No. 10, 1973, pp. 6–10.

20 G. N. Zeynalov, "Birthrate in Azerbaydzhan SSR," in M. A. Adonts and L. M. Davtyan (eds.), *Materialy vsesoyuznoy nauchnoy konferentsii po problemam narodonaseleniya zakavkaz'ya* (Yerevan: Nauchno-issledovatelskiy

Institute Ekonomiki I Planirovaniye Gosplana Armyanskoy, SSR, 1968), pp. 41–42.

21 I. N. Zhelokhovtseva, *et al.*, "On the Interconnection of Marital Fertility of Young Women with Social-Hygienic Conditions of Family Life," *Sovetskoye zdravookhraneniye*, No. 12, 1973, pp. 31–37.

22 Abdullin, 1973. Other findings relevant to this point for the Kirgiz are found in S. P. Ryspayev, "Birthrate and its Outlook in Kirgiziya," in Yakimov, *et al.*, 1972, pp. 86–88. For results of analogous studies in Uzbekistan, see N. M. Aliakverova, "Dynamics and Regional Differences in Birthrate of the Population of Uzbekistan," in Yakimov, *et al.*, 1972, pp. 65–69; I. R. Mullyadzhanov, Yu. V. Voronovskii, and T. S. Tsepkovskaya, *Naseleniye uzbekskoy SSR* (Tashkent: Uzbekistan, 1973), p. 36; and I. R. Mullyadzhanov, *Narodonaseleniye uzbekskoy SSR. Sotsial'no-ekonomicheskiy ocherk* (Tashkent: Uzbekistan, 1967), p. 107.

It should be noted that the urban–rural differentials for Central Asia that are based on pre-1970 birth registration materials may be affected by the rural underregistration problem noted in Chapter 1. Reported 1959 data for general fertility for the Tadzhiks in Tadzhikistan reveals higher urban natality; both Kirgizia and Uzbekistan have higher reported urban birth rates for 1939. Soviet demographic specialists frankly attribute these patterns to less complete registration in the countryside.

23 K. D. Abdullin, "Studying the Reproductive Arrangements of Married Women in Kirgizia," *Zdravookhraneniye kirgizii*, No. 5, 1977, pp. 8–12.

24 M. R. Buriyeva and S. N. Kononenko, "Women of Uzbekistan," in *Nashi zhenshchiny* (Moscow: Finansy i Statistika, 1984), pp. 90–7.

25 M. K. Karakhanov, *Nekapitalisticheskiy put' razvitiya i problemy narodonaseleniya* (Tashkent: Fan, 1983), pp. 147–48.

26 L. P. Shakot'ko, *Rozhdayemost' v belorussii* (Minsk: Nauka i Tekhnika, 1975), pp. 72, 91.

27 V. V. Boyko, *Malodetnaya sem'ya. Sotsial'no-psikhologicheskoye issledovaniye* (Moscow: Statistika, 1980), pp. 43–44. Western studies of the relationship between fertility and migration have also found that the impact of migration varies from region to region and also with the nature of the migration – that is, whether it involves upwardly mobile individuals or not. Georges Sabagh and Sun Bin Yim, "The Relationship Between Migration and Fertility in an Historical Context: The Case of Morocco in the 1960s," *International Migration Review*, Vol. 14, No. 4, Winter 1980, pp. 525–38.

28 Reported differences in the standards for allocating population points to the urban and rural categories are conveniently summarized in B. S. Khorev, *Problemy gorodov* (Moscow: Mysl', 1975), p. 58.

29 Sifman, *Dinamika rozhdayemosti* 1974, pp. 61, 128, 141.

30 Belova, "Differentiation of Opinions," 1973.

31 R. I. Sifman, "Birthrates and Material Safeguarding," in L. Ye. Darskiy (ed.), *Rozhdaymost'. Problemy izucheniya* (Moscow: Statistika, 1976), pp. 76–92. See also R. I. Sifman, "Variations in Fertility Trends by Female Cohort," *Vestnik statistiki*, No. 4, 1973, pp. 27–38.

32 Patterns of differential fertility by social class are reported for the

Naro-Fominsk area of Moscow oblast in Zotina, 1972; Udmurt ASSR in Vasil'yevna, 1975, pp. 58–66; a 1962 budget sample in V. Ye. Ovsiyenko, "Influence of Social and Economic Factors on Demographic Indicators," *Voprosy narodonaseleniya i demograficheskoy statistiki* (Moscow: Statistika, 1966), pp. 125–36; Azerbaydzhan in Zeynalov, 1968; and Yakutia in Tomskiy, 1979, pp. 122–29.

33 V. S. Steshenko (ed.), *Demograficheskaya politika: osushchestvleniye i sovershen-stvovaniye v usloviyakh razvitogo sotsializma* (Kiev: Naukova Dumka, 1982), p. 242.

34 Buriyeva and Kononenko, 1984.

35 T. V. Ryabushkin, *et al.*, *Regional'nyye osobennosti vosproizvodstva i migratsii naseleniya v SSSR* (Moscow: Nauka, 1981), p. 262.

36 Darskiy, "Marital Fertility," 1971.

37 Darskiy, *Formirovaniye sem'i*, pp. 121, 128–50.

38 Sifman, *Dinamika rozhdayemosti*, 1974, p. 62.

39 I. Katkova and A. Mamatokhunova, "Several Aspects of the Formation of Contemporary Large Families," in D. I. Valentey (ed.), *Demografi-cheskaya situatsiya v SSSR* (Moscow: Statistika, 1976), pp. 81–89.

40 R. I. Sifman, "Fertility of Women in Baku," in Volkov, 1971, pp. 21–34.

41 R. I. Sifman, "Dynamics of Fertility in Central Asian Republics and Methods of Studying It," in *Problemy narodonaseleniya. Trudy vsesoyuznoy mezhvuzovskoy nauchnoy konferentsii, posvyashchennoy problemam narodonaseleniya sredney azii* (Moscow: Izdatel'stvo Moskovskogo Universiteta, 1970), pp. 297–301.

42 Shlindman and Zvidrin'sh, 1973, p. 122. Other regional level studies that reveal a moderate inverse relationship between natality and marital age include Udmurt ASSR (Vasil'yevna, 1973, p. 70); and Moscow city (V. A. Belova and L. Ye. Darskiy, "Opinion as a Method of Studying Family Planning," in *Izucheniye vosproizvodstva naseleniya* (Moscow: Nauka, 1968), pp. 285–96).

43 A convenient summary of findings on the work–fertility relationship is available in Robert H. Weller, "Demographic Correlates of Woman's Participation in Economic Activities," *International Population Conference. Mexico 1977*. Vol. 3, pp. 497–515. See also Hamed Abou-Gamrah, "Fertility and Childhood Mortality by Mother's and Father's Education, in Cairo, 1976," *Population Bulletin of ECWA*, Vol. 19, December 1980, pp. 81–90.

44 On the issue of causality in the work–fertility link, see James De Fronzo, "Female Labor Force Participation and Fertility in 48 States," *Sociology and Social Research*, Vol. 64, No. 2, January 1980, pp. 263–78; James C. Cramer, "Fertility and Female Employment: Problems of Causal Direct-ion," *American Sociological Review*, Vol. 45, No. 2, April 1980, pp. 167–90; and James A. Sweet, "Work and Fertility," in Greer Litton Fox (ed.), *The Childbearing Decision: Fertility Attitudes and Behavior* (Beverly Hills, Califor-nia: Sage Publications, Inc., 1982), pp. 197–218.

45 Helen Ware, "Women's Work and Fertility in Africa," in Stanley Kupinsky (ed.), *The Fertility of Working Women* (New York: Praeger, 1977), pp. 1–34. Even in developing areas where an inverse work–fertility

relationship has been found, this may be due more to income levels than to the impact of employment. In rural Java, for example, low-income women, who have fewer births and fewer children for health reasons, are forced to work. See Valerie J. Hull, "Fertility, Women's Work, and Economic Class: A Case Study from Southeast Asia," *ibid.*, pp. 35–80.

46 Douglas T. Gurak and Mary M. Kretz, "Female Employment and Fertility in the Dominican Republic: A Dynamic Perspective," *American Sociological Review*, Vol. 47, December 1982, pp. 810–18.

47 P. M. George, G. E. Ebanks, and Charles Nobbe, "Labor Force Participation and Fertility, Contraceptive Knowledge, Attitude and Practice of the Women of Barbados," *Journal of Comparative Family Studies*, Vol. 7, No. 2, Summer 1976, pp. 273–84; Akbar Aghajanian, "Fertility and Family Economy in the Iranian Rural Communities," *Journal of Comparative Family Studies*, Vol. 9, No. 1, Spring 1978, pp. 119–27. G. B. Terry, "Rival Explanations in the Work–Fertility Relationship," *Population Studies*, Vol. 29, No. 2, July 1975, pp. 191–205; John D. Kasarda, "Economic Structure and Fertility: A Comparative Analysis," *Demography*, Vol. 8, No. 3, August 1971, pp. 307–17; and Nadia H. Youssef, "Rural Women: Factors Affecting Fertility," *Draper Fund Report*, Vol. 9, October 1980, pp. 11–13; and Renee Chahil, "The Status of Women, Work, and Fertility in India," in Stanley Kupinsky (ed.), *The Fertility of Working Women: A Synthesis of International Research* (New York: Praeger, 1977), pp. 146–71.

48 Karen Oppenheim Mason, "Female Employment and Fertility in Peninsular Malaysia: The Maternal Role Incompatibility Hypothesis Reconsidered," *Demography*, Vol. 18, No. 4, November 1981, pp. 549–75.

49 Constantina Safilios-Rothschild, "The Relationship Between Women's Work and Fertility: Some Methodological Issues," in Kupinsky, 1977, pp. 355–68.

50 "A Demographic Problem: Female Employment and Birthrate," *Voprosy ekonomiki*, No. 5, 1969, pp. 157–59. For material on leave patterns among new mothers in Moscow and Kaluga, see I. Katkova, "Maternal Care of Newborns," in D. I. Valentey (ed.), *Zhenshchiny na rabote i doma* (Moscow: Statistika, 1978), pp. 38–46.

51 A. I. Salatich, "Study of Birthrate in Rural Localities," *Zdravookhraneniye rossiyskoy federatsii*, No. 4, 1971, pp. 18–23.

52 V. I. Perevedentsev, *Naseleniye i khozyaystvo* (Moscow: Znaniye, 1971); pp. 13–14; and Yu. Bzhilyanskiy, "Economic Laws and Questions of Population Development," in *Zakony i zakonomernosti razvitiya narodonaseleniya* (Moscow: Statistika, 1976), pp. 38–54.

53 A. A. Vostrikova, "Methods of Research and Indicators of Birthrate in the USSR," in *Voprosy narodonaseleniya i demograficheskoy statistiki* (Moscow: Statistika, 1966), pp. 29–38.

54 L. M. Davtyan, "Influence of Socio-Economic Factors on Birth Rate, with the Example of Armenian SSR," *ibid.*, pp. 47–54; and L. M. Davtyan, "On the Dependence Between Well-being and Birthrate," in A. G. Volkov (ed.), *Problemy demograficheskoy statistiki* (Moscow: Nauka, 1966), pp. 146–60.

55 Shlindman and Zvidrin'sh, 1973, pp. 74–75. Similar findings were reported in a 1960 study of blue and white-collar social classes in Zhukov, a city in Moscow oblast: N. A. Tauber, "Marital Fertility of Women in Connection with Their Life Conditions," *Sovetskoye zdravookhraneniye*, No. 6, 1965, pp. 22–26; a 1970 study of natality in Kalmyk ASSR: E. L. Kasparov, *Dinamika rozhdayemosti i brachnosti v kalmytskoy ASSR* (Elista: Kalmytskoye Knizhnoye Izdatel'stvo, 1974), pp. 90–92; a 1970 study of Moscow city: N. Tauber, "Conditions of Family Life and Average Number of Children," in D. I. Valentey (ed.), *Demograficheskiy analiz rozhdayemosti* (Moscow: Statistika, 1974), pp. 3–19; and Georgia: V. M. Tsabadze, *Materialy izucheniya zdorov'ya naseleniya gruzinskoy SSR* (Tbilisi: Sabchota Sakartvelo, 1973), pp. 15–17.

56 A. A. Akhmedov, "Marital Fertility among Rural Women in Azerbaydzhan SSR," *Sovetskoye zdravookhraneniye*, No. 3, 1974, pp. 43–49. See also A. A. Akhmedov, "Several Results of an Investigation on Opinions of Young Women on the Number of Children in the Family," *Vestnik statistiki*, No. 8, 1974, pp. 16–21; and I. V. Dzarasova, "On the Influence of Social-economic Factors on Birthrate," in *Naseleniye i narodnoye blagosostoyaniye* (Moscow: Vysshaya Shkola, 1968), pp. 64–80.

57 Akhmedov, "Several Results," 1974.

58 I. N. Zhelokhovtseva and L. Ye. Svidova, "To the Question of the Possibilities of Realizing the Desired Number of Children in the Family," *Sovetskoye zdravookhraneniye*, No. 4, 1973, pp. 24–27; and Zhelokhovtseva, *et al.*, "On the Interconnection," 1973.

59 *Sotsial'no-ekonomicheskoye aspekty vosproizvodstva i zanyatosti naseleniya kazakhskoy SSR* (Alma-Ata: Izdatel'stvo Nauka Kazakhskoy SSR, 1980), p. 53.

60 N. Kh. Dzhangishiyev, "Social-hygienic Characteristics of the Birthrate in the Leninski Rayon of Dagestan ASSR," *Zdravookhraneniye rossiyskoy federatsii*, No. 3, 1973, pp. 16–19.

61 Karakhanov, 1983, p. 152.

62 M. Karakhanov and N. Aliakberova, "Several Results of a Monographic Study of Birthrate in Rural Localities in Uzbekistan," in *Problemy narodonaseleniya. Trudy vsesoyuznoy mezhvuzovskoy nauchnoy konferentsii, posvyashchennoy problemam narodonaseleniya sredney azii* (Moscow: Izdatel'stvo Moskovskogo Universiteta, 1970), pp. 283–88.

63 N. M. Aliakberova, "Fertility in Rural Families," in O. B. Ata-Mirzayev, *et al.* (eds.), *Demografiya sem'i* (Tashkentskiy Gosudarstvennyy Universitet. Sbornik nauchnykh trudov No. 604) (Tashkent, 1980), pp. 14–26.

64 Z. A. Yankova, *Gorodskaya sem'ya* (Moscow: Nauka, 1979), pp. 60–62.

65 G. P. Kiseleva, *Nuzhno li povyzhat' rozhdayemost'?* (Moscow: Statistika, 1979), pp. 57–60.

66 Smirnova, in J. K. Gardanov (ed.), *Kul'tura i byt narodov severnogo kavkaza. Sbornik statey* (Moscow: Nauka, 1968), pp. 185–273.

67 See Chapter 4, p. 231.

68 Yankova, 1979, pp. 16–62; D. M. Heer and Nadia Youssef, "Female Status Among Soviet Central Asian Nationalities: the Melding of Islam and Marxism and its Implications for Population Increase," *Population*

Studies (London), Vol. 31, No. 1, 1977, pp. 155–79; and Z. A. Yankova, "The Development of the Personality of Women in Soviet Society," *Sotsialisticheskiye issledovaniya*, No. 4, 1975, pp. 42–51.

69 G. A. Slesarev, "Demographic Changes in an Industrial Region," in AN SSSR. Institute Konktretnikh Sotsiologicheskikh Issledovaniya, *Sotsiologiya i ideologiya* (Moscow: Nauka, 1969), pp. 118–25.

70 Shlindman and Zvidrin'sh, 1973, p. 75; Zotina, 1972; and A. A. Petrakov, "Actual and Desired Number of Children," in *Izucheniy vosproizvodstva naseleniya* (Moscow: Nauka, 1968), pp. 297–306.

71 O. Ye. Chernetskiy and A. I. Salatich, "Marriage and Fertility among Various Social Groups," *Sovetskoye zdravookhraneniye*, No. 6, 1971, pp. 19–22.

72 A. A. Khmedov, "Opinion of Women in Baku about the Number of Children in the Family," *Azerbaydzhanskiy meditsinskiy zhurnal*, No. 11, 1975, pp. 80–85.

73 V. I. Lukina, "The Number of Children in the Family and the Social–Professional Mobility of the Parents," *Sotsiologicheskiye issledovaniye*, No. 4, 1979, pp. 129–31. See also E. K. Vasil'yevna and M. A. Shustova, "The Interaction of Fertility and Social Mobility," in *Sotsial'no-ekonomicheskoye osobennosti vosproizvodstva naseleniya v usloviyakh razvitogo sotsializma*, Vol. 2 (Kiev: Institut Ekonomiki AN USSR, 1970), pp. 10–13. Western studies investigating this relationship have produced conflicting results. (B. G. Zinner, "The Impact of Social Mobility on Fertility: A Reconsideration," *Population Studies*, Vol. 35, No. 1, March 1981, pp. 120–36.)

74 Safilios–Rothschild, 1977.

75 Steshenko, 1982, p. 242.

76 Tauber, "Conditions of Family Life," 1974.

77 V. Sysenko, "Differentiation of Birthrate in a Large City," in *Demograficheskiy analiz rozhdayemosti*, pp. 30–44. See also Tauber, "Conditions of Family Life," 1974.

78 Boyko, 1980, p. 140.

79 Chahil, 1977. See also Abou-Gamrah, 1980.

80 Suhas L. Ketkar, "Determinants of Fertility in a Developing Society: The Case of Sierra Leone," *Population Studies*, Vol. 33, No. 3, November 1979, pp. 479–88.

81 Wayne A. Schutjer, C. Shannon Stokes and Gretchen Cornwall, "Relationships Among Land, Tenancy, and Fertility: A Study of the Philippine Barrios," *Journal of Developing Areas*, Vol. 15, No. 1, October 1980, pp. 83–96.

82 Thomas E. Dow, Jr and Linda H. Warner, "Modern, Transitional, and Traditional Demographic and Contraceptive Patterns Among Kenyan Women," *Studies in Family Planning*, Vol. 13, No. 2, January 1982, pp. 12–23.

83 J. Mayone Stycos, "The Decline of Fertility in Costa Rica: Literacy, Modernization and Family Planning," *Population Studies*, Vol. 36, No. 1, March 1982, pp. 15–30.

84 Peter M. Blau and Otis Dudley Duncan, *The American Occupational Structure* (New York: John Wiley and Sons, Inc., 1967), pp. 363–67; and

Stanley Kupinsky, "The Fertility of Working Women in the United States: Historical Trade and Theoretical Perspectives," in Kupinsky, 1977, pp. 188–249.

85 Ronald R. Rindfuss, Larry Bumpas, and Craig St John, "Education and Fertility: Implications for the Roles Women Occupy," *American Sociological Review*, Vol. 45, June 1980, pp. 431–47.

86 Betty E. Cogswell and Marvin B. Sussman, "Family and Fertility: The Effects of Heterogeneous Experience," in Wesley R. Burr (ed.), *Contemporary Theories About the Family* (New York: The Free Press, 1979), pp. 180–202. See also John H. Kasarda, "How Female Education Reduces Fertility: Models and Needed Research," *Mid-American Review of Sociology*, Vol. 4, No. 1, Spring 1979, pp. 1–22.

87 The changing relationship between education and natality is reviewed in Serim Timur, "Demographic Correlates of Woman's Education, Fertility, Age at Marriage, and the Family," *International Population Conference. Mexico 1977*, Vol. 3, pp. 463–95.

88 Belova, "Differentiation of Opinions," 1973.

89 Sifman, "Birthrates and Maternal Safeguarding," 1976.

90 Shlindman and Zvidrin'sh, 1973, p. 81.

91 Steshenko, 1982, p. 242.

92 L. A. Arutyunyan, *Sotsialisticheskiy zakon narodonaseleniya* (Moscow: Nauka, 1975), p. 70. See also Davtyan, "Influence of Socioeconomic Factors," 1967, and Davtyan, "On the Dependence," 1966.

93 Tsuladze, 1982, pp. 62–66, 76, 80, 93–97.

94 Belova, *Chislo detey*, 1975, p. 166. See also G. A. Bondarskaya, *Rozhdayemost' v SSSR* (Moscow: Statistika, 1977), p. 78. Data from the 1979 census on number of children ever born display a similar inverse relationship between education and fertility, with the lowest number of births occurring among women with the highest level of education and the highest number of births among women with only elementary education or less. See Mullyadzhanov, 1983, p. 84. These data, however, are not age standardized and should be interpreted with caution.

95 As with the national survey findings, several of the regional studies suggest that the link between education and fertility among Muslim women is nonlinear. The women in the very lowest educational category (elementary and less) sometimes have lower natality indicators than do women with incomplete secondary education. This seems particularly true for older age cohorts. For example, the 1962–63 rural Uzbekistan study found that, among Uzbek women above the age of 30, those with at least some secondary education had a higher number of children ever born than did those with less education, holding age and employment status constant. Karakhanov and Aliakberova, 1970. These findings may have more to do with health and living standards than the effects of education on natality.

96 Akhmedov, "Marital Fertility," 1974.

97 O. Ata-Mirazayev, "The Mother of Large Families: Demographic Analysis," in Valentey, *Zhenshchiny na rabote i doma*, 1978, pp. 28–37.

98 L. Akinfiyeva, "Socio-Demographic Investigation of the Population of

Odessa Oblast,." in Valentey, *Demograficheskaya situatsiya v SSSR*, 1976, pp. 90–106.

99 Women surveyed in this study were Uzbeks and members of other Islamic ethnic groups. M. Buriyeva, "Large Families in Uzbekistan," *Naseleniye sredney azii* (Moscow: Finansy i Statistika, 1985), pp. 29–34.

100 Sifman, "Fertility of Women in Baku," 1971.

101 Akhmedov, "Several Results," 1974.

102 A. A. Akhemdov, "Opinion of Women in Baku on the Number of Children in the Family," *Azerbaydzhanskiy meditsinskiy zhurnal*, No. 11, 1975, pp. 80–85.

103 N. A. Kravchenko and I. P. Katkova, "To the Question of Complex Evaluation of the Influence of Socio-Economic Factors on the Family Planning Process," *Zdravookhraneniye kazakhstana*, No. 6, 1976, pp. 88–89.

104 Zhelokhovtseva and Sviridova, 1973. See also Zhelokhovtseva, *et al.*, "On the Interconnection," 1973.

105 R. I. Sifman, "Dynamics of Birthrate and Tempo of Family Formation in the USSR," in Valentey, *Demograficheskaya situatsiya va SSSR*, 1976, pp. 54–69.

106 Sifman, *Dinamika rozhdayemosti*, 1974, p. 139.

107 Sifman, "Dynamics of Birthrate," 1976. See also, Sifman, *Dinamika rozhdayemosti*, 1974, pp. 135–36.

108 Belova, *Chislo detey*, 1975, pp. 149–65.

109 Tauber, "Conditions of Family Life," 1974.

110 Akinfiyeva, 1976.

111 Tomskiy, 1979, p. 138. For other regional studies in highly developed areas that show the diminished impact of educational level on natality see O. V. Larmin, *Metodologicheskiye prolemy izucheniya narodonaseleniya* (Moscow: Statistika, 1974), p. 168; and Belova and Darskiy, "Opinion Research," 1968, pp. 285–96.

112 P. A. Eglite, *et al.*, *Faktory i motivy demograficheskogo povedeniya* (Riga: Zinatne, 1984), p. 111. See also Z.Zh. Gosha, "Actual and Desired Number of Children in the Family in Latvia," *Izvestiya AN latviyskoy SSR*, No. 4, 1982, pp. 23–24.

113 *Sotsial'no-ekonomicheskiye aspekty vosproizvodstva i zanyatosti naseleniya kazakhskoy SSR* (Alma-Ata: Izdatel'stvo Nauka Kazakhskoy, SSR, 1980), p. 58.

114 James Allman, "The Demographic Transition in the Middle East and North Africa," in James Allman (ed.), *Women's Status and Fertility in the Muslim World* (New York: Praeger Publishers, 1978), pp. 3–32.

115 Peter Zvidrin'sh, "The Dynamics of Fertility in Latvia," *Population Studies*, Vol. 33, No. 2, July 1979, pp. 277–82.

116 Karakhanov, 1983, pp. 149–51.

117 Shlindman and Zvidrin'sh, 1973, pp. 48–50. See also P. Zvidrin'sh, "From the Experience of Conducting a Socio-Demographic Investigation in the Latvian SSR," *Vestnik statistiki*, No. 2, 1973, pp. 28–35.

118 Akinfiyeva, 1976.

119 Tsuladze, 1982, pp. 83–87.

120 Belova, *Chislo detey*, 1975, p. 151.

121 Vasil'yevna, 1975, p. 15.

Part 2

Public policy and population dynamics

4

Social policy, family values, and fertility change

Demographic modernization in the USSR, as in other national settings, is closely linked with socioeconomic development. On the eve of the Bolshevik Revolution, the vast majority of the tsar's subjects lived out their lives as peasants in patriarchal families. Only the small proportion of the population who resided in the empire's urban centers in the north and west had been touched by industrialization, and it was there that fertility decline began. The social and demographic changes associated with modernization penetrated the vast and culturally-diverse Russian hinterlands only gradually. It was a process punctuated by revolution, civil upheaval, and world war.

This process of social and demographic modernization is also closely linked with public policy. The structural trends commonly associated with modernization – urbanization, industrialization, the spread of mass education – took place in a political setting very different from those in Western Europe. The Bolshevik political leadership was deeply committed, as a matter of Marxist ideology and of elemental political survival, to rapid modernization. Moreover, the leadership had, by virtue of state ownership of much of the economy and a coercive control network, a far more powerful set of policy levers than its West European counterparts. Many of the socioeconomic changes that propelled Russia's demographic modernization were accomplished by sheer physical coercion and at great cost in human suffering and social chaos.

The pace and nature of socioeconomic change in the post-Stalin period has been very different. The USSR's political institutions are now firmly entrenched and its leaders more cautious, more supportive of a moderate pace of change. In the absence of Stalinist terror,

195

the political elite has relied on a mix of economic, political, and social policies to achieve its more conservative goals. In this portion of the book, we turn our attention from the relationship between socioeconomic change and fertility transition to the link between public policy and demographic modernization. How has governmental policy shaped Soviet demographic trends in the post-Stalinist era? To what degree is the Soviet pattern of fertility transition a direct result of deliberate population policy and to what degree is it the unintended consequence of other policies?

In examining the policy dimension of Soviet demographic modernization, we are in effect placing fertility transition within a political framework. The analysis in Chapters 2 and 3 underlined the importance of modernization and, especially, the erosion of patriarchal family values in propelling demographic change. Chapter 4, therefore, is devoted to an examination of Soviet social policies and their impact in promoting the structural and value changes associated with fertility decline. Its main focus is on the effects of modernization programs designed to bring the late-developing (and high fertility) southern tier areas up to the socioeconomic levels of European Russia. None of the policies discussed in this chapter are explicitly designed to modify natality trends. In examining these policies and their social consequences, we are analyzing the indirect effects of social policy on natality. In Chapter 5, the focus shifts to demographic policy *per se*, that is, to programs directly targeted at natality. Taken together, the material in these two chapters allows us to explore more fully the influence of public policy on fertility.

A lively debate on this issue has developed in the non-socialist world. Much of the controversy surrounds fertility reduction programs, rather than pronatalist programs, but the implicit assumptions embedded in the debate go to the very heart of the fertility–social change issue. The argument revolves around the question of what causes fertility decline. One group of scholars emphasizes the salience of family planning programs in bringing about fertility decline.[1] Availability of effective fertility control techniques, they argue, is the single most important factor producing fertility decline in developing countries, particularly in the short run. There is some empirical support for this position, particularly in less-developed regions. Several cross-national studies conducted in the mid-1970s found that family planning efforts explained a larger portion of the variance in fertility across countries than did social indicators. All of these studies, however, have been subject to methodological criticism.[2]

Another group of scholars, embracing what has been termed the "motivational" view, place primary emphasis on socioeconomic trends within a given society that lead to changes in the reproductive incentive system.[3] Families begin limiting their childbearing activity because the economic and value systems supporting large families have eroded. The family implements these decisions through the family planning techniques that are available. If "modern" birth control technology is unavailable, "folk" methods – such as rhythm and withdrawal – are used to achieve the new, smaller family size; and, although these techniques are less effective than, for example, oral contraceptives or the IUD, the net effect of their employment by large numbers of couples within society can be a dramatic decline in aggregate fertility. According to this view, availability of modern birth control technology is neither a necessary nor sufficient condition for fertility decline. This is not to say, of course, that widely available, safe, convenient, and effective contraceptive technology has no impact whatsoever on natality. Given a socially motivated desire to limit births, fertility decline will likely proceed more rapidly in areas with easily available, modern family planning technology. This view, too, has some empirical support. Hernandez, after examining twenty-six studies of family planning and fertility in developing countries, concluded that there was little evidence supporting the hypothesis that family planning programs *per se* contributed significantly to fertility decline.[4]

In theory, of course, these two positions are not mutually exclusive. It may be suggested, and indeed it seems to us most sensible to do so, that *both* socioeconomic change and availability of family planning programs affect natality. Indeed, case studies of fertility decline in less developed countries are consistent with this interpretation. In Taiwan, for example, the fertility decline began in 1958, six years before family planning programs were expanded. However, fertility decline was accelerated by this expansion.[5] The role of family planning programs may also vary with the pattern of fertility transition. In cases where initial fertility declines are achieved by postponing marriage, the availability of modern family planning techniques may be less important than socioeconomic factors associated with changing roles for women. In cases where fertility decline is achieved by birth limitation in the mid and later reproductive years of married women, the availability of effective family planning techniques can be a critical factor.[6]

Our findings on the link between social change and natality in the Soviet Union suggest that direct government efforts to modify natality have met with only marginal success. The fact that such an overwhelming portion of the variance in fertility can be accounted for by the social position of women does not leave a great deal of room for direct efforts – either pronatalist or antinatalist – to intervene in fertility trends. This doesn't mean that Soviet policymakers have been unable to modify fertility. Indeed, the erosion of traditional family values that produced the substantial fertility decline in European Russia and are now producing similar patterns in the southern tier areas are the direct result of state-sponsored social and nationality policies. One may say, then, that Soviet policy produced fertility decline as an indirect (and, to some degree, unintended) result of social and ethnic policies. It is to these policies that we now turn.

NATIONALITY POLICY AND MODERNIZATION IN THE SOVIET SOUTHERN TIER

As discussed in Chapter 2, the USSR's southern periphery posed a difficult problem for early Soviet policymakers. These areas were in a much earlier stage of economic development than the European regions to the north and west. A key goal of Soviet domestic policy was to bring the periphery up to the level of the center. The Soviet term for this goal is *sblizheniye* (convergence). It is a key component of contemporary Soviet nationality policy, and it entails a series of programs aimed at promoting socioeconomic development in the late-modernizing hinterlands. This was no easy task and the process is still going on. The consequences of these programs are, however, crucial to the breakdown of patriarchal family values and, in turn, to natality dynamics. In this section, we examine the impact of the Party's nationality policy in the late-modernizing Islamic republics. We are concerned only with policy impact and with those aspects of modernization that are associated directly with family values and indirectly with natality. Therefore, our discussion is primarily limited to the measures of modernization, such as urbanization, education, functional specialization, and geographic mobility that were found to be important predictors of fertility. Other measures that have attracted Western interest, such as investment patterns, income transfers, and regional budgets, are inappropriate for our particular purposes, since they are part of the government strategy to achieve its objectives (both related and unrelated to nationality policy), rather than measures of policy impact.

A brief explanation of our approach is in order. In this section (which examines modernization trends) and in the one that follows (which focuses on family values), we are concerned with absolute, rather than relative, changes. This strategy is based on our findings in the two previous chapters which demonstrated the importance of socioeconomic modernization and value change in propelling demographic modernization. The relevant issue for fertility transition is absolute change in modernization levels and value systems. For this reason, we do not use the statistical tests of convergence often employed by Western scholars, ourselves included, when seeking to measure ethnic equalization.[7] Instead, our primary focus here is the spread of modern institutions and values within late-modernizing areas and groups across time, *not* how these groups are faring relative to European Russia.

The data presented below attest to how far the late-modernizing Islamic southern tier has come in the last several decades. On balance, it is difficult to escape the conclusion that the Soviet strategy of promoting ethnic and regional equalization has produced significant change in the USSR's late-modernizing, high-fertility periphery. This conclusion is based on multiple measures of four separate aspects of modernization; urbanization, education, functional specialization, and geographic mobility.

Level of urbanization is a classic indicator of modernization. Urban life styles are very different from those in the countryside and are associated with a wide range of changes in attitudes and behaviors.[8] Trends in urbanization thus have much to tell us about changing levels of modernization in the southern tier. Table 4.1 provides data on urbanization by nationality from 1959 to 1979. As these data make clear, all ethnic groups became more urban over the past two decades. The weighted average in urbanization level for the Islamic minorities increased from 28.6 in 1959 to 32.4 in 1970 to 35.9 in 1979. Similar trends are evident in urbanization data by region. The weighted average for the six southern tier republics increased from 39.5 in 1959 to 43.9 in 1970 to 47.5 in 1984.[9] The republic data allowed us to examine trends involving more precise measures of

Table 4.1. *Urbanization among Soviet ethnic groups, 1959–79*

Nationality	% urban		
	1959	1970	1979
Slavs			
Russian	57.7	68.0	74.4
Ukrainian	39.2	48.5	55.6
Belorussian	32.4	43.7	54.7
Balts			
Lithuanian	35.1	46.7	57.3
Latvian	47.5	52.7	58.0
Estonian	47.1	55.1	59.1
Muslim			
Uzbek	21.8	24.9	29.2
Kazakh	24.1	26.7	31.6
Azeri	34.8	39.7	44.5
Kirgiz	10.8	14.6	19.6
Tadzhik	20.6	26.0	28.1
Turkmen	25.4	31.0	32.3
Balkar	19.3	28.4	n.a.
Tatar	47.2	55.0	62.8
Chechen	22.3	21.8	25.3
Dargin	16.2	22.7	n.a.
Kumyk	33.0	40.3	n.a.
Lezgin	23.3	30.5	38.3
Ingush	38.7	38.7	n.a.
Kabardinian	14.7	23.9	37.2
Avar	10.6	18.7	24.9
Adygir	15.1	21.6	n.a.
Karachayev	10.9	16.5	n.a.
Cherkess	16.5	21.1	n.a.
Karakalpak	19.8	30.5	41.2
Abkhazy	27.8	34.5	40.5
Bashkir	19.7	26.6	36.8
Other			
Georgian	36.1	44.0	49.1
Moldavian	12.9	20.4	26.8
Armenian	56.6	64.8	69.7
Buryat	16.9	24.6	34.8
Komi	29.5	36.5	n.a.
Mari	11.7	20.5	31.2
Udmurt	22.2	32.1	41.6
Chuvash	19.6	29.1	38.8
Yakut	17.1	21.1	25.3
Jew	95.3	97.9	98.8

Table 4.1. (*cont.*)

Nationality	% urban		
	1959	1970	1979
Mordva	29.1	36.1	47.4
Kalmyk	24.0	35.9	43.4
Karelian	30.9	44.9	55.1
Osetin	34.9	53.3	60.1
Tuvin	9.0	17.1	22.4
Altay	10.6	14.7	n.a.
Khakas	19.0	25.7	n.a.
Komi-Permyak	14.3	22.9	n.a.

Source: Data refer to the proportion of total population residing in cities and urban settlements. The 1959 data computed from *Itogi vsesoyuznoy perepisi naseleniya 1959 goda. SSSR* (Moscow: Gosstatizdat, 1962), pp. 184–95. The 1970 data computed from *Itogi vsesoyuznoy perepisi naseleniya 1970 goda*, Vol. 4 (Moscow: Statistika, 1973), pp. 20–34. 1979 data extracted from V. I. Kozlov, *Natsional'nosti SSSR. Etnodemograficheskiy obzor* (Moscow: Finansy i Statistika, 1982), p. 100.

Table 4.2. *Educational trends, 1959–79 (per 1,000 persons aged 10 and over)*

Republic	Number with completed secondary education and above		
	1959	1970	1979
Slavic			
RSFSR	146	238	390
urban	208	311	466
rural	74	110	218
Ukraine	140	258	408
urban	228	368	521
rural	64	122	236
Belorussia	117	224	386
urban	240	379	545
rural	60	103	198
Balt			
Lithuania	96	185	327
urban	193	295	433
rural	35	70	170

Table 4.2. (*cont.*)

Republic	Number with completed secondary education and above		
	1959	1970	1979
Latvia	171	271	404
urban	244	359	492
rural	76	119	217
Estonia	172	265	392
urban	243	338	468
rural	82	129	219
Muslim			
Uzbekistan	129	237	422
urban	219	331	491
rural	79	172	367
Kazakhstan	126	221	386
urban	175	288	459
rural	87	144	293
Azerbaydzhan	169	262	419
urban	242	354	513
rural	94	153	305
Kirgizia	130	222	393
urban	210	318	494
rural	86	155	320
Tadzhikistan	106	193	345
urban	196	287	438
rural	59	130	289
Turkmenistan	124	213	375
urban	186	276	425
rural	67	147	325
Other			
Georgia	253	371	514
urban	383	507	640
rural	153	238	379
Moldavia	88	170	334
urban	227	344	517
rural	43	83	214
Armenia	208	315	486
urban	297	410	567
rural	112	160	331

Sources: The 1959 and 1970 educational data from *Itogi. 1970*, Vol. 3, pp. 206–357. The 1979 educational data from *Chislennost' i sostav naseleniya SSSR. Po dannym vsesoyuznoy perepisi naseleniya 1979 goda* (Moscow: Finansy i Statistika, 1984), pp. 24–41.

Table 4.3. *Generational change in educational attainment, 1970 (number per 1,000 persons)*

Nationality	Complete secondary and above			Higher		
	16–29	30–49	50+	20–29	30–49	50+
Slav						
Russian	459	309	128	5	82	31
Ukrainian	497	274	87	4	63	22
Belorussian	454	227	73	4	51	18
Balt						
Lithuanian	341	206	45	5	60	10
Latvian	395	333	134	4	75	18
Estonian	389	343	138	6	88	19
Muslim						
Uzbek	475	232	38	5	54	9
Kazakh	417	242	37	5	67	9
Azeri	436	306	97	5	73	30
Kirgiz	459	232	25	5	58	5
Tadzhik	400	187	41	4	44	8
Turkmen	412	195	32	5	56	9
Bashkir	309	139	39	3	31	6
Balkar	415	176	50	7	51	13
Tatar	357	179	56	3	42	12
Chechen	201	70	18	2	15	3
Dargin	254	132	20	3	38	4
Kumyk	317	187	44	3	47	9
Lezgin	371	230	63	5	66	13
Ingush	263	116	47	3	28	8
Kabardinian	397	247	45	3	57	10
Avar	283	162	25	3	39	5
Karakalpak	399	219	24	5	70	6
Abkhazy	443	322	101	7	85	26
Other						
Georgian	623	545	248	8	146	78
Moldavian	277	101	18	3	28	4
Armenian	532	404	187	7	99	55
Buryat	477	275	70	9	102	17
Komi	320	209	74	4	40	12
Mari	245	98	35	2	22	6
Udmurt	301	127	41	3	27	7
Chuvash	327	165	52	2	32	11
Yakut	382	247	57	5	75	11

Table 4.3. (*cont.*)

	Complete secondary and above			Higher		
Mordva	297	116	28	2	21	6
Kalmyk	350	111	50	6	30	11
Karelian	309	133	48	3	22	6
Osetin	518	401	160	6	95	45
Tuvin	276	136	41	3	40	9

Source: Computed from educational data provided in *Itogi, 1970*, Vol. 4, pp. 549–66 and nationality age data provided in *Itogi*, 1970, Vol. 4, pp. 360–82.

urbanization, such as the proportion of the population residing in cities over 20,000, over 50,000, and over 100,000. In every case, the data point to increasing urbanization in the late-modernizing southern tier. For example, the weighted average of the populace living in cities of 100,000 and larger for the six southern tier republics increased from 17.3 per cent in 1959 to 22.2 per cent in 1970.[10] These data suggest that, while the late-modernizing regions and groups still lag far behind the European north and west, these areas and groups are becoming increasingly affected by urbanization.

Another factor that we found to be statistically related to both measures of traditional familial systems and measures of natality was education. Here, the trend since 1959 has been one of rather dramatic gains among high-natality regions and groups. This finding applies to republic, nationality and oblast data. Table 4.2 provides educational attainment data by republic for one variable – completed secondary education. As these data demonstrate, Soviet policies promoting "universal" secondary education have resulted in significant increases in educational level in the late-modernizing regions. The weighted average for the six Muslim republics increased from 13.2 per cent in 1959 to 39.9 per cent in 1979. Similar trends are evident for all other measures of education, and for all other data sets. For example, the weighted average for completed secondary education for the Muslim minorities increased from 9.0 in 1959 to 18.4 in 1970. These trends are due in large degree to striking educational increases among the younger generation of the less-modernized groups and regions. This point is demonstrated by a comparison of educational attainment by generation (Table 4.3). To be sure, there are still substantial differences in educational achievement between the late-modernizing groups and the Russians. For example, several of the Muslim groups, such as the Chechen, Bashkir, and Tadzhiks, still have attainment levels for college graduates that are less than half those of the Russians. Still, these data provide striking evidence of Soviet nationality policy in action. They attest to the leadership's willingness and ability to effect social change in the Soviet periphery.

Other measures of modernization display similar patterns. Functional specialization – a third indicator of modernization – refers to the development of modern occupations and social classes. Virtually all trend data since 1959 attest to dramatic increases in such occupations and classes among the late-modernizing southern tier ethnic groups and regions. Table 4.4 presents ethnic data for the two social class categories associated with modern occupations: blue and white-collar groups. As these data demonstrate, most Islamic minorities made substantial gains during the 1970s in the proportion of the population belonging to these two social classes. The weighted average for white-collar workers increased from 18.2 per cent in 1970 to 20.7 per cent in 1979. Non-Russians also made substantial increases in their representation in the non-collective farm workforce and in white-collar employment.[11] Fragmentary data on individual minorities suggests that the increased representation by the later-modernizing groups in the blue-collar category has been paralleled by increasing representation in the "modernized" segments of the blue-collar workforce.[12] The late-modernizing minorities also increased their representation in the professional and semi-professional components of the white-coller workforce (Table 4.5). Other measures of functional specialization for the republic and oblast data sets, such as the proportion of labor force engaged in mental labor or in white-collar occupations displayed similar trends.[13] An analogous pattern was noted for industrial employment.[14]

Another measure of modernization is the extent of geographic mobility. This is of particular importance for rural residents.[15] Individuals who have lived their entire lives in the same small village are apt to be less receptive to new values than those who have moved, particularly to the city. The 1979 census provided dramatic evidence of the relative stability of rural communities in the southern tier. Respondents were asked whether they had lived in the same populated point since birth. (Those who had left their home village for military service as a draftee and those who had visited outside their

Table 4.4. *Changing social class composition among Soviet nationalities*

Nationality	Blue-collar workers (%)		White-collar workers (%)	
	1970	1979	1970	1979
Slavs				
Russian	63	63	25	31
Ukrainian	47	56	16	23
Belorussian	53	59	15	23
Balt				
Estonian	57	57	25	32
Latvian	54	58	23	28
Lithuanian	52	56	18	27
Muslim				
Uzbek	39	50	16	18
Kazakh	65	64	22	28
Azeri	50	58	21	23
Kirgiz	41	56	15	20
Tadzhik	37	55	15	15
Turkmen	32	39	17	16
Other				
Georgian	41	49	26	32
Moldavian	32	54	7	15
Armenian	60	62	25	31

Source: Yu. V. Arutyunyan, "Root Changes in the Social Composition of Soviet Nationalities," *Sotsiologicheskiye issledovaniya*, No. 4, 1982, pp. 21–27. The weighted averages we report in the text were computed on the basis of the total population as reported in *Itogi, 1970*, Vol. 4, pp. 9–11; and *Chislennost' i sostav naseleniya SSSR. Po dannym vsesoyuznoy perepisi naseleniya 1979 goda* (Moscow: Finansy i Statistika, 1984), pp. 71–73.

home area for less than six months were not counted among those who had moved).[16] Figure 4.1 displays graphically the results of this census question. All of the Islamic southern tier republics had low levels of geographic mobility. In rural Azerbaydzhan, 91 per cent of the population had lived in the same locale since birth, compared to only 41 per cent in European Estonia. Unfortunately, analogous questions were not asked in previous censuses, so there is no way to measure change over time. However, another measure of mobility – the proportion of the population living in the locale for less than two

Table 4.5. *Specialist employment in the USSR (per 1,000 persons)*

Nationality	Semi-professional specialists			Professional specialists		
	1959	1970	1979	1959	1970	1979
Slav						
Russian	53	100	122	39	73	98
Ukrainian	38	78	102	30	58	78
Belorussian	37	76	99	27	53	71
Balt						
Lithuanian	34	82	108	28	62	86
Latvian	51	92	107	39	73	90
Estonian	56	103	126	43	86	111
Muslim						
Uzbek	19	46	60	23	59	91
Kazakh	28	61	77	30	70	97
Azeri	38	72	78	50	78	109
Kirgiz	23	50	62	36	65	96
Tadzhik	21	39	48	23	52	75
Turkmen	23	44	54	27	64	89
Bashkir	22	50	65	17	37	53
Balkar	37	69	96	18	71	118
Tatar	31	65	84	25	48	66
Chechen	4	24	39	3	20	37
Ingush	10	28	46	7	32	53
Kabardinian	30	59	74	40	58	88
Other						
Georgian	48	73	87	81	114	144
Moldavian	18	38	56	12	32	52
Armenian	40	68	81	68	101	130
Buryat	40	90	99	42	127	165
Mari	22	42	54	12	26	38
Udmurt	29	54	68	18	32	44
Chuvash	30	58	76	23	41	53
Yakut	54	100	116	35	86	119
Mordva	19	46	62	11	27	37
Kalmyk	22	66	96	11	50	83
Karelian	40	81	107	17	35	51
Osetin	42	85	102	62	97	127

Sources: for 1959, *Narodnoye khozyaystvo SSSR v 1959 godu* (Moscow, 1960), p. 617; for 1970, *Narodnoy obrazovaniye, nauka i kul'tura v SSSR* (Moscow, 1971), p. 240; for 1975, *Narodnoye obrazovaniye, nauka i kul'tura v SSSR* (Moscow, 1977), p. 296.

The data for semi-professional specialists were standardized to the male population aged 20–59 plus the female population aged 20–54. The data for professional specialists were standardized to the male population aged 25–59 plus the female population aged 25–54.

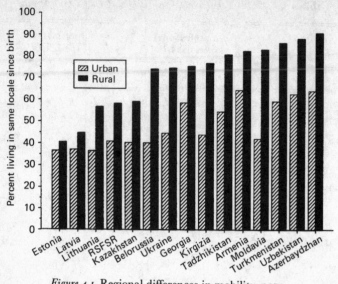

Figure 4.1 Regional differences in mobility, 1979

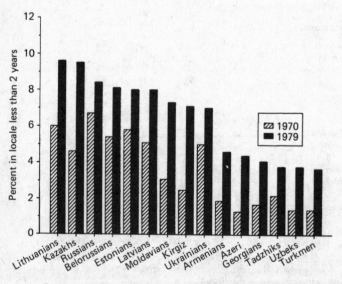

Figure 4.2 Ethnic differences in geographic mobility

years – is available for the two most recent Soviet censuses (Figure 4.2). As these data indicate, the late-modernizing groups are considerably less mobile than their European counterparts, but the trend during the 1970s was one of increasing mobility for all groups.

These data provide persuasive evidence that Soviet policies to promote modernization among the late-modernizing groups and regions have done precisely that: these groups are becoming steadily more modern across a variety of measures. Given the moderately strong statistical connection between modernization and natality, we should expect this trend to be mirrored in post-1970 natality declines for many of the late-modernizing groups who are still in the intermediate stages of the fertility transition.

THE EROSION OF TRADITIONAL FAMILY VALUES

If Soviet nationality policies have been fairly successful in promoting modernization among the late-modernizing groups and regions, Soviet social policies have produced even more striking results in affecting change in the traditional, patriarchal family systems of the Islamic southern tier. This process, it should be noted, has been an extremely difficult one.[17] Soviet policies aimed at "liberating" Muslim women struck at the very heart of the traditional social system. They were (and are) resisted fiercely by both men, who had much to lose in the short run in terms of prestige and preferential access to high-status roles, and by many of the women themselves, for whom "liberation" meant a loss of security and traditional identity. Any assessment of the effectiveness of Soviet social policies in eroding traditional family values and gender roles must consider the extent to which such norms and values were deeply embedded in the social, cultural and religious fabric of southern tier society.

Sex roles

One aspect of family traditionality is a strictly defined series of gender roles which assign women an exclusively domestic role. Educational opportunities for women in patriarchal cultures tend to be far more limited than for men – a factor usually reflected in low female attainment. Female educational levels thus provide a surrogate measure of traditionality in sex roles. One dramatic manifestation of the persistence of traditional gender roles in the USSR's

Table 4.6. *Trends in female education, 1959–79 (per 1,000 women aged 10 and over)*

Nationality	Number with incomplete secondary education and above		
	1959	1970	1979
Slav			
Russian	366	487	626
Ukrainian	314	425	558
Belorussian	282	400	543
Balt			
Lithuanian	204	341	511
Latvian	411	474	598
Estonian	352	454	574
Muslim			
Uzbek	240	356	566
Kazakh	191	332	545
Azeri	268	344	569
Kirgiz	220	342	540
Tadzhik	230	326	510
Turkmen	302	378	551
Balkar	165	297	505
Tatar	308	417	581
Chechen	26	133	403
Dargin	132	191	376
Kumyk	159	274	479
Lezgin	163	259	462
Ingush	55	162	427
Kabardinian	260	375	559
Avar	141	217	404
Adygir	285	386	538
Karachayev	160	278	474
Cherkess	260	370	552
Karakalpak	160	311	536
Abkhazy	300	406	593
Bashkir	237	335	526
Other			
Georgian	457	558	698
Moldavian	175	303	487
Armenian	423	500	694
Buryat	254	392	604
Komi	295	398	584
Mari	172	270	486
Udmurt	225	335	525
Chuvash	278	374	536

Table 4.6. (*cont.*)

| Nationality | Number with incomplete secondary education and above | | |
	1959	1970	1979
Yakut	197	356	577
Jews	754	809	871
Mordva	172	273	437
Kalmyk	105	265	544
Karelian	211	314	484
Osetin	423	497	618
Tuvin	126	336	528
Altay	156	268	498
Khakas	167	280	506
Komi-Permyak	183	265	408

Source: Zhenshchiny i deti v SSSR. Statiticheskiy sbornik. (Moscow: Finansy i Statistika, 1985), pp. 37–8.

Muslim southern tier was the strong resistance to early Soviet efforts there to extend state-sponsored educational programs to young girls. This resistance is reflected in the lower educational attainments of Islamic women in 1959 (Table 4.6). Islamic women, however, have made rapid gains in educational attainment since 1959. A similar trend is evident for other measures of female education. As shown in Table 4.7, for ethnic groups, the most striking disparities in female educational attainment are in higher education. In 1959, the rate at which Georgian women completed college was more than 200 times greater than the rate for Chechen women: 47 per 1,000 women over the age of 10 for Georgians; only 0.2 for the Chechen. In the last two decades, however, the late-modernizing groups have registered substantial gains. As one would expect, most of the advances in overall female education are due to greater female access to education among the younger generation.

Even more striking are the trends in 'emancipation': a series of measures computed as a ratio of female-to-male educational attainment. Table 4.8 provides representative data. As these data demonstrate, women in the late-modernizing regions have made striking gains in educational levels relative to males. These data attest to the success of Soviet authorities in promoting the breakdown of traditional gender roles in these regions.

Table 4.7. *Female education by nationality (per 1,000 women)*

Nationality	High-school graduate and above		College graduate	
	1959	1970	1959	1970
Slav				
Russian	158	258	23	42
Ukrainian	113	216	13	28
Belorussian	107	202	10	24
Balt				
Estonian	165	256	16	40
Latvian	155	251	17	37
Lithuanian	83	177	11	30
Muslim				
Uzbek	42	136	3	12
Kazakh	51	151	4	17
Azeri	86	155	13	22
Kirgiz	47	139	4	14
Tadzhik	32	108	2	7
Turkmen	37	116	3	9
Bashkir	58	118	4	11
Balkar	30	125	1	15
Tatar	83	162	9	20
Chechen	4	36	0	2
Dargin	17	55	1	8
Kumyk	40	114	3	14
Lezgin	39	101	3	12
Ingush	15	62	2	7
Kabardinian	68	167	4	15
Avar	17	64	1	8
Adygir	84	199	6	27
Karachayev	35	126	2	21
Cherkess	59	161	2	22
Karakalpak	27	106	2	12
Abkhazy	122	231	11	41
Other				
Georgian	284	401	47	75
Moldavian	38	98	3	11
Armenian	210	308	33	49
Buryat	93	206	13	40
Komi	112	170	11	21
Mari	37	75	3	8
Udmurt	62	113	5	12
Chuvash	70	127	5	11
Yakut	71	184	7	25

Table 4.7. (*cont.*)

Nationality	High-school graduate and above		College graduate	
	1959	1970	1959	1970
Jews	606	687	240	304
Mordvinian	42	96	2	7
Kalmyk	29	116	2	16
Karelian	63	117	4	12
Osetin	198	312	24	46
Tuvin	26	150	1	18
Altay	57	112	4	15
Khakas	52	111	6	20
Komi-Permyak	54	94	1	6

Source: Itogi, 1970, Vol. 4, pp. 393–548.

Another measure of the erosion of female roles that is associated with fertility decline is female participation in the modernized workforce. An analytical distinction is made here between labor force participation *per se*, and participation in "modern" occupational roles. The Soviet strategy has been to promote both female employment *and* female participation in the modernized labor force. Soviet studies have found that women in a formal work situation are much more accessible to Soviet socialization programs. Soviet survey researchers have discovered that full-time homemakers have higher levels of religiosity than their employed counterparts; and they are more apt to pass religious traditions and other behavioral patterns and attitudes repugnant to Soviet authorities to their children.[18] For these reasons and others, the Soviet leadership is anxious to attract women from late-modernizing areas and groups into the labor force.

Available data suggest that the Soviets have succeeded in these efforts. Republic data indicate extremely high female labor force participation rates. Table 4.9 presents the proportion of working-age women (16–54) who are in the labor force; these data exclude women working on private agricultural plots, students, and those dependent on either government payments or another individual. The trend during the 1960s is one of increased female labor force participation in all regions. This pattern is mirrored in other measures of labor force participation that show steady increases in the late-modernizing

Table 4.8. *Female emancipation (completed secondary education)*

Republic	Ratio of female to male completed secondary education 1959–79		
	1959	1970	1979
Slavic			
RSFSR	98	99	97
urban	101	101	99
rural	91	95	87
Ukraine	87	86	87
urban	95	93	94
rural	77	75	70
Belorussia	95	94	92
urban	106	100	100
rural	88	88	74
Balt			
Lithuania	102	110	104
urban	97	108	107
rural	109	126	93
Latvia	103	104	103
urban	102	102	100
rural	97	115	105
Estonia	112	107	105
urban	111	105	104
rural	112	114	108
Muslim			
Uzbekistan	60	68	82
urban	81	85	91
rural	34	50	75
Kazakhstan	84	93	96
urban	93	99	101
rural	69	81	86
Azerbaydzhan	69	67	77
urban	84	82	86
rural	39	39	63
Kirgizia	70	83	90
urban	87	96	96
rural	53	66	83
Tadzhikistan	59	65	78
urban	80	81	88
rural	30	46	69
Turkmenistan	67	69	83
urban	84	80	89
rural	34	53	77

Table 4.8. (*cont.*)

Republic	Ratio of female to male completed secondary education 1959–79		
	1959	1970	1979
Other			
Georgia	100	97	95
urban	103	100	99
rural	95	89	87
Moldavia	97	94	94
urban	102	101	102
rural	87	84	80
Armenia	94	95	99
urban	103	101	103
rural	74	79	85

Sources: 1959 and 1970 educational data from *Itogi. 1970*, Vol. 3, pp. 206–357. 1979 educational data from *Chislennost' i sostav naseleniya SSSR. Po dannym vsesoyuznoy perepisi naseleniya 1979 goda* (Moscow: Finansy i Statistika, 1984), pp. 24–41.

southern tier. The average number of years spent by women in the labor force in Uzbekistan, for example, increased from 25 in 1959 to 32 in 1979. Women in Uzbekistan averaged 11.4 years as full-time homemakers in 1959, compared to only 5.5 years in 1979.[19] Current female labor force participation rates, even among the late-modernizing minorities within the southern tier republics, are surprisingly high. A mid-1970s study of rural Uzbek families revealed that 26.4 per cent of the married women surveyed were full-time homemakers. In other words, nearly three-quarters of the rural Uzbek married women were employed outside the home, compared to a US labor force participation rate for married women of 44 per cent.[20] These data suggest a dramatic weakening in cultural barriers to female labor force participation.

But female labor force participation, as we have seen in Chapter 2, may not necessarily be a reliable indicator of female roles. For these reasons, we examined other, less ambiguous, measures of female status: female employment in the non-agricultural workforce, female employment in well-paid blue-collar jobs, and female access to sought-after white-collar jobs. For female employment in the non-

Table 4.9. *Working-age women in the labor force (%)*

Republic	% in the paid labor force		% in the non-agricultural workforce	
	1959	1970	1959	1970
Slav				
RSFSR	69.2	87.8	47.4	74.9
Ukraine	69.4	86.7	31.8	60.5
Belorussia	75.8	89.1	27.3	58.7
Balt				
Lithuania	66.3	86.8	29.4	62.2
Latvia	68.4	94.2	43.5	78.9
Estonia	69.1	94.9	48.0	83.4
Muslim				
Uzbekistan	65.0	80.9	22.8	45.0
Kazakhstan	55.0	79.4	36.3	66.9
Azerbaydzhan	60.3	70.1	25.3	41.8
Kirgizia	64.2	80.7	28.6	53.6
Tadzhikistan	67.9	73.8	21.4	38.2
Turkmenistan	59.9	78.7	27.4	46.2
Other				
Georgia	63.6	80.2	27.3	49.6
Moldavia	81.4	92.5	18.9	43.5
Armenia	57.2	75.0	26.6	53.7

Sources: Number of women employed in 1959 and 1970: *Itogi, 1970*, Vol. 6, pp. 6–13. The 1959 data is standardized to females aged 16–54 and adjusted to reflect the women under 16 and over 54 in the labor force based on data in Table 39 of *Itogi, 1959*, republic volumes. 1959 and 1970 data on employment in non-agricultural labor force computed from data on employment in physical labor in agricultural occupational force. The latter data were extracted from *Itogi*, Vol. 11, pp. 170–244. The data were age-standardized and adjusted as described above.

agricultural workforce, only republic data were available. These data (Table 4.9) reveal a pattern of increasing levels of female employment in the modernized workforce for all regions. Similar trends are evident for female employment in the non-collective farm labor force (Table 4.10), although the trend between 1970 and 1979 was one of increasing regional disparity. Women in all republics are still substantially underrepresented in the well-paid blue-collar jobs in industry (in 1959, only 39 per cent of the industrial workforce was

Table 4.10. *Females in the non-collective farm labor force (by republic)*

Republic	%age of working-age women in the non-collective farm labor force				
	1959	1970	1975	1979	1983
Slav					
RSFSR	53.0	77.0	80.3	81.6	84.6
Ukraine	35.2	59.9	66.3	70.4	73.7
Belorussia	37.7	65.4	70.6	73.9	78.5
Balt					
Lithuania	36.0	66.5	72.4	76.5	78.6
Latvia	54.4	82.0	85.9	90.0	90.6
Estonia	61.7	85.8	87.6	91.9	93.4
Muslim					
Uzbekistan	29.8	43.6	46.3	46.7	49.0
Kazakhstan	43.5	68.1	69.4	68.9	74.1
Azerbaydzhan	28.7	46.3	47.2	47.7	48.5
Kirgizia	33.1	54.5	56.2	56.9	62.6
Tadzhikistan	23.4	36.4	38.2	40.2	40.1
Turkmenistan	28.6	40.7	41.5	42.4	44.0
Other					
Georgia	31.0	50.3	56.6	60.2	66.0
Moldavia	22.2	47.9	58.0	62.8	70.2
Armenia	33.8	57.3	60.2	63.3	63.9

Sources: Data includes blue-collar workers and white-collar employees. 1959: Data from *Itogi. 1959*, Table 33 of each republic census volume, standardized to the number of women aged 16–54 as reported in *Itogi, 1970*, Vol. 2, pp. 16–75.
1979: Data extracted from *Itogi, 1970*, Vol. 5, pp. 26–33, standardized to the number of women aged 16–54 as reported in *Itogi, 1970*, Vol. 2, pp. 16–75.
1975 and 1979: Data extracted from *Narodnoye khozyaystvo SSSR v 1979 g.*, (Moscow: Statistika, 1980), p. 392 and standardized to women aged 16–54 using FDAD estimates.
1983: Data extracted from *Narodnoye khozyaystvo SSSR v 1983 g.* (Moscow: Finansy i Statistika, 1984), p. 390 and standardized to women aged 16–54 using FDAD estimates.

female), but the trend (Table 4.11) is one of gradually increasing access in all republics. The share of the female labor force that is engaged in mental labor and other measures of female participation in the modernized workforce also display similar trends. A similar pattern can be seen for the nationality data on female specialists. As indicated in Table 4.12, female participation rates in the specialist

Table 4.11. *Women in the industrial labor force (per 1,000)*

Republic	1959	1970
Slav		
RSFSR	365	413
Ukraine	222	332
Belorussia	170	316
Balt		
Lithuania	190	336
Latvia	307	404
Estonia	338	421
Muslim		
Uzbekistan	153	200
Kazakhstan	272	310
Azerbaydzhan	173	235
Kirgizia	185	272
Tadzhikistan	136	192
Turkmenistan	185	220
Other		
Georgia	165	231
Moldavia	86	193
Armenia	213	342

Sources: "Industrial" labor force refers to women employed in industry, construction, transport, and communications. 1959: Data extracted from Table 33 of republic volumes, *Itogi, 1959.* 1970: Data extracted from *Itogi, 1970*, Vol. 5, pp. 203–94.

workforce nearly doubled between 1959 and 1970; and some of the most dramatic gains in access to such occupations were registered by women from late-modernizing ethnic groups and regions.

It would seem from these data, then, that the Soviets are making a fair amount of progress in promoting female participation in modern Soviet society among women from late-modernizing regions and groups. The data on female educational attainments indicates that the Soviet policy of promoting enhanced female access to educational institutions has worked fairly well. Both the republic and ethnic labor force data reveal increasing levels of female entry into the modernized labor force, even in the traditional areas in the Soviet southern tier where cultural restrictions limited female access. These trends are persuasive evidence of a salient shift in popular attitudes regarding appropriate female public and private roles; the system of values governing gender roles for the less modernized areas and groups is gradually becoming more similar to that of the early-modernizing Europeans.

But while the trend is one of convergence in value systems, substantial differences still remain.[21] Data on female educational levels indicate that the late-modernizing groups still have a long way to go before educational opportunities in the Soviet southern tier are on a par with those of either European women or of their male counterparts. The Soviet press still contains stories critical of Muslim parents who neglect to send their daughters to schools and husbands who interfere with their wives' desire for further education.[22] In some rural schools in the Islamic southern tier, the female-to-male ratio declines after grade four, because parents are withdrawing their daughters from class. Even in those cases where the parents allow their daughters to finish the local school, they refuse to allow them to finish their studies in the neighboring city.[23] Similarly, late-modernizing women are far from being as fully integrated into the paid labor force as their Russian counterparts in Moscow. Soviet press references to cases of Muslim husbands forcing their wives to quit work or parents refusing to allow their daughters to commute to a factory job would suggest that there are still very real social strictures against female employment in this area.[24]

Popular acceptance of working wives and mothers

Another aspect of the breakdown in patriarchal family values is the degree of popular acceptance of wives and mothers who are employed outside the home in modernized work roles. Soviet ethnographic surveys typically include at least two questions touching on this issue. In one, respondents are asked which of two family life styles is most attractive to them. Two women with an identical speciality marry and have children. In one family, the wife works; she, the husband, and a grown son all share the housework equally. In the other family, the wife is a full-time homemaker. Given the traditional stress in Islamic areas on the importance of motherhood and the extent to which Muslim women were excluded from the public domain, one would expect a lower level of approval of the employed mother. In fact, however, Islamic respondents displayed strong support for combining a career with motherhood. In the Uzbekistan study,

Table 4.12. *Female specialist participation rates (per 1,000 women)*

Nationality	Specialists	
	1959	1970
Slavs		
Russian	106	190
Ukrainian	71	141
Belorussian	71	136
Balt		
Estonian	109	213
Latvian	103	191
Lithuanian	74	164
Muslim		
Uzbek	20	62
Kazakh	36	100
Azeri	58	101
Kirgiz	32	77
Tadzhik	16	40
Turkmen	15	47
Bashkir	36	86
Balkar	49	101
Tatar	63	118
Chechen	4	19
Dargin	n.a.	n.a.
Kumyk	n.a.	n.a.
Lezgin	n.a.	n.a.
Ingush	5	37
Kabardinian	61	92
Avars	n.a.	n.a.
Adygir	n.a.	123
Karachayev	n.a.	93
Cherkess	n.a.	154
Karakalpak	n.a.	64
Abkhazy	n.a.	121
Other		
Georgian	110	169
Moldavian	33	70
Armenian	96	151
Buryat	84	214
Komi	130	260
Mari	29	65
Udmurt	46	96
Chuvash	45	91

Table 4.12. (*cont.*)

Nationality	Specialists	
	1959	1970
Yakut	79	176
Jews	n.a.	452
Mordvinian	28	73
Kalmyk	38	115
Karelian	65	144
Osetin	100	170
Tuvin	33	113
Altay	n.a.	172
Khakas	n.a.	127
Komi-Permyak	n.a.	n.a.

Sources: The number of specialists per 1,000 women aged 20–54. Specialist data derived from *Zhenshchiny v SSSR*, pp. 76–77. Nationality age groups derived from: *Itogi*, 1970, Vol. 4, pp. 360–82; and *Itogi vsesoyuznoy perepisi naseleniya 1959 goda SSSR*, pp. 211–25; and *Itogi*, 1959, *RSFSR*, pp. 388–409.

64 per cent of the urban respondents and 72 per cent of the rural respondents favored employment for the wife.[25] The higher rural percentage may reflect the greater ease with which many rural wives and mothers can integrate both family and employment responsibilities; female employment in an urban environment more often means non-agricultural employment, with regular work hours and greater potential conflict between work and domestic responsibilities. These findings compare with the Estonian rural sample, in which 65 per cent of the women and 53.3 per cent of the males reported a preference for the employed mother.[26] This pattern of higher approval among females for the employed mother role was found in Islamic Uzbekistan. In both rural and urban samples, support for the employed mother was stronger among females than males.

Similar findings emerged from another question, which asked respondents whether they favored employment for the mother even if family finances didn't require it, or was it enough if she was "fully occupied" with housework and children. Under these conditions, 59 per cent of the rural Muslim respondents and 56 per cent of the urban Muslim respondents in Uzbekistan still favored employment outside the home; 62 per cent of the urban Muslim women in Islamic

Table 4.13. *Women's attitudes toward labor force participation in Dagestan*

Response	Dagestani women	Russian women	Other women
(1) Attitude toward participation of women in "social labor:"			
Consider it necessary	64.9	85.6	68.5
Do not consider it necessary	27.8	13.2	25.4
No answer	7.3	1.2	0.1
(2) Motives for participating in "social labor:"[a]			
Desire to use one's skills	27.5	38.2	27.2
Desire to be useful to society	49.2	53.0	51.3
Family financial needs	61.2	56.1	59.8
Desire to be financially independent	15.8	16.9	16.3

[a] Respondent could give more than one response.
Source: T. A. Abdusalamova, "Labor Activity of Women in Dagestan," *Sotsiologicheskiye issledovaniya*, No. 4, 1981, pp. 140–43.

Kirgizia endorsed the working mother.[27] This compares to 57.3 per cent of the females and 47.4 per cent of the males in the rural portion of the Estonian study.[28] In the Moldavian study, 67 per cent of the Russians and 57 per cent of the Moldavians favored employment over full-time homemaking. It is not clear, however, whether they were responding to the first question or to the more stringent conditions of the second question. Higher status and better-educated respondents tended to be more in favor of an active professional life for the woman. This was noted in studies from both European and Islamic areas.[29] In the Moldavian study, younger women were more likely to favor a combination of work and motherhood than their middle-aged counterparts; only 16 per cent of the young Moldavian women, compared with a quarter of the middle-aged women, favored the full-time homemaker role.[30]

Strong support for paid employment was also found among women in a separate study conducted in Dagestan ASSR. Conducted between 1973 and 1978, the study surveyed women employed in various fields. Respondents were asked about their attitudes toward the participation of women in the paid labor force; 76 per cent of the urban respondents and 61 per cent of the rural residents considered such participation "necessary." Data provided by nationality group indicated stronger support for female employment among Russian women (Table 4.13). Eighty-six per cent of the Russian women, compared to 65 per cent of the Islamic Dagestanis, considered employment a necessity for women. Only 3 per cent of the Russians felt that a woman should confine herself only to housework, compared with 26 per cent of the Dagestanis. Women of both nationalities, however, reported a similar pattern of motives for working: 61 per cent of the Dagestanis and 56 per cent of the Russian women cited financial pressure. The desire for financial independence was noted by 16 per cent of the Dagestanis and 17 per cent of the Russians. Russian women were slightly more likely to be motivated by the "desire to be useful to society" or the "desire to use her skills." Social class, not nationality, was the major factor differentiating employment motives, with women in white-collar jobs more likely to report that they were motivated to work by a combination of financial reasons *and* the desire for self-realization.[31] The Dagestan study is particularly revealing because this area is among the most traditional of all Muslim regions (in terms of the gender role measures of native women), yet acceptance of the dual mother–worker role among employed Dagestani women is remarkably strong.

A 1976 study of rural Tatar women in Islamic Tataria found a similar strong commitment to participation in the paid labor force. When asked what motivated them, 80 per cent of the women replied that they wanted to be part of the collective, rather than a housewife, while 16 per cent cited financial needs, and the remaining 4 per cent, the desire to be financially independent of their husbands.[32]

These data suggest a relatively high degree of acceptance of the employed wife and mother, even among the late-modernizing groups and even when the family does not need her income. How do these findings compare to attitudes toward working wives and mothers in other industrialized countries? A 1975 European Economic Community poll of ten European countries also included questions designed to tap popular attitudes toward working wives.[33] In this case, each male respondent (married men only) was asked whether he preferred his wife to work; and each female respondent (married women only) was asked whether she preferred to work. Only 41 per cent of the males favored employment for his wife. As in the Uzbekistan data, women more readily endorsed employment; 64 per cent of the married women preferred to be employed. The American public is still strongly supportive of the full-time homemaker, especially if she has children. A 1978 *Time* magazine survey of Americans revealed that 77 per cent of the sample agreed that a mother with young children should not work outside the home unless financial need required it.[34] Because the questions used in these surveys are not identical to those employed by Soviet ethnographers, these findings are not directly comparable to the Soviet data. But they do permit us to place the Soviet data in better perspective, highlighting the relatively strong public support for working wives and mothers in the USSR even among late-modernizing groups and areas. The Soviet data show that modernization, coupled with economic necessity and an energetic socialization program stressing labor force participation even for mothers of small children, has produced strong approval for working mothers, even among the most traditional Islamic groups.

Other data suggest that an important corollary to working motherhood – communal child care – receives generally favorable support among Soviet mothers, including those from late-modernizing groups. One study of high-parity Islamic women in Uzbekistan revealed that while 60 per cent of the mothers favored caring for infants (up to one year) in the home; only 31 per cent favored family care for children aged one to three.[35] Attitudes towards communal child care varied with the mother's employment history; 82 per cent of the wives who had been employed outside the home throughout their marriage felt communal child care was best for children aged one to three, compared with only 46 per cent of the full-time housewives. Similar findings were reported in a study of Russian and Islamic (Kazakh) families in Kazakhstan. Fifty-one per cent of the urban respondents and 40 per cent of the rural respondents favored communal care for one to three year olds, while a large majority in both areas (92 per cent urban, 85 per cent rural) advocated communal child care for three to seven year olds.[36] In the study of Islamic Tatars, Russian and Tatar urban residents had virtually the same proportions of children in institutional child-care facilities.[37] These findings, although far from conclusive, suggest a relatively high level of receptivity to communal child care, even for very young children, among groups that might be expected to advocate that mothers remain in the home caring for their small children. Resistance to communal child care, it seems, has not been a strong barrier to increased labor force participation by mothers in the late-modernizing southern tier.

Marriage and divorce

Another aspect of the patriarchal family value system is the complex of values, norms, and behaviors surrounding the institution of marriage. One behavioral indicator of traditionality in this area is the frequency of early marriage. The stress on the women's role as wife and mother was coupled in many areas with social pressures to marry at an early age. In the Islamic southern tier, young girls were often married in their early teens, sometimes against their will. This practice was one of the early targets of Soviet authorities; the legal age of marriage was raised to 16 for females in Turkestan and the northern Caucasus.[38] But legislating the marital age upwards in the Soviet southern tier proved difficult. Many Muslim families simply ignored the marriage law, and avoided prosecution by not registering the marriage with civil authorities.[39] Nonetheless, the proportion of early marriages (in which the bride is younger than 20) decreased dramatically among Soviet Muslims and other traditional minorities during the 1960s (Table 4.14). For several of the late-modernizing Muslim groups, the proportion of teenage brides dropped by more than half.[40] Fragmentary ethnographic data indicate that this trend continued in the 1970s.[41] The marriage data reinforce the conclusion – drawn from the educational and occupational data – that a gradual breakdown in traditional female roles is occurring in the late-modernizing Muslim areas.

Patriarchal norms and values regarding marriage are also reflected in attitudes and behavior with regard to divorce. Divorce rates are frequently used by Western scholars as an indicator of family modernism.[42] Given the strong emphasis on family in Soviet Asia, low social acceptance of divorce can be expected there. Indeed, Soviet survey research reveals that respondents from the late-modernizing groups are considerably less willing to terminate an unhappy marriage. A higher percentage of Uzbeks reject the possibility of a divorce if the couple has children; 87 per cent of the rural Uzbeks and 84 per cent of the urban Uzbeks rejected divorce under these conditions. Again, Georgians were somewhat less strongly committed to maintaining family integrity even if one partner was no longer happy; 73 per cent of the urban Georgians rejected divorce under these conditions. This compares with 67 per cent of the urban Moldavians, 54 per cent of the urban Russians, and 51 per cent of the urban Estonians.[43] In the Estonian study, older respondents were

Table 4.14. *Early marriage rates by nationality (per 1,000 women)*

Nationality	Early marriage	
	1959	1970
Slavs		
Russian	93	91
Ukrainian	101	112
Belorussian	70	76
Balt		
Estonian	42	49
Latvian	45	59
Lithuanian	48	54
Muslim		
Uzbek	318	217
Kazakh	287	123
Azeri	278	183
Kirgiz	442	201
Tadzhik	366	249
Turkmen	320	191
Bashkir	130	85
Balkar	70	60
Tatar	80	71
Chechen	404	199
Dargin	208	186
Kumyk	214	152
Lezgin	185	130
Ingush	149	90
Kabardinian	111	140
Avar	202	185
Adygir	n.a.	n.a.
Karachayev	n.a.	n.a.
Cherkess	n.a.	n.a.
Karakalpak	395	231
Abkhazy	102	95
Other		
Georgian	107	134
Moldavian	149	119
Armenian	158	152
Buryat	80	40
Komi	69	61
Mari	61	56
Udmurt	70	69
Chuvash	44	63

Table 4.14. (*cont.*)

Nationality	Early marriage	
	1959	1970
Yakut	55	32
Jew	n.a.	n.a.
Mordvinian	71	67
Kalmyk	115	56
Karelian	58	59
Osetin	35	53
Tuvin	157	84
Altay	n.a.	n.a.
Khaka	n.a.	n.a.
Komi-Permyak	n.a.	n.a.

Source: The number of women married aged 16–19. *Itogi, 1970,* Vol. 4, pp. 383–92.

more insistent on keeping the marriage intact; for the urban portions of the sample, 65 per cent of the over-60 respondents, compared to only 48 per cent of the 20 to 24-year-olds rejected divorce if there were children.[44] Again, the pattern of Russian responses to this question reveals the strong impact of regional norms on Russian attitudes. As with the issue of parental authority, Russian attitudes toward divorce vary with the region they live in. Sixty-three per cent of the Russians residing in Uzbekistan rejected divorce if children were involved; this compares with 58 per cent of the Russians in Georgia and Moldavia, 54 per cent of the Russians residing in RSFSR, and 50 per cent of those residing in Estonia.[45]

These ethnic differences in attitudes toward divorce are reflected in behavior. Figure 4.3 depicts trends in divorce rates over a three-decade period. Divorce rates in all areas of the Soviet Union have risen significantly since 1950. This trend is due partly to socio-economic factors involving attitudes toward marriage and the status of women and partly to changes in the divorce law. The quickening pace of divorce in the late 1960s resulted primarily from a simplification of divorce procedures adopted in December 1965.[46] This change was reflected in divorce rates throughout the Soviet Union, including the southern tier regions. The lowest level of divorce, as measured by the number of divorces per 1,000 married couples

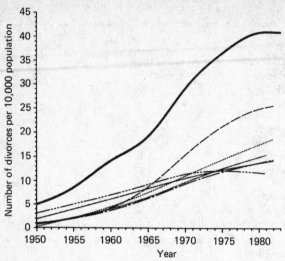

Figure 4.3 Trends in divorce rates, 1950–83

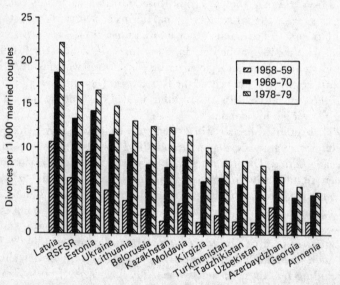

Figure 4.4 Regional trends in divorce

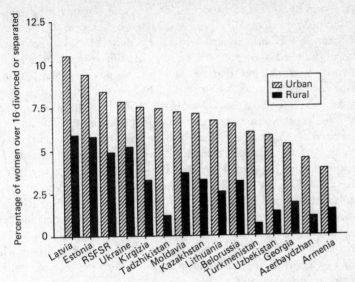

Figure 4.5 Urban–rural variations in divorce, 1979

(Figure 4.4) is in Central Asia and the Caucasus. Data from the 1979 census (Figure 4.5) demonstrates the extent to which the attitudes discussed above are mirrored in divorce statistics. The proportion of separated and divorced women is dramatically lower in rural regions in all republics, and especially low in Central Asia and the Caucasus.

All three Figures (which embody three different measures of divorce) attest to the lower level of divorce in the late-modernizing southern tier regions. To be sure, frequency of divorce in these areas mirrors the general trend in the European areas – all are moving upward and slowly converging. Despite these trends, striking differences in divorce remain, providing additional evidence that patriarchal norms and values regarding family life continue to affect behavior among Soviet Muslims.

Other aspects of divorce also reveal the continuing persistence of traditional, patriarchal values in the late-modernizing areas. Among late-modernizing groups, women appear to be much less likely to initiate divorce than their European counterparts. For example, 35–40 per cent of the Uzbek divorces were initiated by the wife; in the Azeri mining town mentioned above, only 25–30 per cent of the divorces were initiated by the wife.[47] These figures may be contrasted with various studies of divorce in western and central USSR where 50–70 per cent of the divorces are initiated by the wife.[48]

Reasons for both divorce and family dissatisfaction also reveal ethnic differences. Alcoholism is a somewhat more frequent cause for divorce and marital disharmony in European families.[49] One Moscow study found, for example, that 63 per cent of the wives seeking divorces cited alcoholism of the husband as the main factor.[50] Among late-modernizing families, conflict between the wife and her husband's parents is more frequently cited. This is related in part to the greater frequency of extended families among such groups; for instance, in 34 per cent of the rural Uzbek families and 25 per cent of the urban Uzbek families, the parents live with their married children. This pattern was found in only 10 per cent of the Russian urban families residing in Uzbekistan. Differences in lifestyle between the generations – particularly between the young wife who wishes to assert her independence and the husband's parents who wish to assert their traditional prerogatives – often lead to conflict between Muslim couples.

The material surveyed above on marriage and divorce indicates that patriarchal values with regard to the institution of marriage persist in the Islamic southern tier and are reflected in ethnic and regional differences in attitudes and behaviors. Still, salient changes in behavior – as reflected in early marriage and divorce rates – have occurred in the late-modernizing southern tier, attesting to the power of Soviet economic and socialization programs to produce significant change in life styles.

Family life

Another aspect of traditionality is the nature of family life itself – the distribution of authority and responsibility between spouses. Although data on family authority patterns is sparse, that which exists indicates that exposure to modern institutions has resulted in some erosion of the husband's traditional dictatorial authority over his wife. To be sure, while husbands in Islamic families no longer enjoy dictatorial power within the household, the traditional view regarding the husband as the head of the family remains strong in many parts of the Soviet southern tier.[51] For example, 44 per cent of the rural respondents and 33 per cent of the urban respondents in the 1974 Uzbekistan survey reported that in their family, the important family issues were decided by the husband. In a five-city study of ethnic convergence conducted in the early seventies and repeated in the early eighties, sex researchers found little change in the distribution of authority between spouses. In Tashkent, husbands took the lead in deciding family issues ten times more frequently than wives.[52] This pattern also persists within non-Islamic groups that have a strong tradition of patriarchal family systems. In a study of family life and gender roles among the Gagauz in Moldavia, for example, 33 per cent of the rural respondents chose this response.[53] However, these traditional patterns of family authority are less pronounced for younger and better-educated Muslims. While deference to the father and husband remains strong in Islamic Dagestan (even among young and middle-aged couples), younger husbands in a 1969 survey of rural Muslim couples in this area were more likely to consult with their wives and placed a higher value on her opinion than did the older-generation husbands.[54] A similar pattern linking educational levels to family decision-making was found in the Georgian, Moldavian, and Estonian studies.[55] In Islamic Kirgizia, researchers found only marginal differences between Islamic and European attitudes on whether the husband should always act as the head of the family. In the study of family life in Osh oblast, 31.6 per cent of the Kirgiz respondents and 36.8 per cent of the Russian respondents stated that the husband must always be the head of the family. Sharing family authority between husband and wife was advocated by 21 per cent of the Kirgiz and 36.8 per cent of the Russians.[56] Ethnographic surveys in Muslim Uzbekistan reveal that, as in European areas of the USSR, the more modernized couples were more likely to share family decision-making authority.[57]

This trend may be due to the wives' increasing financial contribution to the household budget. Soviet researchers claim that wives who contribute more to the family budget enjoy more influence in family financial decisions.[58] If this is true, it suggests that the increasing labor force role of women in the late-modernizing areas may help to modify patriarchal authority patterns within the family. For example, in rural Uzbekistan, 20 per cent of the wives had higher incomes than their husbands.[59] A study in rural Turkmenistan revealed that in 57 per cent of the cases, the wife's earnings were equal to or greater than those of the husband.[60]

Somewhat greater change has taken place in the distribution of domestic responsibilities within the household. In traditional patriarchal family systems virtually all domestic tasks were the woman's responsibility. Soviet studies make clear that this is one area that was very resistant to change; and change was particularly difficult to achieve in the late-modernizing areas of the Soviet southern tier where patriarchal family patterns and customs defining the sexual division of labor were most deeply ingrained.[61] By the post-war period, Soviet ethnographic studies of southern tier cultures indicate that some husbands, particularly the younger husbands, had begun to assist their wives in tasks that had earlier been considered "women's work," such as tending the children.[62] This was particularly true in families where the young wife was employed outside the home. But many men, particularly those in the older generation, still scorned such necessary, but mundane, chores as demeaning.[63] And in many rural Tadzhik families, for example, the husband's mother, who generally was not employed, stayed home and handled most of the domestic responsibilities when the young wife went out to work.[64]

By the middle 1970s, some limited progress in more equitable distribution of domestic labor had been made. Most Soviet husbands, including Muslim husbands, now display at least a limited willingness to share the domestic labor.[65] A study of family life among urban Kazakh couples in Chimkent oblast (a region in Islamic Kazakhstan) found that a large majority of both male and female respondents felt that housework should be shared equally or divided between the spouses on the basis of professional responsibilities. The pattern of responses by Kazakhs in Chimkent was very similar to those found in an analogous study conducted in Moscow. There were only marginal differences indicating greater persistence of traditionality in Chimkent. For example, 15.5 per cent of the Kazakh women (compared to only 7 per cent of their counterparts in Moscow) agreed with the statement that women should do women's work and men should do men's work. In this study, 22 to 45 per cent of the Kazakh wives in Chimkent reported that their husbands either did or assisted them in doing such traditional female tasks as food preparation, dish washing, house cleaning, and laundry.[66]

Other studies in Islamic regions also suggest significant erosion in traditional norms regarding domestic tasks. A study of family life among urban residents in the Islamic regions of Dagestan found that 85 per cent of the husbands claimed to help with the housework.[67] Another study of family life, this time in Islamic Kirgizia, found that husbands performed household tasks, such as food preparation, dish washing, cleaning, and laundry in 36.8 per cent of the Russian households, compared to 22.1 per cent of the Islamic (Kirgiz) families.[68] Fifty-eight per cent of the urban respondents in the Uzbekistan study reported that in their family, the husband helped with both the housework and child care.[69] Another question asked in several surveys allowed the respondent to specify the extent of that help. In 21 per cent of the Uzbek families, couples shared household chores equally; in 52 per cent of the families, the husband assisted his wife; and in 7 per cent, husbands did not help at all.[70]

Egalitarian patterns of family life were more common among higher status, more modernized families in both European and non-European regions. In the Georgian study, the higher status husbands were more willing to help; only 7–10 per cent of the husbands who worked as scientific researchers did not help at all, compared to 17 per cent of the factory workers.[71] Similar patterns were found in another Kirgizia study, this time conducted in the early 1970s and involving a survey of 1,226 industrial and state farm workers in Kirgizia; 17.2 per cent of the Russian husbands and 16.8 per cent of the Kirgiz husbands performed household tasks that are traditionally defined as "woman's work:" laundry, food preparation, cleaning and mopping. In addition, 47.8 per cent of the Russian and 47.6 per cent of the Kirgiz husbands assisted their wives with such tasks. Sharing of the household chores was much more common among urban families of both nationalities.[72] Supporting this finding is a mid-1970s study of rural Muslim families; in a third of the families surveyed, the husbands did a significant portion of the housework, but husbands whose wives contributed a large portion of the family income were the most likely to take a more active role in household chores.[73]

The particular pattern of distribution of tasks varies with cultural tradition. Because it was traditional for Uzbek men to do the cooking at holiday time, in Uzbek families, the husband is somewhat more likely to feel at ease in the kitchen. Georgian husbands are more likely than Russian husbands residing in Georgia to do the shopping; this relates to a custom common in some areas of the Caucasus and Soviet Asia for males to do the shopping in the bazaar.[74]

The available data on sharing of tasks in families in the late-modernizing southern tier suggests that patterns of family responsibility here are similar to those in central and western USSR. Of course, what is missing from all of these surveys is an actual breakdown of time spent by each spouse on each task. Individual perceptions of "assistance" and "equal sharing" are highly subjective. Soviet studies that present results broken down by husband and wife reveal substantial differences in perceptions. A Belorussian study, for example, found that 26 per cent of the husbands reported that they shared equally in housework; 56 per cent of the husbands claimed they helped their wives; and seven admitted that they did nothing at all. The wives, however, reported a far different situation; 27 per cent of the wives claimed that their husbands did nothing at all to help them with household chores. A similar discrepancy was found in a Euro-barometer poll conducted in the fall of 1977. In this study, 15 per cent of the husbands (compared with 27 per cent of the wives) reported that the husband never helped with the housework. Husbands and wives in both the USSR and Western Europe, it seems, have differing perceptions of how much the husband shares the burden of housework.[75]

Moreover, results of Soviet time-budget surveys reveal huge disparities in the actual amount of time spent by each spouse on domestic obligations. Women typically spent far more time on housework than men. A late 1960s study found that wives spent on average over 27 hours per week on housework (not counting time for childcare), while their husbands spent less than 12 hours.[76] In another study of domestic responsibilities, this time in one of the European republics of the Baltic, the average number of hours spent by men on housework was 11 per week; women, by contrast, spent 31.4 hours per week.[77]

A study of working-class families in the southern tier found a similar pattern among couples in a mining town in Azerbaydzhan; the average time spent by males on housework was 12–13 hours per week, compared to 34–35 hours for women.[78] A study of the division of labor in Osh oblast (in Islamic Kirgizia) found that mothers spent an average of six hours and 43 minutes a day on housework – on the average 2.5 times more than their husbands.[79] As such studies make clear, the typical Soviet husband may be fairly willing to lend a hand, but the bulk of the time spent by the family on housework is done by his wife. Closer examination of nationality-based differences in the distribution of household labor must await the publication of results of time-budget surveys by nationality. However, the information that is available suggests that while the Soviet wife still suffers from a double burden of job and housework, her husband's willingness to share at least some of the domestic tasks depends less upon his nationality than on his social status and place of residence.

Attitudes toward family planning

The material summarized above covering sex roles, attitudes toward employed mothers, attitudes toward marriage and the nature of family life suggests that there have been important changes in patriarchal value systems affecting life styles in the late-modernizing areas. These changes have been accompanied by changes in attitudes and behaviors regarding family limitation techniques. Attitudes toward family planning methods are of particular importance since achievement of the smaller family sizes that free married women for a more active occupational role is not possible without broad acceptance of family limitation techniques. Such acceptance, however, runs counter to conservative norms and values in the Muslim areas, where birth control and, especially, abortion have traditionally been condemned, partly on religious grounds.[80] While cross-cultural data on family planning are extremely limited, it appears that use of family planning among late-modernizing groups, as among other Soviet women, is most widespread among better educated, employed urbanites. Those studies that provide results tabulated separately by nationality suggest that European women are more frequent users of family planning techniques of any kind than their late-modernizing counterparts. For example, a 1972 study of Russian and Kirgiz women in Kirgizia showed that, among indigenous nationalities, 50 per cent of the urban respondents and 27 per cent of the rural respondents used family planning methods. The corresponding percentages for Russian women were 76 and 69.[81] A study of married women in Karaganda (Kazakhstan) revealed a similar pattern; among those with secondary education, 45 per cent of the Islamic Kazakhs compared to 67 per cent of the Russians regulated childbearing. The corresponding percentages for those with higher education were 60 and 64.[82]

Women from both early and late-modernizing groups who want to limit their families appear to rely heavily on abortion as a means of family planning. This conclusion is based on several dozen regional or clinic studies of abortion and must be regarded as tentative because data derived from such studies must be approached with a great deal of caution. Because neither Soviet nor Western researchers who have examined the abortion issue have exercised this caution, a few comments on Soviet abortion data are in order. Most Soviet studies from which abortion data can be derived are of two types: cohort studies (generally regional in scope) and clinic studies.

Cohort studies, which are undertaken primarily to examine the birth histories of a specific marital or age cohort, sometimes include questions on abortion history as well.[83] It is tempting to compare figures on abortion frequency across several cohort studies, but the temptation should be resisted. The Latvian study, for example, revealed an average of almost four abortions for women married 16 to 20 years.[84] The 1973 Uzbek study revealed an average of 0.6 abortions per woman.[85] Because of significant differences between the two samples, the two figures cannot be validly compared. The Uzbek study was limited to women who had given birth to their fourth child just prior to the survey. The 1972 survey of expected family size revealed that Uzbek urban women expected, on the average, five children.[86] Clearly then, many of the Uzbek women surveyed had only just completed their families while others were still in the process of doing so. These women were in their prime reproductive period and many of the reported abortions were likely to have been for spacing purposes. The abortion frequency among a sample of Uzbek women that was not limited to women with four or more children (such as was the case in the Latvian study) would probably yield quite different results.

Similarly, one cannot compare abortion rates or abortion-to-birth ratios derived from samples drawn from different stages of reproductive life. An example from reported US abortion data will illustrate why. In 1978 (the latest year for which data are provided), the abortion-to-birth ratio ranged between 1.15 for teenagers under 15 to 0.22 for women aged 25 to 29.[87] These differences reflect current patterns of fertility and exposure to pregnancy. Among very young women who are sexually active, first pregnancies are often terminated in abortion, producing a relatively high abortion-to-birth ratio. The ratio goes down for women in the key childbearing years, since the denominator (births) is higher. After age 30, the abortion ratio increases again, since many women have completed their desired family size and are more likely to terminate an unwanted pregnancy with abortion. For women over 40, the ratio was 0.79. This pattern will clearly be quite different in areas with different fertility patterns.

The US data do, however, dramatize the danger of comparing abortion data across samples in different stages of reproductive life. For example, a 1978 study of student females at the Karaganda Medical Institute revealed an abortion-to-birth ratio of 0.4, while a 1977–79 study based on marriage, birth, and abortion registration in Ryazan oblast (RSFSR) revealed an abortion-to-birth ratio of 2.28.[88] The low ratio found in the study of student females is probably due to the fact that it was limited to an age group for which abortion-to-birth ratios are relatively low.

Another difficulty with Soviet abortion studies is that virtually all that have been reported are limited to one geographical area. One regional study of pregnancy outcomes was provided by N. S. Sokolova on Leningrad city and Leningrad oblast.[89] Sokolova, using data derived from the city and oblast health departments, calculates an abortion-to-live-birth ratio of 3.2:1 for 1962 and 4:1 for 1967. The author of a Soviet medical text, A. F. Serenko, citing Sokolova, reports these ratios in a context that suggests that such data can be seen as characteristic of the USSR as a whole.[90] There are two major problems with Serenko's statement. First, he neglects to note that the abortion data used included some miscarriages (spontaneous abortions). For induced abortion, the ratio for 1967 is actually 3.59:1. But the major problem in generalizing from the Leningrad data to the entire country is that it rests on the assumption that abortion ratios for Leningrad are representative of all other parts of the USSR. The shakiness of this assumption can be demonstrated by using US abortion data. In 1978, abortion rates (abortions per 1,000 females aged 15 to 44) in Alaska were 6 per 1,000 women aged 15 to 44; the analogous figure for New York state was 38, about 6.3 times higher. Regional variation in abortion-to-birth ratios was even more dramatic. In Alaska, the abortion ratio was 0.075, in New York State, 0.657 – nearly nine times higher![91] Attempting to estimate overall US abortion rates and ratios from individual state data is clearly a hazardous business, yet this is precisely what Serenko has done in generalizing from the Leningrad data. There is little reason to think that Leningrad is any more representative of the USSR than New York is of the USA.

Quite aside from the issue of generalizing from regional surveys is the even more troubling problem that many of the Soviet studies that have been used to generate estimates of abortion rates and ratios were not designed to provide insight into abortion frequency, but rather to examine why the women who aborted did so. Most Soviet abortion surveys are based on samples of women who request abortions at specific medical facilities or in a general region.[92] One mid-1970s study, for example, reports results of interviews with women who requested abortions between 1963 and 1966 in Aginsk National Okrug.[93] The sample, which included women aged 15 to 49, averaged 2.4 abortions for Russian women; 1.1 abortions for Buryat women. However, the survey results provide no clues as to the percentage of women of either nationality who had not had an abortion. Therefore, it is not possible to generalize from such surveys to the entire population of females in that region. Some Soviet scholars, undaunted by these limitations, have gone ahead and done so anyway; and their comments have contributed to the general level of misinformation on the subject.

Finally, there is the issue of the validity of the data themselves. Both cohort studies and studies based on the histories of women requesting abortion rely on self-reporting. There will clearly be some cases in which the woman will conceal previous abortions, particularly illegal abortions. Studies based on medical records of pregnancy outcomes generally include both legal abortions and illegal ones – i.e., those that occur outside of a hospital. Those illegal abortions are registered when the woman is given medical care for subsequent complications. Again, there is likely to be some under estimation. Moreover, a larger proportion of abortions in the late-modernizing areas occur outside of hospitals. In Tashkent oblast, for example, 49 per cent of the registered abortions in 1959 and 52 per cent in 1973 occurred outside the hospital.[94] These data raise the issue of reporting accuracy, since it is likely that some abortions performed outside of a hospital setting will not find their way into medical records at all – thus distorting findings that are based on medical records. Moreover, given the traditional prohibition against abortion in the southern tier region, it is likely that Islamic women questioned on their pregnancy history are more likely than their European counterparts to conceal previous abortions – thus distorting findings based on interviews. We cannot, therefore, exclude the possibility that studies of abortion frequency in the Islamic regions may underestimate abortion rates.

In spite of all these problems, there are a limited number of studies that allow one to draw at least tentative conclusions regarding abortion use among traditional and non-traditional women. In general, women in the late-modernizing southern tier republics have abortions much less frequently than those in the European areas. Abortion is said to be three to four times more rare in Azerbaydzhan, Kirgizia, and Turkmenistan than in the European republics. There are, however, some indications that Kirgiz women use abortions more frequently than other Muslim women. Moreover, within southern tier republics, Islamic women have recourse to abortion less than their Russian counterparts.[95] Surveys that provide separate tabulations by status indicators suggest that abortion use among the more traditional women, including Muslims, is directly related to education and status. A study of family formation among urban Uzbek women with four or more children, for example, found a higher incidence of abortion among the most highly educated women; 26 per cent of the entire sample married fifteen years or more had had at least one abortion, compared to 79 per cent of the well-educated women.[96] The well-educated group having abortions averaged 3.4 previous abortions per woman, as compared to 2.4 abortions per woman for those with secondary education or less.

A study of childbearing activities in the first seven years of marriage among Kazakh women in Alma Ata revealed a similar pattern. Kazakh women with higher education averaged 2.28 abortions; those with secondary education only 1.99 abortions.[97] The Kazakh and Russian women in this study reported nearly identical abortion rates. At the time of the survey, Alma Ata had the highest abortion rate in the republic, so these rates should not be generalized to all Kazakh women. Another study of abortion frequency in Kazakhstan, this time in Karaganda, revealed that the abortion/live birth ratio for the first five years of marriage was 1.16 for Russian women and 0.79 for Kazakh women. Given the ethnic difference in family size expectations in urban areas of this size, it is likely that the abortion rates for the Russian and Kazakh women in the sample are very similar.[98]

Another study focusing on Azerbaydzhan suggests similar patterns there. In a study of women seeking abortions at medical institutions, the most successful use of contraception, as well as the most frequent recourse to abortion, was found among highly educated women and among urban residents.[99] Data from the Azeri Health Ministry indicate an increasing demand for contraceptive means in the late 1960s and early 1970s; during this same period, the number of reported abortions increased by 8 per cent.[100] A sample survey of pregnancies and birth histories at gynecological clinics in the four Central Asian republics also reported a direct relationship between status and abortion use. The survey found that pregnancy outcomes for Muslim women were differentiated by employment status and occupation; among professional women, second pregnancies terminated in birth at a rate 25–30 per cent lower than for other women, with a corresponding increase in the frequency of abortion. By the third pregnancy, this tendency was even more pronounced.[101] A 1975 study of pregnancy outcomes in rural Uzbekistan found a similar link between status indicators and family limitation. Although frequency of both abortion and contraceptive use was extremely low, working women, particularly those in higher status occupations, were more likely to regulate births.[102] Measures of modernized life style, then, such as urban residence, education, employment and high status occupations, are consistently related to higher abortion use among the late-modernizing groups of the Soviet southern tier.

In European families, by contrast, abortion use is inversely related to status. Comparative data for Moscow, Vilnius, Tambov, and Russian women in Alma Ata reveal that highly educated women had fewer abortions.[103] For example, in a Moscow study of childbearing behavior in the first five years of marriage, 88 per cent of the women with secondary education or less had had at least one abortion, compared to only 67 per cent of those with specialized secondary and higher education.[104] These lower abortion frequencies for better educated, non-Muslim women are due to more successful use of contraception among these women.[105]

Muslim women appear to make less frequent use of contraception than their European counterparts. A 1976–78 study in Tadzhikistan revealed that the majority of women used abortion as a means of family planning, with European women making better use of contraception than their Islamic counterparts.[106] In the study of Uzbek mothers of four mentioned above, only 16 per cent of the total sample used contraceptives. While no directly comparable data for other nationalities are available, several studies of family planning practices in other areas of the USSR revealed that 70–80 per cent of the women studied used contraceptives.[107] Higher status women of all nationalities, however, report more frequent use of contraception. In the Uzbek study, 27 per cent of the working wives and only 4 per cent of the housewives reported use of contraceptives.[108] In the Tambov,

Vilnius, and Alma Ata studies, highly educated women report more frequent use than their less-educated counterparts.[109]

Use of family planning methods of any kind (either contraception or abortion) in the more traditional areas of the southern tier appears to be much less common among rural women, particularly house-wives. The abortion ratio in one rural and predominantly Muslim area in Dagestan ASSR, for example, was 0.12.[110] A study in rural Uzbekistan indicated that less than one per cent of the Muslim women who visited the women's clinics used contraceptive devi-ces.[111] Mid-1960s data from the Main Pharmaceutical Directorate of Uzbekistan indicated that sales of contraceptive materials were significantly lower in rural areas.[112] A recent study of Kazakh families found that 19 per cent of the married women in the countryside had no knowledge of contraceptive methods.[113] In Turkmenistan, the abortion-to-birth ratio was 0.98:1 in urban areas and 0.005:1 in rural areas in 1970. The corresponding figures for 1975 were 0.91 and 0.01. In Tadzhikistan, the 1970 ratio was 1.11:1 in the cities and 0.14:1 in the countryside. The 1975 Tadzhikistan ratios were 1.02:1 and 0.188:1. In Uzbekistan, the urban abortion rate was 122 in 1970 and 118.6 in 1975, compared to only 16.1 and 19.9 in the country.[114]

All of these data attest to the more widespread use of abortion as a family planning method in the more modern urban areas. The material presented above suggests a pattern of family planning usage in which women from late-modernizing areas and groups have much lower levels of usage, with the lowest levels among the less-modernized components of these groups. This pattern may be due partly to the conservatism of rural communities and partly to religious and cultural values condemning birth control practices and abortion. But, just as cultural strictures against both have not deterred Catholic women from obtaining abortions in the US, cultural taboos against family planning have clearly not prevented the more Sovietized Muslim women from using these techniques to achieve their smaller family size preferences.

The authority of the older generation

Another manifestation of traditional patriarchal family values in the late-modernizing areas is deference to the older generation.[115]

Table 4.15. *Deference to parental authority by nationality*

Nationality (within titular republic)	Percentage agreeing that parental approval is obligatory before getting married				
	City dwellers	Rural residents			
		20–24	30–39	64+	Total
Estonian	22.0	13.1	21.2	33.3	24.9
Russian	37.7	27.8	27.4	48.5	34.4
Moldavian	40.7	30.5	53.2	65.6	52.4
Georgian	61.2	56.3	75.0	78.4	71.1
Uzbek	87.6	89.9	92.6	94.0	92.0

Source: Yu. V. Arutyunyan, "National-regional Variation in the Soviet Village," *Sotsiologicheskiye issledovaniye*, No. 3, 1980, pp. 73–81.

Respect for and subordination to elder family members remains one of the strongest traditions affecting Muslim family life in the Soviet southern tier.[116] Deference to parental wishes is particularly strong in the area of marriage; in many patriarchal communities, particularly in the southern tier, marriages were arranged by the family. While there is evidence that the motives for marriage among Islamic groups at the present time mirror those of their European counterparts (love and compatible interests), the tradition of gaining parental blessing for one's choice of a spouse remains strong in many late-modernizing areas.[117] To tap these values, Soviet ethnographers typically ask whether parental approval was necessary to get married. As expected, the proportion of positive answers varies inversely with measures of modernization (i.e., urban residence) and age. For example, a survey of Osetin couples in the North Caucasus revealed that 43 per cent of the rural women aged 60 and over married men chosen by their parents, compared to 5.3 per cent of the rural women aged 20 to 24. Urban women in this study reported lower levels of parental deference regarding choice of a marital partner, but again older women were more apt to have married men chosen for them by their parents.[118]

There are also regional and ethnic differences in deference to parental authority. Respondents from Central Asia and the Caucasus are predictably more deferential to parental authority than are their counterparts in European areas of the Soviet Union (Table 4.15). The highest levels of parental authority were found among the Uzbek respondents; 92 per cent of the rural and 88 per cent of the urban Uzbeks said that it was necessary to obtain the parents' approval before marrying.[119] Georgians were somewhat less likely to seek parental approval; 61 per cent of the urban Georgians (in Georgia) said they felt parental approval was necessary. This compares with 43 per cent of the rural Gagauz (in Moldavia), 41 per cent of the urban Moldavians, 38 per cent of the urban Russians (in RSFSR), and 22 per cent of the urban Estonians (in Estonia). In all five of the regional surveys, urban respondents and young people were slightly less concerned with parental attitudes than rural residents and older respondents.[120]

But adherence to traditional values is still striking, even among the youngest Uzbeks sampled; 90 per cent of the 20 to 24-year-olds in the rural portion of the Uzbekistan survey said they felt parental approval was a prerequisite to marriage, compared with only 13 per cent of their counterparts in rural Estonia.[121] For urban Uzbeks, the analogous percentages were 83 for 20 to 24-year-olds and 91 for Uzbeks over 60 years old.[122] In another study of Muslim attitudes, over 80 per cent of the respondents said that the opinion of elders should be respected if it did not conflict with the "Soviet" way of life, but only 60 per cent said they felt free to express their opinion if it conflicted with those of their elders.[123]

Attitudes toward parental authority also appear to vary with social class and occupation. In the Georgian survey, 31 per cent of the researchers at one institute and 19 per cent at another said they considered parental approval obligatory; this compares with 54 per cent of the Georgian farmers.[124] The cultural norms of the surrounding region also have a salient impact on attitudes toward parental authority. Russians residing in the European areas of the Soviet Union are less likely to think that parental approval is necessary than are Russians in Uzbekistan. Only 35 per cent of the Russians in Estonia, compared with 55 per cent of their counterparts in Uzbekistan, felt that parental approval was a prerequisite for marriage.[125] These findings suggest that cultural heritage interacts with the prevailing value system in the immediate social environment.

Another indicator of the strength of traditional values is the strength of family and kinship ties epitomized by persistence of the extended family in the late-modernizing regions.[126] As shown in

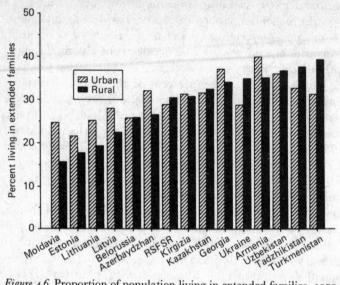

Figure 4.6 Proportion of population living in extended families, 1970

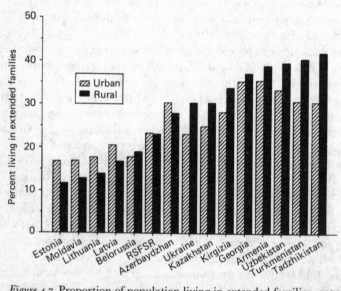

Figure 4.7 Proportion of population living in extended families, 1979

Figures 4.6 and 4.7, the proportion of individuals living within extended families varies widely, with the highest figures recorded in the rural regions of Central Asia, in both 1970 and 1979. In fact, the proportion of the rural population residing in non-nuclear families in these regions increased between 1970 and 1979, primarily due to an increase in the young marriageable cohorts, coupled with the cultural tradition of young couples continuing to live with their parents after marriage.[127] In most cases, the extended family in rural areas of Central Asia consists of the older parents living with one or more married sons.[128] In 1979, 40 per cent of the rural population of Uzbekistan, 41 per cent in Turkmenistan, and 42 per cent in Tadzhikistan resided in non-nuclear families.[129] These data provide some measure of the continuing strength of the extended family in rural Central Asia and the Caucasus.

The extended family helps perpetuate traditional values, since the older generation is better placed to enforce patriarchal life styles.[130] This conservatism is apparent in choice of clothing. Islamic women who live with their husband's relatives are more likely to wear more traditional clothing.[131] Such women are also more likely to conform to patriarchal norms governing women's roles. The young Soviet wife, like her counterpart in other areas, is more vulnerable to pronatalist pressures from her husband's family when she resides with them in an extended family.[132] Indeed, the influence of the older generation on family values has complicated efforts by Soviet researchers to gather valid data on family size orientations. In one study of desired family size in rural Uzbekistan, the interviewers were unable to discover the family size desires of young wives living with their husband's family; the pronatalist mothers-in-law would typically interrupt the respondent and answer for her.[133]

Continuity and change in family life styles

The evidence examined in this section points to both continuity and change in family life styles among the less-modernized groups and regions. Of course, what is missing from all of the attitudinal data examined here is relevant time series data, enabling us to track trends in attitudes over time. Without such data, we are unable to assess whether the traditional patterns of parental and gender authority within the family and traditional concepts of marital roles have declined along with other indicators of traditionality among the

Table 4.16. Regional links between modernization and sex roles. Nationalities (Zero order correlation with urbanization)

Measure of female roles	1959			1970		
	USSR	Non Muslims	Muslims	USSR	Non Muslims	Muslims
Female/male inc. sec. and above	0.47[b] (45)	0.68[b] (24)	0.09 (21)	0.43[a] (45)	0.40 (24)	0.19 (21)
Female/male complete sec. and above	0.45[b] (45)	0.48 (24)	0.29 (21)	0.37 (45)	0.12 (24)	0.31 (21)
Female/male inc. higher and above	0.54[b] (45)	0.53[a] (24)	0.50 (21)	0.43[a] (45)	0.28 (24)	0.34 (21)
Female/male higher educ.	0.59[b] (45)	0.63[b] (24)	0.56[a] (21)	0.46[b] (45)	0.33 (24)	0.37 (21)
Female/male specialists	0.48[a] (31)	0.45 (19)	0.43 (12)	0.37 (40)	0.12 (23)	0.37 (17)
Female college graduates	0.75[b] (45)	0.79[b] (24)	0.50 (21)	0.70[b] (45)	0.74[b] (24)	0.18 (21)
Early marriage	-0.22 (45)	0.02 (24)	-0.20 (21)	-0.23 (45)	0.19 (24)	-0.33 (21)

[a] Significant at 0.005 level.
[b] Significant at 0.001 level.
Figures in parenthesis refer to number of cases.

Table 4.17. *Regional links between modernization and sex roles. Oblasts (Zero order correlation with urbanization)*

Measure of female roles	1959			1970		
	USSR	European areas	Muslim areas	USSR	European areas	Muslim areas
Female specialized sec. attainment	0.79^b (169)	0.84^b (108)	0.82^b (54)	0.77^b (169)	0.77^b (108)	0.82^b (54)
Female/male inc. sec. and above	0.54^b (169)	0.60^b (108)	0.44^a (54)	0.54^b (169)	0.59^b (108)	0.39^a (54)
Female/male complete sec. and above	0.35^b (169)	0.30^b (108)	0.43^b (54)	0.45^b (169)	0.34 (108)	0.45^b (54)
Female/male inc. higher and above	0.30^b (169)	0.16 (108)	0.46^b (54)	0.42^b (169)	0.15 (108)	0.53^b (54)
Female/male higher educ.	0.40^b (169)	0.33^b (108)	0.53^b (54)	0.48^b (169)	0.22 (108)	0.60^b (54)

[a] Significant at 0.005 level.
[b] Significant at 0.001 level.
Figures in parenthesis refer to number of cases.

247

late-modernizing groups. These data do, however, allow us to point to those areas where patriarchal values have persisted most strongly. Three areas in particular may be singled out: family planning use, attitudes regarding patriarchal patterns of family power distribution, and patriarchal attitudes concerning the role of marriage and family. Among the late-modernizing groups, use of family planning techniques, both contraception and abortion, is less prevalent than among European Soviets. Traditional minorities still espouse patriarchal authority patterns within the family; erosion of these attitudes is evident among the more Sovietized segments of the Georgians, but young Soviet Uzbeks display few differences from the older generation. Both Georgians and, to an even greater extent, Uzbeks favor a view of marriage that places most emphasis on the spouses' parental responsibilities and less on their happiness as individuals. These values are reflected in regional differences in divorce rates. Although there have been significant increases in southern tier divorce rates over the last twenty-five years, they remain substantially lower than in European regions. Another indicator of the persistence of traditional attitudes toward the family is the high proportion of extended families in Central Asian areas.

The evidence also points, however, to major shifts in values relating to family and sex roles. While use of family planning techniques is relatively limited among the late-modernizing groups, the younger, better educated, and employed women within these groups display patterns much more similar to their European counterparts. Public attitudes toward the working mother do not seem to be very different in the traditional areas than in the European regions to the north and west. Distribution of household tasks seems to be determined more by socioeconomic variables than by ethnic affiliation or region of residence. Many women from even the most traditional areas exhibit a surprisingly high degree of acceptance of institutional childcare. These factors point to aspects of life style and values that are generally compatible with the "Soviet" family system in central USSR.

DOES MODERNIZATION LEAD TO VALUE CHANGE?

The evidence above suggests that ethnic and regional differences in levels of socioeconomic development and traditionality have declined over the past two decades. Much of the decline in each is due to socioeconomic change among the late-modernizing minorities on the southern tier who are becoming more modern in both public life styles and family values. To what degree are these two trends linked causally? Does modernization – increasing urbanization, education, and functional specialization – help erode patriarchal values? This hypothesis was posed in Chapter 1:

Hypothesis 3. The greater the level of modernization, the greater the erosion of patriarchal family values. This relationship will be mediated by cultural heritage.

The first part of the hypothesis indicates that we should find moderately strong statistical relationships between measures of modernization and measures of family values. Representative findings for nationalities and oblasts are displayed in Tables 4.16 and 4.17. For the nationality data set, the strength of the modernization–values relationship depends on how the concepts are operationalized. Although not all correlations are statistically significant, all are in the expected direction. For 1959, the strongest correlation ($r=0.59$) was between urbanization and the female-to-male ratio for higher education (45 cases). The link between modernization and gender roles was somewhat stronger for the oblast data. The correlation between urbanization and female specialized secondary education was 0.79 in 1959 and 0.77 in 1970. These findings suggest that, as hypothesized above, there is a moderate statistical link between measures of modernization and measures of family values.

Analysis of the statistical relationship between modernization level (as measured by percentage urban) and traditionality (as measured by female education and early marriage rates) provides findings that, although not overwhelmingly strong, are generally consistent with the hypothesis that exposure to modernizing institutions produces more modern values. Our findings are consistent with those of Western social scientists who have studied the impact of modern institutions on the values, behaviour, and personality of "traditional" men.[134] Those studies have consistently found that exposure to modern institutions – school, factory, and city – increased individual modernity. The most powerful predictor of modern values across a variety of national settings was education.[135] Some of the modernity studies included questions similar to the Soviet ethnographic survey questions. For example, Kahl's study in Mexico included a series of questions on family modernism, tapping acceptance of divorce as a way of resolving an unhappy marriage, beliefs regarding parental authority, and attitudes toward working wives. Composite scores on this measure were positively related to socioeconomic status.[136] Other studies by Western scholars that focus more narrowly on gender roles reveal a similar nexus between exposure to modern institutions, particularly school, and support for egalitarian sex roles.[137] The Soviet data, which reveal a moderate link between exposure to modern institutions and modern family and sex role values and behavior lend limited support to the modernization hypothesis.

It may be argued, however, that the hypothesis should be tested dynamically. Accordingly, we computed change scores for level of urbanization and for female participation rates. Correlation of change in the urban percentage with change in the various measures of female participation provides results that are either weak or contrary to the hypothesis. For example, the correlation between change in urbanization and early marriage rates is 0.55, that is, in the direction opposite to that expected: those ethnic groups with the smallest increases in the urban percentage showed the greatest decline in early marriage rates. The urbanization level of the Chechen, for example, actually declined between 1959 and 1970, yet their early marriage rate declined by 51 per cent, from 404 per 1,000 women in 1959 to 199 in 1970.

Results more consistent with the modernization hypothesis were obtained when we controlled for modernization level through the use of two-stage regression. First, female change scores were regressed on the analogous male rates for the same indicator, and then the residuals were regressed on change in urbanization. In other words, the modernization level of the group as indicated by the appropriate male rate was removed from the analysis to determine the independent contribution of urbanization. The rationale for this procedure is that groups where males have much higher levels of achieved education than their female counterparts are qualitatively different in terms of modernization from groups where both sexes have nearly equivalent (either high or low) educational achievement.

Change in urbanization explains 14 per cent of the variance in the residuals when change in female specialized secondary education is the dependent variable ($t=2.74$; $p<0.01$). Analogous two-stage regressions for change in female college and specialist participation produced weaker results; change in urbanization explains 5 and 8 per cent of the variance in the residuals respectively. In sum, statistical tests of the modernization/traditionality link provide limited support for the hypothesis that levels of traditionality are statistically related to modernization levels.

The second part of the hypothesis involves the role of cultural heritage in mediating the modernization/value change relationship. This part of the hypothesis rests on the assumption that some societies are less willing to accept egalitarian gender roles and family authority patterns than others. Such societies ascribe more import- ance to traditional family patterns, slowing the process of value change. Given cross-cultural findings revealing the persistence of traditional gender roles in Muslim societies, we expect slower rates of acceptance of modern family values in the Muslim portions of the USSR. "Muslimness" acts as a cultural "filter" mediating the link between modernization and value change. To test this hypothesis, we first examined the link between Muslim cultural heritage and measures of family values. Simple correlations between a dummy "Muslim" variable and thirty-three measures of traditionality in gender roles produced thirty-three statistically significant relation- ships; Muslim groups are more traditional.

Nor are these results an artifact of the level of modernization of Muslim groups or regions. The relationships between "Muslimness" and modernization are relatively weak, since there is considerable diversity in levels of modernization among Muslim groups. These findings indicate that the relatively low levels of socioeconomic development of some Muslim groups is insufficient to explain the low Muslim scores on measures of family value modernity. Among groups at a similar level of modernization, Muslims tend to be more traditional. This suggests that both modernization level and "Mus- limness" are important in explaining modernity of family values. Indeed, combining modernization level with a dummy "Muslim" variable to predict measures of gender role produces substantially stronger results (Table 4.18). For example, the urban percentage (1959) and the dummy variable combine to explain 65 per cent of the variance in female-to-male higher education ratios in 1959.

This finding accords with those of Western researchers examining the correlates of individual modernity. The results of Inkeles and Smith's six-nation study revealed substantial differences in modern- ity scores by country. These differences persisted, although at reduced levels, when characteristics such as educational attainment

Table 4.18. *Regression summary: modernization, culture, and gender roles*

Variables	Multiple R	R Squared	R Square change
Emancipation 1 (1959)			
(Female/male incomplete secondary and above)			
1 % urban, 1959	0.47	0.22	0.22
Muslim dummy variable	0.67	0.45	0.23
2 Semiprofessional participation			
rate, 1959	0.71	0.51	0.51
Muslim dummy variable	0.76	0.58	0.07
Emancipation 2 (1959)			
(Female/male complete secondary and above)			
1 % urban, 1959	0.45	0.20	0.20
Muslim dummy variable	0.76	0.58	0.37
2 Semiprofessional participation			
rate, 1959	0.70	0.49	0.49
Muslim dummy variable	0.81	0.66	0.17
Emancipation 3 (1959)			
(Female/male incomplete higher and above)			
1 % urban, 1959	0.54	0.29	0.29
Muslim dummy variable	0.77	0.60	0.31
2 Semiprofessional participation			
rate, 1959	0.71	0.50	0.50
Muslim dummy variable	0.80	0.64	0.14
Emancipation 4 (1959)			
(Female/male higher and above)			
1 % urban, 1959	0.59	0.35	0.35
Muslim dummy variable	0.81	0.65	0.30
2 Semiprofessional participation			
rate, 1959	0.70	0.49	0.49
Muslim dummy variable	0.80	0.64	0.15

and occupation were controlled. Respondents in an Islamic country (Bangladesh), for example, scored significantly lower on modernization even when groups were matched across key measures of structural modernization. Within Bangladesh, however, the pattern of individual modernity was virtually identical to that in the five other nations – men with the most exposure to modern institutions had the most modern values, beliefs, and behavioral patterns.[138]

The USSR's late-modernizing ethnic groups, then, do not appear to be an exception to the generalization that contact with modern socioeconomic settings tends to produce individuals with less traditional, more modern values. This is not to say that cultural differences in values and associated behavior disappear when measures of "structural modernity" (such as, urban residence and education) are held constant. It is true that some of the more dramatic cultural differences in the Soviet findings virtually disappear when key socioeconomic variables are controlled. The identical pattern of abortion use by young Kazakh and Russian women in the Alma Ata study and the similarity of family size desires among young Azeri and Russian women in Baku are two examples. Other survey results, however, like those relating to parental authority, suggest minimal erosion of traditionality among even those members of the late-modernizing groups most exposed to modern institutions – i.e., young urban residents. Ethnic differences remain strong in those areas. The cultural heritage of Islam has made some of the USSR's Muslim regions more resistant to the erosion of traditional family values associated with modernization. Islamic heritage has not, however, rendered those groups immune to the effect of socioeconomic development. Exposure to mass communications, education, urban life, modern occupations, and the modern bureaucracy has produced dramatic change in family patterns and gender roles. In sum, both structural modernization *and* cultural heritage play a role in the formation of family values.

SOCIAL POLICY AND DEMOGRAPHIC MODERNIZATION

This chapter has provided strong evidence of the ability of Soviet policymakers to influence basic social changes, affecting both structural modernization levels, such as urbanization and industrialization, and basic values and attitudes. What do these trends, in turn, mean for Soviet natality? First of all, it is difficult to escape the conclusion that the modernization in life styles and erosion of family values that have occurred in the high fertility areas since 1959 will have an impact on natality patterns. Many of the empirical indicators that were found to be most closely associated with natality decline have recorded dramatic change over the last two decades. This would imply significant fertility decline among the late-modernizing groups in the 1970s and 1980s. At the same time, the review of evidence bearing on the erosion of family values revealed important aspects of persistence of patriarchal value systems, well into the mid and late 1970s. This would in turn suggest that the most likely natality patterns of the 1970s and 1980s will be ones of continuing, although perhaps diminishing, ethnic and regional differences. In other words, we should expect post-1970 natality declines for most of the high fertility groups, but fertility among these groups is still expected to far exceed that of those in areas where the fertility decline is about stabilized.

This analysis, however, has so far ignored an important dimension of the policy–family values–natality relationship: the potential effects of direct government intervention on fertility. So far we have examined nationality and social policies. These policies have had a major cumulative impact on Soviet society and have produced important changes among the late-modernizing groups – changes that will almost surely be reflected in reduced natality. The Soviet leadership also has at its disposal some potentially powerful policy levers to modify fertility directly. These include: financial and other material incentives to promote or inhibit childbearing and measures to encourage or discourage use of effective family planning techniques. The Soviet leadership also enjoys a near-virtual monopoly over mass communications and educational institutions. These socialization mechanisms could be used to either encourage or discourage social support for large families. It is to these direct efforts to intervene in demographic developments that we turn in Chapter 5.

NOTES

1 A good discussion of the relative contribution of family planning programs and socioeconomic development is Robert D. Retherford and James A. Palmore, "Diffusion Processes Affecting Fertility Regulation" in Rodolfo A. Bulatao and Ronald L. Lee, *Determinants of Fertility in Developing Countries* (New York: Academic Press, 1983), Vol. 2, pp. 295–339.
2 Scott Menard and Elizabeth Moen, "The Relative Importance of Family Planning and Development for Fertility Reduction: Critique of Research and Development Theory," *Studies in Comparative International Development*, Vol. 17, No. 3–4; Fall–Winter 1982, pp. 22–43.
3 Donald J. Hernandez, "The Impact of Family Planning Programs on Fertility in Developing Countries: A Critical Evaluation," *Social Science Research*, Vol. 10, 1981, pp. 32–66.

4 Hernandez, 1981.
5 T. H. Sun and Y. L. Soong, "On Its Way to Zero Growth: Fertility Transition in Taiwan, Republic of China," in *Fertility Transition of the East Asian Populations* (Honolulu: The University Press of Hawaii, 1979), pp. 117–48.
6 Charles Hirschman, "Premarital Socioeconomic Roles and the Timing of Family Formation: A Comparative Study of Five Asian Societies," *Demography*, Vol. 22, No. 1, February 1985, pp. 35–39.
7 See, for example, Ellen Jones and Fred W. Grupp, "Modernisation and Ethnic Equalisation in the USSR," *Soviet Studies*, Vol. 36, No. 2, April 1984, pp. 159–84; and Donna Bahry and Carol Nechmias, "Half Full or Half Empty?: The Debate over Soviet Regional Equality," *Slavic Review*, Vol. 40, No. 3, September 1981, pp. 366–83.
8 Alex Inkeles and David H. Smith, *Becoming Modern: Individual Change in Six Developing Countries* (London: Heinemann Educational Books, Ltd., 1974), *passim*.
9 Computed from 1959, 1970, 1979, and 1984 population data in *Narodnoye khozyaystvo SSSR v 1983 g.* (Moscow: Finansy i Statistika, 1984), pp. 8–9.
10 Computed from data on population in both cities and urban-type settlements in *Itogi vsesoyuznoy perepisi naseleniya 1970 goda*, Vol. 1 (Moscow: Statistika, 1972), pp. 61–75.
11 See data provided in M. I. Kulichenko (ed.) *Natsional'nyye otnosheniya v razvitom sotsialisticheskom obshchestve* (Moscow: Mysl', 1977), pp. 93, 95.
12 See, for example, A. M. El'darov, *Rost rabochego klassa azerbaydzhana na etape razvitogo sotsializma*, 1959–1975 (Baku: Elim, 1978), p. 68.
13 Data on 1959 and 1970 white-collar employment was extracted from *Itogi, 1970*, Vol. 5, pp. 26–45. The 1979 data (available by republic) is from *Chislennost' i sostav naseleniya SSSR. Po dannym vsesoyuznoy perepisi naseleniya 1979 goda* (Moscow: Finansy i Statistika, 1984), pp. 155–6. Data on 1959 and 1970 mental labor (available by republic) is from *Itogi, 1970*, Vol. 6, pp. 6–13. The 1979 data is from *Chislennost'*, p. 181.
14 M. N. Rutkevich, "Convergence of National Republics and Natives of the USSR in Social-Class Structure," *Sotsiologicheskiye issledovaniya*, No. 2, 1981, pp. 14–24.
15 G. P. Kiseleva and A. Ya. Krasha, *O chem rasskazyvayut perepisi naseleniya* (Moscow: Finansy i Statistika, 1983), p. 81.
16 Also excluded were rural residents who had moved from one rural settlement to another within the same administrative region (apparently from one populated area to another that was subordinate to the same village council). "Instructions on Procedures for Conducting the 1979 All-Union Population Census," *Vestnik statistiki*, No. 5, 1978, pp. 28–46.
17 See, for example, S. Bekhodzhayeva, *Sotial'no-ekonomicheskiye problemy truda zhenshchin v narodnom khozyaystve kirgizii* (Frunze: Ilim, 1978), pp. 25–43.
18 See, for example, O. Pal'vanova, "Some Results of a Concrete Sociological Study of the Level of Religious Belief Among Women in the Turkmen Village," *Izvestiya akademii nauk turkmenskoy SSR. Seriya obshchestvennykh nauk*. No. 4, 1979, pp. 13–19.

19 R. A. Ubaydullayeva, "To the Problem of Improving the Effectiveness of Utilizing Female Labor in the USSR," *Obshchestvennyye nauki v uzbekistane*, No. 10, 1980, pp. 44–49.

20 The US figure is based on the Current Population Survey and applies to married women over 16 with husband present. See *Employment in Perspective: Working Women*. Summary 1980. US Department of Labor, Bureau of Labor Statistics, Report 643.

21 Nancy Lubin, "Women in Soviet Central Asia: Progress and Contradictions," *Soviet Studies*, Vol. 33, No. 2, April 1981, pp. 182–203.

22 See, for example, *Turkmenskaya iskra*, 7 April 1979, p. 2; and "To the History of the Emancipation of Karakalpak Women," *Obshchestvennyye nauki v uzbekistane*, No. 4, 1974, pp. 41–43; V. Kolesnikova, "Our Khamis," *Nauka i religiya*, No. 7, July 1982, pp. 13–15; and T. S. Saidbayev, *Islam i obshchestvo*, Second edition (Moscow: Nauka, 1984), p. 253.

23 M. V. Bagabov, *Islam i sem'ya* (Moscow: Nauka, 1980), p. 143.

24 Yu. Shokin, "Not a Special Case," *Turkmenskaya iskra*, 14 June 1979, p. 2; T. Ruzibayov, "For a Cup of Fresh Tea," *Pravda*, 21 May 1979, p. 2; and A. L. Mogilevskiy, *Okhrana prav zhenshchin v turkmenskoy SSR* (Ashkhabad: Ilym, 1979), pp. 69–70.

25 S. M. Mirkhasilov, "On Several Tendencies in the Development of Contemporary Families in Uzbekistan," *Sotsiologicheskiye issledovaniye*, No. 1, 1979, pp. 121–23.

26 Yu. Arutyunyan and Yu. Kakhk, *Sotsiologicheskiye ocherki o sovetskoy estonii* (Tallin: Periodika, 1979), pp. 54–55.

27 S. I. Karakeyeva, "The Experience of Studying the Cultural and Life Style of Kirgiz Urban Families," *Polevyye issledovaniya instituta etnografii 1977* (Moscow: Nauka, 1979), pp. 149–56; S. I. Karakeyeva, *Sovremennaya kirgizskaya gorodskaya sem'ya* (Frunze: Ilim, 1981), pp. 42–43; Mirkhasilov, "On Several Tendencies," 1979 and S. M. Mirkhasilov, "Social-Cultural Changes and Their Reflections in the Contemporary Family of the Rural Population of Uzbekistan," *Sovetskaya etnografiya*, No. 1, 1979, pp. 3–15.

28 Arutyunyan and Kakhk, 1979, pp. 54–55.

29 Yu. V. Arutyunyan, "Ethno-social Aspects of the Development and Rapprochement of Nations in the USSR," *Sovetskaya etnografiya*, No. 3, 1972, pp. 3–19; Yu. V. Arutyunyan, "On Several Tendencies in a Nation's Cultural Pattern," *Sovetskaya etnografiya*, No. 4, 1973, pp. 3–13; and Mirkhasilov, "Social–Cultural Changes," 1979. A similar link between professional status and positive attitudes toward female labor force participation was found in a 1970s study of the Gaguaz in Moldavia. S. S. Kuroglo and M. V. Marunevich, *Sotsialisticheskiye preobrazovaniya v bytu i kul'ture gagauzskogo naseleniya MSSR* (Kishiniv: Shtintsa, 1983), p. 169.

30 Yu. V. Arutyunyan (ed.), *Opyt etnosotsiologicheskogo issledovaniya obraza zhizni (po materialiam moldavskoy SSR)* (Moscow: Nauka, 1980), p. 92.

31 T. A. Abdusalamova, "Female Labor Activity in Dagestan," *Sotsiologicheskiye issledovaniye*, No. 4, 1981, pp. 140–3. See also T. A. Abdusala-

mova, "Female Labor Force Participation and Motivations," *Sotsial'noetnicheskoye i kul'turnoye razvitiye gorodskogo naseleniya dagestana* (Makhachkala, 1978), pp. 85–98.

   Financial reasons for working were also important for the lower income respondents in a study of Georgian women in Tblisi. See G. V. Tsulaya, "Contemporary Ethnodemographic Situation in Georgia in the Georgian Ethnographic Literature: 1964–1974," *Etnicheskiye i kul'turnobytovyye protessy na kavkaze* (Moscow: Nauka, 1978), pp. 255–79.

32 Z. Z. Mukhina, "Changes in the Role of Tatar Women in the Years of Soviet Power," *Voprosy etnografii srednogo povolzh'ya* (Kazan: Izdatel'stvo Kazanskogo Universiteta, 1980), pp. 69–81.

33 Data from Euro-barometer 3, a survey of ten European nations, conducted by the Commission of European Communities in the spring of 1975. The data were made available by the Inter-University Consortium for Political and Social Research, University of Michigan.

34 Deborah Barron and Daniel Yankelovich, *Today's American Woman: How the Public Sees Her* (study prepared for the President's Advisory Committee for Women, December 1980), p. 61.

35 I. Katkova and A. Mamatokhunova, "Several Aspects of the Formation of Contemporary Large Families," in D. I. Valentey, *Demograficheskaya situatsiya v SSSR* (Moscow: Statistika, 1976), pp. 81–89.

36 I. N. Zhelokhovtseva and L. Ye. Sviridova, "To the Question of Realizing Desired Family Size," *Sovetskoye zdravookhraneniye*, No. 4, 1973, pp. 10–14.

37 Yu. V. Arutyunyan (ed.) *Sotsial'naya struktura selskogo naseleniya SSSR* (Moscow: Mysl', 1971), pp. 185–86.

38 B. P. Pal'vanova, *Emansipatsiya musul'manki. Opyt raskreposhcheniya zhenshchiny sovetskogo vostoka* (Moscow: Nauka, 1982), pp. 33–34. On current legal marriage ages, see M. V. Matevosa, "Legal Regulation of Age of Marriage," *Sovetskoye gosudarstvo i pravo*, No. 1, 1976, pp. 125–28.

39 E. G. Filimonov, *et al.* (eds.), *Islam v SSSR* (Moscow: Mysl', 1983), p. 59; Ya. S. Smirnova, "Changes in the Marital Age of Peoples of the North Caucasus in the Years of Soviet Power," *Sovetskaya etnografiya*, No. 1, 1973, pp. 122–27; and M. V. Vagabov, *Islam i sem'ya* (Moscow: Nauka, 1980), pp. 139–43.

40 These data are derived from self-reports of marital status taken from the Soviet census. Average age of marriage derived from the citizen registry is usually inaccurate for many areas where, until recently, at least, it was common practice to delay the registry of the marriage until the birth of the first child. See S. M. Abramzon, *et al.*, *Byt kolkhoznikov kirgizskikh seleniy darkhan i chickkan* (Moscow: AN SSSR, 1958), p. 242.

41 G. I. Gadirzade, "Dynamics of Average Marital Age of Azeris," *Polevyye issledovaniya instituta etnografii, 1979* (Moscow: Nauka, 1983), pp. 134–37.

42 Alex Inkeles, "The Responsiveness of Family Patterns to Economic Change in the United States," in Jesse Pitts (ed.), *The Tocqueville Review*, Vol. 11, No. 1, Spring–Summer 1984, pp. 5–50.

43 Mirkhasilov, "Social-Cultural Changes," 1979; Yu. V. Arutyunyan, "International and National-specific in the Soviet Way of Life," *Sotsialis-*

ticheskiy obraz zhizni i voprosy ideologicheskoy raboty (Moscow: Politizdat, 1977), pp. 244–46. In a recent US survey, only 39 per cent of the respondents rejected divorce if young children were involved, Barron and Yankelovich, 1980, p. 84.

44 Arutyunyan and Kakhk, 1979, pp. 51–52.

45 Arutyunyan and Kakhk, p. 119.

46 Yu. A. Korolev, *Brak i razrod. sovremennyye tendentsii* (Moscow: Yuridicheskaya Literatura, 1978), pp. 126–31; and A. M. Chechot, *Brak, sem'ya, zakon. Sotsial'no-pravovyye ocherki* (Leningrad: Izdatel'stvo Leningradskogo Universiteta, 1984), p. 165.

47 U. Tashtemirov, "Reasons for Divorce in Uninational Uzbek Families," *Sotsiologicheskiye issledovaniya*, No. 2, 1981, pp. 115–18; and A. A. Abbasov, *Sovremennyy byt i kul'tura gornopromyshlennykh rabochikh azerbaydzhana (po materialam dashkesanskogo gornorudnogo rayon)* (Baku: Elm, 1980), p. 65.

48 Z. A. Yankova, *Gorodskaya sem'ya* (Moscow: Nauka, 1979), pp. 150–51; L. V. Chuyko, *Braki i razvody* (Moscow: Statistika, 1975), pp. 145, 163; and Korolev, 1978, pp. 143–49; S. N. Burova, *Sotsiologiya i pravo o razvode* (Minsk: Izdatel'stvo BGU im V. I. Lenin, 1979), pp. 19–20; and P. Zvindrinsh, "Several Results of an Investigation of Differential Divorce and Reasons for the Breakup of Marriages in Latvia," *Sotsial'no-demograficheskiy issledovaniya sem'i v respublikakh sovetskoy pribaltiki* (Riga: Zinatne, 1980), pp. 110–20.

49 See, for example, Vladimir Voyna, "Is the Family the Formula for Happiness?" *Literaturnaya gazeta*, 11 May 1983, p. 14.

50 V. A. Sysenko, "Divorce: Dynamics, Motives, Consequences," *Sotsiologicheskiye issledovaniya*, No. 2, 1982, pp. 99–104.

51 Yu. V. Arutyunyan and L. M. Drobizheva, "Ethnosociological Research in the USSR," *Sotsiologicheskiye issledovaniya*, No. 1, 1981, pp. 64–70; and O. B. Naumova, "New and Traditional in the Contemporary Kazakh Family," *Polevyye issledovaniya instituta etnografii, 1980–1981* (Moscow: Nauka, 1984), pp. 71–78.

52 Mirkhasilov, "On Several Tendencies," 1979; and Yu. V. Arutyunyan, "National Peculiarities of Social Development," *Sotsiologicheskiye issledovaniya*, No. 3, 1985, pp. 28–35.

53 S. S. Kuroglo, "The Changing Social and Family Situation of Gagauz Women in the Years of Soviet Power," *Narodnyye traditsii i sovremennost'* (Kishinev: Shtintsa, 1980), pp. 38–47. In most European families, the majority of family decisions are decided by both spouses. See, for example, A. Kelam, "Structure and Function of the Family," in *Trud zhenshchin i sem'ya* (Tallin: AN Estonskoy SSR, 1978), pp. 43–100.

54 S. I. Golod, *Stabil'nost sem'i: Sotsiologicheskiy i demograficheskiy aspekty* (Leningrad: Nauka, 1984), p. 140 and M. A. Abdurakhimov, "The Role of Moral Duty in Family Everyday Ethics," *Sotsiologicheskiy sbornik* (Makhachkala: Dagestanskiy Filial AN SSSR, 1970), pp. 117–35.

55 Mirkhasilov, "Social–cultural Changes," 1979; Arutyunyan and Drobizheva, 1981; and O. A. Gantskaya, "Ethnicity and Family in the USSR," *Sovetskaya etnografiya*, No. 3, 1974, pp. 20–29.

56 Toktosun Attokurov, *Sem'ya i kommunisticheskoye vospitaniye* (Frunze: Kyrgyzstan, 1983), pp. 94–96.

57 Yu. V. Arutyunyan and L. M. Drobizheva, "Soviet Form of Life: General and Nationality-Specific," *Sovetskaya etnografiya*, No. 3, 1976, pp. 10–21; and Mirkhasilov, "On Several Tendencies," 1979.

58 Mirkhasilov, "On Several Tendencies," 1979. See also V. M. Ivanov, *Novoye vremya–novaya zhizn. Etnograficheskiy ocherk o byte rabochevo klassa belorussii perioda kommunisticheskogo stroitel'stva* (Minsk: Nauka i Tekhnika, 1968), pp. 76–77.

59 Mirkhasilov, "Social-Cultural Changes," 1979.

60 G. P. Vasil'yeva, "Women of the Republics of Central Asia and Kazakhstan and their Role in Transforming the Life Style of the Rural Population," *Sovetskaya etnografiya*, No. 6, 1975, pp. 17–27. Western studies of the link between contributions to the family budget and family decision-making come to conflicting conclusions; some researchers report a direct relationship between budgetary contributions and the woman's power within the family, while others have found no relationship. Marilyn H. Buehler, Andrew J. Weigert and Darwin L. Thomas, "Correlates of Conjugal Power: A Five Culture Analysis of Adolescent Perceptions," *Journal of Comparative Family Studies*, Vol. 5, No. 1, Spring 1974, pp. 5–16; and George H. Conklin, "Cultural Determinants of Power for Women Within the Family: A Neglected Aspect of Family Research," *Journal of Comparative Family Studies*, Vol. 10, No. 1, Spring 1979, pp. 35–53. A review of recent literature is presented in Gerald M. McDonald, "Family Power: The Assessment of a Decade of Theory and Research, 1970–1979," *Journal of Marriage and the Family*, Vol. 42, No. 4, November 1980, pp. 841–54.

61 A. Kh. Khashimov, *Formirovaniye novykh semeyno-bytovykh otnosheniy u narodov sredney azii* (Dushanbe: Irfon, 1972), pp. 107–13.

62 S. Sh. Gadzhiyeva, *Sem'ya i semeynyy byt narodov dagestana* (Makhachkala: Dagestanskoye Knizhnoye Izdatel'stvo, 1967), pp. 62–63.

63 A. Dzhumagulov, *Sem'ya i brak u kirgizov chuyskoy doliny* (Frunze: AN Kirgizskoy SSR. Institut Istorii, 1960), p. 60; and O. A. Sukhareva and M. A. Kikhanova, *Proshloye i nastoyashcheye seleniya aykyran. Opyt etnograficheskogo izucheniya kolkhoza im stalina chartakskogo rayona namaganskoy oblasti* (Tashkent: Izdatel'stvo A. N. Uzbeksoy SSR, 1955), pp. 190–91.

64 N. A. Kislyakov (ed.), *Kul'tura i byt tadzhikskogo kolkoznogo krestyanstva* (Moscow: Izdatel'stvo AN SSSR, 1954), p. 169.

65 Kh. A. Argynbayev, "Family-Marital Relations Among Kazakhs in the Soviet Era," in *Aktual'nyye problemy istorii sovetskogo kazakhstana* (Alma-Ata: Nauka, 1980), pp. 302–15.

66 M. D. Dzhunusbayev, "Distribution of Housework in Kazakh Families," *Sostiologicheskiye issledovaniya*, No. 1, 1985, pp. 106–09. Findings on ethnic differences in division of household chores appear to vary depending on the wording of the questions. The five-city survey of ethnic convergence revealed that the husband did "a significant part" of household tasks in 45 per cent of the Saratov (located in the Russian republic) families, compared with only 5–6 per cent in Tashkent. Arutyunyan, 1985.

67 A. A. Magidyev, "Several Aspects of Family–Marital Relations in Cities of Dagestan," in *Sotsial'no-etnicheskoye i kul'turnoye razvitiye gorodskogo naseleniya dagestana* (Makhachkala: Dagestanskiy Filial AN SSR, 1978), pp. 99–112.

68 Attokurov, 1983, pp. 87–88.

69 Mirkhasilov, "On Several Tendencies," 1979.

70 S. M. Mirkhasilov, "Contemporary Families of the Rural Population of Uzbekistan," *Obshchestvennyye nauki v uzbekistane*, No. 4, 1977, pp. 36–41.

71 Arutyunyan, "On Several Tendencies," 1973.

72 Reported in A. G. Kharchev, *Brak i sem'ya v SSSR* (Moscow: Mysl', 1979), pp. 259–60. The pattern of male involvement in various household tasks is consistent with the findings of study conducted between 1977 and 1981 in six cities in the Urals. B. S. Pavlov, "Materi, otsy, deti: Sotsiologicheskiy ocherk (Moscow: Sovetskaya Rossiya, 1984), p. 98.

73 M. Sushanlov, *Sem'ya i semeynyy byt dungan* (Frunze: Ilim, 1979), pp. 45–51.

74 Mirkhasilov, "Social–cultural Change," 1979; and Arutyunyan and Drobizheva, 1976, pp. 10–21.

75 N. G. Yurkevich, *Sovetskaya sem'ya* (Minsk: Izdatel'stvo BGU im V. I. Lenin, 1970), pp. 189–90. Data on Eurobarometer 8 made available by the Inter-University Consortium for Political and Social Research, University of Michigan.

76 R. S. Rotova (ed.), *Osobennosti demograficheskogo razvitiya v SSSR* (Moscow: Finansy i Statistika, 1982), p. 60.

77 These figures refer to parents of juvenile children only. A. Klinchyus, "Several Peculiarities of Family Lifestyle in Small Cities," in P. Gulyan *et al.* (eds.), *Sotsial'no-demograficheskiye issledovaniya semi'i v respublikakh sovetskoy pribaltiki* (Riga: Zinatne, 1980), pp. 32–39. See also V. D. Patrushev, *Ispolzovaniye sovokupnogo vremeni obshchestva* (Moscow: Mysl', 1978), *passim*, and *Byudzhet vremeni zhiteley g. Pskova* (Novosibirsk, 1973), *passim*.

78 These figures refer to the winter season only. In the summer, females spent 38–40 hours per week, males 15–16 hours. A. A. Abbasov, 1980, p. 57.

79 Attokurov, 1983, pp. 54–55.

80 S. Khakimova, "Family Limitation of Birth in Tadzhikistan," in *Naseleniye sredney azii* (Moscow: Finansy i Statistika, 1985), pp. 35–42; and N. M. Aliakberova, "Fertility in the Rural Family," in *Demografiya sem'i* (Tashkent: Tashkent State University, 1980), pp. 14–26.

81 K. D. Abdullin, "Study of the Reproductive Situation of Married Women in Kirgizia," *Zdravookhraneniye kirgizii*, No. 5, 1977, pp. 8–12.

82 Ye. I. Chuykina, *et al.*, "Some Data on Social-Hygienic Study of Abortions Among Women in the City of Karaganda," *Zdravookhraneniye kazakhstana*, No. 7, 1973, pp. 8–9.

83 Cohort studies that include questions on abortion include: Sh. Shlindman and P. Zvidrin'sh, *Izucheniye rozhdayemosti* (Moscow: Statistika, 1973), p. 145; Katkova and Mamatokhunova, "Several Aspects," 1976; Ye. I. Chuykina, "Level of Knowledge of Youth on Questions of Family Planning and Reproductive Activity of Young Married Couples," *Zdra-*

vookhraneniye kazakhstana, No. 12, 1979, pp. 17–19; Chuykina, *et al.*, 1973; I. Katkova, "Particularities of Demographic Behavior of Families in the First Years of Marriage," in *Molodaya sem'ya* (Moscow: Statistika, 1977), pp. 84–95; I. P. Katkova, *Rozhdayemost' v molodykh sem'yakh* (Moscow: Meditsina, 1971), *passim*; M. S. Tsirulnikov and R. A. Khentov, "On Application of Some Contraceptive Means and Calculating Their Effectiveness," *Voprosy okhrany materinstva i detstva*, No. 6, 1960, pp. 49–51; L. Ye. Dakrsiy and V. A. Belova, "Social–Hygienic Questions Connected with Marriage and Birth of Children in Families," *Zdravrookhraneniya rosskiyskoy federatsii*, No. 3, 1969, pp. 14–17; I. P. Katkova and S. G. Frolov, "Sanitary Socialization Work in the Struggle Against Abortions," *Feldsher i akusherstvo*, No. 3, 1968, pp. 39–41.

84 Shlindman and Zvidrin'sh, 1973, p. 145.

85 Katkova and Mamatokhunova, "Several Aspects," 1976.

86 V. A. Belova (ed.), *Skol'ko detey budet v sovetskoy sem'ye (resultaty obsledovaniya)* (Moscow: Statistika, 1977), p. 76.

87 US Department of Health and Human Services. Public Health Service. Centers for Disease Control, *Abortion Surveillance. Annual Summary 1978*, p. 35. A second source of national data on US abortions is the Alan Guttmacher Institute. Data reported by the Institute are generally higher than those reported by the Centers for Disease Control, because the Institute surveys organizations that provide abortions directly, while the CDC cumulates data reported by the states. Comprehensiveness of abortion reporting seems to vary substantially from state to state. These comments underline the difficulties of achieving accurate reporting of abortion, even in the United States where the overall comprehensiveness of reporting is considered quite high. See Stanley K. Henshaw, "Abortion Services in the United States, 1979 and 1980," in *Family Planning Perspectives*, Vol. 14, No. 1, January/February 1982, pp. 5–15.

88 Ye. I. Chuykina, "Some Data on the Formation of Student Families: Social Hygiene and Demographic Aspects," *Zdravookhraneniye rossiyskoy federatsii*, No. 1, 1981, pp. 24–27; and L. V. Anokhin and L. D. Sarayeva, "Variation in the Level of Several Demographic Indicators by Rayons of an Oblast," *Zdravookhraneniye rossiyskoy federatsii*, No. 1, 1981, pp. 21–24.

89 N. S. Sokolova, "Statistical Analysis of the Outcome of Pregnancy," *Zdravookhraneniye rossiyskoy federatsii*, No. 3, 1970, pp. 38–40. There are only five other studies of which we are aware that provide data on "pregnancy outcomes;" all except one cover much more limited geographical areas. The first provides data drawn from records of pregnancy maintained at three gynecological clinics in Leningrad city. (N. Tutoverova, "Characteristics of the Contingent of Post-war Births in Leningrad," in *Zdravookhraneniye rossiyskoy federatsii*, No. 1, 1967, pp. 10–13). The second provides partial results of a study using pregnancy records, abortion records, and disease data for a small city and the surrounding rural rayon in Altay Kray. (I. A. Danilov, "Frequency and Outcomes of Pregnancy Among Urban and Rural Residents," *Zdravookhraneniye rossiyskoy federatsii*, No. 6, 1972, pp. 26–28). The third, noted above, provides data for Ryazan oblast. See Anokhin and Sarayeva, 1981. The fourth is an

analysis of pregnancy outcomes in the Islamic southern tier. Data were collected in 1974 in Frunze, Ashkhabad, and Dushanbe and in 1975 in oblast centers and rural population points in Uzbekistan. See N. M. Aliakberova, "Analysis of Contemporary Tendencies of Birthrate in Central Asia," in O. B. Ata-Mirzayev (ed.), *Regional'nyye demograficheskiye issledovaniya* (Tashkent: Tashkent State University, 1978), pp. 18–26. The fifth study examines pregnancy outcomes for women employed in one Leningrad factory. N. S. Sokolova, "Questions of the Study of Pregnancy Outcomes of Women," *Zdravookhraneniye rossiyskoy federatsii*, No. 3, 1980, pp. 13–15.

90 A. F. Serenko and V. V. Yermakova, *Sotsial'naya gigiena i organizatsiya zdravookhraneniya* (Moscow: Meditsina, 1977), p. 392.

91 *Abortion Surveillance*, p. 30. Regional variations in abortion rates as revealed in the Guttmacher data are similar to those evident in the CDC data. In 1980, for example, abortion rates ranged from 7 per 1,000 fertile-age women in West Virginia to 45.9 in New York State. Henshaw, 1982.

92 Published results of studies relying on data collected at medical facilities from women requesting abortions include: K. I. Zhuravleva and Ts. D. Tsydypov, "Reasons and Results of Abortion," *Zdravookhraneniye rossiyskoy federatsii*, No. 2, 1971, pp. 22–5; Ye. A. Sadvokasova, "Several Social-hygienic Aspects of the Study of Abortion," *Sovetskoye zdravookhraneniye*, No. 3, 1963, pp. 45–50; A. I. Markov, "Social-hygienic Aspects of Abortion in the Tambov Rayon of Amur Oblast," *Sovetskoye zdravookhraneniye*, No. 7, 1973, pp. 43–46; M. S. Tsirulnikov and R. A. Khentov, "On the Applications of Several Contraceptive Means and Calculation of their Effectiveness in Gynecological Clinics," *Voprosy okhrany materinstva i detstva*, No. 6, 1960, pp. 49–51; M. T. Inderbiyev, "Social-hygienic Characteristics of Abortion in Chechen-Ingush ASSR," *Zdravookhraneniye rossiyskoy federatsii*, No. 5, 1975, pp. 24–26; S. L. Polchanova, "Several Social-Psychological Aspects of Birthrate," *Sovetskoye zdravookhraneniye*, No. 5, 1972, pp. 15–19; I. V. Polyakov and A. P. Kovaleva, "To the Social-hygienic Characteristics of Abortion in Leningrad," *Sovetskoye zdravookhraneniye*, No. 12, 1976, pp. 43–46; V. L. Krasnenkov, "Several Social-Hygienic Aspects of Abortion Among Women of Kalinin Oblast," *Sovetskoye zdravookhraneniye*, No. 5, 1973, pp. 20–24; V. K. Kuznetsov, "On a Factor Influencing the No. of Abortions," *Zdravookhraneniye rossiyskoy federatsii*, No. 9, 1969, pp. 9–10; and I. M. Starovoytov, *et al.*, "Reproductive Functions of Women and Abortion Motives," *Zdravookhraneniye belorussi*, No. 5, 1981, pp. 25–27.

There are also studies where the method for collecting the data is not clear. The first is a study of Magadan; it provides data on the outcome of pregnancies without specifying the source of the figures. However, the author goes on to describe a survey done using anonymous questionnaires directed at women who had an abortion in Magadan abortion facilities in 1970, suggesting that the outcomes of pregnancy data are derived from a clinic or regional study of women having abortions. V. D. Vlasov, "Several Results of Social–Demographic Research in the Far

North," *Zdravookhraneniye rossiyskoy federatsii*, No. 8, 1972, pp. 26–30. The second study, conducted in 1962, provides no information on methodology. A. A. Verbenko, *et al.*, "On the Social-Hygienic Significance of Abortion," *Zdravookhraneniye rossiyskoy federatsii*, No. 6, 1966, pp. 22–26. The third study, which covered all of the RSFSR, was described as a sample survey, but we have no details about the survey. See M. S. Bednyy, *Demograficheskiye faktory zdorov'ya* (Moscow: Finansy i Statistika, 1984), p. 111; and N. A. Shneyderman, "Social-hygienic Factors of Birthrate and Formation of the Able-bodied Population in the RSFSR," *Zdravookhraneniye rossiyskoy federatsii*, No. 1, 1982, pp. 25–28.

93 Zhuravleva and Tsydypov, 1971.

94 A. A. Popov, "On Frequency of and Reasons for Outside-of-Hospital Abortions," *Zdravookhraneniye rossiyskoy federatsii*, No. 6, 1982, pp. 27–30.

95 V. I. Grishchenko, *Nauchnyye osnovy regulirovaniya rozhdayemosti* (Kiev: Zdorov'ya, 1983), p. 15; and Aliakberova, 1978.

96 Katkova and Mamatokhunova, "Several Aspects," 1976.

97 Katkova, "Particularities of Demographic Behavior," 1977.

98 Chuykina, *et al.*, 1979.

99 K. V. Mamedov, "Several Methodological Aspects of Studying the Impact of Social–economic Factors on the Reproductive Functions of Women," in *Sotsial'no-ekonomicheskiye osobennosti vosproizvodstva naseleniya v usloviyakh razvitogo sotsializma*, Vol. 2 (Kiev: Institut Ekonomiki AN USSR, 1976), pp. 41–43.

100 A. M. Guseynova, "On Factors Influencing the Level of Fertility," *Sotsial'no-ekonomicheskiye osobennosti vosproizvodstva naseleniya v usloviyakh razvitogo sotsializma*, 1976, pp. 136–37.

101 N. M. Aliakberova, "Fertility Trends in Central Asia," *Sotsial'no-ekonomicheskiye osobennosti vosproizvodstva naseleniya v usloviyakh razvitogo sotsializma*, 1976, pp. 134–36.

102 Aliakberova, 1980.

103 Katkova, "Particularities of Demographic Behavior," 1977.

104 Katkova, 1971, pp. 70–71.

105 L. A. Arutyunyan, "Several Peculiarities of Family Planning in Armenia," in M. A. Adonts and L. M. Davtyan (eds.), *Materialy vsesoyuznoy nauchnoy konferentsii po problemam narodonaseleniya zakavkaz'ye* (Yerevan: Scientific Research Institute of Economy and Planning, 1968), pp. 37–40.

106 Khakimova, 1983.

107 See, for example, Shlindman and Zvidrin'sh, 1973, pp. 134–45; and Darskiy and Belova, 1969.

108 Katkova and Mamatokhunova, "Several Aspects," 1976.

109 Katkova, "Particularities of Demographic Behavior," 1977.

110 Ya. Golin, "Birthrate in Dagestan," *Zdravookhraneniye rossiyskoy federatsii*, No. 12, 1971, pp. 9–13.

111 M. Buriyeva, "Family Formation in Rural Uzbekistan," *Lyudi v gorode i na sele* (Moscow: Statistika, 1978), pp. 95–102.

112 M. K. Kharakhanov, "Dynamics of Population in Central Asia," in *Problemy narodonaseleniya. Trud vsesoyuznoy mezhvuzovskoy nauchnoy konferent-*

sii posvyashchennoy problemam narodonaseleniya sredney azii (Moscow: Izdatel'stvo Moskovskogo Universiteta, 1970), pp. 6–26.

113 N. S. Yesipov and A. M. Yelemesova, "Several Problems in the Development of Kazakh Families," in *Sovremennaya sem'ya* (Moscow: Finansy i Statistika, 1982), pp. 82–90.

114 M. K. Karakhanov, *Nekapitalisticheskiy put' razvitiya i problemy narodonaseleniya* (Tashkent: Fan, 1983), p. 141. Results of a study of pregnancy outcomes in Tadzhikistan suggest an abortion to birth rate of 0.83 to 1, with lower abortion usage among Islamic women than among their European counterparts. See Khakimova, 1985.

115 K. Shaniyazov, "Socialist Transformation of Social and Family Life of the Uzbek People," *Obshchestvennyye nauki v uzbekistane*, No. 11–12, 1972, pp. 44–49.

116 Boris Pshenichnyy, "The Paradoxes of the Saidov Family," *Zhurnalist*, No. 2, February 1983, pp. 25–27.

117 Golod, 1984, p. 30.

118 Ya. S. Smirnova, *Sem'ya i sem'eynyy byt narodov severnogo kavkaza* (Moscow: Nauka, 1983), pp. 191–92.

119 Mirkhasilov, "On Several Tendencies," 1979, Yu. V. Arutyunyan and S. M. Mirkhasilov, "Ethno-sociological Research of Culture and Life Style in Uzbekistan," *Obshchestvennyye nauki v uzbekistane*, No. 1, 1979, pp. 36–41; Mirkhasilov, "Social-cultural Changes," 1979; A. I. Ginzberg, "Influence of the Urban Environment on Rural Migrants. On the Results of an Ethno-sociological Study in Uzbekistan," *Polevyye issledovaniya institut etnografii, 1977* (Moscow: Nauka, 1979), pp. 147–48; Arutyunyan, 1977; and O. M. Guseynov, "International Contacts in Life Style," *Nauchnyy kommunizm*, No. 6, 1981, pp. 53–58.

120 Arutyunyan and Kakhk, 1979, p. 116; Kuroglo, 1980; and Yu. V. Arutyunyan, "National-Regional Variation in the Soviet Countryside," *Sotsiologicheskiye issledovaniya*, No. 3, 1980, pp. 73–81.

121 Arutyunyan and Kakhk, 1979, p. 119.

122 L. M. Drobizheva, *Dukhovnaya obshchnost narodov SSSR. Istoriko-sotsiologicheskiy ocherk mezhnatsional'nykh otnosheniy* (Moscow: Mysl', 1981), p. 165.

123 D. Kh. Aybazov, "Experience of Sociological Study of International Socialization of Workers in a Multi-ethnic Work Collective," *Sotsiologicheskiye issledovaniya*, No. 1, 1979, pp. 115–18.

124 Arutyunyan, "On Several Tendencies," 1973; and Arutyunyan and Drobizheva, 1976.

125 Arutyunyan and Kakhk, 1979, p. 119.

126 On family ties and respect for the elderly among the Islamic Abhazians, see G. V. Smyr, *Islam v abkhazii i puti preodoleniya ego perezhitkov v sovremennykh usloviyakh* (Tblisi: Izdatel'stvo Metsinereba, 1972), pp. 179–80.

127 A. G. Volkov and G. I. Kolosova, "Marital Status of the Population and Family Composition in the USSR," in *Vsesoyuznaya perepis' naseleniya 1979 goda. Sbornik statey* (Moscow: Finansy i Statistika, 1984), pp. 194–214.

128 I. I. Kashtanenkova and Kh. Nazarova, "Comparative Social-

Demographic Analysis of Urban and Rural Families in Uzbekistan," in *Demografiya sem'i* (Tashkent: Tashkent State University, 1980), pp. 27–42; and R. D. Artykbayev and Kh. Ishkhodzhayeva, "Features of Formation of the Rural Family in Surkhandarinsk Oblast," in *loc. cit.*, pp. 97–109.

129 The 1970 and 1979 data presented in Figures 4.6 and 4.7 cannot be directly compared. The 1970 data includes types II and III (families with one married couple, with or without children, with one of the parents of the couple and/or with other relatives); type IV (two or more married couples, with or without children, with or without one of the parents of the couple, with or without other relatives); and types VII and VIII (mother/father with children, with one of the parents). In contrast, the 1979 data does not include types VII and VIII since figures for these families were not provided in the 1979 census results. The 1979 rates, therefore, understate the share of the population living in non-nuclear families. For a description of the categories of families, see Volkov and Kolosova, 1984.

130 Karakhanov, pp. 149–50. See also, "What Price Happiness?" *Komsomol'skaya pravda*, 17 August 1983, p. 2.

131 G. P. Vasil'yeva, "The Reflection of Ethnosocial Processes in the Material Culture of the Contemporary Rural Family," *Sovetskaya etnografiya*, No. 5, September–October 1982, pp. 41–51.

132 On pronatalist pressures in Soviet extended families, see M. K. Karakhanov, *Nekapitalisticheskiy put' razvitiya i problemy narodonaseleniya* (Tashkent: Fan, 1983), pp. 147–48; and M. Buriyeva, "Large Families in Uzbekistan," in *Naseleniye sredney azii* (Moscow: Finansy i Statistika, 1985), pp. 29–34. On similar pressures in non-socialist countries, see Linda J. Beckman, "Communication, Power, and the Influence of Social Networks in Couple Decisions on Fertility," in Bulatao and Lee, Vol. 2, pp. 415–43.

133 M. R. Buriyeva, "Opinion of Rural Women on the Number of Children in the Family," in *Demografiya sem'i* (Tashkent: Tashkent State University, 1980), pp. 69–81.

134 Inkeles and Smith, 1974, *passim*.

135 David B. Holsinger and Gary L. Theisen, "Education, Individual Modernity, and National Development: A Critical Appraisal," *Journal of Developing Areas*, Vol. 11, No. 3, April 1977, pp. 315–33.

136 Joseph A. Kahl, *The Measurement of Modernism: A Study of Values in Britain and Mexico* (Austin, Texas: The University of Texas Press, 1968), pp. 33; 47–8.

137 See, for example, John H. Scanzoni, *Sex Roles, Life Styles, and Childbearing* (New York: The Free Press, 1975), pp. 19–62.

138 Alex Inkeles, "Understanding and Misunderstanding Individual Modernity," *Journal of Cross-Cultural Psychology*, Vol. 8, No. 2, June 1977, pp. 135–76.

5

Soviet demographic policy and fertility transition

As the foregoing chapters demonstrate, the main engine propelling the fertility transition in the USSR has been social change and the erosion of traditional family values. These trends were the result of public policy that first placed European Russia on the path of rapid modernization and then promoted socioeconomic development in the late-modernizing southern tier. Accelerating social change in each case was a deep commitment, born partly of ideology and partly of practical need, to full female participation in the public domain – a goal that necessitated a breakdown in patriarchal family values in both European Russia and the Islamic southern tier. In the latter case, however, as documented in Chapter 4, the division of status and labor on the basis of sex and the subordinate role and physical segregation of women were critical elements in Islamic social systems and have proven extremely resistant to change. The erosion of patriarchal family values that has occurred in these southern tier regions, despite these very powerful cultural barriers, is a tribute to the effectiveness of Soviet ethnic and social policies.

The Soviet political elite has been less successful in its direct efforts to modify fertility. This is partly because Soviet demographic policy is at odds with social policy: in effect, Soviet population programs are intended to moderate the fertility declines produced by socioeconomic modernization. The limited success of demographic policy is also partly due to the fact that the Soviets do not have a comprehensive, internally consistent set of programs to modify fertility. As will be detailed below, there is deep disagreement over both goals and means. Moreover, the goals of the individual programs that constitute demographic policy are in conflict with each other. In addition, many of the Soviet programs have been half-hearted ones, since the political leadership has been unwilling to make the changes in economic priorities necessary to field a more effective set of policies. They have been unwilling, for example, to address the longstanding housing and consumer shortages that plague young Soviet families. Finally, in the absence of Stalinist terror, Soviet officials are discovering that in matters affecting the most private of all personal decisions – whether or not to have a child – public policy is not all-powerful.[1]

GOALS, STRATEGIES, AND TACTICS OF SOVIET DEMOGRAPHIC POLICY

Evaluation of Soviet demographic policy must begin with an examination of both its goals and the programs that have been adopted to achieve these goals. Here we run into an immediate problem, because neither Soviet officials nor Soviet demographers are in complete agreement over either goals or means. This is due in part to an implicit conflict between long-term and short-term Soviet goals.

The immediate cause of Soviet official concern over demographic developments is the dramatic and sustained fertility decline in the modernized areas of the USSR.[2] There does not seem to be a great deal of concern about the high fertility rates in the southern tier, although many Soviet commentators seem to concur that overly large families of five or more children place a financial burden on the parents and inhibit the wife's participation in society: "Large families in contemporary circumstances, as is known, hinder participation of the women in social production, and deprive the woman of creative growth and full harmonic development as an individual."[3] Nonetheless, Soviet demographers and officials explicitly reject measures to help promote fertility decline in the high-natality southern tier areas: "Demographic policy measures cannot be used with a view toward artificially accelerating a decline in the birthrate in areas where its level is high, for this would clash with the essence of socialist social and national policy."[4] Most Soviet demographers, moreover, subscribe to the belief that fertility decline in these areas is inevitable and that lower rates will occur without direct intervention:

Slightly expanded reproduction is provided by Central Asia and Azerbaydzhan ... Yet I believe no demographer challenges the fact that these republics will inevitably change to the new kind of reproductive situation that now characterizes the central and Western parts of the country. It is simply that the demographic revolution in Central Asia is being completed somewhat later than in other areas.[5]

Indeed, some articles are now appearing that bemoan the rapidity with which the fertility transition is occurring in some parts of the southern tier. The implicit (and sometimes explicit) message of these demographers is: the high natality of the southern tier area has so far cushioned the drop in overall USSR birth rates, but even these areas will inevitably follow the European regions in fertility decline and, to the extent that they do so at a rapid pace, the overall USSR decline will accelerate:

The beginning of a limiting of the number of children in a family has become clearly noticeable among Kazakhs recently ... at present, many young persons consider two children optimum. However, they are very wrong in this view. We must see that our young people carry on the very fine tradition of our people, the tradition of raising large numbers of children.[6]

There is, however, little evidence supporting the image sometimes presented in the Western press of a Soviet officialdom alarmed by the imminent prospect of a USSR swamped by non-Russians.[7] In spite of the reservations about the impact of large families on sexual equality, most leaders would probably echo former Party leader Brezhnev in acknowledging the positive results of high fertility in the southern tier and for a very pragmatic reason – continued high fertility there serves to moderate the low fertility in European Russia.[8] Indeed, as we shall see below, if the Soviets were seriously interested in stemming the demographic "yellowing" of the USSR, one wonders why they have adopted programs whose effects are in precisely the opposite direction. Either the Soviet leadership is very stupid indeed, or the set of motives attributed to it by Western commentators is very much mistaken!

If there seems to be some unanimity on the major problem confronting Soviet demographic development (the declining European birth rate), there is little unanimity of response. Some Soviet demographers exhibit a strong pronatalist orientation in their grim assessment of the implications of the fertility decline and enthusiastic espousal of remedial measures.[9] These commentators point to the negative economic consequences of fertility decline. Declining fertility, they argue, will inevitably produce an aging population. This, in turn, will lead to a decline in labor force growth, an increase in the proportion of pensioners in the population, and an increasing economic "burden" on the remaining able-bodied populace.[10] Demographers also warn of the potential decreases in occupational mobility involved in an aging labor force. The new occupational skills required by technology-generated jobs are easier to provide to young people prior to labor force entrance than to older workers in obsolescent positions who must be retrained later in their career.[11] Certain types of expenditure, such as those for defense or science, do not depend on the size of the population; the larger the labor force, or so goes the argument, the easier these expenditures will be absorbed by society. Moreover, a declining birth rate also means that the Soviet Union will comprise a smaller share of the world population – a factor of considerable symbolic importance in a nation self-consciously proud of its claim to great-power status.[12]

Other Soviet demographers counsel moderation. The fertility decline, they argue, is a natural part of the overall modernization process that has resulted in substantial increases in the quality of life for all Soviet citizens.[13] They point out that an increase in labor force size is only one way to achieve economic growth. An alternative strategy, and one which is more in tune with the leadership's stress on intensive economic development, is improved labor productivity.[14] Economic growth, from this perspective, depends less on labor force quantity that on labor force quality.[15] These demographers note that current manpower shortages are due, not to insufficient numbers of able-bodied workers, but inefficient use of those workers who are available.

These moderate pronatalists note that a gradual aging of the population is inevitable unless one is able to achieve the high natality that characterized the USSR in the interwar period – a practical impossibility. Similarly, they note that concerns about the declining USSR share of the world population are based on the untenable assumption that the high population growth rates in the developing countries will be maintained indefinitely. This, they argue, is most unlikely; and the USSR's future share of the world population is likely to be much higher than that projected from current growth rates in the developing world. In any case, keeping up with the current Third World growth rates would entail raising the birth rate to 35 or 40 per 1,000; and this, they contend, is hardly a viable goal.[16]

Some of the moderate pronatalists place explicit emphasis on an issue underlying the entire demographic debate: the role of women. The strong pronatalists in their enthusiastic espousal of "pro-family" programs, seem to disregard the implications of their proposals for sexual equality; they give lip service to the woman's role in social "production," but are clearly ready to sacrifice that role for what they see as the more important role of reproduction. The moderates, by contrast, argue that any measures to moderate or stabilize the fertility decline in low-fertility areas must be fully consistent with the broader goals of Soviet society, in particular those relating to sexual equality.[17] Proponents of this approach recognize the woman's dual role as worker and parent, but oppose any programs that would stimulate fertility by sacrificing female participation in society. They point out, for example, that extending paid maternity leave to three years is incompatible with the desire women have to participate fully in the paid labor force. Such officials advocate instead an expansion of day care programs and improvement of household services to ease the conflict between work and motherhood.[18]

The proponents of both groups seem to regard an average family size of two to three children as the ideal.[19] Attainment of this ideal would require a major behavioral shift for both the European areas where the single child is becoming increasingly popular, particularly among young professional women, and the Muslim regions, where extremely large families are still the norm for rural couples. Here again, Soviet demographers are not agreed on the most appropriate strategy to achieve the two-to-three child average. The mix of programs in existence up to the mid-1980s may be described as moderately pronatal. Most of these programs were not explicitly designed to raise fertility but rather (1) to improve living standards for the poorest families and (2) to ease the burden of the working mother. Moreover, the programs in existence were not targeted toward producing more of the medium-sized families so favored by demographers, but rather toward encouraging high-parity families to produce even more children. Several such programs have had a disproportionate impact on high fertility, southern tier areas; and even those programs limited to employed mothers have had a disproportionate impact on low-income, non-professional women.

These contradictions between goals and means have not escaped

Soviet demographers; and a brisk debate on the most appropriate strategy to achieve "optimum population growth" has emerged in the demographic press. One group of demographers is sharply critical of programs focused exclusively on large families; these demographers favor a "differentiated" approach, that is, differentiated by parity, with resources devoted primarily to encouraging low-fertility women (who now constitute 80 per cent of the Soviet fertile-age populace) to continue childbearing after the first baby. This position – as articulated by one of its most forceful proponents, B.Ts. Urlanis (now deceased) – involves tailoring incentives to local conditions.[20] Urlanis, for example, suggested a partially paid maternal leave system in which working mothers in urban areas would receive 70 per cent of their salary while on leave to care for the infant, while working mothers in rural areas would receive only 50 per cent. Urlanis saw no need to stimulate the birth of the first baby, so he suggested linking maternal leave payments to the number of previous children – i.e., providing 40 per cent of salary for maternal leave for the first birth, 60 per cent of the salary for the leave following the second birth, and 80 per cent after the third. These suggestions would have a disproportionate impact on urban areas and on those regions with a high proportion of urban population.

Other demographers criticize this "differentiated" approach, primarily because they object to programs that would refocus resources away from high parity families (predominantly concentrated in the southern tier areas) and toward mothers with small families (who predominate in the European areas). Supporters of the high-parity focus of most Soviet population programs, such as Kazakh demographer Tatimov, note that all Soviet demographic policy is regionally differentiated within the broader framework of a unified policy:

In circumstances of such a large country as the USSR with its many-sided demographic characteristics, significant place must be made for a regional population policy, functioning only within the limits of a unified population policy and governed by its purposes.[21]

Tatimov freely acknowledges that policy to encourage migration to labor-poor areas is regional policy. But policy toward natality is "unified" in the sense that there is a single program which applies to all Soviet women, regardless of their region of residence or ethnicity.[22] Tatimov, and other supporters of the high-parity focus of Soviet population policy, are determined to keep it that way, and for good reason. The so-called "unified" policy has differential impact; and, as we shall see below, a disproportionate share of the program ruble goes to the southern tier area. Tatimov and other defenders of the "unified" policy frankly acknowledge the disproportionate benefits to high-parity (primarily southern tier) mothers, but defend the programs as necessary to the income levelling required by Soviet nationality policy. In other words, their defense of the programs is couched primarily in terms of the positive social welfare benefits provided, rather than impact on overall Soviet fertility.[23]

It should be emphasized that, although Soviet demographers generally present the major policy options in terms of a dichotomy – "differentiated" vs. "unified" – the real choice is between programs that favor the low-parity families throughout the USSR (the so-called "differentiated" approach) and those that favor high-parity families (the so-called "unified" approach). Both approaches, while "universal" in eligibility standards, are "differentiated" in their impact, with programs focused on the low-parity families having a greater impact on European regions and ethnic groups and those favoring high-parity families having a greater impact on southern tier regions and Muslim nationalities.[24]

Thus far the Soviet leadership has not resolved either the disagreement between demographers on the best population strategy or the basic conflict between the social welfare and the fertility goals of most Soviet policies affecting the birth rate. The latest modifications in the grab-bag of programs affecting policy were announced in 1981[25] and included in the "Basic Directions" for the 11th Five Year Plan (1981–85).[26] The dual goals of previous policy in this area are maintained. The primary goals of the new policy are (1) to enhance social welfare, (2) to promote population growth, and (3) to improve "upbringing."

The Communist Party and the Soviet state, consistently pursuing a course toward increasing the people's well being, pay great attention to creating the most favorable conditions for population growth and the rising generation's education.

Regarding assistance to families in educating children as an important avenue of the social program for our society's development, the CPSU Central Committee and the USSR Council of Ministers deemed it expedient to implement further measures to increase state assistance to families with children so as to ensure a rational combination of public and family education, alleviate the position of working mothers, and create favorable conditions for young families' life and living conditions.[27]

In other words, the conflicting goals of welfare and fertility increase were preserved.

What was added in the 1981 program was a series of one-time payments for first and second children (previously the child assistance payments had begun with the third child), but the graduated payments for higher-parity mothers were retained, as was the monthly allowance system which, as before, begins with the birth of the fourth child. Also added was a system of extended, part-paid leave for employed mothers. Unlike the 112 day pregnancy leave, however, which is paid at full salary, the extended leave payment is not geared to the mother's wage at all, but provides simply a flat 32 ruble per month payment until the child is a year old. This means that the incentive effect, if any, will be limited almost entirely to low-income women whose opportunity costs of staying home to care for their infant are much lower than those of higher-income mothers.

On the whole, then, the policies adopted in 1981 do not represent a major shift in demographic policy at all, but a continuation of the rather modest efforts to ease the financial plight of families with children (particularly low-income families) and the physical burden on the mother with a young infant. While the program mix specified in the resolution is basically a compromise between those who favored a refocusing of resources toward the medium-sized family and those who favored retaining the high-parity focus of previous population policy, the real victory seems to lie with the defenders of the status quo, the "unified" approach to fertility policy focused on high-parity families.[28] First of all, the basic child allowance and income assistance programs for low-income families were retained; both programs had been strongly supported by proponents of a unified policy for their role in helping to "level" out differences in living standards. Advocates of a "differentiated" policy – i.e., a policy focused on providing incentives for the second and third births – had urged that these programs be shifted to aid small and medium sized families; they had argued that the sharp drop in living standards that generally accompanies the birth of the first child must be attenuated by public assistance to the young family.

Nowhere in the mix of programs is there any mention of Urlanis' policy of focusing on second and third births and urban women. The only bow to those who had advocated a shift in resources to the mid-size family was the timing of implementation. The extended leave program was phased in gradually, beginning (in November

1981) with low-fertility Siberian areas and ending (in November 1983) with the higher-fertility southern tier areas. The program has now been implemented throughout the country.[29] This regional phase-in is not unique.[30] For example, the 1973 resolution, establishing sick-leave privileges for females with children under fourteen, was also phased-in in three stages, beginning with the far north.[31]

Proponents of the "differentiated" approach have continued to agitate for programs that would provide incentives to produce the ideal mid-size family, pointing to the dual rate system for maternity leave as precedent for the restructuring of the demographic policy they advocate.[32] They advocate a series of state-financed incentives for the second and third births, including a system of special salary raises for working parents.[33] Such demographers are calling for an increase in the length of both fully-paid maternity leave (from four to at least six months) and subsequent childcare leave (from one to at least two years), with a shift from flat allotments to payments geared to the woman's salary. Also advocated is a system that would institute monthly allowances for working women on childcare leave that would be highest for second and third births and would decrease with subsequent births. All of these proposals are targeted at low-parity, rather than high-parity families.[34]

The debate over demographic policy, then, is complicated by an increasingly clearcut conflict of regional interests. The willingness of officials like Tatimov to invoke the goals of nationality policy is a suggestion of the potential political problems of reorienting existing programs away from the high-fertility borderlands. The large proportion of children in the southern populace automatically lowers all per capita indicators of living standards, fueling arguments in favor of redistributive programs favoring these areas. Southern tier officials can buttress their requests for more of the social welfare ruble with references to the social and economic disparities in their provinces and the long-term Soviet promise to ameliorate these disparities in ways that officials from the European areas of the USSR cannot. Demographic policy in the Soviet Union thus remains hamstrung by the continuing effort to link it with both social welfare and the ideological commitment to equality.

The current mix of programs as modified by the latest changes, include: economic incentives (including those to ease the conflict between work and motherhood), socialization programs, and family planning programs. Much of the explicit discussion in the Soviet press has focused on the first factor. There is less overt discussion of the impact of socialization and family planning availability on the birth rate, but these factors are important, if less publicized, aspects of population policy.

Economic incentives

Most of the programs explicitly linked in the Soviet press with population policy are really social welfare programs.[35] There are two major family income supplement programs. The first is a series of one-time and monthly payments granted at the birth of a child and designed to partly offset the additional expenses occasioned by the birth. The program was originally adopted, with very modest payments, in 1936. In 1944, the program was revamped and payments increased; but a 1948 revision cut those payments in half. Nonetheless, the payment schedule represented at that time a rather substantial supplement to family income. Steady increases in average monthly wage, coupled with inflation, have steadily eroded the economic significance of the payments.[36] Moreover, the program was deliberately designed to meet the needs of large families, not to encourage mothers of small families to bear an additional child. One-time payments (of 20 rubles) were given for the third child. Mothers giving birth to the fourth were given both a one-time payment, followed by monthly payments until the child reached the age of five. Soviet demographers understandably raised questions about the effectiveness of this program as a stimulus to the birth rate; and some called for a revamping of the entire program to concentrate resources on lower-order births.[37] Demographers argued that the program provides virtually no incentive for the one and two child families to have that needed second or third child, and urged adoption of programs similar to those in Hungary and Bulgaria which provide maximum benefits for the second and third child, with decreased benefits for higher-parity children.[38] But other demographers vigorously defended the graduated system, arguing that it is meeting its major goal of ameliorating the strained economic circumstances of many large families.[39]

The compromise adopted at the 26th Party Congress and embodied in the 1981 decree was largely a victory for the defenders of the status quo. The graduated benefits for high-parity mothers were retained as before and an additional payment schedule for the first through third births was added.[40] For mothers who are employed or engaged in full-time study, payment for the first birth is 50 rubles, for the second and third births, 100 rubles. Non-working mothers receive a lump sum of 30 rubles each for the birth of the first, second, and third children.[41] One consolation to those who have been advocating policies which focus on the medium-sized family was the timing of implementation; like the part-paid leave (discussed below), the new birth payments were introduced in a three-stage process; and were extended to the high-fertility southern tier areas in 1983.

Under the new system, the schedule of one-time and monthly payments for fourth and higher order births was preserved as before, with no income criteria for participants. This portion of the program applies to both housewives and working mothers.[42] With the birth of a fourth child, the woman is given a one-time payment of 65 rubles and a monthly payment of 4 rubles beginning when the child reaches age one and extending to the child's fifth birthday. A mother giving birth to her fifth child receives 85 rubles and a monthly payment of 6 rubles. If her fourth child is still under five, she will continue to receive the 4 ruble a month payment for that child until the fifth birthday is reached.[43] Thus, the payments are additive and increase with the number of children previously born up to a ceiling of a one-time payment of 250 rubles and a monthly payment of 15 rubles for the eleventh and subsequent children.

This program is not tremendously expensive. In 1983, 544 million rubles (less than two-tenths of 1 per cent of the total budgetary expenditures for that year) were allocated for child allowance payments and for single mothers, another category of welfare recipients designated in the 1970 law.[44] In 1983, 1.9 million mothers received monthly income supplement payments for the fourth and higher-order children.[45] The role of these sums allocated in providing real economic incentive to have another baby is clearly limited. In 1983, the average monthly income of blue and white-collar class workers was 182 rubles.[46] Assuming that average female salaries are substantially lower, perhaps as low as 70 per cent of the overall average paycheck, the average Soviet women may make perhaps 127 rubles per month. The 4 ruble monthly allocation for the fourth child is only three per cent of the average female monthly wage. Moreover, the payments only make a very slight dent in the estimated costs of supporting a young child. Soviet demographers estimate that expenditures for a child up to the age of three or four were about 65 to 70

Table 5.1. *Distribution of expenditures for child allowance and assistance to single mothers (1980)*

Republic	Number of children under 5 (1,000s)	Rubles expended in programs (millions)	Children under 5 (%)	Total program ruble (%)
RSFSR	10604	67.1	45.4	21.6
Ukraine	3679	19.3	15.7	6.2
Belorussia	760	4.1	3.3	1.3
Uzbekistan	2503	87.4	10.7	28.1
Kazakhstan	1749	38.7	7.5	12.4
Georgia	460	2.5	2.0	0.8
Azerbaydzhan	742	20.2	3.2	6.5
Kithuania	259	1.9	1.1	0.6
Moldavia	395	3.6	1.7	1.2
Latvia	169	1.1	0.7	0.4
Kirgizia	520	16.1	2.2	5.2
Tadzhikistan	652	28.0	2.8	9.0
Armenia	334	2.8	1.4	0.9
Turkmenistan	449	17.5	1.9	5.6
Estonia	104	0.8	0.4	0.3
USSR	23379	311.1		

Sources: Data on the under-five population extracted from unpublished estimates and projections (medium estimates), dated March 1977, provided by the Foreign Demographic Analysis Division. Program expenditures compiled from *Gosudarstvennyyi byudzhet SSSR i byudzhety soyuznykh respublik 1976–80 gg. Statisticheskiy sbornik*. (Moscow: Finansy i Statistika, 1982), pp. 27, 78, 85, 92, 99, 106, 113, 120, 127, 134, 141, 148, 155, 162, 169, and 176.

rubles per month in the mid-1970s. Additional costs accumulate if the parents must take frequent sick leave at less than full-salary reimbursement.[47] If the primary cause of low fertility in European USSR is the employed mother who decides against having a second or third child because of the potential decline in living standards, this particular schedule of payments is clearly not going to change her mind.

It is only at the higher parities that such a program can have any fertility-stimulating effect. A woman with seven children, for example, receives 27 rubles per month if three children are under five. This 27 rubles may represent an appreciable enhancement to the family income and a substantial proportion of what this woman could make in the paid labor force, particularly if, as is the case for many such mothers, educational and occupational qualifications are low. For this family, the graduated child allowance payments may indeed provide some small incentive to have an additional child.

These considerations mean that the impact of the child allowance program has been limited primarily to high natality areas. This is demonstrated by 1980 data on the geographical distribution of recipients and of funding for the program. Data on expenditure associated with the child allowance program itself are not available. Soviet budgetary sources do, however, provide figures on aggregate expenditures for both the child allowance program and the welfare assistance program for single mothers.* These data are presented in Table 5.1 and are standardized to the number of children under five – the target groups for the child allowance program. Two-thirds (208 million rubles) of the expenditures for the two allowance programs go to Muslim republics, although only 28 per cent of the under-five population is located in this area. Tadzhikistan, Turkmenistan, and Uzbekistan, in particular, receive a disproportionately large share of program funds. Note that the data in this table probably understate the extent to which southern tier areas are affected by the child allowance program, since the funding includes welfare payments to single mothers. While data on the geographical distribution of single mothers is not available, it is quite likely that they are concentrated in European areas where marriage rates among fertile-age women are relatively low. If this is the case, the geographical distribution suggested by the funding data probably understates the extent to which program rubles are concentrated in the Muslim republics.

The geographical concentration of the child allowance program suggested by the funding data is confirmed by an examination of the geographical distribution of program recipients. Table 5.2 presents a breakdown of mothers receiving a monthly child allowance by republic. Nearly 70 per cent of the recipients were in the six Muslim republics; 84 per cent of the recipients receiving the more generous

---

*Soviet budgetary allocations for these two programs are budgeted exclusively through the republic budgets, making it possible to track geographic distribution of all expenditures included under the budget category "government grants to mothers with many children and single mothers." This category may not, however, include all funds allocated for these programs. Some funding, for example, is derived from the all-union collective farm social welfare fund; and it is not clear from Soviet budgetary sources in precisely which budgetary category these funds are included.

Table 5.2. *Regional distribution of recipients of monthly child allowances*
(1980)

Republic	% 0–5 year olds	% Recipients	% with four children	% with five children	% with six children	% with seven or more children
RSFSR	45.4	21.2	27.8	25.6	17.5	12.4
Ukraine	15.7	5.8	9.3	6.5	4.1	2.3
Belorussia	3.3	1.4	2.2	1.9	1.0	0.5
Uzbekistan	10.7	29.0	21.6	28.4	34.8	34.8
Kazakhstan	7.5	12.9	10.7	12.1	13.2	15.9
Georgia	2.0	1.5	2.5	1.5	1.0	0.5
Azerbaydzhan	3.2	7.5	6.8	7.0	7.8	8.4
Lithuania	1.1	0.7	1.1	0.7	0.5	0.3
Moldavia	1.7	1.3	1.8	1.4	1.1	0.8
Latvia	0.7	0.3	0.4	0.3	0.2	0.1
Kirgizia	2.2	5.0	3.7	4.1	5.0	7.0
Tadzhikistan	2.8	8.2	5.9	6.9	8.9	11.4
Armenia	1.4	n.a.	n.a.	n.a.	n.a.	n.a.
Turkmenistan	1.9	5.4	5.6	4.3	5.1	6.2
Estonia	0.4	0.2	0.3	0.2	0.1	0.1

Sources: Population data extracted from Table 5.1.
RSFSR: *NK RSFSR v 1980 g.* (Moscow: Finansy i Statistika, 1981), p. 256.
Ukraine: *NK Ukrainskoy SSR* (Kiev: Tekhnika, 1982), p. 284.
Belorussia: *NK Belorusskoy SSR v 1981 g.* (Minsk: Belarus, 1982), p. 162.
Uzbekistan: *NK Uzbekskoy SSR v 1981 g.* (Tashkent: Uzbekistan, 1982), p. 213.
Kazakhstan: *NK Kazakhstana v 1981 g.* (Alma Ata: Kazakhstan, 1982), p. 167.
Georgia: *NK Gruzinskoy SSR v 1980 godu* (Tbilisi: Sabchota Sakartvelo, 1981), p. 170.
Azerbaydzhan: *NK Azerbaydzhanskoy SSR za 60-letiyu obrazovaniya SSR* (Baku: Azerbaydzhanskoye Gosudarstvennoye Izdatel'stvo, 1982), p. 220.
Lithuania: *NK Litovskoy SSR v 1981 godu* (Vilnius: Mintis, 1982), p. 174.
Moldavia: *NK Moldavskoy SSR v 1981 g.* (Kishinev: Kartya Moldovenyaskie, 1982), p. 182.
Latvia: *NK Latviyskoy SSR v 1980 godu* (Riga: Avots, 1981), p. 264.
Kirgizia: *NK Kirgizskoy SSR* (Frunze: Kyrgyzstan, 1982), p. 184.
Tadzhikistan: *NK Tadzhikskoy SSR v 1980 g.* (Dushanbe: Irfon, 1982), p. 203.
Armenia: N.A.
Turkmenistan: *NK Turkmenskoy SSR v 1981 godu* (Ashkabad: Turkmenistana, 1983), p. 131.
Estonia: *NK Estonskoy SSR v 1979 godu* (Tallin: Eesti Raamat, 1980), p. 222. [1979 data].

payments provided to mothers of seven or more children lived in these regions. Two republics, Uzbekistan and Kazakhstan, alone (with only 18 per cent of the under-five target population in 1980) accounted for over 40 per cent of the total recipients and over half of those recipients received payments for seven or more children. Both sets of data, then, suggest that the impact of the child allowance program has been limited primarily to high-parity areas.

The child allowance system, even as modified in 1981, can hardly be expected to have a significant effect on natality. The monthly payment schedule (for fourth and higher order births) has not been increased since 1948; in the intervening years average salaries have increased substantially. The payments represent, then, a declining portion of average earnings; and, as such, their limited economic significance has lessened. Moreover, neither the one-time payment nor the monthly payment schedule make any adjustment for variable cost of living. Soviet pay schedules reflect rather substantial differences in cost of living by incorporating regional wage coefficients designed to adjust salary levels to real living costs. For example, workers in regions of the far north receive an additional 50 to 70 per cent wage differential.[48] Because the child assistance payments are provided on a flat scale for the entire country, the real economic impact of the payments is lowest in the high-cost areas.

The other major family income supplement program – aid to low-income families with children – was introduced in 1974. Although linked by Soviet demographers with Soviet population policy, the low income assistance program is primarily a social welfare measure. Its goals are: "to create better conditions for socialization of the younger generation and to increase material help to low-income families with children."[49] There are no complex schedules linking allowances and benefits with income. There is only one income ceiling – average total income per family member must be below 50 rubles per month.[50] Income calculations to determine eligibility are made on the basis of the previous year's income history. For example, a couple applying for assistance in 1976 must have an average per capita family income of less than 50 rubles per family member in 1975. In calculating family income, both wages (including bonuses) and other social welfare benefits (such as, student stipends and child allowances) are included. All dependent children under age 18 are included in the calculation of per capita family income, as well as parents and other nonworking family members living with the couple but not drawing a pension of their own. For those families that qualify, a flat payment of 12 rubles per month is provided for each child under the age of eight.[51] The Soviets apparently intend to expand the program in the 12th Five Year Plan (1986–90) by including children up to age twelve.[52]

One of the shortcomings of the income supplement program was the failure to adjust program standards to regional variations in living costs. This problem was partly addressed in 1984 with the introduction of a proviso raising the income ceiling to 75 rubles per month per family member for families in the far east and Siberia.[53] However, the new provision applies only to the income ceiling that determined eligibility for the program. It does not raise the payment schedule for these families.

This program represents a somewhat larger financial commitment than the child allowance program. In 1983, a total of one billion rubles were expended for family income assistance from all sources. Of this total, 740 million rubles were allocated through the state budget for social insurance. Allocations for the program have declined by about 17 per cent since the program was first introduced in the mid-1970s, as fewer families fall below the income floor.[54] This may be due to hidden inflation or to real increases in wellbeing, or (as is more likely) to a combination of both factors.

Like the child allowance program, the family assistance program is mainly geared for large families. Even relatively low-income families with only one child will find it difficult to qualify. As noted above, the average monthly salary in 1983 was 182 rubles; and average family income, given the prevalence of two-worker families, is significantly higher and is increasing steadily. In 1965, only 4 per cent of the population had an income of over 100 rubles per family member per month; by 1970 this share had increased to 18 per cent; and by 1983, about 60 per cent of the population had reached this income level.[55] These data suggest, then, that the poverty level of 50 rubles per family member per month (75 in the far east) is substantially lower than average income levels. Even for a one-worker family with one child, the employed family member would have to make less than 150 rubles per month to qualify. High-parity families, however, particularly those with only one worker employed are far more likely to meet income standards. Consider, for example, a family with five children in which the husband, a transport worker, makes 200 rubles per month, the wife, a teacher, makes 130 rubles per month, and the child allowance program provides an additional 17 rubles. This family of seven falls just under the income ceiling of 350 rubles for a seven-member family, even though both spouses have relatively good jobs. If all five of their children are under eight, they will receive an additional 60 rubles a month in assistance. The two income supplement programs together raise their monthly income by a hefty 23 per cent.

Clearly, then, the program standards are weighted not only toward low income families, but also toward large families, even those with a relatively prosperous total family income. It is not surprising to find a disproportionate share of program funds flowing into the high natality southern tier areas. In 1981, for example, 760 million rubles were allocated through state budget social insurance funds for the family assistance program; Uzbekistan, Kazakhstan, Turkmenistan, Tadzhikistan, and Azerbaydzhan, accounted for half. More than a quarter of these funds went to Uzbekistan alone.[56] More precise analysis of the geographical distribution of the low-income assistance program must await the publication of additional republic expenditures data for the program. Nonetheless, it seems fairly clear that this program, like the child allowance program, is disproportionately focused on high natality areas.[57] This is not surprising, given that the primary goal of the program is income assistance. To the extent that the family assistance program stimulates the birth rate at all, its impact is largely limited to high parity women in the southern tier areas. Since the major concern of Soviet demographers is to increase natality among the low fertility women of European USSR, one is hard pressed to give either income assistance program anything but very low marks as elements of population policy.

There are several other related measures either already implemented or promised which involve efforts to ease the financial strain of parenthood. The most important has to do with housing allocation. Soviet demographers have linked the unwillingness to have the second or third baby with housing shortages. Noting various provisions now in effect in East Europe, these commentators have called for preferential access of young families to both state and cooperative housing.[58] The January 1981 Central Committee decree unveiling the new mix of population/welfare programs did indeed include some movement in this direction. Young families are to be given preference in access to housing-construction cooperatives and some financial assistance in purchasing apartments in cooperative housing. Young couples with one child can get an interest-free home loan for home improvements or for making the initial payments to a housing construction cooperative, with portions of the loan forgiven if the couple have a second or third child.[59]

The 1981 decree did not, however, address the issue of preferential access to state and "social" housing (the latter category refers to residential buildings belonging to collective farms, trade unions, and other "social" organizations). The new basic legislation on housing, adopted in June 1981, gave scant attention to problems of preferential housing allocation to newlyweds and young families seeking accommodation in state and social housing. Deputy Council of Ministers Chairman Arkhipov, who formally introduced the measure, noted in passing that more should be done to ameliorate housing conditions of large families and newlyweds.[60] The legislation itself listed nine categories of citizens who were to enjoy preference in housing assignments; the list included families with twins, single mothers, large families (not further specified, but, given accepted Soviet usage, probably families with four or more children), and "heroine" mothers (mothers with ten or more children).[61] Again, this provision is a far cry from the preferential system urged by Litvinova and Urlanis. The priority list adopted by the new housing legislation benefits large families, while Litvinova and Urlanis had advocated measures targeted to aid the medium-sized family. Again, the probable motive in retaining the current focus on large families, as in all economic incentive measures, is social welfare. These families are most in need of benefits from a financial standpoint. The goal of maintaining a minimal floor on living standards, particularly for large families and single parents who undoubtedly are over-represented among the Soviet Union's poor, is apparently more pressing than the goal of achieving the demographic "optimum" – the medium sized family.

Easing the conflict between motherhood and employment

Most of the resources devoted to what may be roughly termed population policy involve a series of measures to lighten the physical and financial burden of the employed mother. As noted in Chapter 4, female labor force participations rates, even in the traditional southern tier areas, are extremely high by US standards. Implementation of more vigorous pronatalist measures, such as fully-paid, extended maternity leave (until the child is, for example, three or four years old), would conflict with both the pragmatic need for female labor and the ideological imperative, stressed by some of the moderate pronatalists, to support female equality. Nonetheless, the plight of the typical Soviet mother, faced with an additional four to six hours of housework and childcare after a regular working day, seems to have captured the attention of Soviet demographers; and many of the proposed and actual measures to stimulate the birth rate involve attempts to ease the work-motherhood conflict.

These programs include, first, a series of protective labor laws specifically targeted at pregnant women, nursing mothers,* and mothers with children under the age of one.[62] Employers are forbidden to fire or decrease the wages of such women, unless they can show that the action was unrelated to the pregnancy or nursing status. Pregnant women and new mothers are exempt from mandatory overtime and night work. They cannot be assigned to evening shifts that end later than ten in the evening, nor can they be sent on extended business trips. Women with children over one, but under eight, can be asked to work overtime or participate in business trips, but cannot be compelled to do so.

There are also provisions in the protective labor codes designed to deal with more direct health hazards. A pregnant woman may, on advice of her physician, demand transfer to lighter work for the duration of her pregnancy, without loss of pay. Nursing mothers and mothers with children under one who are not able to perform their normal jobs are transferred to more appropriate positions until the child reaches age one or they cease to breastfeed it. Women who remain at their original jobs are given less demanding work norms. Pregnant women are not allowed to work in areas where they are exposed to radiation or other health hazards. Specific industries have individual guidelines covering pregnant women involving limits on weight lifting, the temperature of the workplace, and so forth.[63]

Other provisions have been made to assist the working mother at the workplace. Nursing mothers and mothers with children under the age of one are provided with thirty-minute break periods every three hours to feed their infants. They are compensated for these breaks at a wage level equal to the average pay they received for the two months previous regular service. Additional periods of break time

---

*The protective benefits extend to women who continue to breastfeed their infant, even if the child has passed its first birthday.

can be provided for the mothers who must travel to a childcare center or home to feed their babies and for those whose babies require more frequent feedings. Mothers employed in positions not allowing them to take breaks are transferred to more appropriate jobs (at the same salary) for the duration of the nursing.

Some modest efforts have also been made to deal with one of the perennial problems of working parents – the need to stay home and care for sick children. Leave to care for a sick family member is provided on the same basis as other sick (temporary disability) leave.[64] Leave is provided to all workers regardless of work tenure but the size of the grant paid to cover the salary loss varies with work tenure and union membership, from 50 per cent of full salary for workers with an uninterrupted tenure of under three years to 100 per cent for those with eight or more years of uninterrupted service. The leave is granted to all family members living together in a household unit, not just to mothers. (There are, however, special provisions for single parents that apply only to single mothers.) For children up to age fourteen, the leave for a single episode of illness is seven calendar days (ten for single mothers); for children over fourteen, a three day limit is in effect. There are no limits on the number of episodes covered. Like all "temporary disabilities," granting of childcare leave requires a medical certificate of the child's illness.

The major shortcoming of the system is that many women with children most susceptible to frequent childhood illnesses are young women who have not yet earned eight years uninterrupted work tenure; taking repeated series of half-pay sick leave to care for a small child represents a real financial hardship for such women. To help deal with this problem, the Soviets adopted in 1975 a system that allows full salary sick leave (90 per cent for collective farmers) for family members with three or more dependent children under the age of sixteen.[65] (If the children are in school, the age cutoff is raised to eighteen.) This provision applies to all leave for "temporary disability," including incapacity caused by the need to stay home and care for a sick family member. There are also plans to extend the maximum number of sick days per episode to fourteen, with the additional seven days compensated at half pay. This provision was originally planned for implementation in the 11th Five Year Plan (1981–85).[66] It now appears to have been postponed to the 12th Five Year Plan (1986–90).[67]

Additional privileges and protection varies from republic to republic. In Lithuania and Tadzhikistan, for example, women with children under eight must be given preferential placement in day shifts. In Estonia, women with children under three are given preference in scheduling of annual leave during summer vacation.[68] The January 1981 population/welfare program included a promise to make the young mother's priority right to annual leave at a time convenient to her a nation-wide policy. The package also includes a provision, implemented in late 1981, for a more liberal annual leave policy for mothers with young children. Now, mothers with two or more children under twelve are provided three extra days of annual paid leave; they may also take an additional two-weeks leave without pay.[69]

Another important consideration for working mothers is the opportunity for part-time work, flexible working hours, and work within the home. The 1981 population/welfare program included a provision promising wide availability of such programs.[70] A limited number of workers, mostly women, are already employed within the home. In the RSFSR, for example, there were 200,000 home workers in local industry alone in the late 1970s.*[71] The RSFSR Ministry of Local Industry goal was to increase this number to 250,000 by 1985.[72] Many of these workers are concentrated within industries, such as the textile industry and electronic industry, where certain operations appear to be particularly suited for home workers. Home work, however, is still a tiny proportion of total labor. The limited opportunities in this area stem in part from the difficulty of regulating labor conditions and in part from the meager incentives to encourage industrial managers to make the necessary arrangements for such programs. Moreover, Soviet economists fear that expanded opportunities for home work, intended primarily to bring nonworking women into the labor force, might result in some women now employed in the plant or office streaming back into the home as home laborers.[73] Such a development may not be positive from a purely economic standpoint, but it would surely help ease the burden of the working mother. The fact that expanded opportunities for home work were included within a program designed to help the working mother

---

*The term "local industry" (*mestney promyshlennost'*) is frequently encountered in the Soviet press. It does not refer to a particular branch of industry but to the administrative status of the enterprises involved. Local industry includes only those facilities that are administered by the republic level Ministries of Local Industry; factories within this system produce a wide variety of products: textiles, chemicals, construction materials, school supplies, and so on.

suggests that the Soviet leadership may now be willing to sacrifice the economic goal of maintaining high full-time, on-the-job employment for the humanitarian one of assisting the working mother combine labor with motherhood.

Another plank in the 1981 population/welfare program was increased flexibility in working hours. As noted above, one of the advantages of work as a collective farmer for women with children lies in the flexibility and variability of working hours. The full-time, non-collective farm worker has no such options and at present, opportunities for part-time work in the non-collective farm labor force in the USSR are very limited. In 1973, some 170,000 workers in the RSFSR – less than one-half of one per cent of the state labor force – were employed on a part-time basis.[74] Efforts over the past decade to widen part-time opportunities have probably increased that figure to some extent, but a labor economist writing in 1978 indicated that only 0.41 per cent of the total USSR labor force was employed on a part-time basis "at the present time," suggesting that the improvement, if any, has been relatively small.[75] In 1980, a new statute on part-time work for women with children was introduced.[76] Its provisions were designed to make part-time work more attractive to mothers. The woman negotiates an agreement with the enterprise administrator to set up a part-time schedule. The woman can work standard workdays with a shorter workweek or a standard work week but shorter days. Under the new measure, the minimum workday is generally four hours and the minimum workweek is generally twenty to twenty-four hours with five or six workdays. Part-time workers employed under this statute receive annual leave, regular breaks for feeding their infants, and other labor privileges. Part-time work is included in computation of work longevity and the woman's labor book contains no notation that a particular period of work was part-time.

The statute was a start in the right direction, but the real problem with part-time work is availability. At the present time, most of the opportunities for part-time work are in limited industrial and service occupations, such as morning and evening mail delivery and sales jobs. Studies in the European regions of the USSR have shown that many working mothers would prefer part-time employment while their children are young. One study of Latvian women, for example, found that 40 per cent of the women with higher education preferred returning to work on a part-time basis after the child was a year old.[77] Such women, however, still have virtually no opportunity to switch to part-time work within their own occupational speciality. This is particularly hard on the professional woman; offering a chemist or engineer the opportunity to work part-time as a mail carrier is not the same as allowing her to continue in her regular position, but working reduced hours. Employers, moreover, have resisted the expansion of part-time employment in part because they fear that many women working full-time would switch to part-time work.[78] Their resistance underlines the real demand for part-time work among Soviet women.

A 1977 survey of both full and part-time employees in ten republics found that 76.1 per cent of the women now working full-time would prefer a part-time schedule; most favored a six or seven hour workday and were motivated by the presence of small children in the home.[79] The study also revealed that 46 per cent of the part-time workers had not been employed at all prior to their part-time employment and 54 per cent had previously worked full-time.[80] These findings suggest that expanded part-time opportunities may result in some net loss to the labor force. Nonetheless, economists who favor expansion of part-time opportunities point to substantial benefits in improved labor productivity for part-timers.[81] It remains to be seen how vigorously Soviet officials will pursue their promise to achieve this expansion in the face of management resistance and the possibility of a substantial short-term decrease in the labor force as full-time women move into part-time work while their children are young.

One of the most important in the Soviet mix of programs to ease the workplace/motherhood conflict is the provision of maternity leave, generous by US standards, but quite modest compared to some of the more liberal East European programs.[82] The past decade has, however, seen some modest efforts to improve benefits. Pre-birth maternity leave was extended from five to eight weeks in 1956. Until 1973, however, the amount of salary provided during the leave depended on duration or overall and uninterrupted work status, trade union membership, and age; the program provided from two-thirds to full pay for the leave period. In 1 December 1973, the provisions became more generous. Currently all working women (including *kolkhozniks*) regardless of work tenure are allowed maternity leave of 112 calendar days – two months before and two months after the birth with full salary. Women are paid at rates equal to their previous salary.[83] An additional two weeks is provided for difficult birth and twins; and the woman may tack her yearly allotment of annual leave onto the end of the maternity leave to postpone return to work for an additional month.[84] Salaries for the maternity leave programs are provided from social insurance funds. The four month period is credited to the women as uninterrupted employment, an important factor, since pension rights and other social welfare benefits are often linked to employment duration.

While Soviet labor law does provide several provisions (enumerated above) to ease the burden of trying to combine employment with the upbringing of a small infant, the most difficult and demanding time for working mothers is often the first year or two of the child's life. Soviet demographers have urged that maternity leave be extended along lines similar to those provided by the more generous East European programs.[85] Most East European countries provide paid maternity leave of four to six months. Several have supplemented this with a childcare allowance, enabling the mother to rear her child at home until it is one to three years old. Hungary, for example, provides a supplementary leave program (with payments keyed to parity, not mother's salary) that extends until the child is three.[86] Czechoslovakia's program covers the first two years.[87] Bulgaria keys the duration of its supplemental leave program to parity: mothers of first children get six months; of second, seven months; of third, eight months; and of four or more, six months.[88] The German Democratic Republic introduced a program in 1976 that extended paid maternity leave to twenty-six weeks of full salary for mothers of more than one child. This is followed by a part-paid leave (65 to 90 per cent of salary) until the child is at least a year old.[89]

The strong pronatalists among Soviet demographers have long espoused such extended leave systems for Soviet women. Urlanis, as noted above, proposed a system tying the payment during extended leave to birth order, with women giving birth for the second and third time receiving 70 and 80 per cent of their regular salaries respectively.[90] Most of the European systems provide flat rates regardless of the woman's regular salary, and of course such payment schedules provide more incentive to lower-income women. Urlanis' advocation of payments linked to wages was obviously a way to provide equal levels of incentives regardless of the woman's occupational level.

In response to the demand for longer maternity leave, the Soviet leadership included as part of its January 1981 package of population/welfare programs, a plan to phase in part-paid maternity leave. The leave program, which was introduced in three stages beginning with the northern regions in 1981 and ending with the southern tier in 1983, covers the period after the four-month maternity leave is completed to the child's first birthday. Until that time, women who wished to stay home with their baby after the four-month paid leave had to go on leave without pay. This preserved their jobs, but left them in financial difficulties. The new payment schedule, however, consists of a flat monthly allowance of 35 rubles (50 rubles for the Siberian and far north areas). The higher rates for the Siberian areas are clearly an attempt to adjust for the higher living costs in these areas; but, given current wage rate coefficients, the differential is not large enough to cover the higher living costs in these areas. Still, the dual rate system is a start, at least, in the direction of adjusting for variable regional living costs. All working mothers (including collective farmers) with at least one year's job seniority are covered by the program.[91] Part-time as well as full-time workers are eligible for the payment and are allocated the same flat rate as full-time workers.

The sums provided in lieu of wages cover only a fairly small portion of the lost wage. With a current minimum wage of 80 rubles and an average wage of 177 rubles, a 35 ruble per month stipend scarcely compensates most young mothers for the loss of her regular wage. The payment covers less than half of the estimated costs of providing for a young infant. Thus the payment must be seen primarily as an attempt to ameliorate the frequently onerous financial burdens of parenthood, rather than to obliterate entirely the financial burdens of raising a young child.

How will the new part-paid leave system affect the Soviet birth rate? Full analysis must wait until the program has had several years to work throughout the USSR and until data on program users are available. Nonetheless, some suggestion of the natality effect of the program can be gleaned from the early Hungarian experience.[92] The Hungarian system provides a far lengthier leave opportunity and far more generous payments than the new Soviet system. The Hungarians introduced their system in 1967 as a supplement to the twenty-week postnatal maternity leave. The 1967 measure introduced a 600 forint per month leave payment (which has since been raised to 910 forints per month for the first child) for working mothers who wished to stay home and care for their babies. The allowance is granted until the child is three. The system achieved almost instant popularity. In 1969, two-thirds of the eligible women were participating. But use of the program, as revealed by a study undertaken several years after it began, varied by social class. Three-fourths of the blue-collar mothers chose to remain home and collect the leave allowance. Only 58 per cent of the white-collar mothers took advantage of the program. Similar patterns emerged in an analysis of program users by educational level; 62–73 per cent of those mothers with primary education chose the extended leave program, compared to only 30 per cent of the university graduates. Income, too, was closely associated with program use; lower-income women were more frequent users of the leave program than were their middle and upper income counterparts. Drop out rates (the proportion of women who returned to full-time work before the child's third birthday) were twice as high for women in intellectual occupations. Although the proportion of women making use of the program had increased substantially by 1973, the occupational and educational differences remained; 73 per cent of the eligible women employed in mental labor used the program, compared to 83 per cent of their counterparts in physical labor. Among women with college degrees, 56 per cent took advantage of the leave program, compared to 85 per cent of women with elementary education and 67 per cent of those with secondary education.

Hungarian demographers interpreted these findings in terms of the opportunity costs – both economic and social – of remaining at home versus returning to the workplace. For manual workers and clerical employees, the two to three year work interruption is not seen as a break in the career; the sums paid by the allowance program covered at least half of the wages these women would have received had they returned to work immediately after their twenty-week maternity leave. Professional women, by contrast, not only take a larger pay cut, they also perceived the lengthy absence from the workplace as a barrier to career advancement. It is interesting to note that fertility increases after the program was introduced were fairly modest. Hungary's birth rate climbed by 8 per cent in 1967, by 4 per cent in 1968, and remained stable in 1970. Hungarian demographers generously attribute these increases to the impact of the program. Even if this assumption is a valid one, the program produced only a relatively modest net increase. Moreover, the increase came mostly from increased fertility among lower-status, manual workers. Further expansion of pronatalist measures, undertaken in 1973, produced a temporary upsurge in fertility (total fertility increased 22 per cent, from 1.95 in 1973 to 2.38 in 1975), followed by a sharp decline. Hungary's total fertility rate decreased to 1.92 in 1980, a 19 per cent decline. Hungarian officials now concede that the net long term effect of their ambitious pronatalist policies has been primarily that of improving the living conditions of affected families, with relatively limited impact on fertility.[93]

Similar patterns of differential use of the part-paid leave program are evident in Czechoslovakia. A 1975 study found that women with higher education returned to work sooner. Eighty-one per cent of eligible women with elementary education, 76 per cent of those with secondary, and 63 per cent of those with higher chose to take the full two years of the part-paid leave. Use of the program was also related to salaries; those women with the highest salaries made less use of the program.[94]

These findings have direct relevance for the Soviet case. The new part-paid leave will almost surely ease the financial situation of those mothers who would have taken a ten-month unpaid leave. Some mothers whose financial situation would have forced them into an early return to work will now be able to remain at home to care for their babies. But it is questionable whether the modest 35 rubles per month payment will, in and of itself, convince many women to have an additional child. To the extent that it does, the greatest impact will be on low-income and part-time workers who have less to lose, financially and socially, from a lengthy absence from work. To the extent that many women who fulfill these qualifications are older, high-parity, rural women from the southern tier area, the natality impact will again be concentrated in these areas, where the program may moderate the fertility declines now underway.

The new part-paid leave program, then, does not get very high marks from the standpoint of a natality-stimulation program. We should remember, however, that population growth is not the only goal, and probably not the major goal, of this measure. The two other stated goals of the program mix embodied in the January 1981 decree are to improve social welfare and to improve conditions surrounding the upbringing of young children. In terms of these two goals, the program is almost sure to be a success.

Maternity leave, however, covers only a small portion of the young child's life. Soviet children do not enter school until age seven (age six under the 1984 educational reform program), and between the end of the maternity leave and the beginning of primary school, the working Soviet mother must find a source of childcare. In many Soviet families, particularly those in urban areas where relatives are not available to mind the children, the mother remains at home with the child until it is a year old. A Ukrainian study found that 80 per cent of the children under one from white-collar families and 70 per cent of those from blue-collar families were cared for in the home.[95] A study of urban families in Latvia found that for 77 per cent of those surveyed, infants under the age of one were cared for by the mother at home. (Both studies were conducted in 1978–79, prior to the part-paid leave program; and the proportion of mothers remaining at home with their infants has almost surely increased since this program was instituted.) In the Latvian study, a fifth of the families surveyed relied on nannies to care for their infant while the parents were at work. Only 3 per cent placed their babies in childcare facilities.[96]

Once the child reaches his first birthday, many mothers return to work. In the Latvian study cited above, only 11 per cent of the children aged one to three and 3 per cent of those aged three to school age were cared for by the mother at home. The remaining mothers had returned to the labor force and had to find an alternate source of childcare. Childcare for working mothers, in the USSR as in other industrialized societies, can take several forms. Care can be provided within the family itself, by other adults in the household, older children, or the father. The child may be cared for by a paid nanny, either inside or outside the household. Another alternative is communal day care. In the Latvian study cited above, about half of the one to two-year-olds and nearly three-quarters of the older pre-schoolers were cared for in childcare facilities.[97] Care by a nanny or an arrangement in which both parents traded off childcare duties made up the balance.[98] In the Ukrainian study, 50 per cent of the children aged one to two are cared for in group care facilities. At age three to four, the proportion rises to 80 per cent of the children of white-collar employees and 60 per cent of those of workers. The analogous percentages for five to six-year-old children were 91 and 83.[99]

Communal childcare facilities, then, represent a primary source of childcare for pre-schoolers over the age of one. Provision of a large, state-subsidized childcare system for working mothers involves a substantial financial commitment by the Soviet leadership. In 1983, the system included a year-round pre-school program covering 15.5 million pre-school children. For children under three, there are over 10,000 creches or nurseries (*detskiy yasli*) with an enrollment of

Table 5.3. *Enrollment in Soviet day care centers, 1965–85*

Year	Number of children enrolled in year-round pre-school facilities[a] (1,000s)	Estimated number of children aged two months through age six[b] (1,000s)	% coverage
1965	7,673	33,002	23.3
1970	9,281	28,351	32.7
1975	11,523	29,045	39.7
1976	12,108	29,564	41.0
1977	12,672	30,103	42.1
1978	13,177	30,602	43.1
1979	13,778	31,179	44.2
1980	14,339	31,868	45.0
1981	14,755	32,485	45.4
1982	15,093	33,110	45.6
1985[c] (planned)	17,580	34,494	51.0

[a] Enrollment data provided for the end of the year, in *Narodnoye khozyaystvo v 1980 g.*, p. 409; and *NK v 1982 g.*, p. 415.
[b] Age data refers to 1 January of the following year and was computed based on the medium estimates of the Foreign Demographic Analysis Division, US Bureau of Census (March 1977). Infants to the age of two months were calculated as 0.1666 of the estimated number of infants under age one.
[c] Computed from *Ekonomicheskaya Gazeta*, No. 48, November 1981, p. 3.

756,000 children. Children from the age of three to entry into primary school are accommodated in 31,000 kindergartens, with a total enrollment of 2.2 million youngsters. A third type of facility, combined creche–kindergartens, constitutes the majority of pre-school institutions. These combination facilities accommodate nearly 13 million pre-school children.[100]

While these figures seem rather impressive, the actual proportion of pre-school children covered by the year-round institutions is surprisingly low, given the high female labor force participation rates. Table 5.3 provides estimates of coverage from 1965 to 1985, based on Foreign Demographic Analysis Division age projections for the relevant years. Also provided are projected growth rates based on the 11th Five Year Plan. Between 1965 and 1982, the proportion of pre-school youngsters enrolled in year-round childcare facilities doubled, from 23 per cent in 1965 to 45 per cent in 1982. If the Soviets are able to meet their planned goals for expansion of the pre-school program, about 51 per cent of the eligible population will be provided for in 1985. As a point of comparison, in 1958, 5 per cent of the US children under six of mothers working full-time were cared for in a group care center. This percentage increased to 15 by 1977. Care in the child's home and care in another home (either by relatives or nonrelatives) plays a far more important role in childcare arrangements in the US than the USSR.[101]

In spite of the increasing proportion of youngsters enrolled in year-round facilities in the USSR, the demand far outstrips the supply.[102] The availability of childcare varies substantially by the age of the child. In 1977, the latest year for which age breakdowns of pre-school pupils has been published, an estimated 52 per cent of the three to six-year-olds, but only 29 per cent of the children under three, were enrolled in public childcare. Waiting lists for available places are lengthy.[103] Demand for Soviet public childcare, then, continues to outpace supply, in spite of real Soviet efforts to expand the network. There were also large differences in availability of childcare in cities as opposed to the countryside. Soviet officials estimate that 77 per cent of the urban children, compared to only 23 per cent of the rural children, were enrolled in childcare centers.[104]

Regional variations in enrollment are also striking (Table 5.4). The highest coverage is in European areas, the lowest in the southern tier. This is partly due to lower demand in the southern republics. The level of female participation in the paid labor force is lower, with many high-parity women remaining home to care for their larger families and work the private plot.[105] Moreover, as noted in Chapter 4, the proportion of extended families is significantly higher; and a larger proportion of the mothers who are in the labor force can depend on relatives (i.e., parents and older children) to help with childcare during working hours.

Year-round facilities, however, are not the only available institutionalized childcare. There are also seasonal pre-schools that serve (1983) an estimated one million children.[106] For families with school age children, there is a network of extracurricular educational and recreational programs, as well as summer camp.[107] These activities served 43.9 million children in 1983, including 13.4 million visitors to summer Pioneer camps, which provide recreational programs during summer holidays.[108]

Most important of the part-time childcare facilities are the pro-

Table 5.4. *Regional variation in day care enrollment*

	1970			1980		
	Number of children	Number enrolled	% coverage	Number of children	Number enrolled	% coverage
RSFSR	12,878	5,666	44.0	14,453	8,148	56.4
Ukraine	4,777	1,574	33.0	5,025	2,444	48.6
Belorussia	1,022	274	26.8	1,040	488	46.9
Uzbekistan	2,594	348	13.4	3,407	915	26.9
Kazakhstan	2,114	564	26.7	2,384	877	36.8
Georgia	604	116	19.2	629	169	26.9
Azerbaydzhan	1,029	111	10.8	1,013	147	14.5
Lithuania	370	80	21.6	355	152	42.8
Moldavia	409	91	22.3	537	266	49.5
Latvia	223	72	32.2	232	114	49.1
Kirgizia	571	90	15.8	709	151	21.3
Tadzhikistan	682	68	10.0	884	109	12.3
Armenia	402	90	22.4	456	135	29.6
Turkmenistan	479	78	16.3	611	138	22.6
Estonia	135	59	43.9	143	86	60.4

Notes: Number of children aged two months through six years in thousands. Data refers to 1 January of the following year and was computed based on the medium estimates of the Foreign Demographic Analysis Division projections, dated March 1977. Infants to the age of two months were calculated as 0.1666 of the estimated number of infants under age one. Enrollment data are for the end of the year. See *NK SSSR v 1980 g.*, p. 410.

longed day schools that provide supervised educational and recreational programs for the period after school is dismissed but before the parents return home from work. Begun as a limited experiment in the mid-1950s, the program was endorsed by the leadership in a 1960 joint Central Committee/Council of Ministers resolution.[109] It has expanded rapidly in the last decade. In the 1970–71 school year, only 13 per cent of the first to eight graders participated; by the 1983–84 school year there were 12.4 million pupils enrolled in prolonged day programs; one in every three children in the first eight grades attends such a program.[110] The 11th Five Year Plan includes a targeted 28 per cent increase in the number of pupils covered by the program by 1985.[111] These programs are particularly important for very young schoolchildren whose classes may end long before the parents return home. Participation is apparently highest for the young age groups. In Moscow, for example, nearly half of the first to third graders were enrolled during the 1978–79 school year, compared to a third of all the pupils in grades one to eight.[112] The programs include scheduled periods to complete homework assignments, plus time for supervised recreation and hobbies.[113]

While most of these programs are not free, they are heavily subsidized. The fee is waived entirely for children from families with a monthly income of less than 60 rubles per person. Higher-income families pay according to a sliding scale based on income.[114] Parents currently pay only about 20 per cent of the costs of maintaining a child in a pre-school institution with the state absorbing the balance.[115] While total costs to the state are not known, budgetary expenditures for maintenance of children in pre-school facilities, summer camps, and after school activities (not counting capital investment costs) was 7.5 million rubles in 1981, compared to less than 3 million rubles for the maternity leave, nursing breaks, child allowances, and low-income family supplements combined.[116]

The most recent innovation is the plan to integrate six-year-olds into the regular school system. The five-year plan directives for 1981–85 called for progress "to create the basis for the gradual transition to the teaching of six-year-olds in preparatory classes of general education schools."[117] Experimental classes in both preschool institutions and within the school system began over a decade ago.[118] These experimental groups were gradually expanded and modified. In Estonia, for example, school officials found that the program for six-year-olds had to coincide with the parent's workday, so children were kept in school until their parents could pick them up at five or six o'clock in the evening.[119] Plans announced in early 1982 by the Belorussian Education Ministry involved ambitious goals. By 1985, the Belorussians hoped to enroll 70 per cent of their six-year-olds in the new preparatory classes, with the remainder being covered by preparatory work of some kind in nursery school.[120]

The integration of six-year-olds into the regular school system was endorsed as a nation-wide goal in the "Basic Directions" for the reform of the educational system, approved at the April 1984 Central Committee Plenum and Supreme Soviet meetings. The school reform, which was implemented through a series of Council of Ministers and joint CC/Council of Ministers resolutions, will be phased in gradually between now and 1990.[121] Full implementation of that portion of the program affecting six-year-olds will mean that Soviet families will have one year less to worry about finding child care for their pre-schoolers.

None of the policies discussed here involve a serious, sustained effort to ameliorate what is probably one of the most important factors contributing to the work/family conflict: the low priority accorded to consumer goods and services in Soviet economic policy. The absence of household goods like automatic washers and other labor-saving devices means that domestic responsibilities – cleaning, cooking, and laundry – consume enormous amounts of time. Soviet sources estimate that about one-third of the nonworking time of the workforce is spent on housework. One study found that the average wife spent nearly four hours per weekday and nearly seven hours on nonwork days on household chores.[122] Meal preparation in particular is extremely time consuming. One Ukrainian study found that the average family spent two to two and a half hours per day preparing meals.[123] Perennial shortages of food and consumer items means that shopping (for many Soviet women a daily necessity) involves standing in an endless series of queues.[124] In the Ukrainian study, the typical wife spent about an hour on food shopping alone.[125] The burden of these tasks, which falls largely on women, increases with the number of children in the family.[126] Remedies to these problems would entail major shifts in priorities that the Soviet leadership has been unwilling to make.

This review of Soviet policies relating to employed mothers suggests that conflict between family and employment responsibilities, despite Soviet policies designed to ease it, remains a source of anguish for many Soviet working mothers and that such conflicts undoubtedly play some role in the decision not to have a second or third child. Nonetheless, the long-term commitment to female labor force participation has meant that both school and employer have been forced to assume some of the responsibility for easing the employment/family conflict. Maternity leave has been liberalized and the need to care for sick children has been incorporated into rules governing regular sick leave. The educational hierarchy – through the prolonged day program – has been assigned a major role in the supervision of children after school hours. The rapid expansion of this program in the 1970s suggests that the educational system is seen as a caretaker, not just an educator, of Soviet children. The expansion and extension of some of these programs during the 1980s may well help stabilize the birth rate in the European areas of the USSR.

Socialization for motherhood

A growing body of Western research attests to the role of socialization in producing young women who define themselves primarily as mothers.[127] It comes as no surprise that strikingly similar strategies are used in the Soviet Union. Rosenhan's analysis of the content of four Soviet children's readers provides persuasive evidence of how the formal education process is used to underline the importance of mothering.[128] Like many Western readers (at least until the 1970s when increased awareness of sexual and racial stereotyping in school textbooks produced substantial revisions), Soviet readers have fewer female than male characters; and males are presented in a much broader range of occupations. Unlike most traditional American texts, however, which present few working mothers, adult women in Soviet textbooks are usually employed outside the home. Nonetheless, the young Soviet reader is provided with few details of the woman's work role. The emphasis is on her mothering role. Rosenhan's count revealed that 41 per cent of the actions associated with female characters (compared with 5 per cent of those associated with male characters) involved the traditional woman's role: child care, housework, and nurturance.

O'Dell came to similar conclusions from an analysis of Soviet children's literature that included both readers and the children's periodical press; Soviet readers may differ from Western readers in the extent to which males and females share instrumental roles (i.e., wage earning), but the expressive function (i.e., childcare and nurturance) is still monopolized almost exclusively by female characters and the idealization of motherhood is a strong theme in children's literature.[129] By presenting the mother–job pattern as the norm, with the mother role as the primary identity, Soviet socializers are encouraging young Soviet girls to define their adult lives in terms of a dual mother–worker role.[130] The ideal Soviet woman is expected to hold a job, but also – and more important – to be a good mother.

Soviet attitudinal surveys reveal that few Soviet women reject the motherhood role entirely. Studies of ideal and desired number of children have repeatedly found only a very low proportion (well under 5 per cent) who do not wish to have any children at all.[131] So, whether this value is a result of formal socialization at school or informal socialization by family and peers, the Soviet woman seems to have accepted the dual role.

What worries Soviet demographers is that neither the formal nor the informal socialization systems have produced a strong desire for the ideal "three"-child family in the modernized areas. Soviet women from European USSR want the experience of motherhood, but most are unwilling to have more than one or two children. So, together with economic incentives, Soviet demographers urge stepped up socialization efforts to promote the "mid-size" family of two or preferably three children.

There has already been some movement in this direction. The Soviet popular press is replete with reminders that marriage is the desired state and that young couples should begin a family early. Couples who postpone parenthood are criticized as selfish consumerists, ignoring their duty to society. Most of these warnings are directed at the woman, who is told that true happiness resides in mothering:

Some people decide to postpone the birth of a child for an indefinite period of time; first, they say, we have to live a little "for ourselves." And such women do not understand that, in fact, they are living "against themselves," since the joys of marriage, as a rule, begin to be experienced only after a woman has become a mother.[132]

Professional women worried about combining a career with mothering are advised that even the most fulfilling career is no substitute for a family of two or three children: "one child is not enough. It is not enough from the standpoint of population reproduction and it is not enough for the creation of a normal and real family, for the full enjoyment of the joys of motherhood."[133] Because Soviet demographers realize that there are not enough marriageable men to go around (particularly for those women who are "not too sociable"), unmarried women as well are urged to have babies. Pronatalist Urlanis voiced special concern with convincing pregnant unmarried women not to have abortions: "She should know that motherhood sometimes brings more joy (or, in any case, no less) than marriage, especially if the marriage is not accompanied by love and respect."[134] Soviet discussions on family size in the popular press contain dire warnings of the potential problems of the only child. The only child, it is said, becomes the center of the family, frequently growing spoiled and egotistical, and turning into a family "despot."[135] It is showered with too much attention and material objects when what she/he really needs is a little brother or sister:

parents of single children have more anxiety and trouble than those of two or three. Mothers with one child are generally too suspicious and nervous and are not able to perceive motherhood as the joy it should be. Naturally, all the attention centers on the only child. He is too protected, they are afraid to harden him; this constant surveillance deprives him of self-reliance by creating greenhouse conditions for him. As a result, the resistance suffers. Only children, accustomed to being the center of everyone's concern, often develop egoistic character traits ... In an effort to ensure the physical and psychological well-being of the child and his future, one must strive to ensure that he will not be an only child![136]

Young women are warned that rejection of childbirth is bad for their physical and mental health. Bearing a child, they are told, will make them prettier and healthier. The optimal number of children, from a health standpoint, is said to be two or three, with birth intervals of three to four years:

It is no accident that after childbirth, many functional disorders and neurosis previously distressing to the woman disappear, she feels better, and her endurance increases. After childbirth a woman generally is prettier, stronger, and more gentle in nature. In other words, childbirth has a vivifying, rejuvenating effect.[137]

The medium-sized family, then, is presented as the ideal from both the standpoint of the parents and the child: "And so, Papa, Mama and three kids – that's the ideal pattern."[138]

Pronatalist demographers urge that more systematic efforts be made to promote the joys of parenthood in the educational establishment and mass communications.[139] Valentey and Kvasha urge incorporation of "marriage and the family" courses in the school

system to prepare youngsters for family life.[140] The 1981 population/
welfare program did indeed include a vague promise to

increase the publication of literature on questions of demography, the family,
marital hygiene, child raising; on improving the population's health; on
organizing their proper relaxation and leisure; and on increasing educational
work with the aim of consolidating the family as one of the supreme moral
assets of socialist society.[141]

In 1981, the Ministry of Education introduced (on an experimental
basis) a required course on hygiene and sex education for eighth-
graders and another on the ethics of family life in the ninth and
tenth grades. The goals of the latter program are:

The formation in boys and girls of the demand to create a family and have
children, the formation of readiness to marry and socialize their own future
children; and the creation of an irreconcilable relationship to bourgeois
conceptions of the family, theories of "free love," and other immoral aims.[142]

In Estonian high schools, an elective course called "Preparation for
Family Life" has been introduced in the senior classes; the course
includes lectures and a planned practical exercise in which students
learn to manage household finances and care for small children.[143] In
the early 1980s, the Moscow school system introduced a similar
course that included a section on the problems of the single-child
family and the need for each couple to have two or three children in
order to create a normal family life.[144] In June 1983, the Ministry of
Education adopted a time-table for introducing the "Ethics and
Family Life" course. The schedule called for development of teaching
materials in 1983, the expansion of experimental courses in 1984, and
the nation-wide introduction of the course in the 1984–85 school
year.[145] The family life course, however, is still in an evolutionary
stage. The course content is still under development, and it is not yet
clear how strong a case the course material makes for the ideal
"mid-size" family.

   In sum, Soviet socialization efforts to promote the mid-size family
thus far fall far short of the goals advocated by pronatalist demographers. What is needed, of course, is not just one "family life" course
in the middle-teens, but the incorporation of values embodying not
just motherhood in general, but the "ideal three children" family into
the entire school curriculum, in the same way "military–patriotic"
virtues are stressed in readers and textbooks beginning with the
primary grades. The very modest Soviet socialization effort is

unlikely to produce significant change in the family size aspirations of its youth.

Family planning availability

Another key factor in public policy toward fertility is the extent to which the state encourages or inhibits access to modern family planning techniques. Much of the debate over fertility programs and their effectiveness in the West stems from disagreement over how important the technology of fertility control is to fertility dynamics. Assessing Soviet policy in this area is difficult because top Soviet officials have not made the sort of public statements of policy preferences associated with other aspects of demographic policy. Nonetheless, there are indications that Soviet officials, at least those charged with implementing policy in this area, are not in complete agreement about how available family planning technology ought to be in a period of low natality.

Another difficulty is the absence of data that would provide insight into the actual availability of various types of family planning technology in the USSR. The Soviets have not, to our knowledge, published nationwide data on use/non-use of family planning methods; and the regional surveys that have been published cannot validly be generalized (for reasons similar to those noted with regard to the abortion data). Assessing the availability of contraceptive devices is difficult because many are presumably distributed through the medical hierarchy; other devices are sold through the retail pharmacies, but no data are available here either.

Trends in official policy toward one aspect of family planning – abortion – are easier to track since abortion policy is embodied in public legislation. Abortion was first made legal in the USSR by an 18 November 1920 decree. The purpose of the measure was to minimize health hazards of abortion; the legalization of abortion, then, was not a population measure per se, but a social welfare measure.[146] In 1936, abortion was again made illegal. The measure was accompanied by the introduction of family allowances and promises to expand the childcare network. Under the 1936 provision, abortions could be performed only with a medical certificate; and each case was determined by an abortion commission composed of three medical specialists. Studies on the frequency of abortions (both induced and spontaneous), based on records of both medically-certified abortions and of women seeking medical care due to miscarriages or complications of illegal abortions, revealed a sharp drop in abortion frequency in 1937; the number of recorded abortions declined by a factor of three in the cities and a factor of four in rural areas. Abortion frequency soon started to increase, however; recorded abortion rates (abortions per 1,000 women aged 15 to 49) in urban areas reached 36.5 by 1939.[147] (These data considerably understate actual abortion frequencies since they include only those women hospitalized in connection with an incomplete abortion plus the much smaller number of therapeutic abortions). The decree restricting access to legal abortion was apparently interpreted rather narrowly by most commissions; and few abortions were granted for "social" reasons; only about 10 per cent of the recorded abortions were induced abortions performed on medical certificate. As a result, the number of illegal abortions soared, as did illnesses and deaths associated with abortion complications; in 1954, non-hospital (illegal) abortions constituted an estimated 80 per cent of all abortions.

The high number (and undesirable consequences) of illegal abortions was the major reason for the re-legalization of abortion, which took place in 1955.[148] Since 1955, abortion has been available during the first trimester of pregnancy (gestation up to twelve weeks), and in the second trimester if special permission is obtained. Women may not have abortions more frequently than once every six months. Although recent information is not available, most abortions in the 1960s appear to have been performed on an in-patient basis, with average stays of about three days.[149]

In the decade following re-legalization, the number of legal abortions increased rapidly; there was an 82 per cent increase between 1955 and 1956 alone.[150] As noted in Chapter 4, Soviet-wide data on abortion frequency are not available. As a result, there is a great deal of erroneous and misleading information regarding Soviet abortion in Western literature. Christopher Davis and Murray Feshbach, in their study of infant mortality in the Soviet Union, cite the Serenko material, claiming "a lifetime average of six abortions for every Soviet woman." Given the fact that abortion is viewed as a crime by Muslim women, they conclude that abortion levels for non-Muslim women "must be substantially higher than the overall average."[151] Richard Pipes goes several steps further. He portrays the USSR's "fantastic abortion rates" as a manifestation of a deeper systemic crisis. Although no documentation is provided, he asserts that current abortion frequency is "estimated at 10 per Russian female."[152]

The evidence suggests that these estimates fall far wide of the mark. A 1982 sample survey of abortion-to-birth ratios in the RSFSR revealed a ratio of 2.08:1, with the lowest rates in the North Caucasus and Tuvin regions and the highest in Magadan (3.3:1), Kamchatka (3.2:1), and Kaliningrad oblasts (3:1).[153] A separate study, also conducted in the late 1970s, in one oblast of the RSFSR (Ryazan) revealed abortion-to-birth rates of 2.28 to 1.[154] None of the data in either of these surveys support the average lifetime abortion figures proposed by either Davis and Feshbach or Pipes. The validity of the Davis/Feshbach figures appear to be limited to those areas in the RSFSR where abortion rates are highest and are invalid for both the RSFSR and the Soviet Union as a whole. Nor is there any data that will support Pipes' estimate of ten abortions per Russian female.

Despite the fact that abortion frequency in the USSR has been wildly exaggerated in the West, the fragmentary evidence that is available suggests that abortion does remain a major means of fertility control in the Soviet Union, in at least some areas. Data from Latvia indicate that women married twenty years or more had 7.5 pregnancies, of which 4.4 ended in abortion. A 1960 study of Tbilisi women aged 40 to 46 revealed an average of 11.9 pregnancies, of which 7.8 ended in abortion. A study of Moscow working women showed that 11 per cent had five or more abortions.[155] The Leningrad data yield an estimated abortion rate of almost 165 in 1967.[156] A later Leningrad study, this time of pregnancy outcomes of women aged 30 to 50, revealed that the average woman had five pregnancies and three to four abortions during her childbearing years.[157] A study of medical data in five Soviet cities indicates an estimated rate of about 128 (per 1,000 women of childbearing age).[158] Data provided on abortions to births for Moscow City in the late 1970s yield an estimated rate of about 100.[159] These data suggest wide variation in abortion frequencies that are similar to US patterns. In 1978, the reported abortion rate for Washington, DC was higher than Moscow's – 173.4 compared to 100. The abortion rate for DC residents only was a lower 82.5, still well above the overall US metropolitan area rate of 36.4.[160] In short, although we cannot validly generalize from this fragmentary data to the entire Soviet Union, the data we do have suggest widespread reliance on abortion in at least some metropolitan areas. Abortion in the USSR, like abortion in many other industrialized states, must rank as one of the primary methods of family planning.

This does not mean, of course, that either the Soviet leadership or the Soviet medical establishment are pleased with the heavy reliance on abortion, at least in some areas. Pronatalist demographers bemoan high abortion frequencies because of the impact on the birth rate. Health care specialists point to the medical consequences of abortion, particularly repeated abortions. High abortion frequency also places a burden on the health care network. One 1970 text providing average hospitalization rates for urban areas indicated a planning factor of 68.7 hospital stays for abortions (at an average of three days each) per 1,000 women per year.[161]

The alternative to abortion being promoted by the medical establishment is fuller, and more effective, use of contraceptives.[162] In the 1920s, Soviet medical authorities began promoting and distributing contraceptive devices; a special commission on the issue was created in the Institute for Maternal and Child Health. Other socialization programs were sponsored by the Central Commission for the Struggle Against Abortions. On the eve of the restrictive abortion legislation of 1936, the Soviet Union (or so it is claimed by Soviet medical specialists) was producing large quantities of contraceptive devices at the technological levels of the period. But the prohibition of abortion, ironically, curtailed many of these activities; and doctors at gynecological clinics ceased to promote contraceptive techniques among their patients.

The re-legalization of abortion in 1955 produced renewed efforts to promote contraception. Most of these activities were keyed to voluntary limitation of abortion services. In 1956, the health ministry endorsed a new series of initiatives promoting fuller use of contraceptives. In 1962, the USSR Academy of Medical Sciences set up a special laboratory to develop more effective contraceptive techniques. Experimental programs in gynecological clinics to cut down the number of abortions through wider use of contraceptives were set up in the Ukraine, Moscow, Belorussia, and elsewhere; and the results were publicized in the Soviet medical press. The popular medical journal "*Zdorovye*" (*Health*) began publishing articles stressing the dangers of abortion and the joys of motherhood. Documentaries on the subject and a series of special brochures on abortion were produced in the 1960s.

These efforts have continued in the 1970s and 1980s. Efforts continue to focus on the two major problems: availability of effective techniques and public awareness. Research on contraceptive technology is directed by the Allunion Scientific-Research Chemical-Pharmaceutical Institute in Moscow.[163] Available contraceptive devices include condoms, diaphrams, cervical caps, and various spermicidal agents (pastes and tablets); these devices are distributed through maternity centers and the network of pharmacies run by the Ministry of Health.[164] Intrauterine devices are now available. These are apparently imported, although reportedly plans are afoot to manufacture copper IUDs in the USSR. Oral contraceptives, primarily the minipill, are also prescribed, but only for a limited period and on a very limited scale.[165] Supplies of contraceptives, like most Soviet consumer goods, are subject to perennial shortage and distribution problems. They are not consistently available in many areas. Also, like most Soviet consumer items, Soviet-made contraceptive devices are of much lower quality than Western-made goods. Soviet medical specialists and Soviet women complain with cause that effective, convenient birth control devices are still not widely available; and Soviet commentators continue to call for stronger socialization programs, beginning with sex education in the school system.

Whether these efforts will bear fruit in expanded use of reliable birth control techniques is open to question. It might be concluded from the relatively high frequency of recorded abortion (in areas like Leningrad and Moscow at least) that contraceptive use is necessarily low. However, the relationship between abortion and contraception is by no means this simple. Even the most reliable reversible method of contraception does not provide full protection against pregnancy over long periods. This means that a typical couple completing a family of three when the woman is in her late twenties can expect to have at least one additional pregnancy before she reaches menopause.[166] For many women, the only recourse to an unwanted birth is abortion (legal or illegal). High abortion frequencies, then, are not necessarily incompatible with high and/or increasing rates of contraceptive use. In fact, the experience of Great Britain in the nineteenth century and of Korea, Latin America, and Japan in the mid-twentieth century suggests that both abortion and contraceptive use rise together when a society first starts to regulate its fertility.[167]

Table 5.5. _Contraceptive use in the Soviet Union_

Method	% Contraceptive users employing each method, according to studies reported by:			
	Bykov, 1928[a]	Tsirulnikov, 1960[a]	Yakovleva, 1962[a]	Shlindman, 1973[b]
Condoms	10	51	37	34
Withdrawal	22	29	45	56
Diaphrams	3	3	4	3
Chemical means	39	13	10	6
Douche	19	2	3	
Rhythm		2	1	
Other	7	3		

[a] S. M. Yakovleva, _Sposoby i sredstva kontratseptsiy_ (Leningrad: Meditsina, 1970), p. 132.
[b] Sh. Shlindman and P. Zvidrin'sh, _Izucheniye rozhdayemosti_, (Moscow: Statistika, 1973), pp. 134–41.

It has been suggested that societies typically pass through several stages in family planning. In the first, family planning is minimal and fertility is high. In the intermediate stages, there is primary reliance on induced abortion. Abortion rates decline in the later stages, as contraceptive use becomes widespread; but abortion continues to be a major "back-up" to deal with unwanted pregnancies that result from contraceptive failure.[168] In short, high abortion rates are not necessarily incompatible with relatively high (and increasing) contraceptive use.

The high abortion rates revealed by the Leningrad and Moscow data, then, may not necessarily indicate low contraceptive use. In fact, regional studies of contraceptive use in the Soviet Union reveal fairly high rates of usage, between 70 to 90 per cent for most studies of urban, European women (Table 5.5). One recent study of couples residing in large cities found that 88 per cent employed some type of contraceptive method.[169] But many of the couples who do use some form of contraception either do not use it consistently, or use a method which is not particularly effective.[170] For example, a 1966 Moscow study revealed that only 49 per cent of the sample used contraception consistently.[171] The Moscow study of young families during their first five years of marriage revealed that only 8 per cent of the women and 44 per cent of the men used contraceptive techniques

Table 5.6. *Estimated use of family planning methods among Soviet women*

Method	% of women at risk of unwanted pregnancy relying on given method
Abortion, rhythm, withdrawal	<50
Condoms	15–18
IUDs	12–15
Diaphrams	8
Hormonal methods	8

Source: Adopted from Ira Lubell, "IUDs and Family Planning in the USSR," in E. S. E. Hafez and W. A. A. van Os (eds.) *IUDs and Family Planning* Vol. 2. (Boston: Massachusetts, 1980), pp. 137–39. The estimates given are based on Lubell's personal communications with representatives of the All-Union Institute of Research in Obstetrics and Gynecology. Since there are no indications in the Soviet medical press that the Soviets have conducted a recent, Soviet-wide survey of contraceptive and abortion users, the Soviet medical officials who provided these data are apparently basing their estimates on regional surveys. For this reason, the figures should be interpreted as very rough estimates only.

Table 5.7. *Family planning methods as reported by couples, 1981[a]*

Method	Women	Men
Full or partial abstention	2.3	5.0
Rhythm	40.7	42.0
Withdrawal	20.8	22.8
Chemical means (spermicides)	13.6	7.3
Mechanical means (condoms, cervical caps)	18.1	38.8
Intrauterine devices	8.6	9.6
Hormonal methods	3.6	4.6
Abortion	33.9	19.3

[a] Columns do not add up to 100 per cent because the respondents, all residents of large cities, could choose one or more answers from an eight-item list.

Source: S. D. Golod, *Stabil'nost' sem'i: sotsiologicheskiy i demografichesky aspekty* (Leningrad: Nauka, 1984), pp. 109–10.

in the first year of marriage. After five years, these usage rates had increased to 40 per cent for women and 88 per cent for men, but almost three-fourths of the sample had been forced to interrupt an unwanted pregnancy with abortion.[172] The primary reasons for the relatively low levels of effective contraceptive use are lack of knowledge and difficulty in obtaining necessary devices. In a study of contraceptive use and abortion in Magadan, for example, 24 per cent of the non-users cited lack of knowledge, and an additional 22 per cent cited limited availability of contraceptive means.[173]

In addition, many Soviet couples who do use family planning techniques rely on methods that Soviet authorities consider unreliable (Tables 5.6, 5.7). Some women are apparently under the impression that they cannot get pregnant while nursing and extend the duration of breastfeeding for this purpose.[174] The most popular contraceptive methods appear to be rhythm, withdrawal and condoms.[175] Soviet medical officials have been hesitant to promote widespread use of oral contraceptives because of related health hazards; and the use of intrauterine devices appears to be quite limited.[176]

One strategy of dealing with the abortion problem is criminalization or imposition of stringent restrictions on abortion. Roumania outlawed abortion in 1967; in the early 1970s, Hungary and Czechoslovakia passed measures that severely restricted abortion access.[177] How likely is it that the Soviet Union will follow suit? Soviet press discussions of the East European experience suggest that a recriminalization of abortion is not a step the Soviets would undertake lightly. Even the most vehement critics of abortion concede that legal abortions fill an important need; and that de-legalization would result in an upsurge in illegal abortions, with all the attendant health hazards:

Disturbed by (alarming abortion statistics), certain countries have considered it necessary to limit the freedom of abortions ... Of course, such measures do have some effect, and they restrain some persons from taking a false step. But, of course, as is well known, there are two sides to this coin ... It sometimes happens that, when she fails to obtain official permission, a woman seeks out illegal ways and has recourse to the aid of non-professionals. Need we say what harm this causes to health? ... In short, such a way [restrictions on abortions] is scarcely a panacea or way out of the problem situation. Each family must decide on its own how many children to have – depending on its own opportunities, relations, and living conditions ... the right to an abortion is an important right.[178]

Soviet commentators also tend to link legal abortions with the concept of personal freedom: the woman's right to choose motherhood.[179] To some degree, the Soviet decision on abortion will hinge on trends in abortion frequency. Continued high or increasing abortion rates could very well provide supporters of de-legalization with an important argument in favor of more restrictive measures. Soviet officials will also be monitoring the East European experience. It remains to be seen whether the Soviet leadership will bow to pronatalist pressures and criminalize abortions. So far it has not been willing to do so.

EVALUATING THE IMPACT OF DEMOGRAPHIC POLICY ON SOVIET FERTILITY

Soviet population programs, then, do not constitute a unified, consistent policy. First, none of the programs are designed exclusively as population programs. Second, the programs, in so far as they affect fertility at all, sometimes work in opposite directions. Availability of abortion on demand and the more limited availability of effective birth control technology through the health care network can hardly be viewed as pronatalist in intent or effect; both policies are supported as health measures. All other programs, however, are explicitly designed to (among other things) promote fertility. The series of economic incentives – both the direct income subsidies and the measures to ease the conflict between work and motherhood – and the socialization programs are intended to bolster fertility, especially in modernized areas where small families have become the norm.

Assessing the impact of this mix of economic, social, and legal measures on Soviet fertility is made difficult by the total absence of Soviet program evaluation studies. What indirect evidence does exist, however, suggests that most of the economic programs at least are based on a premise of questionable validity. Most of the measures associated with population policy in the USSR fall under the general rubric of economic programs. They are based on the assumption that the fertility decline is due primarily to economic causes: for many young couples, the birth of the first child leads to dramatic declines in living standards and the decline continues with subsequent children. Government subsidies of all or part of the direct economic costs of children, so runs the argument, will remove the major barrier to the mid-sized family.[180] Proponents of this view note that the practical problems of rearing a child in Soviet society and the financial difficulties of parenthood are frequently noted by women when asked why they do not want another child. Young Soviet couples begin marriage wanting a mid-sized family, but pare back their family size desires after they realize how demanding parenthood is. For example, in a survey of rural couples in Rostov oblast, the desired family size in the first year of marriage was 2.54 children. But when the same couples were re-surveyed four years later, their desired family size had declined to 2.15. Most of the couples surveyed pointed to low living standards and the practical problems of bringing up children when the wife is working as the explanation for their reduced family size desires.[181] Low living standards were cited by the majority of women in a study of family limitation in Chuvash ASSR.[182] Studies of motives for seeking an induced abortion also reveal the importance of living standards – low income, poor housing, and problems with childcare availability are frequently cited as justification for an abortion.[183]

Proponents of the economic incentive approach to population policy are also able to point to studies showing that many European women expect to have fewer children than they "desire." For example, the 1969 study by the Central Statistical Administration on desired and expected number of children revealed consistently lower family size expectations than family size desires for women surveyed in Belorussia. In explaining this discrepancy, women surveyed noted low living standards and difficulties in raising a child.[184] A study of urban families in Latvia conducted in 1978–79 found that poor living conditions were cited most often as the main reason for limiting family size. The women surveyed in this study ranked housing conditions, the difficulty of finding childcare, and general "material difficulties" among the leading reasons for limiting the size of their families.[185] Similar findings were reported in a 1978 study of married women with two children in Moscow. These women indicated that what was needed to encourage the birth of a third child was the expansion of maternity leave programs, a shorter work day (at full-time salary) and preferential access to trade, medical, and other commercial services.[186] In a study of families in the Ukrainian capital of Kiev, both husbands and wives cited improved housing and material conditions most frequently as factors necessary for them to have an additional child.[187]

These findings have led Soviet demographers to suggest that the most promising way to promote childbearing among the low-fertility Europeans is to ease the hardships of working mothers, while compensating young families for the economic burdens of parent-hood.[188] The relationship between fertility and living standards, however, is by no means as clear as that implied by the studies cited above. While many Soviet women who curtail their families after one or two children cite the importance of financial hardship, many Soviet studies that have investigated the link between fertility and income suggest that better-off families frequently have fewer children than their lower-income counterparts.[189] It should be noted, however, that there are conflicting findings on this issue and that some Soviet studies have come up with no conclusive results.[190]

Studies of the relationship between natality and income suffer from several methodological weaknesses.[191] One problem is the inter-vening factor of age; older couples who are more advanced in their career professions (and hence more likely to have higher incomes) tend also to have progressed furthest in completing their families. Yet several Soviet studies that use family size or children ever born as a dependent variable fail to adjust for these factors. Another compli-cation in trying to sort out cause and effect is the child allowance system (and, after 1974, the income supplement program); family income is modified by payments keyed to the number of children.

Still another methodological problem is how to measure "family income." In some studies, income per family member is used as a measure of family income. Because a large number of children automatically slices the family income pie into smaller slices, the real relationship between well-being and natality may be obscured. These studies typically find an inverse relationship between income and number of children. A study in Latvia, for example, found a negative relationship between income per family member and number of children in the family ($r=-0.53$ for urban areas, and $r=-0.44$ for the rural areas).[192] Similar results were found in Belorussia;[193] and in the 1960 study of blue and white-collar family size in the Moscow suburb of Zhukov.[194] The 1969 survey of blue and white-collar families found an inverse relationship between expected family size and income per family member, holding constant for education, social class, and urban–rural residence. The inverse income/natality relationship was noted for both low and high fertility minorities.[195] Some of the findings of this study are depicted in Figure 5.1

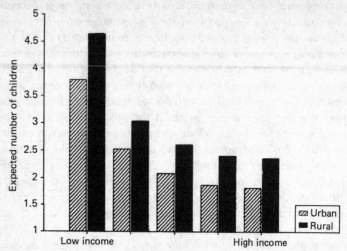

Figure 5.1 Effect of income on family size expectations (workers and employees) 1969

Studies that operationalize income as total family income yield somewhat different results. Slesarov's study of married women in six Gorkiy enterprises found a strong direct relationship between family size and total family income. Slesarov failed, however, to adjust for either age or length of marriage.[196] Nor did he indicate the proportion of high-income families that were extended. This is an important point, because the presence of a nonworking grandparent or other relative may in fact play an important role in determining whether the family decides to have another child. The 1972 nationwide study revealed a weak curvilinear relationship between income and family size for low fertility republics. The results, standardized by length of marriage, showed that families with an income below 150 rubles per month had an average of 2.01 births per woman; those with a total income between 301 and 450 rubles, 1.95 births. At income levels above 450 rubles, however, births per woman were marginally higher.[197] When results were provided separately by education level, only the lowest educational group (elementary education and below) revealed a direct relationship between income and natality. For the two highest educational categories (higher and completed secondary), there was a weak inverse relationship. For women with incomplete secondary education, there appeared to be a weak curvilinear relationship similar to that described for the sample as a whole.[198]

The Latvian study revealed a fairly strong inverse relationship between income and family size, whether income was measured by total family income or as income per family member.[199] A more recent study (1979) of young women with two to three children in Riga (the Latvian capital) provides similar results. Average monthly family incomes varied little according to family size, but the three-children families tended to be marginally less well off. And, when asked if they would consider having an additional child, women with lower incomes were slightly more apt to reply "yes" or "maybe."[200] A 1980 study of ideal, desired, and expected family size in Tbilisi found a moderate inverse relationship between income and family size ideals and desires, but no relationship with family size expectations, when income was measured as total family income. When income was measured per family member, however, the negative relationship was strong with all three family size indicators. In other words, the higher the income per family member, the lower the ideal, desired, and expected family size. This relationship persisted when nationality was controlled. Similar results were found in a 1976 study conducted in rural areas of Georgia.[201]

A similar mixture of contradictory or inconclusive results is evident in a review of Soviet studies examining the impact of housing on family size.[202] Given the frequency with which women cite poor housing as a reason for curtailing their families, one might expect to see a strong empirical link between the quality of living quarters and natality. However, some studies have found that couples with the best housing conditions are least likely to have a third child. For example, a 1970 study of families in Moscow found an inverse relationship between housing space and the desire to have another child.[203] The Latvian study revealed a direct relationship between housing and natality when housing was operationalized as total living space, but an inverse relationship when housing was operationalized as living space per family member.[204] The Riga study found that couples with the less desirable living conditions (smallest living space; fewest number of rooms; shared versus separate apartments) were more likely to consider having an additional child.[205]

A 1973 Leningrad study reported no relationship between housing

space and family size.[206] The Zhukov study found an inverse
relationship between living space per family member and family
size;[207] and another study in the Moscow area found a similar
relationship holding age and rural–urban residence constant.[208]
Slesarov's 1962 Gorkiy study found the lowest number of children
ever born for women with the smallest housing space. Although he
asserts that his findings reveal a direct relationship between housing
quality and natality, his data in fact show a curvilinear relationship.
There is virtually no difference in number of children ever born for
families living in separate apartments and those living in two or more
rooms in a communal apartment. Couples in private apartments and
homes have fewer children still. Similar mixed findings are evident in
Slesarov's data on "communal conveniences."[209] Davytan's study of
natality in urban Armenia found that the fertility of women living in
separate apartments was 35 per cent lower than that of women living
in communal apartments.[210]

Some of the contradictory findings on the relationship between
living standards and family size are due to faulty research design and
the difficulties of measuring living standards with available empirical
indicators. In other cases, it seems fair to conclude that the influence
of living standards varies from group to group and family to family
depending on perceived standards of poverty and plenty.[211] What
may be a perfectly acceptable housing arrangement for one family
may be perceived as substandard by another. On the whole, in spite
of the inconclusive and inconsistent results, the available data
provide little support for the assumption that a threatened drop in
living standards alone prevents the urban Soviet couples from having
a second or third child. The frequency with which this reason is
given, in both formal surveys and informal conversations with Soviet
women, as a justification for not having more children is probably a
reflection of pronatalist values. Poor housing and the difficulty of
obtaining convenient childcare are socially acceptable answers to the
question: "Why don't you have another child?" And, a significant
proportion of Soviet women are refusing to take refuge in such
answers. A 1969 survey of women in Kalmyk ASSR asked under
what circumstances they would be willing to have three children;
although some women replied with the usual references to better
living conditions and housing, 59.4 per cent admitted frankly that
they didn't want to have three children under any circumstances.[212]

These findings provide little support for a pronatalist program based almost entirely on economic incentives; and critics of the economic incentive approach to raising the birth rate claim that family payments have not proven to be particularly effective as a pronatalist measure.[213] They note that the long-term fertility decline in the European areas of the USSR occurred at the same time as did a significant increase in living standards.[214] Other Soviet officials argue that the number of children people have is a reflection of their value for children. The desirability of a small family among many couples in urban European areas is due primarily to a growing orientation toward activities outside the family. Economic incentives, they insist, are of little value in promoting the ideal, mid-size family (of three or four children), because such programs fail to modify the values that have produced a growing preference for small families.[215]

Recent fertility trends in the low-fertility republics are generally in line with these arguments. The 1981 measure, including the introduction of birth payments for low-parity mothers and the extended maternity leave program, was intended to raise fertility in the Slavic and Baltic areas. Indeed, between 1980/81 and 1982/83 total fertility increased by 8 per cent in the RSFSR and Latvia; 5 per cent in the Ukraine; and 3 per cent in Belorussia, Estonia, and Lithuania.[216] Soviet officials, of course, are proudly pointing to these increases as proof of the effectiveness of the 1981 measure.[217] Those increases, however, are very modest. Moreover, the Hungarian experience with expanded maternity leave suggests that even these modest fertility increases may only be temporary.

Definitive assessment of the real role of economic incentive programs must await publication of the results of program evaluation studies. Nonetheless, we feel safe in concluding from the current evidence that financial subsidies and other measures to ease the work/motherhood conflict have probably not made more than a marginal dent in the long-term Soviet fertility decline. For one thing, the programs, as noted above, are relatively modest efforts to cushion what is almost surely a significant decline in living standards. Given the expenses associated with a more vigorous program and the continuing Soviet need for high female labor force participation rates, it is unlikely that the Soviet Union will embrace the more radical pronatalist programs urged by the pronatalist demographers – programs involving large-scale, long-term withdrawal of females from the labor force with payment schedules commensurate with previous salaries. In sum, the impact of Soviet demographic policy has been rather limited and will remain so in the absence of major policy changes.

NOTES

1 G. I. Litvinova, *Pravo i demograficheskiye protsessy v SSSR* (Moscow: Nauka, 1981), p. 31.
2 English-language summaries of Soviet population policy have been compiled by David Heer: "Recent Developments in Soviet Population Policy," *Studies in Family Planning*, Vol. 3, No. 11, November 1972, pp. 257–64 and "Three Issues in Soviet Population Policy," *Population and Development Review*, Vol. 3, No. 3, September 1977, pp. 229–52.
3 G. P. Kiseleva, *Nuzhno li povyshat rozhdayemost'?* (Moscow: Statistika, 1979), pp. 81–82; and A. Ya. Kvasha, "Several problems of the Demographic Situation in the USSR," in *Voprosy filosofii*, No. 9, 1974, pp. 94–97.
4 A. Ya. Kvasha, "The Demographic Optimum," *Obshchestvennyye nauki*, No. 6, 1981, pp. 31–45.
5 V. I. Perevedentsev, "It is Necessary to Stimulate the Growth of the Population in Our Country," *Voprosy filosofii*, No. 11, 1974, pp. 88–92.
6 Maquash Tatimov, "A Family with Children is Like a Bazaar," *Madeniet Jane Turmis*, No. 10, 1980, pp. 20–21. Translated in Joint Publication Research Service, JPRS 77252, 27 January 1981. In this same vein, see Baltaybay Adambayev, "Mother With Children: A Happy Mother," *Sotsialistik Qazaqstan*, 21 March 1981, p. 4. Translated in Joint Publication Research Service, JPRS 78076, 14 May 1981.
7 Murray Feshbach, "Between the Lines of the 1979 Soviet Census," *Problems of Communism*, January–February, 1982, pp. 27–37.
8 See Ye. L. Manevich, "Population Reproduction and Utilization of Labor Resources," *Voprosy ekonomiki*, No. 8, 1978, pp. 34–38.
9 B. Ts. Urlanis, "Dynamics of Fertility in the USSR," in N. P. Fedorenko (ed.), *Vosproizvodstvo naseleneniya i trudovykh resursov* (Moscow: Nauka, 1976), pp. 16–33.
10 V. I. Perevedentsev, *Naseleniye i khozyaystvo* (Moscow: Znaniye, 1971), pp. 8–9.
11 B. Ts. Urlanis, *Problemy dinamiki naseleniya SSSR* (Moscow: Nauka, 1974), pp. 264–65.
12 Urlanis, 1974, p. 271; Perevedentsev, 1974; and K. Vermishev, "Stimulating the Growth of the Population," *Planovoye khozyaystvo*, No. 12, 1972, pp. 102–07.
13 V. A. Boldyrev, "Economic Aspects of the Problem of Birth Rate," in L. Ye. Darskiy (ed.), *Rozhdayemost' (Problemy izucheniya)* (Moscow: Statistika, 1976), pp. 62–75.
14 V. A. Boldyrev, "Tendencies in the Development of the Socialist

Economy and Demographic Policy," *Voprosy filosofii*, No. 11, 1974, pp. 84–88.

15 A. G. Volkov, "On the Influencing of the Birthrate," in Darskiy, 1976, pp. 35–52.

16 Boldyrev, "Tendencies," 1974.

17 G. A. Slesarov, *Demograficheskiye protsessy i sotsial'naya struktura sotsialisti-cheskogo obshchestva* (Moscow: Nauka, 1978), pp. 72–79; L. Ye. Darskiy, "Sociodemographic Studies of Problems of the Birthrate," *Sotsiologi-cheskiye issoledovaniya*, No. 3, 1979, pp. 10–19; and I. V. Bagrova, "To the Question of Choosing a More Advantageous Form of Combining the Woman's Maternal Function with Employment," in *Sotsial'no-ekonomi-cheskiye osobennosti vosproizvodstva naseleniya v usloviyakh razvitogo sotsializma*, Vol. 1 (Kiev: Institut Ekonomiki AN USSR, 1976), pp. 79–82; and V. P. Piskunov and V. S. Steshenko, "On the Demographic Policy of Socialist Society," in V. S. Steshenko and V. S. Piskunov (eds.), *Demograficheskaya politika* (Moscow: Statistika, 1974), pp. 15–27.

18 V. Ye. Khodzhabekyon, Yu. Base, and R. Shefer, *Demograficheskiye problemy i vosproizvodstvo trudovykh resursov* (Yerevan: Izdatel'stvo AN Armyanskoy SSR, 1983), p. 28.

19 D. K. Shelestov, "Study of the Population Problem," *Voprosy filosofii*, No. 10, 1976, pp. 166–72; and G. Kiseleva, "The Status of Women and Demographic Policy," in D. I. Valentey (ed.), *Zhenshchiny na rabota i doma* (Moscow: Statistika, 1978), pp. 3–15.

20 B. Ts. Urlanis, "Demographic Science and Demographic Policy," *Vestnik akademii nauk SSSR*, No. 1, 1980, pp. 41–49.

21 M. B. Tatimov, *Razvitiye narodonaseleniya i demograficheskaya politika* (Alma Ata: Izdatel'stvo Nauka Kazakhskoy SSR, 1978), p. 86.

22 *Ibid.*, p. 87.

23 *Ibid.*, pp. 82–83, 91–92.

24 Robert J. McIntyre, "On Demographic Policy Debates in the USSR," *Population and Development Review*, Vol. 8, No. 2, June 1982, pp. 363–64. For an alternate view that depicts the distinction as one between a policy that is "countrywide in scope" versus one that is "differentiated by region," see Cynthia Weber and Ann Goodman, "The Demographic Policy Debate in the USSR," *Population and Development Review*, Vol. 7, No. 2, June 1981, pp. 279–95.

25 "O merakh po usileniyu gosudarstvennoy pomoshchi sem'jam imeyush-chim detey," 22 January 1981, *Sobraniye postanovleniy pravitel'stva SSSR*, No. 13, 1981, pp. 330–38. (Hereafter cited as 22 January 1981 resolu-tion).

26 "Basic Directions in the Economic and Social Development of the USSR in 1981 to 1985 and the period to 1990," in *Materialy XXVI s"ezda KPSS* (Moscow: Politizdat, 1981), pp. 131–205. The treatment of population/welfare programs for families is on p. 178.

27 22 January 1981 resolution.

28 An alternative assessment of the 1981 program, characterizing it as "a major shift from the de facto uniform approach to demographic policy"

and an endorsement of the "differentiated approach to stimulate fertility," is provided in Weber and Goodman, 1981.

29 *Pravda*, 6 September 1981, p. 1; and 29 January 1984, pp. 1, 3. See also the 2 September 1981 resolution. The actual text of the resolution is available in *Resheniya partii i pravitel'stva po khozyaystvennym voprosam*, Vol. 14 (Moscow: Politizdat, 1983, pp. 178–80). Hereafter cited as 2 September 1981 resolution.

30 For an alternate view, which describes this aspect of the program as a "major shift" in policy, see Weber and Goodman, 1981.

31 "Ob ulushenii obespecheniya posobiyami po beremennosti i rodam i po ukhodu za bolnym rebenkom," 26 July 1973 in *Zakonadatel'stvo o pravakh zhenshchin v SSSR*, pp. 152–53.

32 T. Ryabushkin, "Demographic Policy in Light of the Decisions of the 26th Party Congress," *Vestnik statistiki*, No. 2, 1982, pp. 3–8.

33 T. Ryabushkin, "Dynamics and Structure of the USSR Population over the last 60 Years," *Voprosy ekonomiki*, No. 9, 1982, pp. 10–19.

34 Yu. B. Ryurikov, "A Family Matter? No, a State Matter. A Strategy for Upbringing and Assistance to the Family." *Ekonomika i organizatsiya promyshlennogo proizvodstva*, No. 10, 1982, pp. 149–70.

35 The legal acts embodying this portion of Soviet demographic policy are conveniently listed and described in N. I. Kungurova, *Zhenshchina v obshchestvennom proizvodstve pri sotsializme. Ekonomiko-demograficheskiy aspekt* (Moscow: Finansy i Statistika, 1983), pp. 104–65.

36 Heer, 1977; V. Ts. Urlanis, "Demographic Policy in the USSR," *Vestnik akademii nauk SSSR*, No. 9, 1972, pp. 60–63; and M. D. Solovyeva and Ye. P. Frolova, "Government Help to Families with Many Children," *Finansy SSSR*, No. 9, 1974, pp. 22–25.

37 See, for example, the comment of G. I. Litvinova in "Legal Aspects of Demographic Policy," *Sovetskoye gosudarstvo i pravo*, No. 1, 1975, pp. 28–35.

38 G. I. Litvinova, "Demographic Legislation in European Socialist Countries," *Sovetskoye gosudarstvo i pravo*, No. 7, 1980, pp. 67–75.

39 Tatimov, 1978, pp. 82–83.

40 *Pravda*, 6 September 1981, p. 1.

41 T. V. Ivankina and Ye. F. Chernysheva, *Gosudarstvennaya pomoshch' sem'yam, imeyushchim detey* (Moscow: Yuridicheskaya Literatura, 1985), pp. 31–32; and M. A. Ivanov, *Brak, sem'ya, deit* (Moscow: Pedagogika, 1983), pp. 39–40.

42 "Polozheniye o poryadke naznacheniya i vyplaty posobiy beremennym zhenshchinam, mnogodetnym i odinokim materyam," 12 August 1970, excerpted in *Okhrana detstva v SSSR. Sbornik normativnykh aktov* (Moscow: Yuridicheskaya Literatura, 1979), pp. 187–92; and "Ob uvelichenii gosudarstvenniy pomoshchi beremennym zhenshchinam, mnogodetnym i yedinokim materyam," 8 July 1944, excerpted in *Zakonodatel'stvo o pravakh zhenshchin v SSSR. Sbornik normativnykh aktov* (Moscow: Yuridicheskaya Literatura, 1975), pp. 19–23.

43 G. S. Simonenko, *V interesakh materi i rebenka. Posobiya na detey* (Moscow: Profizdat, 1976), pp. 67–70; and Ye. P. Frolova and O. Yu Biryuleva, *Posobiya na detey* (Moscow: Finansy i Statistika, 1981), p. 41.

44 *Narodnoye khozyaystvo SSSR v 1983 g. Statisticheskiy Yezhegodnik* (Moscow: Finansy i Statistika, 1984), pp. 547, 550–1. Hereafter cited as *NK 1983*.

45 "Women in the USSR," *Vestnik statistiki*, No. 1, 1985, pp. 62–76.

46 *NK 1983*, pp. 393–94.

47 A. Ya. Kvasha, *Demograficheskaya politika v SSSR* (Moscow: Finansy i Statistika, 1981), pp. 162–63.

48 Janet G. Chapman, 'Recent Trends in the Soviet Industrial Wage Structure," in Arcadius Kahan and Blair Ruble (eds.), *Industrial Labor in the USSR* (New York: Pergamon Press, 1979), pp. 151–83.

49 Ukaz Prezidiuma verkhovnogo soveta SSSR 25 Septyabrya 1974 g. o vvedenii posobiy na detey maloobespechennym sem'yam," in *Resheniya partii i pravitel'stva po khozyaystvennym voprosam (1973–1975 gg.)* (Moscow: Politizdat, 1976), pp. 271–72.

50 "Ob utverzhdenii polozheniya o poryadke naznacheniya i vyplaty posobiy na detey maloobespechennym sem'yam," 25 September 1974, *ibid.*, pp. 272–85.

51 Simonenko, 1976, pp. 7–58.

52 *Izvestiya*, 21 May 1985, p. 1.

53 "O vnesenii izmeneniy v ukaz Prezidiuma Verkhovnogo Soveta SSSR. O vvedenii posobiy na detey maloobespechennym sem'yam," *Vedomosti verkhovnogo soveta SSSR*, No. 51, 21 December 1983, pp. 816–17; and "Postanovleniya soveta ministrov SSSR o vyplate posobiy na detey maloobespechennym sem'yam v rayonakh Dal'nego Vostoka i Sibirii, a takzhe v severnykh i drugikh rayonakh strany," *Sobraniye postanovleniy pravitel'stva SSSR*, Part 1, No. 4, 1984, p. 52. See also Ivankina and Chernysheva, 1985, pp. 44–58.

54 *NK 1983*, pp. 549, 552.

55 *NK 1983*, p. 409; and *Narodnoye khozyaystvo SSSR v 1979 g. Statisticheskiy yezhegodnik* (Moscow: Statistika, 1980), p. 406.

56 *NK 1983*, p. 552; and *Narodnoye khozyaystvo uzbekskoy SSR v 1982 g. Statistichskiy yezhegodnik* (Tashkent: Uzbekistan, 1983), p. 292; *NK kazakhstana v 1982 g* (Alma Ata: Kazakhstan, 1982), p. 258; *NK azerbaydzhanskoy SSR k 60-letiyu obrazovaniya SSR* (Baku: Azerbaydzhanskoye Gosudarstvennoye, Izdatel'stvo, 1980), p. 307; *NK turmenskoy SSR v 1982 g.* (Ashkhabad: Turkmenistan, 1983), p. 221; and *NK tadzhiskskoy SSR v 1981* (Dushanbe: Irfon, 1983), p. 268.

57 Tatimov, 1978, p. 92; and G. I. Litvinova, "Influence of State and Law on Demographic Processes," *Sovetskoye gosudarstvo i pravo*, No. 1, 1978, pp. 132–36.

58 Litvinova, "Demographic Legislation," 1980; Urlanis, "Demographic Science and Demographic Policy," 1980; and G. I. Litvinova and B. Ts. Urlanis, "The Soviet Union's Demographic Policy," *Gosudarstvo i Pravo*, No. 3, 1982, pp. 38–46.

59 22 January 1981 resolution. See also Ivankina and Chernysheva, pp. 101–02; V. Stepanov, "Aid to Young Families and Families with Children," *Sovety narodnykh deputatov*, No. 12, 1983, pp. 99–101; *Leningradskaya pravda*, 12 July 1983, p. 2; and *Sovetskaya latviya*, 28 April 1983, p. 4.

60 *Izvestiya*, 24 June 31, p. 3.

61 "Osnovy zhilizhchnogo zakonodatel'stva soyuza SSR i soyuznykh respublik," *Pravda*, 26 June 1981, pp. 1, 2, 3.

62 A. Kozlov, *Zabota o materi rebenke* (Moscow: Moskovskiy Rabochiy, 1984), pp. 16–22; and N. N. Sheptulina, *Pravovoye regulirovaniye usloviy truda zhenshchin* (Moscow: Yuridicheskaya Literatura, 1978), pp. 42–55. See also A. A. Abramova, *Okhrana truda zhenshchin. Spravochnik po zakonodatel'stvu* (Moscow: Politizdat, 1978), pp. 81–94. An example of republic labor code provisions implementing the protective labor measures is "Kodeks zakonov o trude ukrainsoy SSR," in *Sbornik zakonov ukrainskoy SSR i ukazov prezidiuma verkhovnogo soveta ukrainskoy SSR, 1938–1979*, Vol. 1 (Kiev: Izdatel'stvo Politicheskoy Literatury Ukrainy, 1980), pp. 503–65. The relevant articles are article 174 through article 186. Relevant excerpts from the RSFSR codes are provided in *Spravochnik profsoyuznogo rabotnika* (Moscow: Profizdat, 1979), pp. 216–18.

63 "Rekomendatsii po ispolzovaniya trudu beremennykh zhenshchin na predpriyatiyakh legkoy promyshlennosti," excerpted in *Zakonodatel'stvo o pravakh zhenshchin v SSSR*, pp. 105–26.

64 "Polozheniye o poryadke naznacheniya i vyplaty posobiy po gosudarstvennomu sotsialnomu strakhovaniyu," in *Spravochnik profsoyuznogo rabotnika*, pp. 277–300. The relevant sections on temporary work incapacity, including sick leave for care of sick family members, are found on pp. 277 through 290.

65 Simonenko, 1976, pp. 70–75.

66 22 January 1981 resolution.

67 *Izvestiya*, 21 May 1985, p. 1.

68 Sheptulina, 1978, pp. 54–55.

69 See the 2 September 1981 resolution. See also, *Pravda*, 6 September 1981, p. 1.

70 *Pravda*, 31 March 1981, p. 1. It should be noted, however, that this promise is virtually a restatement of a similar promise expressed in the 1976–80 "Basic Directions." See *Materialy XXV s"yezda KPSS* (Moscow: Politizdat, 1976), p. 217.

71 L. Danilov, "Labor at Home: Problems and Prospects," *Khozyaystvo i pravo*, No. 12, 1980, pp. 15–18.

72 V. Uspenskiy, "The Use of Work Done at Home by Local Industry Enterprises in the RSFSR," *Planovoye khozyaystvo*, No. 5, 1984, pp. 80–4.

73 Danilov, 1980.

74 Alastair McAuley, *Women's Work and Wages in the Soviet Union* (London: George Allen and Unwin, 1981), p. 27.

75 L. Kuleshova, "Part-time Work in the Organization of Female Employment," *Planovoye khozyaystvo*, No. 12, 1978, pp. 54–63.

76 Kozlov, 1984, pp. 23–4; *Zakondatel'stvo o trude* (Minsk: Nauka i Tekhnika, 1982), pp. 97–8; and Yu. Korshunov, "In the Interests of Working Mothers," *Trud*, 4 June 1980, p. 4.

77 Z. Zh. Gosha, "Conditions of Combining Professional Employment of Women and Upbringing of Children," in *Lichnoye potrebleniye v mekhanizme vosproizvodstva naseleniya* (Riga: Zinatne, 1983), pp. 109–24.

78 Litvinova, 1981, pp. 97–98.
79 L. M. Kuleshova and T. I. Mamontova, "Employment of Women in Part-time Work," *Sotsiologicheskiye issledovaniya*, No. 4, 1979, pp. 90–92.
80 Kuleshova, 1978.
81 *Ibid.*
82 Simonenko, 1976, pp. 58–63; and Egon Szabady, "Population Policy in the European Socialist Countries in Light of the World Population Plan of Action," *International Population Conference. Mexico 1977* (Liege, Belgium: International Union for the Scientific Study of Population, 1977), Vol. 2, pp. 475–87.
83 "Ob ulushenii obespecheniya posobiyani po beremennosti i rodam i ukhodan za bolnym rebenkom," Council of Ministers resolution of 26 July 1973, excerpted in *Zakonodatel'stvo*, 1982, pp. 152–53. The provision relating to maternity leave went into effect on 1 December 1973. The resolution was implemented through "Polozheniye o poryadke naznacheniya i vyplatu posobiya po gosudarstvennomu sotsialnomu strakhovaniyu," *ibid.*, pp. 153–58. On kolkhoz women, see "Polozheniye o poryadke naznacheniya i vyplatu posobiy po beremennosti i rodam zhenshchinam-chlenam kolkhozov," *ibid*, pp. 161–67. A convenient summary of relevant regulations is provided in A. Ye. Kozlov, *Sotsial'noye obespecheniye v SSSR. Pravovyye osnovy* (Moscow: Nauka, 1981), pp. 120–23.
84 Soviet workers receive at least 15 days paid annual leave per year with additional leave for longevity and harsh work conditions; the average annual leave in 1980 was 24 working days.
85 Litvinova, "Demographic Legislation," 1980.
86 Andras Klinger, "Results of Fulfillment of Decrees in the Area of Population Politics, 1973–1979," translated in A. G. Volkov (ed.), *Demograficheskaya politika. Opyt sotsialisticheskikh stran* (Moscow: Finansy i Statistika, 1983), pp. 93–130; and Vladimir Vinnichuk, "International Comparisons of Population Policy Measures in Europe (1978)," translated in Volkov, *Demograficheskaya politika*, 1983, pp. 165–88.
87 Vinnichuk, 1983.
88 Vinnichuk, 1983 and Litvinova, "Demographic Legislation," 1980.
89 K. Lungvits, G. Vinkler, V. Lebenig and E. Strobakh, "Problems of Demographic Development in Circumstances of a Further Building of Developed Socialist Society in the German Democratic Republic," in Volkov, *Demograficheskaya politika* 1983, pp. 12–49. See also, Vinnichuk, 1983 and Litvinova, "Demographic Legislation," 1980.
90 Urlanis, "Demographic Science and Demographic Development," 1980.
91 M. Yeliseyenkova, "Leave for Mothers to Care for Newborns and Infants," *Khozyaystvo i pravo*, No. 9, 1982, pp. 81–4.
92 E. Sabadi, "Critical Demographic Problems of Hungary," in *Politika narodonaseleniya v stranakh-chlenakh SEV* (Moscow: Statistika, 1977), pp. 24–34; Egon Szabady, "Study of the Impact of a Family Protection Measure: The Selective Role Played by Social Factors in Utilizing the Allowance for Child Care in Hungary," *Journal of Comparative Family Studies*, Vol. 2, No. 2, Autumn 1971, pp. 156–64; and K. Mil'ten'i,

"Demographic and Economic Effectiveness of Maternity Leave," in Steshenko and Piskunov, *Demograficheskaya politika*, 1974, pp. 113–23.

93 Andrash Kliner, "Population Policy in Hungary: Scope and Limits," *New Hungarian Quarterly*, Vol. 23, No. 85, Spring 1982, pp. 115–25; Anrash Klinger and Istvan Monigli, "Demography and Demographic Policies in Hungary During the Decades of the 1970s and 1980s," *Demografia*, Vol. 24, No. 4, 1981, pp. 395–421; *Statisticheskiy yezhegodnik stran-chlenov soveta ekonomicheskoy vzaimopomoshchi. 1984* (Moscow: Finansy i Statistika, 1984), p. 9; and *Narodo-naseleniye stran mira. Spravochnik*, third edition (Moscow: Finansy i Statistika, 1984), p. 49.

94 T. V. Ryabushkiu and R. A. Galetskaya, *Naseleniye i sotsialisticheskoye obshchestvo* (Moscow: Finansy i Statistika, 1983), pp. 231–32.

95 V. S. Steshenko (ed.), *Demograficheskaya politika: osushchestvleniye i sovershenstvovaniye v usloviyakh razvitogo sotsializma* (Kiev: Naukova Dumka, 1982), p. 221.

96 P. A. Eglite, *et al.*, *Faktory i motivy demograficheskogo povedeniya* (Riga: Zinatne, 1984), pp. 163–4; and Charles Y. Nakamura, *et al.*, "Interdependence of Child Care Resources and the Progress of Women in Society," *Psychology of Women*, Vol. 6, No. 1, Autumn 1981, pp. 26–40.

97 Eglite, 1984, pp. 163–64.

98 Shared child care appears to be particularly prevalent among students. A 1979 study of student couples in the same republic revealed that institutionalized child care was used in only 14 per cent of the cases; for the 36 per cent of the respondents, the children were cared for by the spouse during class and study time. Relatives provided care in 44 per cent of the families. P. P. Zvidrin'sh and A. N. Lapinsh, "Investigation of Student Families in Latvia," *Sotsiologicheskiye issledovaniye* No. 2, 1981, pp. 110–12.

99 Steshenko, 1982, p. 221.

100 *Narodnoye khozyaystvo SSSR v 1983 g. Statistickeskiy yezhegodnik* (Moscow: Finansy i Statistika, 1984), p. 445.

101 Arland Thornton and Deborah Freedman, "The Changing American Family," *Population Bulletin*, Vol. 38, No. 4, October 1983, p. 26.

102 K. Bazdyrev, "The Development of Family and Demographic Policy," in *Sem'ya segodnya* (Moscow: Statistika, 1979), pp. 3–16.

103 Gail Warshofsky Lapidus, *Women in Soviet Society: Equality, Development and Social Change* (Berkeley, California: University of California Press, 1978), p. 132.

104 E. K. Vasil'yeva, *Obraz zhizni gorodskoy sem'i* (Moscow: Finansy i Statistika, 1981), p. 37.

105 A. Tkachen, "Concern about the Health of the Population – An Important Social Task," in *Naseleniye i trudovyye resursy RSFSR* (Moscow: Finansy i Statistika, 1982), pp. 70–81.

106 *Vestnik statistiki*, No. 1, 1985, p. 12.

107 *Ibid.*, p. 75.

108 *Ibid.*

109 "Ob organizatsii shkol s prodlennym dnem," CC CPSU/Council of Ministers Resolution, excerpted in *Spravochnik partiynogo rabotnika*

(Moscow: Politizdat, 1961), pp. 435–46; and O. Voldan, "Prolonged Day: What Experience Tells Us," *Narodnoye obrazovaniy*, No. 9, 1980, pp. 46–48.

110 *Vestnik statistiki*, No. 1, 1985, p. 74.

111 *Ekonomicheskaya gazeta*, No. 48, November 1981, p. 3.

112 K. Agafonova, "Prolonged Day – Attention and Concern," *Narodnoye obrazovaniye*, No. 9, 1979, pp. 21–23.

113 V. Saprykin, "Improve Work in Prolonged Day Schools," *Narodnoye obrazovaniye*, No. 10, 1979, pp. 16–20; N. Kibkalo, "School After Lessons," *Narodnoye obrazovaniye*, No. 3, 1982, pp. 19–23; O. Suleyev, "Prolonged-day School – A General Concern," *Narodnoye obrazovaniye*, No. 10, 1981, pp. 22–24; and O. Volodim, "Prolonged Day – To the Level of Contemporary Demands," *Narodnoye obrazovaniye*, No. 7, 1981, pp. 24–27.

114 Ivankina and Chernysheva, 1985, p. 88.

115 *Vestnik statistiki*, No. 1, 1985, p. 74.

116 *Ibid.*

117 "Osnovnyye napravlenye ekonomicheskogo i sotsialnogo razvitiye SSSR na 1981–1985 gody i na period do 1990 goda," in *Materialy XXVI s"yezda KPSS* (Moscow: Politizdat, 1981), p. 181.

118 Sh. Amonashvili, "Such Wise Experience," *Pravda*, 14 March 1981, p. 3; and O. Meshkov, "In School From Age Six," *Pravda*, 14 July 1981.

119 Lilian Kivi, "Five Day School Week Begins for 6-Year-Olds," *Rahva Haal*, 28 July 1981, p. 2.

120 M. Minkevich, "Improve the Style of Leadership," *Narodnoye obrazovaniye*, No. 1, 1982, pp. 14–17.

121 The reform package and the various implementing resolutions are conveniently reprinted in *O reforme obshcheobrazovatel'noy i professional'noy shkoly. Sbornik dokumentov i materialov* (Moscow: Politizdat, 1984). Relevant passages on the integration of six-year-olds are found on pp. 41–42, 65–67.

122 B. M. Levin and M. V. Petrovich, *Ekonomicheskaya funktsiya sem'i* (Moscow: Finansy i Statistika, 1984), pp. 120–21.

123 Steshenko, 1982, p. 28.

124 Alex Holt, "Domestic Labour and Soviet Society," in Jenny Brine, Maureen Perrie, and Andrew Sulton (eds.), *Home, School and Leisure in the Soviet Union* (London: George Allen and Unwin, 1980), pp. 26–54.

125 Steshenko, 1982, p. 218.

126 Z. Zh. Gosha, "Loss of Time for Upbringing Children," in *Trud, byt, otdykh* (Moscow: Finansy i Statistika, 1983), pp. 70–80.

127 *Dick and Jane as Victims. Sex Stereotyping in Children's Readers* (Princeton, New Jersey, 1972), pp. 25–28.

128 Mollie Schwartz Rosenhan, "Images of Male and Female in Children's Readers," in Dorothy Atkinson, Alexander Dallin and Gail Warshofsky Lapidus (eds.), *Women in Russia* (Stanford, California: Stanford University Press, 1977), pp. 293–305.

129 Felicity Ann O'Dell, *Socialization Through Children's Literature* (Cambridge: Cambridge University Press, 1978), pp. 91–94; 227–28.

130 Janet S. Schwartz, "Women under Socialism: Role Definitions of Soviet Women," *Social Forces*, Vol. 58, No. 1, September 1979, pp. 67–88.

131 See, for example, *Skol'ko detey budet v sovetskoy sem'ye* (Moscow: Statistika, 1977), pp. 26–27.

132 Boris Urlanis, "A Wanted Child," *Nedelya*, No. 49, 1–7 December 1980, p. 16.

133 Irina Gerasimova, "Unwanted Dolls," *Zhurnalist*, No. 8, 1982, pp. 50–53.

134 Urlanis, "A Wanted Child," 1980.

135 K. Bazdyrev, "A Single Child. Pros and Cons," *Moskovskiy komsomolets*, 19 May 1982, p. 4; and K. K. Bazdyrev, *Yedinstvennyy rebenok* (Moscow: Finansy i Statistika, 1983), p. 112.

136 D. Orlova and I. Bykova, "One? Two? Three?", *Zdorov'ye*, No. 9, 1978, pp. 2–4.

137 *Ibid.*

138 *Kazakhstanskaya pravda*, 17 October 1981, p. 4.

139 V. Perevedentsev, "The Population and the Party's Demographic Policy," *Politicheskoye samoobrazovaniye*, No. 8, 1981, pp. 45–53; and H. Kovtun, "Flowers of Life," *Radyans'ka ukrayia*, 4 April 1981, p. 4.

140 D. Valentey and A. Kvasha, "Problems of Population and Demographic Policy," *Pravda*, 19 June 1981, pp. 2, 3.

141 *Pravda*, 31 March 1981, p. 1.

142 N. Khromenkov and V. Mysanikov, "Demographic Politics and the School," *Narodnoye obrazovaniye*, No. 2, 1982, pp. 72–77.

143 Quoted in *ibid.*

144 I. Bestuzhev-Lada, "Preparation of Upper Class Students for Family Life," *Vospitaniye shkolnikov*, No. 1, 1982, pp. 33–37.

145 "O podgotovke k vnedreniyu v ix-x klassakh obschcheobrazovatel'noy shkoly kursa 'estetika i psikhologiya semeynoy zhizni', *Byulleten' normativnykh aktov ministerstva prosveshcheniya SSSR*, No. 10, 1983, pp. 38–39.

146 A. A. Verbenko, S. Ye. Il'in, V. N. Chusova, and T. N. Al'shevskaya, *Aborty i protivozachatochnyye sredstva. Kliniko-staticheskoy issledovaniye* (Moscow: Meditsina, 1968), pp. 5–6. See also Henry P. David, *Family Planning and Abortion in the Socialist Countries of Central and Eastern Europe* (New York: The Population Council, 1970), p. 45.

147 Ye. A. Sadvokasova, *Sotsial'no-gigiyenicheskiye aspekty regulirovaniya razmerov sem'i* (Moscow: Meditsina, 1969), pp. 29–32, 118; and Verbenko, *et al.*, 1968, pp. 7–8.

148 "Ob otmena zapreschcheniya abortov," 23 Nov. 1955, in *Zakonodatel'stvo o pravakh zhenshchin v SSSR*, pp. 31–32, and David, 1970, p. 46. See also Mark G. Field, "The Re-legalization of Abortion in Soviet Russia," *New England Journal of Medicine*, Vol. 255, No. 9, 1956, pp. 421–27.

149 N. D. Bogatyrev (ed.), *Zabolevayemost' gorodskogo naseleniya i normativy lechebno: profilakticheskoy pomoshchi* (Moscow: Meditsina, 1967), pp. 218–19.

150 Sadvokasova, 1969, p. 117.

151 Christopher Davis and Murray Feshbach, *Rising Infant Mortality in the*

USSR in the 1970s, US Department of Commerce, Bureau of the Census, International Population Reports, Series P-95, No. 74, p. 13.

152 Richard Pipes, "Can the Soviet Union Reform?", *Foreign Affairs*, Autumn, 1984, pp. 47–61.

153 The sample survey was conducted by Shneyderman and Popov. Details about the survey have not been provided. See M. S. Bednyy, *Demograficheskiye faktory zdorov'ya* (Moscow: Finansy i Statistika, 1984), p. 111; and N. A. Shneyderman, "Social-Hygienic Factors of Birthrate and Formation of Able-Bodied Population in RSFSR," *Zdravookhraneniye rossiyskoy federatsii*, No. 1, 1982, pp. 25–28.

154 About 10 per cent of these abortions began outside a hospital setting. L. V. Anokhin and L. D. Sarayeva, "Variation in the Level of Some Demographic Indicators by Rayons of an Oblast," *Zdravookhraneniye rossiyskoy federatsii*, No. 1, 1981, pp. 21–24.

155 E. K. Vasil'yeva, *Obraz zhizni gorodskoy sem'i* (Moscow: Finansy i Statistika, 1981), pp. 83–84.

156 The estimated rate was computed from the data on pregnancy outcomes provided by Sokolova, plus both birth rate data and data on the age structure of Leningrad. N. S. Sokolova, "Statistical Analyses of the Outcomes of Pregnancy," *Zdrovookhraneniye rossiyskoy federatsii*, No. 3, 1970, pp. 38–40. The birthrate data are from *Naseleniye SSSR. 1973. Statisticheskiy sbornik* (Moscow: Statistika, 1975), pp. 96–99. The sex and age structure data are from *Itogi 1970* Vol. 2, p. 114; and *Itogi 1959 RSFSR*, pp. 62–63.

157 N. S. Sokolova, "Questions of Analyses of Pregnancy Outcomes Among Women," *Zdravookhraneniye rossiyskoy federatsii*, No. 3, 1980, pp. 13–15.

158 Bogatyrev, pp. 194–95.

159 Z. Bashlyayeva, "How Are We Concerned About the Health of Our Children," in *O naselenii Moskvy* (Moscow: Statistika, 1980), pp. 91–98.

160 *Abortion 1977–79. Need and Services in the United States* (New York: Alan Guttmacher Institute, 1981), pp. 2, 20.

161 Bogatyrev, pp. 218–19.

162 This survey of Soviet policy on contraceptives is drawn primarily from Sadvokasova, 1969, pp. 124–29. An example of popular literature designed to promote better use of birth control techniques and more limited recourse to abortion is S. M. Yakovleva, *Protivozachatochnyye sredstva* (Moscow: Meditsina, 1970). The brochure was published in 650,000 copies.

163 Sadvokasova, 1969, p. 180; and *Moskva. Entsiklopediya* (Moscow: "Sovetskaya Entsiklopediya", 1980), p. 637.

164 K. H. Mehlan, "Teaching Family Planning in Eastern Europe: The Significance of the High Abortion Rate," in Janet Leban (ed.), *Teaching Family Planning* (New York: The Joseph Mary Jr Foundation, 1973), pp. 61–76.

165 Ira Lubell, "IUDs and Family Planning in the USSR," in E. S. E. Hafez and W. A. A. van Os (eds.), *IUDs and Family Planning* (Boston, Mass: G. K. Hall Medical Publishers, 1980), pp. 137–39. See also

Barbara Holland, "A Woman's Right to Choose in the Soviet Union," in Brine, Perrie, and Sulton, 1980, pp. 55–69.

166 Malcolm Potts and Peter Selman, *Society and Fertility* (Plymouth, Great Britain: Macdonald and Evans Ltd, 1979), pp. 111–12.

167 *Ibid.*, pp. 203–04.

168 Emily C. Moore, "Inducted Abortion and Contraception: Sociological Aspects," in Sidney H. Newman (ed.), *Abortion, Obtained and Denied: Research Approaches* (The Population Council), 1971, pp. 131–55.

169 S. I. Golod, *Stabil'nost' sem'i: sotsiologicheskiy i demograficheskiy aspekty* (Leningrad: Nauka, 1984), p. 134.

170 Sh. Shlindman and P. Zvidrin'sh, *Izucheniye rozhdayemosti* (Moscow: Statistika, 1973), pp. 134–45; and L. Ye. Darskiy and V. A. Belova, "Social-hygienic Questions Connected with Marriage and Childbirth in Families," *Zdravookhraneniye rossiyskoy federatsii*, No. 3, 1969, pp. 14–17. The major difference between contraceptive use in European Russia and Western developed countries is not the level of use itself, but the fact that most European and US women who use contraception rely on the most reliable techniques. On contraceptive use in the developed countries of the West see Henri Leridon, "Fertility and Contraception in 12 Developed Countries," *Family Planning Perspectives*, Vol. 3, No. 2, March/April 1981, pp. 93–102.

171 Darskiy and Belova, 1969. See also V. D. Vlasov, "Several Aspects of Social-demographic Research in the Extreme North," *Zdravookhraneniye rossiyskoy federatsii*, No. 8, 1972, pp. 26–30.

172 I. P. Katkova, *Rozhdayemost' v molodykh sem'yakh* (Moscow: Meditsina, 1971), pp. 70, 79–80, 85.

173 Vlasov, 1972.

174 Yakovleva, *Protivo-zachatochnyye sredstva*, 1970, p. 21.

175 Results of Soviet studies on contraceptive methods are reported in S. M. Yakovleva, *Sposoby i sredstva kontratseptsii* (Leningrad: Meditsina, 1970), pp. 132; M. S. Tsirulnikov, R. A. Khentov and I. S. Rozovskiy, *Predu- prezhdeniye beremennosti* (Moscow: Gosudarstvennoy Izdatel'stvo Medit- sinksoy Literatury, 1963); M. D. Tsirulnikov and R. A. Khentov, "On the Application of Some Contraceptive Means and Computation of their Effectiveness," *Voprosy okhrana materinstva i detstva*, No. 6, 1960, pp. 49–51; and Shlindman and Zvidrin'sh, 1973, pp. 134–45. See also, *Zdorov'ye vashego rebenka* (Kiev: Zdorov'ya, 1983), pp. 23–25.

Both Soviet officials in the family planning field and their counter- parts in the West rate withdrawal as an unreliable birth control technique. However, "folk" methods, such as withdrawal and rhythm, were the primary techniques used to achieve the long-term fertility decline in France; and failure rates can be surprisingly low. A US study in 1941 found a failure rate of 10 pregnancies per 100 woman-years of use for withdrawal, compared to a rate of 12 for other methods. Like all contraceptive techniques, failure rates vary with the background of the user and the stage of family building. Potts and Selman, 1979, pp. 110–51. A 1935–47 study of contraception in Great Britain revealed that failure rates for withdrawal were only marginally higher than appliance methods (condom, spermicides, diaphram). Christopher Tietze, "The Current Status of Fertility Control," *Law and Contemporary Problems,* Vol. 25, No. 3, Summer 1960, pp. 426–44.

176 Yakovleva, *Sposoby,* 1970, p. 132.

177 G. I. Litvinova, "Demographic Legislation in European Socialist Countries," *Sovetskoye gosudarstvo i pravo,* No. 7, 1980, pp. 67–75; and Barbar Wolfe Jancar, *Women Under Communism* (Baltimore: The Johns Hopkins University Press, 1978), pp. 143–44.

178 Urlanis, "A Wanted Child," 1980.

179 Sadvokasova, 1969, p. 117.

180 B. Ts. Urlanis, "Dynamics of Fertility in the USSR," in N. P. Fedorenko (ed.), *Vosproizvodstvo naseleniya i trudovykh resursov* (Moscow: Nauka, 1976), pp. 16–33; and Bazdyrev, 1979.

181 A. I. Salatich, "Study of the Birthrate in Rural Localities," *Zdravookhraneniye rossiyskoy federatsii,* No. 4, 1971, pp. 18–23. See also Ya. I. Golin, "Indicators of Population Reproduction in Dagestan ASSR," *Zdravookhraneniiye rossiyskoy federatsii,* No. 6, 1972, pp. 6–8.

182 G. P. Kiseleva, "On the Demographic Situation in the RSFSR," in V. N. Yakimov (ed.), *Rayonnyye osobennosti vosproizdovstva naseleniya SSSR. Materialy vsesoyuznogo mezhdvusovskogo nauchnogo simpozium* (Cheboksary, 1972), pp. 46–57. See also G. P. Kiseleva, "From the Experience of a Concrete Socio-demographic Investigation," in *Izucheniye vosproizvodstva naseleniya* (Moscow: Nauka, 1968), pp. 307–16; V. A. Belova, *Chislo detey v sem'ya* (Moscow: Statistika, 1975), p. 160; I. V. Polyakov, "Population Production in Leningrad," *Sovetskoye zdravookhraneniye,* No. 8, 1973, pp. 43–46; G. M. Korostrelev and A. A. Petrakov, "Study of the Practice of Family Planning," *Sovetskoye zdravookhraneniye,* No. 8, 1967, pp. 30–32; N. M. Shishkan, *Trud zhenshchin v usloviyakh razvitogo sotsializma* (Kishinev: Izdatel'stvo Shtiintsa, 1976), p. 100; and I. Ye. Tomskiy, *Sotsial'no-ekonomicheskiye problem zhenskogo truda (na materialakh yakutskoy ASSR)* (Novosibirsk: Nauka, 1979), pp. 130–31.

183 Ye. A. Sadvokasova, "The Role of Abortion in Realization of Motherhood in the USSR," in *Izucheniye vosproizvodstva naseleniya* (Moscow: Nauka, 1968), pp. 207–24; and Ye. A. Sadvokasova, "Several Social-hygienic Aspects of Studying Abortions," *Sovetskoye zdravookhraneniye,* No. 3, 1963, pp. 45–50; and V. K. Kuznetsov, "On Factors Influencing the Number of Abortions," *Zdravookhraneniye rossiyskoy federatsii,* No. 9, 1969, pp. 9–10.

184 V. A. Belova, "Family Size and Social Opinion," in A. G. Volkov (ed.), *Faktory rozhdayemosti* (Moscow: Statistika, 1971), pp. 35–51. See also G. P. Kiseleva, "To the Question of Regional Differences in Soviet Birthrates," in D. I. Valentey (ed.), *Voprosy teorii i politiki narodonaseleniya* (Moscow: Izdatel'stvo Moskovskogo Universiteta, 1970), pp. 141–53.

185 Eglite, 1984, pp. 128–31. See also Yu. P. Siks, "Subjective Evaluation of Material and Housing Conditions as a Factor for Limiting Children," *Izvestiya AN latviyskoy SSR,* No. 4, 1982, pp. 35–45.

186 N. Zvereva, "Demand for Children in the System of Demands of

Working Women," in *Chelovek v aktivnom vozraste* (Moscow: Finansy i Statistika, 1984), pp. 37–47.

187 Steshenko, 1982, p. 227.

188 V. Perevedentsev, "Demographic Policy," *Sotsialisticheskaya industriya*, 9 June 1983, p. 3.

189 I. V. Dzarasova, "On the Influence of Social-economic Factors on Birthrate," in *Naseleniye i narodnoye blagosostoyaniye* (Moscow: Vysshaya Shkola, 1968), pp. 64–80; A. A. Vostikova, "Methods of Research and Indicators of Birthrate in the USSR," in *Voprosy narodonaseleniya i demograficheskoy statistiki* (Moscow: Statistika, 1966), pp. 29–38; and B. Ts. Urlanis, *Narodonaseleniy. Issledovaniya. Publitsistika.* (Moscow: Statistika, 1976), p. 220.

190 L. M. Davtyan, "Influence of Socio-economic Factors on Birthrate, with the Example of Armenia SSR," in *Voprosy narodonaseleniya i demograficheskoy statistiki* (Moscow: Statistika, 1966), pp. 47, 54; G. M. Korostrelov, "To the Characteristic of a Socioeconomic Law of Socialist Society," in *Izucheniye vosproizvodstva naseleniya* (Moscow: Nauka, 1968), pp. 23–36; L. A. Arutyunyan, *Sotsialisticheskiy zakon narodonaseleniya* (Moscow: Nauka, 1975); A. A. Petrakov, "Sociological Study of the Influence of Migration on Birthrate," in *Problemy formirovaniya i razvitiya naseleniya urala* (Sverdlovsk, 1977), pp. 124–31; I. N. Zhelokhovtseva, L. Ye. Sviridova and Yu. D. Shitikov, "On the Interconnection of Marital Fertility of Young Women with their Social-hygienic Conditions of Family Life," *Sovetskoye zdravookhraneniya*, No. 12, 1973, pp. 31–7; and A. A. Akhmedov, "Marital Fertility among Rural Women in Azerbaydzhan SSR," *Sovetskoye zdravookhraneniye*, No. 3, 1974, pp. 43–49.

191 The methodological problems are summarized in Z. A. Yankova, *Gorodskaya sem'ya* (Moscow: Nauka, 1979), pp. 71–73. See also V. P. Tomin, "The All-union Symposium on Demographic Problems of the Family," *Sotsialogicheskiye issledovaniya*, No. 2, 1976, pp. 187–91.

192 P. Zvidrin'sh, "From the Experience of Conducting a Sociodemographic Investigation in the Latvian SSR," *Vestnik statistiki*, No. 2, 1973, pp. 28–35.

193 L. P. Shakhot'ko, *Rozhdayemost' v belorussii* (Minsk: Nauki i Tekhnika, 1975), p. 100.

194 Tauber, 1965; and N. A. Tauber, "Influence of Several Conditions of Life on the Level of Marital Fertility," in A. G. Volkov (ed.), *Problemy demograficheskoy statistiki* (Moscow: Nauka, 1966), pp. 128–45.

195 V. Belova, "Differentiation of Opinions on the Desired and Expected Number of Children in the Family," *Vestnik statistiki*, No. 7, 1971, pp. 27–36; and Belova, *Chislo detey v sem'ya*, 1975, pp. 146–49.

196 G. A. Slesarov, *Metodologiya sotsiologicheskogo issledovaniya problem narodonaseleniya SSSR* (Moscow: Mysl', 1965), p. 117.

197 R. I. Sifman, "Birthrates and Material Well-being," in L. Ye. Darskiy (ed.), *Rozhdayemost'*, 1976, pp. 76–92.

198 *Ibid.*

199 Shlindman and Zvidrin'sh, 1973, pp. 60–67. *Izucheniye rozhdayemosti* (Moscow: Statistika, 1973), pp. 60–67.

200 I. A. Anderson, *Tretey rebenok* (Riga: Liesma, 1979), pp. 20–25.

201 G. Ye. Tsuladze, *Sotsiologo-psikhologicheskoye izucheniye rozhdayemosti* (Tbilisi: Izdatel'stvo Metsniyereba, 1982), pp. 66–73, 77, 99–102.

202 D. L. Broner, "Family and Housing Conditions," in D. L. Broner (ed.), *Problemy demografii* (Moscow: Statistika, 1971), pp. 149–60.

203 G. Kiseleva and I. Rykova, "On the Motives for Limiting Fertility," in D. I. Valentey (ed.), *Razvitiye naseleniya* (Moscow: Statistika, 1974), pp. 55–71.

204 Shlindman and Zvidrin'sh, 1973, pp. 67–72. See also I. Zarinsh, "Social-economic Characteristics of the Family and Its Influence on the Number of Children," in *Sotsial'no-demograficheskiye issledovaniya pribaltiki* (Riga: Zinatne, 1980), pp. 63–75.

205 Anderson, 1979, pp. 25–26.

206 V. V. Boykov, *Malodetnaya sem'ya. Sotsial'no-psikhologicheskoye issledovaniye* (Moscow: Statistika, 1980), pp. 169–80.

207 Tauber, 1956; and Tauber, 1966.

208 R. K. Zotina, "On Social-hygienic Factors Influencing Birthrate," *Zdravookhraneniye rossiyskoy federatsii*, No. 10, 1972, pp. 23–26.

209 Slesarov, 1965, pp. 118–25.

210 L. M. Davtyan, "The Influence of Socio-economic Factors on Natality," in *Proceedings of the World Population Conference. Belgrade, 30 August – 10 September 1965*, Vol. 2 (New York: United Nations, 1967), pp. 73–77.

211 V. I. Lanshina, "Toward a Method to Study the Influence of Housing Conditions on the Birthrate," in A. G. Volkov (ed.), *Voprosy demografiy* (Moscow: Statistika, 1970), pp. 116–23.

212 Ye. L. Kasparov, *Dinamika rozhdayemosti i brachnosti v kalmytskoy ASSR* (Elista: Kalytskoye Knizhnoye Izdatel'stvo, 1974), p. 106–07. See also V. Barthis, "The Experience of Studying the Reproductive Behavior of the Family," in *Sotsial'no-ekonomicheskiye osobennosti vosproizvadstva naseleniya v usloviyakh razvitogo sotsializma*, Vol. 2 (Kiev: Institut Ekonomiki AN USSR, 1976), pp. 93–95.

213 V. Boldyrev, "Action of Economic Laws of Population in Developed Socialist Society," in *Zakony i zakonomernosti razvitiya narodonaseleniya* (Moscow: Statistika, 1976), pp. 21–37.

214 L. D. Araslanova, "Dynamics of the Birthrate in Komi-permyak National Okrug, 1939–1970," in *Zdorov'ye naseleniya permskoy oblasti* (Perm, 1974), pp. 37–41.

215 A. I. Antonov, "Is the Value for Children Being Reduced?" in *Rozhdaye-most': izvestnoye i neizvestnoye* (Moscow: Finansy i Statistika, 1983), pp. 70–79.

216 See Chapter 2.

217 See, for example, "Two Plus Three: On Measures to Encourage Motherhood," *Izvestiya*, 25 June 1984, p. 3.

Part 3

Conclusions

6

Social change and fertility decline in the USSR

With this chapter, we return to the issues raised at the beginning of the book. To what extent does the Soviet experience confirm or refute hypotheses about fertility change generated by findings from other national settings? Does the model of fertility transition outlined in Chapter 1 have relevance for the Soviet case? That is, to what degree have modernization and value change affected demographic dynamics? Has the USSR's extensive capacity for government intervention produced an analogous ability to manipulate demographic trends? In answering these questions we explored the relationship between modernization, value change, and fertility. Three hypotheses were tested:

In the intermediate stages of fertility transition, as modernization level increases, natality decreases.

As modernization level increases, the strength of patriarchal family values decreases. This relationship will be mediated by a "cultural filter."

In the intermediate stages of fertility transition, as patriarchal family values decrease, fertility decreases.

The first hypothesis was tested by examining the published results of Soviet natality studies, as well as through an analysis of the empirical relationships evident in five basic data sets. In general, the hypothesis received moderate to strong support from all sources. Regardless of how the concept of modernization is measured (by urbanization level, level of education, level of functional specialization) and regardless of how these measures are in turn operationalized (i.e., education by proportion of the population with completed higher education or by student enrollment figures standardized to appropriate age groups), and – regardless of how natality was

335

measured – indicators of modernization were found to be moderately correlated with measures of natality for all data sets examined Moreover, these relationships were also found in the published results of Soviet studies that provide individual-level data; the exception to this generalization is analysis confined to the highly modernized European areas. Here, as predicted by the model, the correlation between natality diminishes as small and medium-sized families become more popular among all socioeconomic and educated groups.

The second hypothesis was examined through an analysis of the four contemporary data sets. The data reveal moderate relationships between measures of modernization and measures of the erosion of patriarchal family values and sex roles. We suggested that the impact of modernization on family values might be mediated by a cultural filter; those cultures that place special importance on patriarchal value systems are hypothesized to be particularly resistant to change in family values. In the Soviet context, those groups and regions of Muslim heritage might be especially resistant to social change involving the family and the role of women. To include culture in our equation, we employed a dummy variable for "Muslimness." This variable did not prove to be a good predictor of modernization level. However, Muslimness is related to a moderate degree with the various measures of "traditionality." Multiple regression using both measures of modernization and Muslimness as predictors of patriarchal family values indicated that both factors were indeed important in explaining the erosion of traditional gender role norms. Depending on which measures were employed, the two-variable regression yielded an explained variance between 50 and 70 per cent. These findings indicate that, as suggested by the second hypothesis, cultural heritage does play a crucial role during the modernization process, making some groups and areas more receptive to social changes involving family relationships and gender roles and others more resistant to them.

This finding, of course, simply pushes the analysis back one step, raising the issue of what it is about Muslim cultures that resists erosion of patriarchal family values, even when the classic measures of modernization (urbanization, education, and so forth) are held constant. We assume that there is a reasonable social explanation for the apparent greater rigidity of Muslim cultures in the USSR. Yet the data available in the Soviet case are not precise enough to capture the importance a culture or region attributes to patriarchal values. This issue might be profitably explored in non-Soviet multi-ethnic settings where good individual-level data on both modernization level and values are available and the relationship between the two could be analysed for both Muslims and non-Muslims.

The third hypothesis received extremely strong support by the material analyzed here. Both the individual-level Soviet studies and our own empirical analysis of the five data sets provide persuasive support for the hypothesis that the erosion of patriarchal family values and natality decline are closely linked during the intermediate phases of the demographic transition. To test this hypothesis, we examined socioeconomic variables that have been found in Western social research to be closely linked with gender role ideology. These included female educational attainment and early marriage. We also investigated the relationship between natality and female labor force participation, particularly participation in the modernized sectors of the labor force. As with hypothesis 1, regardless of how the concept of patriarchal family values is measured and regardless of how these measures are in turn operationalized, all available data suggest a close relationship between these measures and natality decline, for all data sets and for all measures of natality (index of total fertility, expected number of children, child-to-woman ratios, general fertility rate, etc.). The most powerful predictor of natality decline, however, was a series of relative female-to-male indices for both educational level and participation in the modernized workforce. For nationalities, a single predictor (female to male complete secondary education) explained about 80 per cent of the variance in fertility ratios. Several of the other ratio variables (which we call "emancipation") yielded similarly strong relationships; and a similar link between the emancipation variables and measures of natality were found for republics, the republic urban–rural data, and the non-European oblasts. These data, supplemented by individual-level findings in published Soviet studies, enable us to conclude that the Soviet case is fully consistent with the relationships specified by the third hypothesis.

These findings, while constituting persuasive evidence of the role of value change in fertility transition, are not inconsistent with an alternate theory of fertility decline. Economists have suggested that the mechanism that produces fertility decline in modernizing areas is the increase in the cost of children and a concomitant decrease in the economic benefits of children as cultures move from premodern to modern socioeconomic systems.[1] Refinements in this theory incorporate the notion of "tastes" for children as an intermediary factor. Our data, unfortunately, are not precise enough to allow us to test the notion, so dear to the hearts of economists, that children can be viewed as a consumer good. However, our findings are not inconsistent with this theory. One could, for example, argue that the link we found between female educational attainment and natality decline is due to the rising economic opportunity costs of children for women with higher levels of education. These women may have smaller families not so much because they are less affected by patriarchal values as the fact that childbearing is a potential disruption of a higher paying job. The less-educated women may also sacrifice her salary temporarily, but since the salary is lower to begin with, it is less of a sacrifice. Similarly, the link between female labor force participation and the stronger relationship between participation in the modernized portions of the labor force may be interpreted, again, in economic terms.

There is one aspect of our findings that may be viewed as at least potentially troubling for the economic explanation of fertility decline – the stronger correlations for the emancipation variables. There are some groups in the Soviet Union that have extraordinarily high levels of female education but only moderate female/male education ratios; an example is the Georgians. There are other groups, like the Karelians and the Komi, with lower female educational attainments (relative to the Soviet mean), but relatively high emancipation scores.* Similar comments apply to indicators of participation in the modernized labor force. If the economic explanation of fertility dynamics is correct, we would expect higher correlations between fertility measures and female education/occupation variables than between fertility and the ratio scores, since these former predictors come closest to capturing the economic opportunity costs of childbearing. In fact, what we found was exactly the opposite. For every single variable (all levels of education, enrollment, all measures of labor force participation), the better predictor of natality is the ratio variable.

* In 1959, Georgian women earned college degrees at the rate of 47 per 1,000 adult women, a rate more than twice the Soviet average. Their female-to-male index score was 68. In contrast, the college graduate rate for Karelian women was 4, one tenth of that of the Georgian women. Yet, the Karelian index score of 67 is virtually identical to that of the Georgians. The respective numbers for the Komi are 11 and 85.

While we have found strong support for the hypotheses tested, we certainly do not rule out the economic component of natality change. To some degree, the norms vs. dollars (or, in the Soviet case, norms vs. rubles) theories are not mutually incompatible. The increasing economic costs of children may well reinforce or modify values supporting a large number of children. But even the most vehement supporters of the costs of children explanation for fertility decline would readily concede that the theory has little explanatory power unless the normative concept "tastes for children" is factored in. Similarly, the most recent studies of the maternal role incompatibility theory have underlined the importance of *perceived* conflict between the mother and worker role: the level of conflict is not mechanistically related to "real" structural or temporal contradictions, but rather to the woman's perception of her mother role. Role conflict, then, depends on both the "real" external conditions and learned norms regarding appropriate mothering behavior.

Our findings with regard to the impact of policy on fertility are mixed. We examined two aspects of policy – social policy and demographic policy. The most important aspect of Soviet social policy, in terms of fertility transition, is the role played by the Soviet government as a champion of socioeconomic development and sexual equality. These policies produced a dramatic, sustained fertility decline in the European areas of the USSR in the decades following the Bolshevik Revolution. In the southern tier area, they produced, in the short run, a fertility increase (among those minorities where poor medical and nutritional conditions had produced a high proportion of sterility and sub-fecundity) and, in the long run, the beginning of a fertility decline quite similar to that which occurred earlier in the European areas.

It is important to note that to a large degree these social policies involved radical change for both the European areas of the USSR and for the even less developed areas of the southern tier. Western scholars are fond of depicting the impact of Soviet social policies in the Muslim areas as a clash between Western (Soviet) values and life styles and Eastern, Islamic ones. Indeed, to some degree, the process of Sovietization in the southern tier may well be perceived in these terms by residents there. But in the larger historical context, this image is both false and misleading. Russia on the eve of the Revolution was a predominantly peasant society; the vast majority of the empire's subjects were part of a patriarchal peasant culture, little touched by the thin veneer of Western-style modernization that had produced the beginning of an industrial revolution in the late nineteenth century.

For both regions, then, the impact of the forced-pace modernization program was a socially disruptive one. Patriarchal family values dominated both areas on the eve of the Revolution. The transition from a mixed, subsistence-market, agricultural society where the patriarchal family functioned as the major social and economic unit to an industrialized, urbanized culture, with the family stripped of many of its former functions, was a socially wrenching experience for the vast majority of Slavic peasants in European Russia. To be sure, the impact of the Soviet regime was probably even more traumatic for the cultures of the southern tier. But the difference was more of degree than kind. Soviet efforts to "level out" the social and economic differences that have historically set these groups apart from the European nationalities have produced rapid social change in the Muslim areas; the Muslim cultural heritage of rigid sex-based roles and (in some cases) strict physical segregation of the sexes has served to moderate, but not eradicate, the effects of socioeconomic development on family systems. This cultural heritage, however, has not made the Islamic groups immune to the consequences of modernization; and patriarchal family values, while still far stronger here than in European Russia, are eroding under the impact of the Soviet efforts to level out ethnic socio-economic differences. This has produced the beginning of rapid fertility decline – a process that has progressed furthest among Azeris, Kazakhs and Tatars. In this sense, then, Soviet social policies have had a significant and sustained influence on fertility.

Soviet demographic policy, by contrast, can be credited with very little of the salient fertility changes that have occurred throughout the country. This policy has been a rather muddled attempt to moderate the fertility decline among those groups that have more or less completed the fertility transition. Because the goals of Soviet demographic programs are multiple – not just to produce higher fertility among low-fertility groups, but to improve welfare as well – most of the program ruble has been channelled, ironically, to the high-fertility southern tier areas! So, while some of the programs have probably served to moderate slightly the natality-inhibiting impact of social and nationality policies in these high-fertility areas, the fertility-encouraging effects on the low-fertility areas have probably been minimal. Awareness of this contradiction has led Soviet demographers to advocate a shifting of program efforts to low-fertility areas, but these proposals have come under opposition from Muslim area officials who support the current mix of programs from primarily a welfare stance. So far, the leadership response to these conflicting policy positions has been a compromise weighted in favor of the supporters of the status quo. Terminating popular social welfare programs, it seems, is a sticky proposition in both capitalist and socialist countries, particularly if the primary recipients of the programs are minority groups with a claim to disadvantaged status. One attractive alternative is to retain the programs but simply fail to adjust benefits to keep pace with average salaries.

Whether Soviet officials will adopt the vigorous pronatalist programs urged by some demographers to promote the mid-sized family is another issue. The programs that were adopted during the 1970s and early 1980s certainly fell far short of the commitments necessary to provide any real stimulation to fertility for the low-fertility European woman. If the East European experience is any guide, low-status, low-salary women will be disproportionately represented among those who choose to take advantage of the new maternity leave program. The program may produce marginal fertility increases among these groups, but will probably do little to stem the long-term fertility decline now beginning in the Soviet southern tier.

What all of this means for post-1970 regional fertility trends in the Soviet Union may be summarized as follows. In European areas and groups, fertility declined further, but at a considerably slower pace than the previous decade, as these areas approached completion of the fertility transition. In the southern tier, reported fertility began what may turn out to be a very rapid decline. The timing of the process is probably quite uneven, reflecting the fact that Soviet Muslim groups differ from each other substantially in levels of modernization as well as adherence to patriarchal family values. Pronatalist Soviet demographic programs have probably had at least a marginal effect in moderating this decline. This assessment suggests that the 1979 census data, when and if it is released, should reveal not only continuing natality differentials, but also the beginning of sustained natality decline among southern tier minorities.

MODELING SOVIET FERTILITY

To explore the statistical linkages between social variables and natality more fully, we developed a series of models using 1959 social variables to predict 1970 fertility. The best predictive model for the 30 case republic urban/rural file is depicted in Table 6.1 and Figure 6.1. The two 1959 variables used in the equation are both measures of the extent to which patriarchal values have been eroded. The first, emancipation (complete secondary), is the ratio of female-to-male populations with completed secondary school and above. The second, emancipation (industrial work), is the ratio of female-to-male participation in the industrial labor force. As is clear for the regression results (Table 6.1), the more powerful predictor is the education ratio, which explains 89 per cent of the variance; the industrial labor factor adds one additional per cent. The reported and predicted total fertility values are plotted in Figure 6.1. The accuracy of the predictions can be measured by the distance from the 45 degree line. If the predictions had been 100 per cent accurate, all of the points would fall on that line. As is illustrated by Figure 6.1, the two factor model generated highly accurate results. The most inaccurate prediction was for the rural Ukraine where fertility was overpredicted. In rural Ukraine, both emancipation scores were relatively low compared to other rural areas in the USSR's north and west. This error aside, the model accurately forecast both urban and rural total fertility in the RSFSR and several of the Islamic regions of the country. Rural Uzbekistan and rural Tadzhikistan, for example, have forecasts very close to the reported fertility levels.

The larger number of cases in the oblast file gave us an opportunity to explore more fully the relationships between fertility, on the one hand, and modernization and the role of women on the other. The first step was to identify the best model of 1970 fertility, using 1959 social and cultural variables. The results appear in Table 6.2 and Figure 6.2. Again, the most powerful predictor is emancipation (complete secondary) – the ratio of female-to-male educational attainment. This single measure of patriarchal family values explains nearly two-thirds (63 per cent) of the variation in fertility for 169 oblast-level units. Inclusion of the Muslim dummy variable, a cultural indicator, adds another 11 per cent. Finally, the urban percentage, an indicator of modernization, contributes an additional 5 per cent of explained variance. The total variance explained is 0.79.

Table 6.1. *Regression of 1970 index of total fertility on two factors*
(30 cases: 15 republics – urban and rural)

Variable	% of variance explained	Regression coefficient (beta)	T-Test	Significance
Emancipation Complete secondary	0.89	−0.833	−11.023	0.0001
Emancipation Industrial work	0.01	−0.173	−2.292	0.0299
Total (adjusted)	0.90			

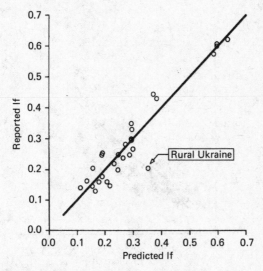

Figure 6.1 Reported and predicted 1970 index of total fertility (30 cases: 15 republics: urban and rural)

While this model is excellent by general social science standards, the logic of the demographic transition model presented in Chapter 1 suggests that what is actually operating here are two separate, though interrelated, processes. For the late modernizing southern tier regions, we expect to find much stronger relationships between measures of patriarchal family values and natality than in the more

Table 6.2. *Regression of 1970 index of total fertility on three factors (169 oblasts)*

Variable	% of variance explained	Regression coefficient (beta)	T-Test	Significance
Emancipation Complete secondary	0.63	−0.386	−7.674	0.0001
Muslim (dummy variable)	0.11	0.487	10.230	0.0001
% urban	0.05	−0.243	−6.390	0.0001
Total (adjusted)	0.79			

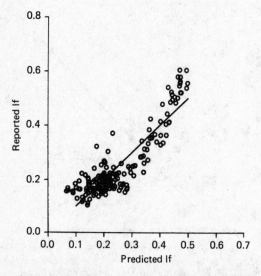

Figure 6.2 Reported and predicted 1970 index of total fertility (169 oblasts)

modernized European areas. In the low fertility European areas, by contrast, we expect that the value for small and medium sized families has already been disseminated throughout most regions. The remaining fertility differentials in the European areas are smaller and they should be less strongly associated with the 1959 measures of modernization and family values. Moreover, the marked

Table 6.3. *Regression of 1970 index of total fertility on percent urban (108 European oblasts)*

Variable	% of variance explained	Regression coefficient (beta)	T-Test	Significance
% urban	0.38	−0.619	−8.111	0.0001
Total (adjusted)	0.38			

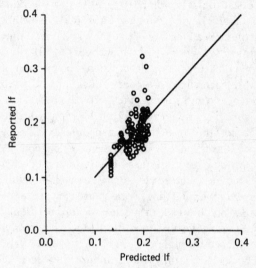

Figure 6.3 Reported and predicted 1970 index of total fertility (108 European oblasts)

curvilinearity shown in the plot of Figure 6.2 suggests that the relationships between the three factors and fertility differ depending on fertility level.

Indeed, when separate regressions are performed on the European and non-European regions, this is precisely what we find. The best model of European fertility contains only one variable – percentage urban, a classic measure of modernization level. The level of urbanization in 1959 in the 108 European oblasts explains only 38 per cent of the variance in 1970 fertility (Table 6.3 and Figure 6.3). The plot of the residuals in Figure 6.3 deserves some elaboration. The column of residuals in the lower left portion of the figure are the seven cities of Leningrad, Moscow, Riga, Kishinev, Kiev, Tallin, and Vilnius, each with a 1959 urbanization score of 100. The six outliers at the top of the figure – those that were most severely underpredicted by our model – are Tuvin ASSR, Kalmyk ASSR, Chuvash ASSR, Yakut ASSR, Moldavia (excluding Kishinev), and Buryat ASSR. While not Muslim, these areas are among the least "European" in the European region; when they are excluded from the regression, the explained variance rises from 38 to 46 per cent.

Far better results are achieved when the analysis is limited to the 61 non-European oblasts, where 91 per cent of the non-European fertility is explained by three factors (Table 6.4). As before, the most powerful predictor is a measure of patriarchal family values, emancipation (complete secondary), which accounts for 81 per cent of the variation. Two measures of modernization – proportion of the adult population with specialized secondary education and the percentage urban – contribute 9 and 1 per cent respectively to the total explained variance. Figure 6.4 provides a plot of the reported and predicted fertility levels for the 61 non-European oblasts. The plot reveals graphically the excellence of the model. The good fit provides additional support for the hypothesis that it is not modernization, but rather value change, that leads to changes in fertility behavior. Nor is it surprising that the modeling works better for the non-European oblasts, since a much larger proportion of those regions are in the intermediate stages of fertility transition. Once the "modern" family values have diffused throughout society, as they have in many of the European oblasts, the family values indicators lose much of their explanatory power.

For the republic and nationality data sets, we used the strong empirical linkages between 1959 social variables and 1970 fertility measures to predict post-1970 fertility developments. We present these models with all due regard for the uncertainties involved in making such predictions. Predicting fertility trends is not a precise science. Fertility dynamics are linked to a multitude of social, political, economic, and demographic factors; and projecting the impact of these factors is a highly speculative exercise. Nonetheless, our analysis of the social correlates of 1970 fertility revealed such strong relationships between 1959 social measures and 1970 fertility, we decided to test these relationships by using 1970 social data to

Table 6.4. *Regression of 1970 index of total fertility on three factors (61 non-European oblasts)*

Variable	% of variance explained	Regression coefficient (beta)	T-Test	Significance
Emancipation				
complete secondary	0.81	−0.664	−12.293	0.0001
Specialized				
secondary educ.	0.09	−0.258	−3.025	0.0037
% urban	0.01	−0.157	−2.222	0.0303
Total (adjusted)	0.91			

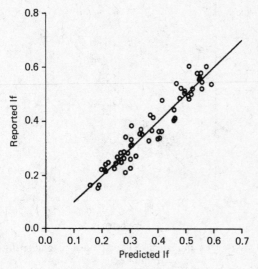

Figure 6.4 Reported and predicted 1970 index of total fertility (61 non-European oblasts)

forecast 1979 fertility. For each data set, the procedure began by identifying the 1959 variables that provide the best predictive model of 1970 fertility. For the 15 republics, the best combination of predictors is emancipation (complete secondary education) and Slav percentage. The regression results are provided in Table 6.5 and

Table 6.5. *Regression of 1970 index of total fertility on two factors (15 republics)*

Variable	% of variance explained	Regression coefficient (beta)	T-Test	Significance
Emancipation				
complete secondary	0.86	−0.879	−13.862	0.0001
% Slav	0.09	−0.291	−4.586	0.0006
Total (adjusted)	0.95			

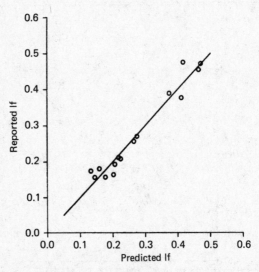

Figure 6.5 Reported and predicted 1970 index of total fertility (15 republics)

Figure 6.5. As Table 6.5 makes clear, the most powerful predictor (explaining 86 per cent of the variance) is the emancipation variable – a measure of patriarchal family values. The cultural variable, the percentage of the population that is Slavic, adds an additional 9 per cent; for a total of 95 per cent explained variance. As with the previous models, the accuracy of the predictions does not depend on the level of modernization. Both highly-modern European republics

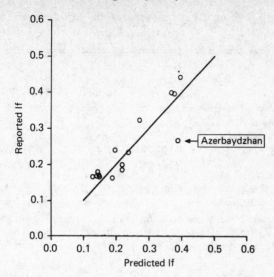

Figure 6.6 Reported and predicted 1980 index of total fertility (15 republics)

(e.g., RSFSR) and late-modernizing republics (e.g., Tadzhikistan) are among the best predicted cases. Conversely, highly modern republics, like Estonia, and less modernized regions, like Turkmenistan, are less well predicted. However, the error rates are very small; the two factor model does extremely well.

The coefficients from the two factor model were used to predict 1980 fertility by inserting the 1970 emancipation and Slav percentage values into the regression equation. The result of these computations is a series of predictions of the 1981 index of total fertility. To derive 1980 fertility, we multiplied the predicted change by 10/11. Figure 6.6 displays the results of the forecast. The predictions were quite good; the correlation between the predicted and actual fertility values is 0.94; or 88 per cent shared variance. The worst prediction is for Azerbaydzhan. The predicted fertility value is 0.388, compared to the reported figure of 0.266 – a substantial overprediction. If Azerbaydzhan is excluded, the correlation between predicted and actual fertility rates rises to 0.96, or 92 per cent shared variance. However, the anomalous prediction for Azerbaydzhan is consistent with other information on fertility trends in this Muslim republic. Fertility is declining there very rapidly, far more quickly than might be expected from measures of either modernization or change in patriarchal

Table 6.6. *Regression of 1970 index of total fertility on three factors (39 nationalities)*

Variable	% of variance explained	Regression coefficient (beta)	T-Test	Significance
Emancipation complete secondary	0.77	−0.551	−6.818	0.0001
Early marriage	0.09	0.421	5.316	0.0001
Slav	0.02	−0.151	−2.595	0.0137
Total (adjusted)	0.88			

Note: Inclusion of the Muslim dummy variable introduced multicollinearity, including sign reversal of the regression coefficient. The three variable model is the most parsimonious and powerful combination of the four variables.

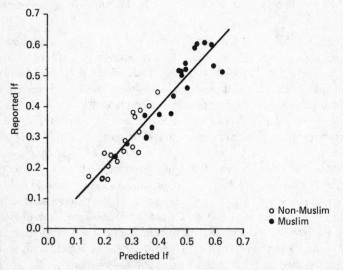

Figure 6.7 Reported and predicted 1970 index of total fertility (39 nationalities)

family values. The dramatic change in Azerbaydzhan natality in the last decade shows that fertility rates in the southern tier may decline very rapidly in the coming decade.

The republic model underestimated fertility in ten republics;

Table 6.7. *Actual and predicted 1970 index of total fertility*

| | | | Index of total fertility | | |
Nationality	Emancipation 1959	Early marriage 1959	Predicted 1970	Actual 1970	Difference (actual minus predicted)
Slav					
Russian	101.3	93	0.175	0.147	−0.028
Ukrainian	83.7	101	0.194	0.166	−0.028
Muslim					
Uzbek	30.7	318	0.528	0.591	0.063
Kazakh	37.5	287	0.495	0.541	0.046
Tatar	97.6	80	0.242	0.240	−0.020
Azeri	41.1	278	0.482	0.502	0.002
Tadzhik	26.4	366	0.563	0.607	0.044
Turkmen	27.8	320	0.536	0.603	0.067
Kirgiz	32.6	442	0.588	0.601	0.013
Chechen	8.5	404	0.627	0.513	−0.114
Avar	16.8	202	0.502	0.460	−0.042
Lezgin	22.0	185	0.480	0.515	0.035
Kabardinian	60.2	111	0.349	0.371	0.022
Kumyk	39.6	214	0.452	0.434	−0.018
Ingush	17.9	149	0.472	0.517	0.045
Balkar	30.0	70	0.401	0.374	−0.027
Dargins	20.2	208	0.497	0.521	0.024
Adygir	69.4	163[b]	0.354	0.300	−0.054
Karachayev	32.4	163[b]	0.444	0.377	−0.067
Cherkess	60.8	163[b]	0.375	0.333	−0.042
Karakalpak	19.6	395	0.595	0.532	−0.063
Abkhazy	84.7	102	0.285	0.281	−0.004
Other					
Armenian	99.5	158	0.278	0.291	0.013
Georgian	100.4	107	0.249	0.223	−0.026
Moldavian	77.6	149	0.326	0.252	−0.074
Lithuanian	101.2	48	0.217	0.208	−0.009
Chuvash	64.2	44	0.305	0.270	−0.035
Latvian	101.3	45	0.215	0.165	−0.050
Estonian	108.5	42	0.196	0.169	−0.027
Udmurt	82.7	70	0.273	0.257	−0.016
Mari	47.4	61	0.354	0.302	−0.052
Osetin	104.0	35	0.203	0.250	0.047
Buryat	68.4	80	0.313	0.367	0.054
Yakut	65.7	55	0.307	0.382	0.075
Komi	101.8	69	0.226	0.244	0.018
Kalmyk	54.7	115	0.364	0.402	0.038
Tuvin	51.0	157	0.395	0.447	0.052
Altay	78.1	163[b]	0.333	0.388	0.055
Khakas	80.0	163[a]	0.328	0.319	−0.009

[a] Based on children under 10.
[b] Value missing, mean score assigned.

overestimated it in only five. While the errors (save for Azerbaydzhan) are all small, the question remains why this is so, particularly since it also occurs if Azerbaydzhan is excluded from the analysis. The answer lies in the change in coefficients between 1970 and 1980. Many of the republics that were underestimated have completed or nearly completed the fertility transition. As fertility rates get lower, it is unreasonable not to expect a slowing down in rates of decline. The resulting errors in prediction, however, are very small and increase our confidence in the validity of the use of social and cultural variables to predict fertility.

A similar strategy was used for the nationalities data. The most parsimonious model of 1970 fertility (using 1959 social variables) is presented in Table 6.6 and Figure 6.7. As with our previous models, the most powerful of the three factors is emancipation (completed secondary education), which explains 77 per cent of the variance in index of total fertility (based on children under 10). This emancipation variable proved to be an excellent measure of traditionality in female roles and was an important predictor in most of the models we present. The second most important variable is also a measure of traditionality in family values – the percentage of 16–19-year-old girls who are married. The early marriage variable adds an additional 9 per cent of explained variance for the 39 nationalities. The dummy Slavic variable contributes 2 per cent to the total of 88 per cent explained variance. As indicated by the data in Table 6.7, this is an extremely efficient model. The worst prediction is for the Chechen, whose fertility was significantly over-predicted. Both of their 1959 traditionality scores point to very high 1970 fertility. The reported rate, while very high, fell significantly below that predicted by the model. The most underpredicted group are the Turkmen, whose reported total fertility rate of 0.603 is moderately higher than the predicted score of 0.536. Despite these outliers, the model is very efficient at predicting 1970 fertility rates.

The coefficients developed by the regression for 1970 fertility were then used to predict a 1979 index of total fertility. We first generated a predicted 1981 index of total fertility by inserting the appropriate 1970 emancipation scores into the equation. We then computed the predicted change in index of total fertility implied by this calculation. Assuming equal change each year, only nine-elevenths of the predicted change would occur by 1979. Accordingly, the predicted change was multiplied by 9/11 (0.8181) to arrive at a prediction for

Table 6.8. *Actual and predicted 1979 index of total fertility*

Nationality	Emancipation 1970	Early marriage 1970	Index of total fertility[a] Predicted 1979	Index of total fertility[a] Estimated 1979	Difference (estimated minus predicted)
Slav					
Russian	102.4	91	0.143	0.155	0.012
Ukrainian	81.8	112	0.204	0.150	−0.055
Muslim					
Uzbek	51.3	217	0.425	0.517	0.092
Kazakh	65.1	123	0.343	0.366	0.022
Tatar	97.6	71	0.237	0.150	−0.087
Azeri	51.5	183	0.497	0.363	−0.045
Tadzhik	46.6	249	0.453	0.526	0.073
Turkmen	50.4	191	0.414	0.488	0.074
Kirgiz	56.7	201	0.404	0.476	0.072
Chechen	31.0	199	0.466	0.343	−0.122
Avar	32.6	185	0.454	0.359	−0.095
Lezgin	39.8	130	0.408	0.294	−0.114
Kabardinian	73.6	140	0.331	0.249	−0.082
Kumyk	57.0	152	0.378	0.310	−0.068
Ingush	38.5	90	0.391	0.283	−0.108
Balkar	57.8	60	0.328	0.200	−0.128
Dargin	33.5	186	0.453	0.393	−0.060
Adygir	75.4	117[b]	0.315	0.197	−0.118
Karachayev	57.8	117[b]	0.358	0.260	−0.098
Cherkess	75.6	117[b]	0.315	0.249	−0.066
Karakalpak	43.8	231	0.451	0.433	−0.018
Abkhazy	92.8	95	0.261	0.195	−0.066
Other					
Armenian	99.0	152	0.276	0.259	−0.017
Georgian	97.8	134	0.269	0.207	−0.063
Moldavian	81.7	119	0.301	0.187	−0.114
Lithuanian	117.0	54	0.181	0.191	0.010
Chuvash	75.6	63	0.287	0.126	−0.161
Latvian	112.1	59	0.196	0.167	−0.029
Estonian	114.7	49	0.184	0.175	−0.009
Udmurt	85.6	69	0.265	0.102	−0.163
Mari	61.5	56	0.317	0.129	−0.188
Ossetin	107.2	53	0.204	0.216	0.012
Buryat	87.3	40	0.246	0.216	−0.030
Yakut	93.8	32	0.226	0.195	−0.031
Komi	112.6	61	0.195	0.104	−0.092
Kalmyk	87.9	56	0.253	0.166	−0.087
Tuvin	114.5	84	0.203	0.256	0.053
Altay	107.7	117[b]	0.237	0.165	−0.072
Khakas	96.5	117[b]	0.264	0.150	−0.114

[a] Based on children under 10.
[b] Value missing, mean score assigned.

nine years of change. This result was then added to the 1970 index of total fertility to yield a predicted fertility value for 1979. Table 6.8 presents the 1970 values for the relevant social variables and the predicted and estimated 1979 index of total fertility.

The basic picture of fertility change that emerges from this model is one of fertility decline. Large decreases in fertility are predicted for virtually all of the Muslim nationalities. For 30 out of 39 ethnic groups, declines are predicted. The increases predicted for the remaining 9 groups are in most cases insignificant. Our predictions involve striking declines for many of the Muslim minorities. For example, the predicted 1979 index of total fertility for the Kirgiz is 0.404, a 33 per cent decline from their 1970 index of total fertility (0.601). Kazakh fertility is expected to decrease from 0.541 in 1970 to 0.343 in 1979, a decrease of 37 per cent. For the other major Muslim groups (Uzbeks, Tadzhiks, Turkmen, and Azeri), fertility is predicted to decline an average of 21.5 per cent. Several of the European minorities, by contrast, are expected to increase their index of total fertility slightly. For example, the Ukrainian index of total fertility is predicted to increase marginally from 0.166 in 1970 to 0.204 in 1979. Russian fertility is expected to remain essentially stable.

The primary factor behind these predicted changes is the changing pattern of female/male educational attainment, the major variable in our predictive equation. Higher 1959 scores on this variable were associated closely with lower 1970 fertility ratios (see Table 6.7). By 1959, for most of the European minorities, there was a rough equality between female and male percentage of completed secondary education. Between 1959 and 1970, the European scores changed very little, producing relative stability in predicted 1979 index of total fertility. The situation for the Muslim minorities was a very different one. In 1959, for many Muslim groups, the proportion of females with completed secondary education and above was less than half that of Muslim males. These extremely low "emancipation" scores in 1959 are associated with extraordinarily high fertility ratios of 1970. For example, the proportion of Tadzhik women with completed secondary education and above was about a quarter that of Tadzhik men; in 1970, the Tadzhiks recorded the highest index of total fertility of all ethnic groups surveyed (0.607). By 1970, the Tadzhik female/male secondary education ratio had increased from 26.4 to 46.6; their early marriage rates had declined from 366 to 249 married

16–19-year-olds per 1,000. These changes suggest a massive transformation in the roles of younger Tadzhik women. Consequently, a substantial decline in fertility is predicted by 1979. The only Muslim group with relatively high female/male education ratios and relatively low early marriage rates for both 1959 and 1970 are the Tatars. The Tatar index of total fertility (0.240) in 1970 was much closer to the European levels than the Muslim. The 1979 Tatar index of total fertility is expected to decline only marginally.

Two caveats regarding our predictions are in order. First, the predicted 1979 fertility scores represent our best estimate regarding general fertility trends among different ethnic groups. Where large decreases in fertility levels are forecast, change in that direction is very likely. When the projected change is near zero, as it is for several of the European groups, neither large increases nor large decreases are deemed probable; in other words, we expect fertility to remain virtually stable among these groups. This caveat is not a disavowal of the accuracy of the predicted change – which rests, after all, on a very good-fitting model – but rather an explicit statement that minor deviations from the forecast figures are to be expected. Second, our predictions for 1979 rest on fertility dynamics between 1959 and 1970. To correct for the possibility of biases in 1970 index of total fertility stemming from assimilation, we excluded six minorities for which we had evidence of substantial levels of assimilation between 1959 and 1970.* However, our predictions do not account for the possibility that some groups may have become increasingly affected by assimilation during the 1970s. For this reason, the predictions are apt to be less accurate for the smaller minorities most vulnerable to assimilation by larger, related cultural groupings. For these groups, our model will tend to over-estimate 1979 fertility. These trends also affect the accuracy of our predictions for groups that are most likely to gain from assimilation (e.g., the Uzbeks); predictions for these groups will tend to underestimate 1979 natality.

Evaluating the accuracy of our 1979 predictions for the nationality groups must await the publication of age-specific nationality data. Nonetheless, there are several sources of data that allow us to assess indirectly the probable accuracy of our results. First, our model rests on the assumption that 1970 ethnic differences in natality were due

---

* The exclusion of these groups does not stem from a desire to eliminate troublesome findings. On the contrary, when the excluded groups are included in the analysis, the explained variance remains virtually unchanged.

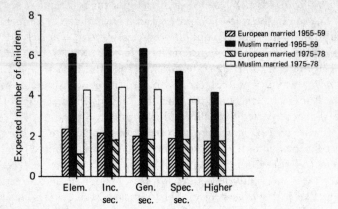

Figure 6.8 Effects of education on ethnic differences in family size expectations, 1978

Source: V. A. Belova *et al.*, "Dynamics and Differentiation of Birth Rate in the USSR," *Vestnik statistiki*, No. 12, 1983, pp. 12–24

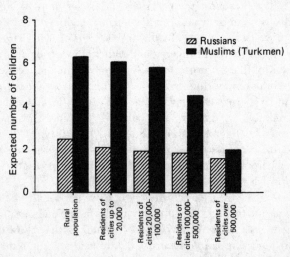

Figure 6.9 Effects of city size on ethnic differences in family size expectations, 1972

Source: Data compiled from V. A. Belova, *et al.*, *Skol'ko detey budet v sovetskoy sem'ye*, Moscow: Statistika 1977, p. 76

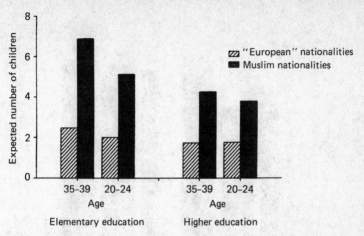

Figure 6.10 Effect of age on ethnic differences in family size, 1972

Source: Data from V. A. Belova, *et al.*, *Skol'ko detey v sovetskoy sem'ye*, Moscow, Statistika, 1977, pp. 63, 64, 69

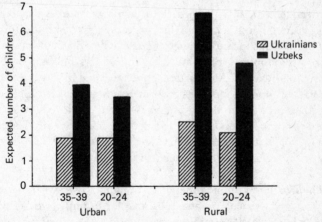

Figure 6.11 Effect of age and region on family size expectations, 1978

Source: Volkov, *et al.*, *Vosproizvodstva*, 1983, pp. 232, 240

primarily to ethnic differences in 1959 socioeconomic factors, particularly those variables involving the role of women in society. As high-natality groups become more "modern" in terms of both structural modernization and family values, we expect a correspond-

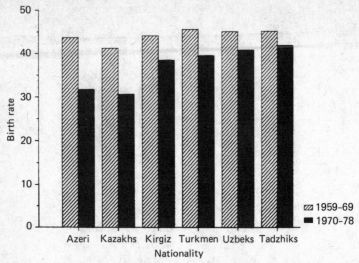

Figure 6.12 Trends in Muslim birth rates

ing decline in natality. Indeed, data from Soviet surveys on expected and desired family size provide persuasive support for this prediction. When educational level or size of city is held constant, ethnic differences diminish dramatically (see Figures 6.8 and 6.9). One study, conducted in Alma-Ata in 1978, revealed that while the ideal number of children for Kazakh women was 30 per cent higher than for Russian women there, among women employed in scientific research institutes and colleges the ethnic difference in ideal family size was only 16 per cent. In sum, the Alma-Ata study clearly shows that ethnic differences diminished for higher-status, better-educated, women.[2]

The decline in ethnic differences in natality is especially striking for younger women. Among Muslims, for example, young women tend to have smaller family size expectations than their mothers and older sisters, regardless of their educational level, residence, or age at marriage (Figures 6.10 and 6.11). One study of young Russian and Azeri women in Baku (the capital of Azerbaydzhan) revealed only marginal ethnic differences in family size expectations. Young Azeri women reported an average expected family size of 2.33, Russian women 2.07. In another Baku study – this time of ideal and desired family size among married women – Azeri women who had married prior to 1940 expressed an ideal family size of 4.3 children and a desired family size of 4.2; the younger Azeri women surveyed had an ideal family size of 2.8 children and a desired family size of 2.2 children.[3] Even in studies limited to Muslim mothers of four or more children, younger women expect to have fewer children than their older counterparts.[4] Similarly, urban Turkmen women aged 23 to 28 reported family size desires and expectations that were 30 per cent below those of their older counterparts over age 39.[5] Similar trends were found in a series of studies of fertility among Uzbek women conducted in 1967–68 and, again, in 1976–78. These studies revealed that natality among older women (those born in the period 1900–09) approached natural limits with virtually no attempt at family limitation. Women born between 1910–39 reported fewer births and some use of family limitation techniques. The younger generation (born between 1940 and 1956) reported a significantly lower ideal family size.[6] Women in their mid-40s (aged 43 to 47) reported an ideal family size of 6.6 children, compared to 5.1 children for women aged 18 to 22. The intended number of children was slightly higher for both groups, 6.9 and 5.3 respectively.[7]

Other statistical data also support our predictions. Two sets of ethnic birth rates have been published; one covering 1959 to 1969 and another covering 1970 to 1978. Figure 6.12 depicts the decline in birth rate for the six Muslim minorities during the 1970s. These data show that the most striking declines occurred among the Azeri – a group for which our model had predicted only moderate natality decreases.

These trends are producing a chorus of complaints from southern tier commentators concerned over the rapid fertility declines. Kazakh demographers complain that rapid fertility decline is taking place among ethnic Kazakhs, particularly urban residents and the rural intelligentsia. Small families of two children are said to be increasingly popular among young Kazakhs. Birth rates for ethnic Kazakhs (within Kazakhstan) fell from 37.2 in 1960 to 24.0 in 1980. Fertility rates for Kazakh women (aged 15 to 49) fell from 220 per 1,000 in 1958–59 to 163 in 1969–70 to 135 in 1978–79, to only 120 in 1980. About 70 per cent of this decline is attributed to family planning, the remainder to late marriage and increasing divorce rates.[8] These assertions are supported by a recent survey of 600 nonmarried Kazakh women aged 18 to 25 who were working or studying in Alma-Ata. Their desired family size was a low 3.28; the majority of those who expressed a desire for large families of five or more children were migrants from isolated rural areas.[9]

Central Asian commentators are now starting to join their Kazakh counterparts in bemoaning the progress of the fertility transition among Islamic groups.[10] As one Turkmen sociologist noted:

it would be a mistake to think that "multi-child" Central Asia, and in particular Turkmenistan, because of the supposed immutability of national traditions, does not have the prospect of changing into a region of small families. Calculations and estimates of our colleagues in the main scientific institutes and sociological research studying the rural family, which are being carried out in our academies, show that such a phenomenon has not only been observed, but is developing rapidly.[11]

The sociologist went on to note that the transition from unlimited to limited natality took almost twenty-five years in Turkmenistan. However, the transition from the large to the medium sized family is likely to proceed more rapidly.[12] These findings provide additional evidence that the basic assumption undergirding our 1979 index of total fertility predictions – that modernization leads to value changes that produce declining fertility – is indeed a valid one.

The second body of data allowing us to test our predictions consists of the reported results of the 1979 census. Although separate age tabulations have not been provided, the preliminary results released thus far do provide overall numbers for each ethnic group in 1979. These data were used in combination with age group data from the 1970 and 1959 censuses to generate estimates of the 1979 index of total fertility. This series of estimates was derived by projecting each age group from the 1970 census nine years, yielding the total estimated number of deaths. This figure was used to calculate the probable number of births between 1970 and 1979; this latter figure, in conjunction with estimated 9-year-olds and females 15 to 49 in 1979 (derived by projecting the appropriate age groups from the 1970 census), yielded an estimated 1979 index of total fertility. Like all estimates of this nature, our estimated 1979 fertility ratios are subject to a number of biases. The estimates rest on USSR survival ratios that are based on Foreign Demographic Analysis Division projections; errors in these data will bias our fertility estimates. This problem is most troubling for those groups with a middle or old age structure. In sum, our estimated series of total fertility indexes should be viewed as a rough projection; this series does, however, enable us to identify probable strengths and weaknesses in the projected

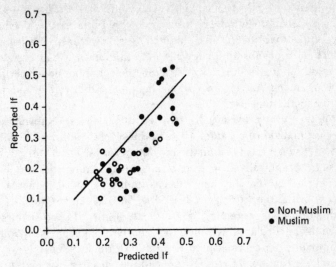

Figure 6.13 Estimated and predicted 1979 index of total fertility
(39 nationalities)

fertility ratios derived from our model. A comparison between the
fertility ratios derived from projections based on reported 1979
census results and our series of predicted ratios derived from the
model are reported in tabular form in Table 6.8 and displayed
graphically in Figure 6.13.

Comparison of the two series suggests that our predictive efforts
have been fairly successful. The large predicted declines in Muslim
indexes of total fertility have, in fact, occurred. The major shortcoming of our predictions is the general tendency to overestimate 1979
fertility levels, particularly among the smaller groups, who have been
subject to assimilation – a process that affects groups unevenly. The
Uzbeks, for example, appear to have their 1979 fertility estimates
inflated slightly by assimilation of Karakalpaks, whose 1979 fertility
estimates are significantly lower than predicted. Such an explanation
does not pertain to another large Muslim group, the Azeris, whose
computed fertility scores are also much lower than predicted. Examination of the 1979 native language and bilingualism results for the
Azeri indicates that probable losses due to assimilation to other
groups are relatively limited; thus, we cannot explain our over-
estimation of Azeri fertility by reference to assimilation. Indeed,

examination of the trends in general and total fertility rates in Azerbaydzhan during the 1970s reveals very rapid fertility declines, suggesting that the results obtained from the census projections reflect real and substantial declines in fertility, rather than losses due to assimilation. In other words, as in the republic model, fertility decline among Azeris is occurring far more rapidly than our predictive model suggests.

Another group for which 1979 fertility levels are substantially over-estimated is the Tatars. In part, this discrepancy may be due to an increasing level of assimilation to other groups. The Tatars are the most geographically dispersed of all Muslim minorities. In some cases, it is clear that they have been assimilating, and at an increasing pace during the 1970s, to Russians, as well as to the "host" nationality. For example, 22 per cent of the 313,000 Tatars in Kazakhstan declared Russian their native language in 1979; an additional 2 per cent declared Kazakh. For the most part, however, our over-estimation of 1979 Tatar fertility stems from the inability of our model to predict with precision the pace of the fertility decline among the more modernized Muslim groups. With the Kazakhs (another modernized Islamic group with moderate to high fertility), these two groups represent nearly half of the Soviet Union's Muslims. Fertility decline among these Islamic minorities is occurring very rapidly indeed.

Another discrepancy between our predicted fertility ratios and the series of fertility estimates generated by reported census results involves Slavic fertility ratios. Indices of total fertility estimated from the 1979 census results reveal that Russian fertility is actually increasing, in contrast to the stability we predicted. Moreover, where we forecast a slight increase in Ukrainian fertility, the estimated fertility scores indicate a slight decline in Ukrainian fertility during the 1970s. The most likely explanation is assimilation. The average republic fertility rates for the RSFSR and the Ukraine were 56 and 56.3 (per 1,000 fertile-aged women); the RSFSR rate represents a combination of ethnic Russian fertility and natality of non-Russian groups from southern tier areas where fertility rates substantially exceeded those of central RSFSR regions. In other words, we may safely assume that ethnic Russian fertility within RSFSR was well below 56 births per 1,000 fertile-age women. In the Ukraine, by contrast, non-Ukrainian groups are at a similar stage in the demographic transition; the Ukraine's fertility rate (56.3) is probably a fair reflection of ethnic Ukrainian fertility. These considerations suggest that real natality levels among Ukrainians are at least as high, and perhaps substantially higher, than among ethnic Russians. Yet, projected 1979 indexes of total fertility are lower for Ukrainians than for Russians, and the average annual Ukrainian growth rate between 1970 and 1979 (0.43) is substantially lower than that of the Russians (0.7). The high and increasing percentage of Ukrainians who identify Russian as their native language (17 per cent in 1979) suggests that the unexpectedly low index of total fertility and growth rates of Ukrainians in the 1970s can be traced to losses due to ethnic assimilation – i.e., children of Ukrainian/Russian parents who declare Russian as their ethnic identity. This same trend, as well as gains due to assimilation from other groups, helps to explain the slight increase in fertility among ethnic Russians.

Full evaluation of the utility of the predictive model presented here must await the publication of the 1979 census.* Nonetheless, estimates generated from the available data suggest that many of our predictions, particularly those for the major nationalities, may be fairly close to the mark. Where the model fails is in our inability to forecast the rapidity with which fertility decline is occurring among those Muslim groups (the Tatars and Azeris) that are already well into the fertility transition. Our predictive model was fairly effective in forecasting the rapid fertility decline among the Kazakhs. Fertility decline among the other four major Muslim groups is occurring more slowly than our model predicted. What this suggests is that fertility decline in the earliest stages of the transition may be relatively slow.

---

* It may be objected that static, cross-sectional analysis is inappropriate for forecasting fertility. Indeed, several of our colleagues have raised this objection. They argue that dynamic analysis of change scores is required to demonstrate causality, noting that static and dynamic analyses frequently produce contrary results. In this case, however, the results of a dynamic analysis lead to similar conclusions. Change in 1959–70 emancipation values predicts 35 per cent of the variance in change in index of total fertility scores between 1970 and 1979. The addition of a dummy variable for whether the group was Muslim or not increases the explained variance to 51 per cent. Despite this confirmation of the importance of female emancipation as an indicator of changing family values that affect fertility, the results are not nearly as compelling as those generated by our static model – i.e., 80 per cent of the variance explained vs. 51 per cent. Furthermore, the basic issue is whether the coefficients generated by regression analysis remain stable from one point in time to another. This is essentially an empirical question, one that also affects dynamic analysis. The closeness of fit between the census-derived estimates of 1979 indexes of total fertility and those predicted by the static analysis indicates that they have remained relatively stable.

Once transition is underway in earnest, however, the momentum shifts in favor of very rapid decreases in fertility. This pattern is clearly evident in a review of Armenian fertility trends. It appears that Kazakh and Azeri fertility may be following a similar path. If so, the overall growth of the Soviet population will slow considerably in the next several decades. The demographic consequences of declining population growth and the uneven timing and pace of fertility transition among Soviet nationalities are discussed below.

DEMOGRAPHIC CONSEQUENCES OF FERTILITY TRANSITION

The foregoing chapters provide persuasive evidence of the consistency of the Soviet fertility experience with the general patterns of fertility transition outlined in Chapter 1. As in many socially and ethnically heterogeneous countries, differences in modernization level and in adherence to patriarchal family values meant that the fertility transition began at different times and proceeded at different rates for different areas and groups. This produced significant variations in regional and minority population growth rates. These differences, in turn, are fueling major changes in the USSR's ethnic composition.

Changes in ethnic composition, however, are nothing new in the USSR. Table 6.9 presents a five-decade overview of ethnic developments. Between 1926 and 1959, the relative positions of each major cultural grouping were fairly stable. The position of individual groups, however, was rather more volatile. For example, between 1926 and 1939, the Ukrainian share of the total populace dropped precipitously, and in fact, the number of individuals identified as Ukrainian decreased by 10 per cent during this period. These and other changes in ethnic composition to 1959 were due to a combination of factors: changes in census definition of nationality, shifts in ethnic categorization, differential fertility and mortality, assimilation, emigration, and the differential impact of forced collectivization and World War II on various regions and groups.[13]

Some of the 1926 and 1939 changes were due to a variation in the wording of the census question relating to minority status. In 1926, the census question asked the respondent to provide ethnicity (*narodnost'*) while in 1939 and later censuses, the question asked for nationality (*natsionalnost'*). This factor may have played a major role in the decline in the Ukrainian share of the population between 1926 and 1959. Assimilation and changes in ethnic categories also had a part in the USSR's changing ethnic mix. The Russians were the major winner in assimilation from the Ukrainian, Polish, Mordvinian, and Karelian minority groups. The low rate of Bulgarian growth was due in part to assimilation to Ukrainian ethnicity. Tatar gains between 1926 and 1939 were partly due to assimilation of several smaller Turkish speaking groups.

Some of the assimilation was due less to intermarriage and consequent shifts in the ethnic affiliation of individuals than to shifts in nationality categories. The number of nationality groups officially recognized by the census audit decreased by almost half from 1926 to 1939. Groups that had been recognized as separate minorities in 1926 were simply folded in, for purposes of census accounting, with larger, culturally-related groups. Into the 1939 count of Uzbeks, for example, went small related groups such as the Kipchaks. This administrative assimilation also helps account for the extraordinarily high growth rates of the Avars.

A key factor in Soviet ethnic trends between 1926 and 1939 was collectivization. The late 1920s decision to reorganize land tenure and agricultural administration was due primarily to the need to gain closer Bolshevik control over the countryside. The main targets of collectivization were ostensibly the *kulaks*, "rich" peasants whose property was confiscated and turned over to the newly created collective farms. In fact, however, peasant resistance to the program was not limited to the so-called *kulaks* (who by official count numbered over 5 million in 1926), but was widespread. Conditions in the countryside between 1929 and 1932 deteriorated to the point of civil war. Violence, looting, and other sporadic acts of peasant retaliation prompted Bolshevik response in kind. The main strategy of most Soviet peasants was passive resistance and refusal to turn over livestock to the new collective farms. Many simply slaughtered their animals, and many other herds and flocks perished in the period of acute grain shortages of the early 1930s. The result was a calamitous decline in agricultural production which reached famine status in some areas. Soviet birth and growth rates plummeted. The winter of 1932 was particularly difficult in the Ukraine, the northern Caucasus, and Kazakhstan. Population losses due to famine are estimated at 4 or 5 million people.[14] These developments played a major role in the population declines charted by the Ukrainians between 1926 and 1939, and in the more dramatic Kazakh declines

Table 6.9. *The USSR's changing ethnic composition (%)*

	1926	1939	1959	1970	1979
Slav	78.0	78.4	77.1	74.6	72.8
Russian	52.9	58.4	54.7	53.4	52.4
Ukrainian	21.2	16.5	17.8	16.9	16.2
Belorussian	3.2	3.1	3.8	3.7	3.6
Polish	0.3	0.4	0.7	0.5	0.4
Bulgarian	0.1	0.1	0.2	0.1	0.1
Other European	5.7	5.9	8.3	8.2	7.8
Armenian	1.1	1.3	1.3	1.5	1.6
Georgian	1.2	1.3	1.3	1.3	1.4
Moldavian	0.2	0.2	1.1	1.1	1.1
Lithuanian			1.1	1.1	1.1
Jews	1.8	1.8	1.1	0.9	0.7
Latvian	0.1	0.1	0.7	0.6	0.6
Estonian	0.1	0.1	0.5	0.4	0.4
Other	1.2	1.1	1.2	1.3	0.9
Muslim	11.8	11.9	11.5	14.2	16.7
Uzbek	2.7	2.8	2.9	3.8	4.8
Kazakh	2.7	1.8	1.7	2.2	2.5
Tatar	2.0	2.5	2.4	2.5	2.4
Azeri	1.2	1.3	1.4	1.8	2.1
Tadzhik	0.7	0.7	0.7	0.9	1.1
Turkmen	0.5	0.5	0.5	0.6	0.8
Kirgiz	0.5	0.5	0.5	0.6	0.7
Avar	0.1	0.5	0.1	0.2	0.2
Other	1.4	1.3	1.3	1.6	2.1
Other	4.5	3.8	3.1	3.0	2.7

during this period. In Kazakhstan, the problems of coerced collectivization were exacerbated by the policy of forcible settlement of nomadic peoples. The resulting disruptions in food supply were catastrophic. The number of Kazakhs declined from nearly 4 million in 1926 to 3.1 million in 1939. Many Kazakhs perished in the violence and famine created by collectivization. Others voted their disapproval of Soviet policies with their feet – by fleeing across the Chinese border.[15]

A major factor in population changes between 1939 and 1959 was, of course, World War II. Although overall Soviet natality and growth rates declined precipitously during the war, some areas and groups were hit harder than others. Large chunks of territory were annexed on the eve of the war and in the postwar territorial settlement. Wartime losses, direct and indirect, were probably heaviest in the western and central areas, particularly those areas that underwent prolonged German occupation or (like Leningrad) blockade. A large, but undetermined, number of Ukrainians, Latvians, and Estonians who occupied areas outside the pre-war Soviet boundaries emigrated to the West rather than face the prospect of becoming Soviet citizens.

These factors make it virtually impossible to evaluate what proportion of the 1926 to 1959 ethnic shifts were due to natality dynamics. After 1959, however, we are on firmer ground. Boundary lines stabilized and emigration has been minimal, affecting primarily Germans and Jews. The list of official nationalities used in the census counts of 1970 and 1979 is quite similar to that used in 1959, so administrative "assimilation" is no longer a major complicating factor in assessing ethnic changes over time. The two major factors accounting for ethnic change after 1959 are natural increase, and (to a much lesser extent) assimilation. Since most assimilation is occurring within the larger ethnic groupings depicted in Table 6.9, focusing on changes in ethnic composition for these larger cultural groupings provides some insight into ethnic shifts that may be attributed wholly to natural increase. Within this context, there are two major trends worth noting in the post-1959 period: a modest, but significant, decline in the European share of the population, and a rather more dramatic increase in the Muslim share.

The European and Slavic declines in population shares between 1959 and 1970, as well as the Muslim gains during this period, were due primarily to differences in natality levels. The shifts between 1970 and 1979 for both Slavs and Muslims were due partly to continuing ethnic differentials in fertility and partly to the demographic impact of differences in age group structure. The high Muslim fertility of the 1960s produced extraordinarily high growth rates between 1959 and 1970 (Table 6.10). Uzbeks, Tadzhiks, and Turkmen, for example, averaged about a 4 per cent annual increase. The annual rate of population increase (unweighted average) for the 36 Muslim minorities was 3.4 per cent; for the group as a whole, the annual increase was 3.3 per cent (weighted average). These rates are all the more astounding when one considers that Muslim age structure was not particularly favorable to high growth rates, although the young age structures of most Muslim groups kept

Table 6.10. *Population trends by nationality*

Nationality	Growth rates		Share of population	
	1959–70	1970–79	1979	2000[a]
Slav			72.20	66.60
Russian	1.12	0.70	52.42	49.07
Ukrainian	0.82	0.43	16.16	14.22
Belorussian	1.23	0.49	3.61	3.24
Muslim			16.40	22.90
Uzbek	3.93	3.43	4.75	7.80
Kazakh	3.52	2.39	2.50	3.32
Tatar	1.62	0.70	2.41	2.26
Azeri	3.69	2.51	2.09	2.84
Tadzhik	3.94	2.51	1.11	1.82
Turkmen	3.90	3.22	0.77	1.22
Kirgiz	3.75	3.07	0.73	1.11
Bashkir	2.07	1.12	0.52	0.53
Chechen	3.52	2.36	0.29	0.38
Avar	3.54	2.22	0.18	0.24
Lezgin	3.44	1.88	0.15	0.17
Kabardinian	2.94	1.57	0.12	0.14
Karakalpak	2.89	2.82	0.12	0.17
Dargin	3.50	2.44	0.11	0.15
Kumyk	3.10	2.12	0.09	0.11
Uighur	5.59	2.21	0.08	0.10
Ingush	3.67	1.86	0.07	0.08
Karachay	3.00	1.68	0.05	0.06
Adygir	2.08	0.98	0.04	0.04
Kurd	3.83	3.00	0.04	0.07
Lak	2.77	1.71	0.04	0.04
Abkhazian	2.21	1.00	0.03	0.03
Balkar	3.13	1.16	0.03	0.03
Tabasarans	4.31	3.47	0.03	0.05
Cherkess	2.46	1.63	0.02	0.02
Dungan	5.29	3.35	0.02	0.03
Nogay	2.71	1.65	0.02	0.03
Abazinian	2.41	1.46	0.01	0.01
Persian	2.59	1.34	0.01	0.01
Rutul	5.45	2.44	0.01	0.01
Tats	3.71	2.83	0.01	0.01
Tsakhur	3.86	2.61	0.01	0.01
Agul	2.53	3.47	0.00	0.01

Table 6.10. (*cont.*)

Nationality	Growth rates		Share of population	
	1959–70	1970–79	1979	2000[a]
Other			11.40	10.50
Armenian	2.25	1.72	1.58	1.83
Georgian	1.71	1.07	1.36	1.38
Moldavian	1.81	1.07	1.13	1.14
Lithuanian	1.24	0.75	1.09	1.03
German	1.20	0.53	0.74	0.67
Jews	−0.48	−1.89	0.69	0.37
Chuvash	1.30	0.37	0.67	0.58
Latvian	0.19	0.07	0.55	0.45
Mordvinian	−0.16	−0.64	0.45	0.32
Poles	−1.51	−0.16	0.44	0.34
Estonian	0.17	0.14	0.39	0.32
Udmurt	1.10	0.15	0.27	0.23
Mari	1.57	0.43	0.24	0.21
Osetin	1.54	1.17	0.21	0.21
Korean	1.19	0.94	0.15	0.15
Bulgarian	0.73	0.31	0.14	0.12
Buryat	2.00	1.29	0.13	0.14
Greek	0.78	0.23	0.13	0.11
Yakut	2.19	1.14	0.13	0.13
Komi	1.05	0.17	0.12	0.10
Tsygan	2.61	1.97	0.08	0.10
Gagauz	2.16	1.11	0.07	0.07
Hungarian	0.67	0.30	0.07	0.06
Kalmyk	2.37	0.77	0.06	0.05
Komi-Permyak	0.59	−0.18	0.06	0.04
Northern peoples	1.56	0.36	0.06	0.05
Tuvin	3.05	1.96	0.06	0.08
Karelian	−1.22	−0.63	0.05	0.04
Romanian	1.05	0.87	0.05	0.05
Finnish	−0.81	−1.06	0.03	0.02
Khakas	1.51	0.69	0.03	0.03
Altay	1.92	0.81	0.02	0.02
Assyrian	0.99	0.32	0.01	0.01
Shor	0.70	−0.34	0.01	0.00
Other	2.41	−0.39	0.09	0.07

[a] Projected.

Table 6.11. *Declining Muslim growth rates*

	Growth rates		
	Actual 1959–70	Hypothetical 1970–79	Actual 1970–79
Uzbeks	3.93	4.02	3.43
Kazakh	3.52	3.50	2.39
Azeri	3.69	3.75	2.51
Kirgiz	3.75	4.01	3.07
Tadzhik	3.94	4.14	3.45
Turkmen	3.90	4.03	3.22
Tatar	1.62	1.61	0.70
Bashkir	2.07	2.86	1.12

Note: The hypothetical growth rate assumes constant fertility for the period 1959 to 1979. In other words, it adjusts for changing age-group structure for the period 1970 to 1979. Except for the Kazakhs and the Tatars, the increasing percentage of women in the fertile childbearing years would have produced even higher fertility in the 1970s than occurred in the 1960s with no change in fertility behavior.

mortality relatively low, the relatively small share of fertility-age women in the population would act to inhibit growth rates. Only 28 per cent of the Uzbeks, for example, were 20 to 49 years old in 1970, compared to 43.3 per cent of the Russians. In 1970, many Muslim females had not yet entered the childbearing years. During the 1970s, these youngsters entered their twenties, the prime childbearing period. An estimated 15 per cent of Soviet Uzbeks were 20 to 29 in 1979, compared with less than 10 per cent in 1970. Given a stable fertility level, the increasingly favorable age group structure of the 1970s would be expected to produce even higher population growth rates for the 1970s than for the 1960s. Table 6.11 provides estimations of population growth rates between 1970 and 1979 for eight major Muslim groups, given stable fertility. The estimates were based on projecting 20 to 49-year-old females in 1979 from 1970 age group structure. Note that estimated growth rates for most groups is about 4 per cent. Applying this figure to the entire Muslim populace would produce, by 1979, a Muslim populace of over 49 million, as compared with 34.7 million Muslims in 1970. In other words, had 1970 natality levels been maintained, the increasingly favorable age group structure of the 1970s would have produced a veritable population explosion in the southern tier by 1979.

This explosion did not, in fact, occur. Average Muslim growth rates declined from 3.4 per cent to 2.2 per cent. The growth rate for Soviet Muslims as a whole declined from 3.3 to 2.5 per cent. The Muslim population increased by 8.5 million; in 1979, 16.3 per cent of the USSR populace was Muslim. These are significant increases, but are much smaller than would have been expected given stable fertility and the large number of females entering the prime child-bearing cohort. Without question, the declining growth rates among Soviet Muslims are primarily due to significant, and in some cases extremely rapid, declines in Muslim natality during the 1970s.

The slowing population growth in the Soviet southern tier during the 1970s has given some pause to Western observers who had been predicting, based on the 1959 to 1970 growth rates, that the USSR would soon be swamped by its burgeoning Muslim population.[16] In the late 1970s, a spate of articles appeared in the Western press predicting imminent minority status for ethnic Russians.[17] Some Soviet specialists in the West were even insisting that, before the end of the century, the three major Slavic groups put together would fall below 50 per cent. Western estimates of the probable Muslim share of the population by the year 2000 ranged from 25 to 34 per cent. Examination of the results of the 1979 census has led to considerable downward revision of these figures.

Our own projections of the 1970 to 1979 growth rates suggest that Muslim minorities will account for 23 per cent of the Soviet populace by the year 2000, assuming stable growth rates (Table 6.10). These projections should be caveated with a number of observations concerning the speculative nature of population projections of this sort. First, the method that we (and others) have used to generate ethnic population estimates to the turn of the century assumes that the minority growth rates of the 1970s will remain stable over the next two decades. There are several reasons to believe that this will not be so. Slavic growth rates, in the absence of additional assimilation from non-Slavic groups, will almost surely decline from their 1970s level. Even if fertility stabilizes (as it seems to be doing), Slavic mortality levels are almost sure to increase due to the gradual aging of the population. The Muslims, by contrast, will continue to enjoy a relatively young age structure to the turn of the century and beyond. During the next two decades, the share of young women in the key childbearing ages will remain high, probably increasing from 1979 levels. These factors suggest increases in growth rates. Coupled with the considerations mentioned above with regard to Slavic growth, these factors indicate a share of somewhat above 23 per cent. On the other hand, the fertility decline, once begun, might proceed very rapidly indeed. This seems to be happening now in Kazakhstan and Azerbaydzhan; and it may well follow a similar pattern in one or more of the other southern republics. If so, this would offset the growth potential of a favorable age structure and produce continuing declines in growth rates. If these declines are more rapid than Slavic and European declines, the Muslim share of the population by the year 2000 will be somewhat less than 23 per cent.

We don't know how rapidly fertility decline will take place among Soviet Muslims over the next two decades. Nor are we willing to guess. Therefore, we will adopt the conservative approach of offering a high and low estimate of the Muslim population share at the turn of the century. If fertility decline among most Muslim groups proceeds at a relatively normal pace, a Muslim share of about 24 per cent is expected. If the pace of fertility decline is more rapid here than it was in the European areas, we predict a Muslim population share of perhaps 21 per cent by the year 2000.

Even the lower level within this range means an extensive shift in nationality composition. Soviet Muslims will have nearly doubled their share of the population in the last forty years of the century. Even if the more extravagant prophesies of the "yellowing" of the Soviet population have not been realized, the more modest changes that have occurred in the two decades since 1959 still have a great deal of economic, social, and political significance.

Most significant from a political and social standpoint, however, are the salient shifts in values that produced the declining southern tier population growth rates between 1970 and 1979. The data presented in the foregoing chapters provide persuasive evidence of the ability of the Soviet leadership to shape values through public policy, even in those areas like family life and gender roles that are resistant to change, even within the most traditional cultures. Our findings indicate that while acceptance of "modern" family values is still far from complete, the trend is one of significant erosion of traditional patriarchal values in both European and southern tier areas. Increasing ethnic homogeneity in values is resulting. Furthermore, the increased opportunities for participation in modern Soviet life that accompany modernization are providing alternate sources of identity (socioeconomic status, gender, occupation) for the more traditional groups. These opportunities for upward mobility will necessarily affect other values as previously traditional elements of society enter the Soviet mainstream.

NOTES

1 A convenient summary of the several schools of thought on the role of child economics in fertility transition is provided in Peter H. Lindert, "The Changing Economic Costs and Benefits of Having Children," in Rodolfo A. Bulatao and Ronald D. Lee (eds.), *Determinants of Fertility in Developing Countries* (New York: Academic Press, 1983), Vol. 2, pp. 494–516.

2 *Sotsial'no-ekonomicheskoye aspekty vosproizvodstva i zanyatosti naseleniya kazakhskoy SSR* (Alma-Ata: Izdatel'stvo Nauka Kazakhskoy SSR, 1980), 56–57.

3 A. A. Akhmedov, "Opinion of Women in Baku About the Number of Children in the Family," *Azerbaydzhanskiy meditsinskiy zhurnal*, No. 11, 1975, pp. 80–85.

4 A. Akhmedov, "Several Results of Research on the Opinion of Young Women About the Number of Children in a Family," *Vestnik statistiki*, No. 8, 1974, pp. 16–21; and I. I. Kashtanenkova, "Social-demographic Analysis of High Fertility Women in Tashkent," in O. B. Ata-Mirzayev (ed.), *Regional'nyye femograficheskiye issledovaniya* (Tashkent: Tashkent State University, 1978), pp. 27–33.

5 The youngest age group surveyed (aged 19–22) expressed a higher expected and desired family size than did the women in their mid-twenties and early thirties. This is probably due to the fact that the sample included only women with children, thus omitting those younger women who had postponed marriage and childbearing. This sample bias skews the findings for the youngest age group. Sh. Kadyrov and Ye. Kubasova, "On the Employment of Turkmen Women in Industry," *Izvestiya AN turkmenskoy SSR. Seriya obshchestvennykh nauk*, No. 5, 1982, pp. 49–55.

6 M. R. Buriyeva and S. N. Kononenko, "Women of Uzbekistan," in *Nashi zhenshchiny* (Moscow: Finansy i Statistika, 1984), pp. 90–92.

7 I. Katanov and I. Kashtanenkova, "Family Marital Relations," in *Naseleniye sredney azii* (Moscow: Finansy i Statistika, 1985), pp. 21–28. See also M. R. Buriyeva, "Opinion of Rural Women on the Number of Children in the Family," in *Demografiya sem'i* (Tashkent: Tashkent State University, 1980), pp. 69–81; and Rahimjon Otayev, "Marriage: Or a Philosophy of Happiness," *Sharq yulduzi*, No. 7, 1984, pp. 184–89, translated in Joint Publication Research Service, JPRS-UPS-85-035, 26 April 1985.

8 Maquash Tatimov, "A Family with Children is Like a Bazaar," *Madeniet jane turmis*, No. 10, 1980, pp. 20–21, translated in Joint Publication Research Service, JPRS 77252, 27 January 1981; "Another Source of Wealth, Motherhood," *Qzazq adebiyet*, 22 April 1983, pp. 10–11, translated in Joint Publication Research Service, JPRS 84175, 23 August 1983; and *Qazaq adebiyeti*, 21 October 1983, translated in Joint Publication Research Service, JPRS-UPS-84-014. See also Azimbay Ghaliev, "The Scientific and Technological Revolution: Hopes and Doubts," *Bilim zhane engbek*, No. 4, 1982, pp. 5–6, translated in Joint Publication Research Service, JPRS 82021, 19 October 1982.

9 N. S. Esipov and A. M. Yelemesova, "Several Problems of the Development of the Kazakh Family," in *Sovremennaya sem'ya* (Moscow: Finansy i Statistika, 1982), pp. 82–90.

10 See, for example, Abdiqadyr Attapkhanov, "The Golden Threshold," *Qazaqstan ayelderi*, No. 6, 1982, p. 18, translated in Joint Publication Research Service, JPRS 82274, 19 November 1982; and *Turkmenskaya iskra*, 24 May 1984, p. 3.

11 *Ibid.*

12 *Ibid.*

13 V. I. Kozlov, *Natsionalnosti SSSR. etnodemograficheskiy obzor* (Moscow: Statistika, 1975), pp. 248–57.

14 Erich Strauss, *Soviet Agriculture in Perspective. A Study of its Successes and Failures* (New York: Frederick A. Prager, 1969), p. 103. Frank Lorimer's analyses of population data from the 1926 and 1939 census suggests an "excess mortality" of about 5.5 million. He attributes this primarily to deaths associated with collectivization and rapid industrialization. Frank Lorimer, *The Population of the Soviet Union. History and Prospects* (Geneva: League of Nations, 1946), pp. 133–34.

15 Kozlov, 1975, p. 252. See also, Lorimer, 1946, p. 40.

16 Murray Feshbach, "Prospects for Outmigration from Central Asia and Kazakhstan in the Next Decade," in *Soviet Economy in a Time of Change* (Washington, DC: US Government Printing Office, 1979), pp. 656–709. See particularly footnote 2, p. 658.

17 James N. Wallace, "In USSR, Minority Problems Just Won't Wither Away," *US News and World Report*, Vol. 82, 14 February 1977; and Herbert E. Meyer, "The Coming Soviet Ethnic Crisis," *Fortune*, 14 August 1978.

Appendixes

Appendix 1 Data sets

Each of the data sets used to test the Soviet findings on fertility and value change raised its own particular set of problems and choices. For the contemporary period, we employed four separate data sets: republic (15 cases), separate republic urban/rural (30 cases), nationality (45 cases), and oblast (194 cases). The first two data sets, both focusing on the republic, posed no problem in terms of case definition since data were consistently available for all 15 republics in the Soviet Union; and republic boundary lines are consistent over time from 1959 to the present. However, use of the republic as a unit of analysis introduced other kinds of uncertainty. Analyses that rely exclusively on the Soviet republic as a unit of analysis are troubled by the extremely small number of cases. There are only 15 Soviet republics: the republic data set includes large republics like the RSFSR (RSFSR's 139 million residents constitute 52.2 per cent of the total Soviet populace) to tiny republics like Estonia, with only 1.5 million residents, or less than 1 per cent of the Soviet populace. Use of the data provided separately by urban and rural portions of each republic increased the number of cases to 30, but limited the types of analyses that could be done since the Soviets provide much less data in separate urban and rural tabulations.

Use of the nationality group as the unit of analysis minimized several of the difficulties encountered through use of republic data. First, we were able to examine cultural groupings directly, without introducing the uncertainties caused by using republic data as a rough surrogate for nationality data. Second, as we have seen, total reliance on republic data would lead us to understate, in some cases quite seriously, some very substantial cultural differences in fertility and value systems. Third, Soviet nationality groups provided a potentially larger number of cases than Soviet republics.

Construction of the nationality data set, however, raised problems of its own. The first involved the choice of which of the USSR's over 100 separate nationalities to include in the analysis. In part, the choice was based on data availability. Age breakdowns and educational attainments are provided (in the 1970 census) for only 52 minorities. Because both types of data were required for our analyses, we were limited to those 52 minorities. We were then faced with the choice of including all 52 or limiting our data set to a smaller number of larger minorities. On the one hand, we wished to maximize the number of cases to make the statistical analysis more rigorous. We also wanted to be as comprehensive as possible. On the other hand, we did not wish to obscure important trends of affecting the major nationalities by patterns that may be particular to the smaller groups. For this reason, we decided to exclude all minorities with a population of less than 25,000 in 1959. This yielded a set of 45 nationalities, comprising 97 per cent of the population in 1959.

Certain types of analyses, however, required a geographical unit of analysis. Analyses of the distribution of medical care facilities or child care facilities obviously require a geographical focus. To meet these needs, we constructed a fourth contemporary data set, this time based on Soviet oblast-type units. The choice of these units requires some explanation. The oblast is the major regional administrative subdivision below the republic in the USSR. There are currently 122 oblasts in the Soviet Union; they range in population size from 6.2 million (Moscow oblast) to 0.2 million (Narynsk oblast).[1] There are, in addition, 6 "krays" whose administrative status in the Soviet federal hierarchy is regulated by the same law governing oblast local government. A third category of oblast-type units consists of the autonomous republics, of which there are 20. They are similar in size, population, and functions to the oblast, although their local government responsibilities are somewhat more extensive than that of the oblast local government. A fourth category of oblast-type units are the 15 republic capitals plus Leningrad, a republic-subordinate city of 'oblast' status; all 16 of these units are directly subordinate to the republic government and separate data is provided in census and statistical sources.

The major problem with an oblast-level approach to the USSR is that not all Soviet republics have oblast-type administrative divisions. The smaller republics, Lithuania, Moldavia, Latvia, Armenia, and Estonia, have no oblast divisions. To deal with this problem, each of these 5 republics was entered into the oblast data set as a separate case; and a residual case (republic minus the capital city) was computed for those instances when we wished to consider the capital separately. In other words, in some analyses it made sense to examine Latvia as a single case; in others, where we had more detailed data, it made more sense to examine it as two cases – i.e., Tallin (the capital city) and the residual population outside of Tallin. In those instances where we did not have separate data for the capital city, we were able to include Latvia in the analysis by selecting out the two sub-cases.

In Georgia, Azerbaydzhan, Kirgizia, Tadzhikistan, and Turkmenistan, the problems were similar, but more complicated. In Georgia, for example, there are two autonomous republics, a capital city, and an autonomous oblast for which data are provided separately. In addition, there are regions in Georgia directly subordinate to the republic government (generally appearing in statistical sources as "rayons of republic subordination"). Data for these areas are often presented separately in statistical tabulations or can be calculated using a residual method. For each of these republics, then, we constructed separate cases for each administrative division provided, in order to yield the finest grained analysis possible with the data at hand. This means that Georgia is divided into 5 cases, Azerbaydzhan into 4, Kirgizia into 6, Tadzhikistan into 6, and Turkmenistan into 6. We also constructed separate cases for Moscow, Leningrad, Kiev, Alma Ata, Tashkent, and Ashkhabad which collapsed the oblast and city data together. This was used to analyse materials, such as access to health care, when it made little sense to consider Leningrad oblast separately from Leningrad. These steps yielded a data base which was both comprehensive and flexible. To make sure we did not "double count" any area in a given analysis we assigned to each unit a type category. In other words, when we wished to treat Leningrad and Leningrad oblast as a single unit, we obviously had to exclude the separate cases from the analysis.

We still had to deal however, with the problems of changing oblast boundaries. Major changes in oblast boundary lines are a fairly frequent occurrence in several of the southern tier areas. In 1973, for example, Guryev oblast in Kazakhstan was divided into two new oblasts, one named Guryev and the other Mangyshlak. At the same time, Karaganda oblast was transformed into a new oblast named Karaganda and an additional one named Dzezkazgansk.[2] Obviously, it is not valid to analyze trends involving Karaganda oblast using early data that applies to the undivided oblast and later data that applies to a smaller oblast (still named Karaganda). To deal with this problem, we created two new oblasts, Guryev 2 and Karaganda 2. Mangyshlak and Dzezkazgansk were added to the file as new oblasts. For post-1973 data, which is broken down according to the new boundary divisions, we estimated appropriate values for Guryev 1 by aggregating data pertaining to Guryev 2 and Mangyshlak. Some pre-1973 data for the four new oblasts have been published in republic statistical handbooks. In other words, Kazakhstan statistical officials, having access to individual rayon data, are able to compute pre-1973 data for the new oblasts; and we have made use of such data wherever possible.

Preserving the "new" and "old" oblast divisions was obviously a compromise. Our preference would have been to incorporate the most current administrative divisions. However, in many cases, retrospective data were not available for the "new" oblasts. In analyzing 1959 to 1970 trends in urbanization and education, for example, data for the "old" oblast divisions were available (from the 1970 census), but not for the "new" oblast divisions. In this case, we selected out the "new" oblasts from the analysis and ran the statistical tests on the "old" oblasts only. This procedure for handling oblast divisions, again, enhanced the flexibility of the oblast file. It yielded a total of 195 oblast-level units. The number of cases in any given single analysis, however, is obviously smaller.

The combination of the four files, three with a geographical focus and one with a nationality group focus, provided us with the ability to perform multiple tests of a single hypothesis. Many of the variables we examined involved at least some measurement problems. Soviet studies, to a perhaps greater degree than most social science, relies on admittedly imperfect indicators. One strategy for dealing with measurement problems is the use of multiple indicators within a given unit of analysis; another is the use of more than one data set.

Appendix 2 Fertility measures

Chapter 1 summarized the fertility measures used as dependent variables in this study and suggested in general terms the strengths and weaknesses of the various measures. This appendix provides more detailed information on how each measure was computed, as well as how the method chosen for the computation in each case may introduce certain biases into the measurement. This material is provided for the benefit of those who might want to replicate and/or extend the analysis of fertility dynamics and fertility–modernization–family linkages. The level of detail incorporated here reflects our conviction that Soviet area studies as a discipline suffers from insufficient attention to data and measurement problems.

METHODS FOR CORRECTING REPORTED FERTILITY INDICATORS

A word should be said first about strategies for correcting reported birth rates that were tried but discarded. Given the abundant evidence of substantial underreporting of births in the southern tier area through at least the mid-1960s, we were unable to use reported republic and oblast-level birth and general fertility rates to track fertility changes in these areas for the pre-1970 period. Because this constituted a substantial gap in our analysis, we examined several techniques that held the promise of "correcting" the reported rates by estimates derived from the census enumeration. Two methods – essentially two ways of doing the same thing – were investigated.

The first involves reverse projection from reported 0–4-year-olds or (in the case of oblast level data) 0–9-year-olds. This technique requires fairly good estimates of mortality within the youngest age groups. Unfortunately, the same data problems that preclude use of birth registry data also affect, and to a much greater extent, reported infant and child mortality data. As we noted in Chapter 1, the births most likely to be unregistered were those in which the infant died soon after birth. In cases where such births were not registered, the infant death was also unrecorded. This aspect of the underregistration problem means that infant and (to a lesser degree) child mortality data for those areas most affected by underregistration are, to put it bluntly, unreliable.

The problem with reported infant mortality data may be demonstrated by noting the discrepancy between *reported* RSFSR and Central Asian infant mortality rates. In 1958, when the reported RSFSR infant mortality rate was 41; Kirgizia's reported rate was 29; Tadzhikistan's was 36. In 1960, the RSFSR reported rate had dropped to 37, higher than the reported rates for four of the Islamic republics, for which we have data. The reported 1960 infant mortality rates were 36.8 for Kazakhstan, 30 for Kirgizia, 30 for Tadzhikistan, and 28 for Uzbekistan.[3] But reported infant mortality rates were higher in Central Asian cities! In 1959, the capital of Kirgizia (Frunze) reported an infant mortality rate of 30.6; Kirgizia as a whole reported substantially lower rates – 28 in 1958 and 30 in 1960.[4] A study of infant mortality in Aktyubinsk oblast in Kazakhstan revealed that the reported 1966 infant death rate in the oblast center was 40 per cent higher than that for the rest of the oblast.[5] The data, then, indicate a significantly lower level of reported infant mortality for the Central Asian republics, with higher reported rates in the major Central Asian cities, where medical care was undoubtedly better.

Are these reasonable findings, given what we know about the relatively high proportion of home and non-medically assisted births in the rural regions of the southern tier, plus known underregistration problems? The answer, quite simply, is no; it is difficult to believe that infant mortality in the RSFSR in the late 1950s was substantially higher than Central Asian mortality. It is clear that these Central Asian data substantially understate real levels of infant mortality. We cannot, then, use reported infant and child mortality to reverse project enumerated 0–4-year-olds; we must instead generate rough estimates of mortality to use as a basis for reverse projection.

The necessity for generating estimates of infant and child mortality has important implications for the reverse projection procedure because birth rate estimates derived from reverse projection of

Table 1. *Natality estimates based on "reverse projection" from census enumerations*

Republic	1954–58 reported birth rates	Birth rate estimates using 1959 mort. assumptions	Birth rate estimates using 1926 mort. assumptions	Birth rate estimates using East model life tables[a]
Tadzhikistan	32.62	37.01	47.01	42.36
Uzbekistan	35.56	36.03	45.76	41.11
Turkmenistan	39.34	36.45	46.30	41.32
Kirgizia	34.22	34.19	43.42	38.76
Azerbaydzhan	38.66	36.08	45.83	40.16
Kazakhstan	36.92	32.29	41.01	35.49

[a] Coale, Anderson, and Harm, p. 239.

0–4-year-olds are very sensitive to mortality assumptions. A simple example will illustrate. Assume, for instance, that in a given republic of total population 100,000, there were 10,000 children ages 0 to 4 recorded for the 1959 census. If we assume an extremely high rate of infant mortality, those 10,000 children would represent the survivors of a very much larger original population, perhaps, say, an original population of 20,000 infants born over the preceding five years, only half of whom survived to be enumerated in the census. Under this assumption, there were 4,000 average births per year, yielding an estimated birth rate of 40. If we assume, however, that infant and child mortality is relatively low, say at about US levels, then our estimates of the original population will be correspondingly lower, say perhaps 10,150. This mortality assumption would yield an estimated average number of births of about 2,000, or an estimated birth rate of about 20. Clearly, then, the estimates derived from reverse projection are very sensitive to mortality assumptions.

To demonstrate how this applies to the Soviet case, we made several different calculations of estimated birth rate, using different assumptions about mortality. Table 1 presents estimated birth rates for six southern tier republics. Column 2 presents reported birth rate; column 3 provides estimates based on reverse projection using mortality data from the 1959 reported rural USSR life tables. Column 4 provides estimates based on reverse projections using reported mortality for European Russia in 1926. As can easily be seen, there are substantial differences in the estimates, depending on which mortality patterns are used to make the projections.

Column 3 represents, in effect, the most positive assessment of mortality in these areas. It assumes that mortality patterns in the southern tier in the mid and late 1950s are about equal to the reported rates for all rural areas in the USSR. There is much evidence to suggest that this assumption cannot be valid. The patterns of prenatal care, hospital births, and medically-assisted births in the southern tier area during this period suggest the real infant and child mortality there was almost certainly higher than the average reported rural rates and, for some republics, substantially higher.

The estimates provided in Column 4 embody the assumption that real infant and child mortality patterns in the mid and late 1950s in the southern tier area were similar to those in the European areas of the Soviet Union in 1926. To evaluate the validity of this assumption, consider for a moment that reported infant mortality for the USSR as a whole in 1926 was 174.[6] But this figure was undoubtedly an understatement of real USSR levels. Table 2 presents selected data for the European areas of the RSFSR. Given the fact that the health care infrastructure was more fully developed in urban areas, lower infant death rates are expected in the urban areas. In fact, for many of the more developed central RSFSR areas, this expectation is fulfilled. But, for many oblasts in the RSFSR's southeastern provincial areas – particularly in the Volga region – reported infant mortality is highest in the capital city and lowest in the rural areas. The fact that reported rates were higher in areas where the medical care system was probably strongest is consistent with the hypothesis of differential underreporting, even in the RSFSR. As the review of available medical surveys in Chapter 2 make clear, there is little doubt that real infant mortality in the southern tier areas in 1926 was substantially higher than the reported European figures, perhaps as high as 400 or 500 in some rural areas of Kirgizia and Turkmenistan.

Reported infant mortality for the USSR as a whole was 181.5 in 1940.[7] The higher 1940 figure may well have been due to increasingly better reporting of infant deaths. Even so, it is fair to assume that the 1940 rate was still artificially low due to unregistered deaths. This may be seen from reported infant mortality rates for Leningrad.[8] Medical conditions in Leningrad, one of the most highly urbanized

Table 2. *Selected data on Soviet infant mortality, 1926*

Region	Total	Urban areas	Of which oblast capital	Rural areas
Saratov	170.4	181.5	173.7	169.0
Astrakhan	195.1	213.8	217.0	185.2
Samara	192.8	227.8	229.8	188.3
Orenburg	191.4	240.7	241.3	175.3
Ivano-Voznesensk	195.0	190.7	213.5	196.4
Tver	155.4	158.2	168.9	155.1
Bashkir ASSR	139.7	195.1		134.5
European RSFSR[a]	190.9	174.1		193.6

[a] Excludes North Caucasus Kray and Dagestan.
Source: Yestyestvennoye dvizheniye naseleniya RSFSR za 1926 god (Moscow: Izdaniye TsSU RSFSR, 1928), pp. 2–9.

and industrialized areas in 1940, were almost certainly better than in much of the remainder of the country. Yet reported infant mortality in Leningrad in 1940 was 196, significantly higher than the overall USSR rate of 181.5. The reported rate in the southern tier autonomous republic of Dagestan, by contrast, was 151, significantly lower than that reported for Leningrad and the reported overall Soviet rate.[9] The reported rate for 1940 in one oblast of Kazakhstan (Aktyubinsk, another southern tier oblast) was only 158.1.[10] The most reasonable explanation is that, in Leningrad, infant deaths were better reported than in Dagestan or Kazakhstan. Underreporting in areas like Dagestan and Kazakhstan kept overall reported USSR rates well below "real" levels of infant mortality. In other words, real USSR infant mortality in 1940 must surely have been substantially above 181.5. Many of the unrecorded infant deaths must have been concentrated in the rural Central Asian and Caucasian republics. O. M. Karyyev provides data allowing us to compute infant mortality from 1939 to 1970 in Ashkhabad, the capital of Turkmenistan.[11] The estimate derived for 1939 is 250 – significantly higher than the Leningrad figure. Even this figure may have been too low, for we cannot rule out some underreporting even in an urban area. Real infant mortality in the rest of Turkmenistan must have been higher than 250, perhaps substantially higher.

What do these pre-war rates suggest about mid to late 1950s rates in Central Asia and the Caucasus? There is evidence to suggest that infant mortality declined very rapidly indeed in Central Russia after the end of World War II. The overall USSR rate had dropped to 80.7 by 1950, to 59.6 by 1955.[12] Reported rates for Leningrad had declined to 148 by 1945; by 1950, Leningrad's reported rate had fallen dramatically, to 82.[13] In Voronezh, the reported infant mortality rate dropped by more than half between 1950 and 1958.[14] Reported rates for Krasnodar Kray showed a similarly rapid decline in the early to mid-1950s.[15] There are several alternative explanations for this trend. First, the immediate postwar decline could be the result of a temporary dislocation in registration procedures in the aftermath of a devastating war. But this can be only part of the reason, since mortality rates continued to drop well into the 1950s and 1960s, well after any temporary disruptions associated with the war would have been operating. The second explanation is that the medical advances impelled by the war (the discovery of penicillin, for example) were disseminated throughout the USSR and had a dramatic impact on infant deaths.

Did real infant mortality in the southern tier experience a similar dramatic decline? We don't know. Karryyev's data are certainly consistent with this explanation; reported infant mortality in Ashkhabad (as derived from Karryyev's figures) had declined to 86 by 1954 and to 68 by 1958.[16] Even assuming that the Ashkhabad figures are complete (and there is every reason to think that they were not), these data would imply a 1954 infant mortality rate in the rest of Turkmenistan of well above 86.

Our estimate of real infant mortality in the 1950s in the southern tier areas hinges on assumptions about the timing and pace of the infant mortality decline in the immediate postwar decades. If we assume that the major portion of the decline had taken place (as it did in central Russia) by about 1955, then we are safe in estimating a real infant mortality somewhat above USSR rates, perhaps 90 to 100. If, by contrast, the decline occurred in the late-modernizing regions at a somewhat later date, then an estimated infant mortality of 90 for some of these republics is clearly far too low. Examination of post-1958 data for Armenia suggests that the decline here took place four to six years after analogous trends in the USSR data.[17] It is not unreasonable to assume that the trends in Azerbaydzhan and Central Asia took place several years after the Armenian trend. If these assumptions are correct, they imply mid-1950s infant mortality rates, for at least some of the Muslim republics of perhaps 110 to 150, perhaps even higher for those areas furthest behind in the modernization process. In other words the 1926 European mortality patterns used to derive the birth rate estimates in Column 3 might not be far off! To date, we have not uncovered any data that would allow us to choose with any kind of confidence in either of these estimates. We may only conclude from the material available to us that infant mortality in the southern tier in the mid to late 1950s was within the range 90 to 170. We suspect further that there was extraordinarily high variation from republic to republic and within republics from region to region, and that at least some of the southern tier areas experienced a rapid decline in *real* rates beginning sometime in the late 1950s.

How does this leave us with regard to the estimates in Table 1. Truth probably lies somewhere in between Column 2 and Column 3. The meager clues to "real" infant and child mortality (and thus to real natality) are clearly insufficient to make an informed estimate. We must therefore reject method one as a means to "correct" for underregistration in vital rates. We have generated "corrected" birth rate estimates for each of the southern tier republics employing several different mortality scenarios. The mortality assumptions implicit in these scenarios are based on the fragmentary data on southern tier infant and child mortality. While these estimates provide a useful way to highlight underregistration problems, we do not have sufficient data to incorporate them into our analyses of contemporary fertility trends.

About method two we will say much less. This procedure involves reliance on model life tables. As such, it raises all of the same problems involved in method one, and introduces several additional uncertainties as well. In order to reverse survive census enumerated 0–4-year-olds using the model life table method, two pieces of data are necessary: the proportion of the population under five and the expectation of life at birth. The first figure can be computed from reported census data. The problem is in obtaining the second. Here we immediately encounter the exact same problem noted above – the lack of reliable mortality data. In this case the problem is an even larger one because estimations of life at birth require not only knowledge of child and infant mortality, but those at later ages as well. Coale, Anderson and Harm, making use of the East model life

Table 3. *USSR natality estimate using East model life tables*

	Reported USSR 1959 females[a]	East model females[b]
Expectation of life at birth	71.70	71.70
Age breakdown		
0–4	10.39	10.39
5–9	9.43	9.67
10–14	6.56	9.03
15–19	7.16	8.42
20–24	8.96	7.85
25–29	8.08	7.31
30–34	9.05	6.80
35–39	6.15	6.32
40–44	5.58	5.86
45–49	6.58	5.40
50–54	5.61	4.94
55–59	5.05	4.48
60–69	6.65	7.37
70–79	3.61	4.55
80+	1.12	1.67
Birth rate	25.64 (reported)[c]	22.29 (estimated)[d]

[a] Age breakdowns are based on reported 1959 date in *Itogi 1970*, Vol. 2, p. 12. Expectation of life at birth for females reported in *Itogi 1959, SSSR*, p. 266.
[b] Data were interpolated from East model life tables provided in Coale and Demeny (1966), pp. 550–52.
[c] Average of reported rates for 1954 to 1958. *Naseleniye SSSR, 1973*, p. 69.
[d] This is the birth rate estimate given an expectation of life at birth of 71.7 and proportion of under five population of 10.39 per cent.

tables for their correction procedures (presented in Column 5 of Table 1), cheerfully acknowledge that they based the estimates on their "guesses about expectation of life" in the southern tier areas.[18] Their methodological discussion (in Appendix A) leaves the reader with little confidence in these "guesses." Indeed, there is no discussion of the available historical, ethnographic, and health care literature that provides the only reasonable basis for mortality assumptions affecting the southern tier regions. We must assume, therefore, that the values for expectation of life at birth were chosen with no reference to the available evidence!

Another uncertainty involved in the model life table method is the reliance on model life tables as opposed to reported (if questionable) Soviet data. Given a choice between working with material closer to the problem at hand (the Soviet Union) and that derived from reported mortality and age structure data in other societies, our preference is to opt for the former. The reasoning behind this preference is demonstrated in Table 3. This table presents the results of birth rate estimates for the USSR derived from reported expectation of life at birth and reported proportion of the population under five for females in 1959. The procedure, analogous to that used by Coale, *et al*. in their corrections for the Central Asian republics, yielded an estimated birth rate of 22.29. In fact, average reported birth rates for the USSR for 1954 to 1958 were 25.64. These deviations between estimated natality and reported natality (in those cases where reported data are available) are due to peculiarities in the USSR age structure that reflect a history more or less unique to the Soviet Union. Obviously, no set of "model" life tables can hope to capture these peculiarities. For this reason, we prefer methods, like method one, that work directly with USSR data. The major problem with the model life table correction method, however, is one it has in common with the first procedure: both necessitate estimations of mortality patterns, which (in the absence of hard data) is a very risky business indeed.

These factors presented what we feel are virtually insurmountable obstacles to "correcting" underregistered births, at least for the purposes of this study. In effect, one is attempting to estimate real fertility through a method based on mortality estimates derived from fragmentary data that are even more suspect than the birth reporting! Keeping close to the reported data and minimizing the problem of underregistration by limiting our pre-1970 analysis to the better reported European areas seemed to us a far wiser course than to generate analyses based on natality estimates that may be as flawed as the reported data.

CALCULATION OF FERTILITY MEASURES

The decision to limit analysis to areas and time periods for which reporting was much less suspect does not mean that the fertility measures used in this study are entirely free from reliability problems. We turn now to the procedures by which the fertility measures used in Chapters 2, 3, and 6 were calculated and an evaluation of the uncertainties involved in these procedures. The measures of natality employed in our analysis were:

Crude birth rate (CBR)
General fertility rate (GFR)
Total fertility rate (TFR)
Child-to-woman ratio (CWR)
Index of total fertility (If)
Expected number of children
Ideal number of children

Crude birth rate (CBR) was extracted directly from Soviet statistical sources. Expected and ideal number of children were taken from reported results of Soviet demographic surveys. The procedures used to derive the other natality measures are detailed below.

General fertility rate

General fertility rates are published for the 15 Soviet republics. For the oblast data set, crude birth rates (only for selected points in time) were available. To convert this to a general fertility rate, we used the following formula:

$$GFR = CBR/D$$

where CBR=crude birth rate and D=the proportion of the total population that is 15–49-year-old females. For 1970, the number of 15–49-year-old females had to be estimated. Estimates of the number of 15–49-year-old females were based on reported age data for the population as a whole. In each case, the number of females was estimated based on republic age and sex ratios. This procedure introduces a small, but unknowable, amount of bias into the results, but we believe that our estimates are so well-grounded on reported data that the error factor is minimal and certainly within acceptable limits.

Total fertility rate

Total fertility rates were computed for the republic data set using the standard procedure: age-specific fertility rates for each five-year group were summed and the result multiplied by five. TFR could not be computed for either the nationality or oblast data sets.

Child-to-woman ratio

For the republic and the republic rural/urban data sets, age and sex-specific data from the 1970 census were used to compute child-to-woman ratios for both 1959 and 1970. Several versions of CWR were computed. The first (CWR1) was computed as follows:

$$CWR1 = \text{children under } 5/\text{women aged } 15\text{--}44$$

The second measure, CWR2, is defined as:

$$CWR2 = \text{children under } 10/\text{women aged } 20\text{--}49$$

In both cases, the necessary data was extracted directly from the census and no adjustment was required.

For the oblast file, 1959 age and sex data are provided in the census publications in enough detail to compute child-to-woman ratios directly from individual age groups. However, for 1970, less detailed material was provided and we were faced with the necessity of estimating the sex structure for the 20–49-year-olds. Here we had available three separate sources of estimation: reported sex structure for the over 10 population in 1970, reported republic 1970 sex structure for 20–49-year-olds, and reported oblast 1959 sex structure for 10–39-year-olds. We compromised by computing a sex ratio from all three measures, according to the following formula:

$$SR = 0.25A + 0.25B + 0.50C$$

where A = 1970 reported oblast sex structure for over 10 population; B = 1970 reported 20–49-year-old sex structure in republic where the oblast is located; and C = reported 1959 sex structure for 10–39-year-olds. The number of 0–9-year-olds for each oblast was provided in the 1970 census, so procedures to derive this figure were unnecessary.

For 21 of the oblasts, 1959 data were not available in the 1959 census. These were oblasts whose boundaries had changed between 1959 and 1970; all were in the southern tier area. Because our data were standardized to 1970 boundaries, we were forced to use the 1959 age data reported in the 1970 census. These data were used – in conjunction with relevant 1959 republic sex ratios – to compute the 1959 child-to-woman ratios for the 21 oblasts. Because our basic procedure for computing 1970 child-to-woman ratios in those districts involved 1959 sex ratios (see above), we had to devise a slightly different strategy to determine the number of 20–49-year-old women among all 20–49-year-olds. For the 21 oblasts, we computed a sex ratio according to the following formula:

$$SR = 0.5A + 0.5B$$

where A=reported oblast sex structure for the over 10-year-old population in 1970 and B=the 1970 reported 20–49-year-old sex structure in the republic where the oblast is located.

The major procedural problem in computing child-to-woman ratios for nationality groups is the lack of sex breakdowns in the 1970 census. For 1959, no estimation procedures were necessary because age and sex specific data by nationality was reported in the census; and child-to-woman ratios could be computed directly from these data. For 1970, the number of 20–49-year-olds of a given nationality could be easily calculated; but we had to generate estimates of sex ratios to yield the number of women aged 20 to 49. To do this, we applied a method of which we make extensive use in this and other computations involving census reported age data – the use of age and sex ratios derived from reported *republic* data and republic-level estimates provided by the Foreign Demographic Analysis Division. For Uzbek child-to-woman ratios, for example, we computed the proportion female 20–49-year-olds from total population 20 to 49 for Uzbekistan. This yielded a republic sex ratio for 20–49-year-olds which was then applied to reported 20–49-year-old Uzbeks to yield an estimate of 20–49-year-old Uzbek women. Republic sex ratios were used for each of the fifteen major nationalities and the overall USSR sex ratio was used for the remaining groups.

A final step in computing 1970 Uzbek child-to-woman ratios was to estimate the number of children 0 to 9. Data are provided only for 0–10-year-olds. Again, we relied on a republic age structure ratio computed from the Foreign Demographic Analysis Division's republic population projections. We first calculated the proportion of 0–10-year-olds in Uzbekistan who were 0 to 9, then used this ratio with the reported 0–10-year-old Uzbeks to estimate the number of 0–9-year-olds Uzbeks. This procedure was applied to the fifteen major nationalities; and a USSR age structure ratio was used for the remaining groups.

Because these estimation procedures are fairly straightforward and well grounded in the data, we have a fair amount of confidence in the validity of the calculations. However, the major source of uncertainty for the nationality child-to-woman ratio lies, not in the assumptions embedded in the calculation procedure, but in the nature of the variable itself. Use of nationality child-to-woman ratios as a measure of fertility is based on the assumption that children are enumerated in the same category (nationality group) as their mothers. Is this a reasonable assumption? A few comments about ethnicity in the USSR are in order. First of all, ethnic identity is not a casual choice for Soviet citizens but an official status that is entered into the internal passport received at age 16. Ethnic data from Soviet censuses, however, like all other data collected by the census takers, are based on self-reports. The official instructions provide no procedure to audit the self-reported answers on this or any other question. Nonetheless, there are some suggestions that such audits may have occurred; some of the ethnic German refugees interviewed by Rasma Karklens claimed that Soviet census enumerators had asked to see their passports during the 1979 census.[19] However, the citizen being enumerated is (officially, at least) not required to show proof that the nationality being claimed is identical to his or her passport nationality.

This raises the issue as to how widespread misreporting of national identity is in the census enumeration. Several factors make it unlikely that misstatement of ethnicity is a common occurrence, even without widespread reliance on on-the-spot audits by the census enumerators. First, the census questionnaire is filled in by an interviewer and, as Soviet experiments with self-administered reports have shown, answers gathered during face-to-face interviews tend to be substantially more reliable than those garnered by independent questionnaires. In many cases, the enumerator will have been familiar with the area and/or its residents, particularly in rural areas. In any event, the interviewer will obviously know in which language the interview was conducted. (Special language questionnaires and instructions are provided for non-Russian areas.) These factors undoubtedly act as a powerful check on capricious or deliberate misstatements. Second, records of ethnic affiliation, as well as educational attainment, age, etc., are maintained by one or more bureaucratic hierarchies in the Soviet government. Whether or not routine spotchecks are made after the census of the accuracy of the self-reported answers, the knowledge that a check could be made also operates to enhance the reliability of the answers. Third, the Soviet census-takers have deliberately framed the question on nationality to elicit "official" nationality.[20] The census questionnaire simply provides a blank after the word *natsionalnost* (nationality). Suggestions to adopt another formulation, such as, "To what nationality do you attribute yourself?" were rejected precisely because this wording would produce less exact results. These factors suggest that the nationality data collected by the census is fairly reliable for most adults; that is, the census-reported nationality coincides in most cases with the nationality designated on the official passport.

For children, the situation is a bit different. The census-reported nationality of each child is designated by the parents. The census instructions provide no indications of any limitations on parental choice. In multinational families, the parents are free to choose the nationality of either spouse. "Only in families where the father and the mother belong to different nationalities and the parents have difficulty themselves in identifying the nationality of the children, is preference given to the nationality of the mother."[21] This passage suggests that, in practice, where both parents belong to the same nationality, the expected ethnic designation of the children will conform to that of the parents. The difficulty arises in enumeration of children of "mixed" marriages. The nationality of children, then, is more likely to be a problem in interpreting census results than that of adults. Some clues to the probable patterns of the ethnic identification of children in census enumerations can be gleaned by examining how ethnic identification is handled for Soviet passports. Although, the "official" passport designation at age 16 may not conform precisely to the ethnicity based on parental choice at census time, a child's choice of nationality at age 16 will almost certainly be affected by parental preferences. So, the problem of ethnic identification as revealed by the passport data is quite certain to be similar to that of the census.

Soviet legal sources make very clear that the data entered in the official passport, including nationality, are not a subject of individual choice. Individuals applying for a passport at age 16 must supply a certificate of birth, which includes the nationality of the parents. This certificate is based on the birth registration, which, in turn, required the submission of the passports of both parents. In other words, the official Soviet procedures are designed to prevent personal choice of nationality and to ensure that the 16-year-old receives the same ethnic identity as one or both parents. Soviet law provides that children born of parents of two nationalities may choose one of these nationalities as their own national identity on their passports. In other cases, there is no choice; individuals are automatically identified on their passports as the nationality of their parents.[22]

The ability to choose a national identification, while restricted to the children of mixed nationality marriages, affects a significant minority of Soviet citizens. In 1970, 13.5 per cent of all families were "interethnic," 11.3 per cent of all family members, and 10.2 per cent of the total population were members of a mixed ethnic family. By 1979, 15 per cent of both families and population were ethnically mixed.[23] We have been unable to locate national-level surveys on the shifts in ethnic identity that result from these marriages. Regional surveys of ethnic choice among children of interethnic marriages, however, have been published. Some focus on interethnic marriage outside the RSFSR, others on autonomous republics within the RSFSR. These surveys reveal wide variation in patterns of ethnic choice.

Outside the RSFSR, in those cases where a member of a titular minority marries a Russian, the children tend to choose the titular nationality. For example, a survey of passport data in the Baltic region between 1960 and 1968 found that 62 per cent of the children of Russian–Estonian marriages in Tallin (the capital of Estonia) chose Estonian as their national identity when applying for their first passport.[24] Choices were more evenly split in Riga (Latvia) and Vilnius (Lithuania), but still favored the titular minority. In Kiev, 60 per cent of the children of Russian–Ukrainian marriages chose Ukrainian. Preference for the titular minority appears to be even stronger in Central Asia. In Ashkhabad, the capital of Turkmenistan, 94 per cent of the children of Turkmen–Russian families chose Turkmen as an ethnic affiliation, while nearly 80 per cent of the children of Tadzhik–Russian marriages in Dushanbe chose Tadzhik.[25] In a study of interethnic marriages in several cities in northern Kazakhstan, 53 to 64 per cent of the children of Kazakh–Russian marriages chose Kazakh.[26] In Belorussia, by contrast, the typical preference for the "root" ethnicity appears substantially lower. In Minsk, for example, only 40 per cent of the children of Belorussian–Russian marriages chose Belorussian.[27]

Preferences also seem to depend on which spouse is the titular minority. In the capital of Moldavia (Kishniev), 74 per cent of the children of mixed Russian–Moldavian marriages chose Moldavian when the Moldavian parent was the father, compared to 57 per cent when the Moldavian was the mother. A similar pattern was noted in rural areas of Moldavia.[28] These findings suggest that preferences for one nationality over another interact with traditional customs favoring one spouse over the other.

Marriages between a titular minority and non-Russians produce a pattern even more heavily weighted in favor of the titular minority. In Vilnius, for example, 80 per cent of the children of Lithuanian–Polish marriages chose Lithuanian.[29] In Kishinev, 80 per cent of the children of Ukrainian–Moldavian marriages chose Moldavian if the father was Moldavian; 60 per cent if the mother was Moldavian.[30]

Outside the RSFSR, marriages between two non-titular nationalities most frequently involve a Russian spouse. In such cases, the children most typically choose Russian as their national identity. Again, the strength of this trend varies from place to place and minority to minority. In Vilnius, the capital of Lithuania, 36 per cent of the children of Russian–Ukrainian marriages chose Ukrainian; the rest chose Russian. But only 11 per cent of the children of Russian–Belorussian marriages chose Belorussian. The preference for Russian is even stronger in Russian–Jewish marriages. In Vilnius, 86 per cent of the children of these partnerships chose Russian and this pattern is even more pronounced in Riga and Tallin.[31]

Patterns within the RSFSR also reveal wide variations in ethnic preferences among the children of mixed ethnic marriages, with preference given in some cases to the nationality of the father.[32] In Chuvash ASSR, nearly all children of Russian–Chuvash marriages chose Russian and a similiar preference for Russian identity is shown among children of Russian–Mordvinian parentage. But in Tataria, the pattern is reversed; the majority of children of Russian–Tatar marriages chose Tatar.[33] A similar preference for the titular nationality is found in Dagestan.[34] As with republic level minorities, in the RSFSR autonomous republics, marriages between Russians and nontitular nationalities produce patterns that favor the Russians. This is particularly true in marriages involving a Jewish spouse. In Ordzhonikdze and Cherkass, cities in the autonomous republic of Dagestan, 100 per cent of the children of Russian–Jewish marriages chose Russian.[35]

How do interesting rates and patterns of ethnic identification among the children of those partnerships affect Soviet nationality data from the census? First, it should be noted that ethnic intermarriage need not always involve assimilation in the aggregate. If, for example, there is a relatively even split between those children who identified as Russian and those whose parents choose another nationality, the net impact on ethnic trends will be minimal. Even patterns favoring one group may not necessarily produce shifts in overall ethnic data. We may find, for example, that for Russian–Ukrainian families, the pattern of ethnic choice favours Ukrainian inside the Ukraine and Russian outside. In this case, the "losses" due to Ukrainian–Russian marriages outside the republic may be balanced by "gains" inside. The critical factor is the extent to which imbalanced losses produce disproportionately low aggregate data for a nationality. In terms of our census-derived fertility data, such losses mean that children of "assimilating" mothers are being counted as the "recipient" nationality. In this case, the fertility rate for the assimilating nationality will be artificially low. Of course, that of the recipient nationality will be artificially high. However, in those cases where the "recipient" of the assimilation process is substantially larger than the assimilating minority, the additional children received by assimilation will not have a statistically significant impact on the fertility ratios of the larger nationality. In other words, the major measurement problem posed by assimilation is that connected with an under-estimation of fertility for the assimilating minority.

Clearly, we need to isolate those cases where this process is taking place and exclude them from the nationality analysis. The analysis above suggested several immediate candidates – the Jews and the Belorussians. Both nationalities appear to be major "losers" in ethnic choice patterns. If, as is likely, patterns of nationality choice at passport time are reflective of patterns of parental choice in the ethnic identity of children during censuses, both the Jews and Belorussians should be excluded from our fertility analyses.

As noted above, the ability to choose official ethnicity operates only in cases of interethnic marriage (excluding shifts in ethnic identity that occur illegitimately). Minorities with a high level of interethnic marriage are most likely to be affected by the ability to choose the ethnic identity of one of the parents. To measure relative intermarriage rates, we computed, from the 1970 census, the proportion of uninational families within the titular republic. The measure was computed as follows. Within each republic or ASSR, the Soviet census reports the number of titular nationalities within uninational

families. For example, in Uzbekistan, there were (in 1970) 7.7 million
Uzbeks, 7.2 million of whom were enumerated as being part of family
units where members were all of the Uzbek nationality. We needed to
determine how many of the 7.7 million Uzbeks in Uzbekistan were
part of families. In other words, we wished to exclude single persons
from the calculations, since the concept of mixed marriage (or, more
accurately, a mixed or interethnic family) is obviously not relevant to
people who do not reside in a family unit. To make this estimation,
we calculated, from republic data, the proportion of Uzbekistan
residents who were single or residing separately from their families
(approximately 4 per cent) and applied this to the total number of
Uzbeks in Uzbekistan to derive a rough estimate of single Uzbeks.
We then calculated an estimate of Uzbeks (within Uzbekistan) who
are part of a family; and this was used, with the reported figure for
Uzbeks within uninational families, to yield an estimated proportion
of Uzbek family members who were in uninational families. In this
case, as expected, the proportion was quite high – 97 per cent. The
major source of uncertainty with this variable is that it rests on the
assumption that the proportion of single persons within a particular
nationality is similar to that reported for the republic. Moreover, the
measure does not address the issue of "mixed" families outside of the
titular republic. Nonetheless, we felt that the measure, particularly in
those cases where a large portion of the nationality resided within its
titular republic, gave a fairly good notion of relative levels of
interethnic families. The procedure can be summarized with the
following equations:

$$U = X/Y \text{ where } Y = (A/B)/C$$

where X=reported number of titular minority within uninational
families inside the titular republic; Y=estimated number of the
titular minority that reside in families; A=estimated number of
family members within the titular republic; B=republic population;
and C=population of the minority within the titular republic. The
results of these calculations are presented in Table 4.

Another rough measure of potential for assimilation is the degree
to which a given minority is shifting its linguistic affiliation. This was
measured by calculating (directly from census records), the proportion of each nationality that declared their "own" language to be
their native tongue. The results for the three census periods are
provided in Columns 3 to 5 of Table 4. We based our use of this
measure on the reasonable belief (confirmed to some degree in Soviet

Table 4. *Measures of potential assimilation*

Nationality	% Of uninational families within titular republic	Native language affiliation		
		1959	1970	1979
Russian	91.1	99.8	99.8	99.9
Ukrainian	86.5	87.7	85.7	82.8
Belorussian	61.7	84.2	80.6	74.2
Uzbek	97.0	98.4	98.6	98.5
Kazakh	98.6	98.4	98.0	97.5
Georgian	94.7	98.6	98.4	98.3
Azeri	98.9	97.6	98.2	97.9
Lithuanian	94.8	97.8	97.9	97.9
Moldavian	91.1	95.2	95.0	93.2
Latvian	87.5	95.1	95.2	95.0
Kirgiz	98.0	98.7	98.8	97.9
Tadzhik	95.5	98.1	98.5	97.8
Armenian	99.2	89.9	91.4	90.7
Turkmen	98.4	98.9	98.9	98.7
Estonian	93.8	95.2	95.5	95.3
Bashkir	85.8	61.9	66.2	67.0
Buryat	97.9	94.9	92.6	90.2
Balkar	92.2	97.0	97.2	96.9
Komi	85.2	88.7	83.7	76.5
Mari	96.8	95.1	91.2	86.7
Tatar	97.6	92.1	89.2	85.9
Udmurt	91.6	89.1	82.6	76.5
Chechen	99.9	98.8	98.7	98.6
Chuvash	97.4	90.8	86.9	81.7
Yakut	94.0	97.6	96.3	95.3
Jews	76.8	21.5	17.7	14.2
Mordva	93.6	78.1	77.8	72.6
Dargin	98.0	98.6	98.4	98.3
Kumyk	92.9	98.0	98.4	98.2
Lezgin	99.6	92.7	93.9	90.9
Ingush	97.2	97.9	97.4	97.4
Kabardinian	97.0	97.9	98.0	97.9
Kalmyk	98.4	91.0	91.7	91.3
Karelian	64.0	71.3	63.0	55.6
Osetin	94.0	89.1	88.6	88.2
Tuvin	99.9	99.1	98.7	98.8
Avar	94.5	97.2	97.2	97.7
Adygir	98.6		96.5	95.7
Altay	91.2	88.5	87.2	86.4
Karachayev	99.9	96.8	98.1	97.7
Khakhas	85.6	86.0	83.7	80.9
Cherkess	82.5	89.7	92.0	91.4
Karakalpak	90.4	95.0	96.6	95.9
Abkhazy	88.8	95.0	95.9	94.3
Komi-Permyak	57.6	87.6	85.8	77.1

ethnographic research) that minorities with extremely high rates of native language affiliation were most unlikely to be experiencing substantial shifts in ethnic affiliation.

Those nationalities with a "uninational family" measure of under 80 per cent and/or a 1970 native language score of less than 80 per cent were excluded from the fertility analysis. The Komi-permyaks, for example, appear to have both low rates of uninational families (under 80 per cent) as do Karelians, Belorussians, and Jews. The Mordva and Bashkir have a low native language rate, but relatively high rates of uninational families. We excluded these six nationalities from our 45 nationality data set for purposes of statistical tests involving fertility. This yielded a data set of 39 minorities which were used in calculating the Pearson's r in Chapter 3 and the projections in Chapter 6.

It should be noted that correlation and regression analysis based on the entire 45-minority data set yielded quite similar results, and in some instances slightly higher correlations. This is because the measures used to exclude the six minorities are themselves highly correlated with measures of modernization found to inhibit fertility. In other words, several of the minorities excluded because of high rates of assimilation were also among the most modernized groups. Because modernization measures proved to be good predictors of fertility decline, the low recorded natality of these groups fits in very well with the pattern high modernization–low fertility. In other words, we excluded the six minorities from the fertility analysis on theoretical grounds, *not* because their inclusion would have weakened the overall statistical relationships discovered for the data set as a whole.

Index of total fertility

For all four data sets (republic, republic urban/rural, oblast, and nationality), we also computed indexes of overall fertility (If). The calculation requires the following data:

Number of births (B)

Number of women in each of seven five-year age groups

$W1 = 15$–19-year-olds

$W2 = 20$–24-year-olds

$W3 = 25$–29-year-olds

$W4 = 30$–34-year-olds

W5=35–39-year-olds
W6=40–44-year-olds
W7=45–49-year-olds

The index of overall fertility was computed, using a method similar to that developed by Ansley Coale, by multiplying the number of women in each age group by the analogous fertility rate from the Hutterite schedule.

Age group

	15–19	20–24	25–29	30–34	35–39	40–44	45–49
Fertility rate	0.300	0.550	0.502	0.447	0.357	0.222	0.061

These computations can be summarized as follows:

$H_1 = W_1 \times (0.300)$
$H_2 = W_2 \times (0.550)$
$H_3 = W_3 \times (0.502)$
$H_4 = W_4 \times (0.447)$
$H_5 = W_5 \times (0.357)$
$H_6 = W_6 \times (0.222)$
$H_7 = W_7 \times (0.061)$

The hypothetical number of births for Hutterite women (Bh) is derived by summing the results:

$Bh = H_1 + H_2 + H_3 + H_4 + H_5 + H_6 + H_7$

The index of overall fertility (If) is derived by dividing the reported births (B) by the hypothetical births (Bh); or,

$If = B/Bh$

For the republic data set, the required age data were reported in the 1959 and 1970 republic censuses, while the birth data were extracted from the relevant statistical series. To compute 1980 If, republic age data were taken from FDAD projections, with the birth data extracted from relevant published Soviet statistical materials.

The procedures used to generate indexes of overall fertility for the nationality data were similar. In this case, however, the Hutterite schedule had to be modified to generate a hypothetical estimate of the number of children born over a ten year period. The calculations were done as follows:*

---

*The appropriate multiplier in each case was computed from the Hutterite fertility schedule summarized above. In this case, however, each group's fertility experience

$$C1 = W1 \times (0.9)$$
$$C2 = W2 \times (3.15)$$
$$C3 = W3 \times (4.86)$$
$$C4 = W4 \times (4.95)$$
$$C5 = W5 \times (4.31)$$
$$C6 = W6 \times (3.35)$$
$$C7 = W7 \times (1.99)$$
$$C8 = W8 \times (0.749)$$
$$C9 = W9 \times (0.122)$$

Where $W1$ = women 15–19; $W2$ = women 20–24; $W3$ = women 25–29; $W4$ = women 30–34; $W5$ = women 35–39; $W6$ = women 40–44; $W7$ = women 45–49; $W8$ = women 50–54; and $W9$ = women 55–59.

The hypothetical number of children born over a ten year period for Hutterite women (Ch) is derived by summation:

$$Ch = C1 + C2 + C3 + C4 + C5 + C6 + C7 + C8 + C9$$

The index of overall fertility is then derived by dividing the reported number of children aged 0 through 9 (C) by the number of hypothetical children (Ch); or,

$$If = C/Ch$$

For 1959, the procedure was relatively straightforward. Children 0 to 9 are reported by nationality in the 1959 census. Females 20 to 59 are reported in five-year age groups. The only adjustment necessary was to estimate the number of 15–19-year-old women from the reported 10–19-year-old women. This was done by applying republic age structure data to each of the 15 titular nationalities, using the overall Soviet age structure values for the remaining groups.

For 1970, the data was less complete, and the necessary adjustments more complicated. First, as noted above, the available age data was not broken out by sex and was not provided in the needed five-year age groups. In order to estimate the number of women in each age group, we had to develop both age structure and sex estimates. We did this in two ways. For the 20–24-year-olds, for example, we calculated the proportion female in the analogous group 10 years earlier (the 10–19-year-olds) using 1959 census data. We

was aggregated over 10 years. In making these calculations, we assumed that women were equally distributed within each five year age group. The two additional age groups (50–54; 55–59) were included since these women were in the fertile ages for some portion of the previous ten years and hence were potential contributors to the supply of childen under age 10.

then multiplied this by the 1970 proportion of 20–24-year-olds in the 20–29-year-old group for each republic. This yielded one estimate of the proportion of 20–24-year-old females in the overall 20–29-year-old age group. We derived an alternate estimate by using the 1970 republic data alone. Each of these estimates was weighted equally to determine the estimated number of women aged 20 to 24 in 1970 – i.e.,

$$\text{Estimated number of females aged 20 to 24 in 1970} =$$
$$[0.5 \text{ (estimated proportion 1)} + 0.5 \text{ (estimated proportion 2)}]$$
$$\times \text{ reported number of 20–29-year-olds}$$

Analogous adjustments were made for the other age groups. The estimate of the number of 15-year-old females from the reported 11–15-year-olds was accomplished by applying republic age and sex ratios to the titular nationalities and the Soviet average for the other nationalities.

The calculations needed to produce the 1979 If estimates were more complex. First, estimates were derived for females in each relevant age group in 1970 and female survival ratios (computed from FDAD USSR rates) were applied to project them to 1970. For the 15–19-year-olds, for example, the 1970 6–10-year-old females were estimated using republic-specific age and sex structure data computed from FDAD material. The estimated number of females 6–10-years-old in 1970 was survived nine years to 1979 using USSR female survival ratios. Similar procedures were used to obtain the following female age groups in 1979: 20–24, 25–29, 30–34, 35–39, 40–44, 45–49, 50–54, and 55–59.

The estimation of the number of children 0–9-years-old was derived in two ways. In the first approach, the individual age groups reported in the 1970 census were simply survived 9 years to 1979, using age-specific USSR survival rates derived from FDAD USSR estimates. These numbers were aggregated to yield that portion of the 1979 population which survived the 9 years from 1970 to 1979. The difference between this number and the reported 1979 nationality population was assumed to be the children born between 1970 and 1979 (the 0–8-year-olds). To this was added an estimate of the 9-year-olds in 1979, to yield an estimate of the number of 0–9-year-olds in 1979.

A second, more precise, method involved first estimating separate male and female five-year age groups in 1970 and surviving to 1979 using more refined age and sex-specific USSR survival rates. This method produced a series of separate male and female estimates for 10–14, 15–19, 20–24, 25–29, 30–34, 35–39, 40–44, 45–49, 50–53, 54–58, 59–63, and 64–68. For the older age groups, it was necessary first to devise a method to break down the age 60 and over population into sex-specific five-year age groups. To do this, age and sex breakdowns for 49 years and over from the 1959 census were survived to 1970 (using USSR age and sex-specific survival rates from data provided by FDAD). These projections were used to disaggregate the single 60 and over number in the 1970 census into relevant age and sex groups: 60, 61–65, 66–70, 71–80, and 81 plus. Then, age and sex-specific survival rates were applied to these groups to project to 1979. This second method was used with those nationality groups with reported 1959 age data. The first method was used for those nationalities for whom 1959 age data was missing.

Methods for deriving both 1979 child-to-woman ratios and index of total fertility suffer from a common weakness – the assumption that the difference between the "survived" population in 1979 and the census reported 1979 population represent the number of births. The assumption that assimilation (changing of nationality identification) during the 9 year period is too small to produce a significant skewing of results is inappropriate. For reasons described above, there is sufficient evidence pointing to assimilation to warrant excluding six nationalities from the data set. In general, it should be pointed out that none of the 1979 natality measures for nationality groups is as well based as the 1959 and 1970 measures.

For the oblast data, the index of total fertility was computed several ways. For 1959, relevant age and sex data were available to insert into the general equations directly. For 1970, relevant age and sex data from the 1959 census were used to generate age and sex structure estimates for 1970. These were combined with 1970 republic age and sex structure data to generate estimates for 1970. For example, to estimate the number of females aged 15–19 of the reported 10–19-year-olds in 1970, the following procedures were used. First, the proportion of females of the 0–9-year-olds in 1959 was computed. This figure was used in conjunction with the proportion of females in the 10–19-year-old group for the republic in 1970. That is, the estimated proportion female of the 10–19-year-olds in 1970 is:

[0.5 (proportion female of 0–9-year-olds in that oblast in 1959)
+ 0.5 (proportion female 10–19-year-olds for that republic in 1970)]

This figure was multiplied by the proportion of 15–19-year-old families of the 10–19-year-old females in 1970 for the relevant republic. For those oblasts formed between 1959 and 1970 (for which 1959 age and sex structure data were not available), a simplified method, using only republic age and sex structure data, was used. The age structure data was used in two ways: with birth data to produce estimates of the ratio of total fertility and with data on the 0–9-year-old population to produce fertility indexes keyed to the child-to-women ratios. The estimation procedures described above to compute fertility indexes for the oblast data set introduce small, but unknowable, errors in the computations.

For the republic data set, an additional form of the index of total fertility was calculated, using the reported number of children ever born as reported in the 1979 census. The procedures used were analogous to those described above, but again, the Hutterite schedule had to be modified. In calculating the appropriate modifier, each group's fertility experience was aggregated over its entire childbearing period. We assumed that women were equally distributed within each five-year age group. These calculations yielded the following:

$$C_1 = W_1 * (0.9)$$
$$C_2 = W_2 * (3.15)$$
$$C_3 = W_3 * (5.756)$$
$$C_4 = W_4 * (8.101)$$
$$C_5 = W_5 * (10.066)$$
$$C_6 = W_6 * (11.446)$$
$$C_7 = W_7 * (12.073)$$
$$C_8 = W_8 * (12.195)$$

Where W_1 = women 15–19; W_2 = women 20–24; W_3 = women 25–29; W_4 = women 30–34; W_5 = women 35–39; W_6 = women 40–44; W_7 = women 45–49; and W_8 = women aged 50 and over.

The index of total fertility is then computed by dividing the reported number of children ever born (CB) (derived by multiplying children ever born by the number of women over age 15 as estimated by FDAD projections) by the hypothetical number of children (CBh); or,

$$If = CB/CBh$$

Estimates of the number of women in each age group were extracted from FDAD projections.

Marital fertility measures

One measure that we decided *not* to use is the index of marital fertility. This measure is the main focus of the Coale study of Russian fertility. Our decision not to make use of the Coale marital fertility data, or to employ similar procedures to generate our own estimates, requires additional explanation. One reason, as suggested in Chapter 1, is that the conceptual focus of our study was very different from that of the Coale team. We were interested more in the relationship between social variables and fertility than in charting fertility trends over time. Because some of the social factors, such as education, operate through age at first marriage, restricting the analysis to marital fertility would not have been appropriate. The second reason to focus on total, rather than marital, fertility has to do with data limitations. To compute the index of marital fertility, you need two series of data beyond those required to compute If. The first is female marital rates by five year age group. Such data are available for 1959 and 1970 for both nationality groups and republics, with separate data provided for the urban and rural portions of each republic. However, the appropriate tables for republics present separate data for 16–17-year-olds and 18–19-year-olds. Data for 15-year-olds are not provided. Moreover, marital data was not provided in any of the Soviet censuses for oblast level units. (In the 1959 census, data were provided for the total number of males and females in each oblast who were married.)

There are several alternate strategies for estimating marital rates by oblast. One is to simply assume that the proportion of women married in each age interval mirrors that in the republic. For 1959, these figures could be adjusted since the total number of women who are married (of all ages) can be calculated by oblast. The Coale team added their own refinements to this process in an effort to adjust for regional differences in the sex imbalances associated with World War II casualties. No matter what adjustment procedure is used, however, one is essentially working with estimates of marital patterns based on the republic data. The basic problem with this approach is that the republic marital pattern conceals huge regional and ethnic variation, as suggested by the data in Table 5. Some of this variation is due, as the Coale team notes, to differences in sex ratios. Some is due to cultural differences. There is simply no valid way to estimate the impact of these differences on oblast level marriage patterns without introducing a series of errors of large, but unknown, proportions. Female marital data by oblast are but one of the dozens of data series we would like to have but don't.

Estimation of 1970 marital patterns by oblast is even more weakly based, since the 1970 census does not provide data on the total number of males and females who are married, by oblast. The Coale team's 1970 oblast estimates were derived by adjusting their 1959 estimates by a factor derived from the observed statistical relationship between the 1959 and 1970 indexes at the republic level. This procedure fails to address the sources of error in the 1959 estimates and, lacking 1970 marital data by oblast, no bounding of the problem is possible.

The data constraints involved in estimating oblast marital patterns, significant as they are, pale in comparison to those involved in estimating illegitimacy. The number of illegitimate births is the second piece of data required to compute marital fertility. The Soviets have not published a data series of illegitimate births during the contemporary period at any level of analysis. How, then, can one go about estimating nonmarital fertility? The Coale team arbitrarily assumed that all births for 1940, 1959 and 1970 were legitimate. No material was presented to justify this incredibly heroic assumption. Indeed, the information that is available casts considerable doubt on its validity. Fragmentary data on illegitimacy for the USSR as a whole and for selected regions reveal that nonmarital fertility is substantial, and that both national and regional rates have varied considerably over time and by region. Estimates of the percentage of illegitimate births in the country as a whole in the late 1950s range from 14 to 20 per cent.[36] Illegitimacy apparently declined during the 1960s. Data on the number of illegitimate births in 1970 suggest a 10 per cent illegitimacy rate.[37] Soviet demographer M. Bednyy, writing in late 1983, noted that the illegitimate birth rate provided roughly 500,000 births per year, or roughly one in ten.[38] A legal monograph signed to press in May 1984 cited the same percentage (10 per cent).[39]

Illegitimacy rates apparently vary substantially by region. Illegitimacy rates are inversely related to the level of the overall birth rate, with the highest levels of illegitimate births occurring in areas such as the central RSFSR, the Ukraine, and the Baltic regions where the overall birth rate is low.[40] Illegitimacy in Belorussia reportedly held stable between 1965 and 1975 at about 7.4–7.9 per cent of all births.[41]

The nonmarital fertility rate for Belorussia in 1970 was 24.7, up from 14.5 in 1959.[42] In the RSFSR, illegitimate births in 1970 comprised 6.2 per cent of all births (5.6 per cent of urban births; 7.2 per cent of rural births). By 1978, the overall proportion of illegitimate births had increased to 11–12.5 per cent. The lowest illegitimacy rates (but not necessarily the least number of illegitimate births) are probably in the high fertility southern tier regions.

Furthermore, these republic figures conceal wide intrarepublic variations.[43] In Saratov oblast, 8.7 per cent of the 1969 births were illegitimate.[44] In the city of Novosibirsk, the percentage of illegitimate births declined from 22.8 in 1950 to 13.5 in 1959 to 11.7 in 1964. In the city of Perm, the illegitimacy rate decreased from 15 per cent in 1959 to 12.1 per cent in 1968.[45] By the late 1970s, illegitimacy was increasing in many regions of the RSFSR, but wide regional variations persisted. In Voronezh oblast, only 3.6 per cent of the urban and 5.6 per cent of the rural births were illegitimate.[46] In Leningrad, the share of illegitimate births in one study was 7 per cent.[47] In Perm and Irkutsk oblasts, by contrast, about one quarter of the rural children were born out of wedlock in the late 1970s, and 18.4 per cent of urban births in Irkutsk oblast were illegitimate.[48] In Tuvin ASSR, 21.5 per cent of the rural births and 18.9 per cent of the urban births were out of wedlock.[49] In Sverdlovsk and Kaliningrad oblasts, one of every six births was illegitimate. In the oblasts of the Central, Volga-Vyatka and Northwestern Economic regions, roughly 10 per cent of the registered births were illegitimate, with higher percentages in Siberia and the Far East.[50] In general, illegitimacy is higher in the rural areas (due to disproportions in the sex and age structure) and in regions with high migration.

How badly does illegitimacy affect the index of marital fertility? Let's take the example of Perm oblast. Assume that the illegitimacy rate of one in four applies to 1970. Assume further that Perm's rural marital pattern mirrors that of the RSFSR. The 46,941 births in Perm in 1970 will be allocated to the urban/rural breakdown for children under 10 as reported in the 1970 census. These assumptions yield a marital fertility rate of 88.3 per 1,000. However, if we arbitrarily (following Coale, *et al.*) consider all births to have been legitimate, the computed marital fertility rate is 117.7 per 1,000. In other words, the error introduced by assuming that all births were legitimate (when clearly a large minority were not) is on the order of

33 per cent. Similar results are obtained from analysis of illegitimate births in Belorussia.

In sum, the crucial assumption of the Coale team estimates – that all the births are legitimate (and, more importantly, that the illegitimacy rate is constant across regions) – introduces substantial error into their estimates of marital fertility. This assumption leads them to overstate marital fertility in regions with a high level of illegitimate births – i.e., areas that have high migration, significant sex or age imbalances, and either high or low overall fertility. The Coale team estimates of marital fertility are of only marginal value as a measure of real natality. There is no valid strategy for estimating illegitimacy rates, given the very fragmentary data available to us. We have opted, therefore, to focus our attention on measures of fertility (such as those discussed above) that can be calculated directly from reported Soviet data.

NOTES

1 *Narodnoye khozyaystvo SSSR v 1980g* (Moscow: Finansy i Statistika, 1981), pp. 12–17, 34.

2 *Kazakhskaya sovetskaya entsiklopediya* (Alma Ata: Glavnaya Redaktsiya Kazakhstkoy Sovetskoy Enstikklopedii, 1981), pp. 646–48, 656–57.

3 Ellen Jones and Fred W. Grupp, "Infant Mortality Trends in the Soviet Union," *Population and Development Review*, Vol. 9, No. 2, June 1983, pp. 213–46.

4 S. I. Imambayev, "Experiences in Lowering Infant Morbidity and Mortality in the City of Frunze," *Sovetskoye zdravookhraneniye kirgizii*, No. 5, 1968, pp. 25–29.

5 V. A. Makatova, "On Infant Mortality in Aktyubinsk Oblast," *Zdravookhraneneye kazakhstana*, No. 12, 1970, pp. 11–12. See also V. A. Makatova, "On Infant Mortality in Aktyubinsk," *Zdravookhraneniye Kazakhstana*, No. 10, 1971, pp. 7–9.

6 *Naseleniye SSSR. 1973, Statisticheskiy sbornik* (Moscow: Statistika, 1975), p. 141.

7 *Naseleniye SSSR. 1973*, 1975, p. 141.

8 B. M. Khromov and A. V. Sveshnikov, *Zdravookhraneniye leningrada* (Leningrad: Lenizdat, 1969), p. 185.

9 F. A. Gamidov, "Infant Mortality in Dagestan ASSR," *Zdravookhraneniye rossiysky federatsii*, No. 9, 1966, pp. 29–31.

10 Makatova, 1970.

11 O. M. Karryyev and N. I. Strygin, "Influence of the Level of Infant

Mortality on the Birthrate in Ashkhabad," *Zdravookhraneniye turk-menistana*, No. 10, 1971, pp. 42–45. Karryyev and Strygin make use of the concept of "useless" birth, which was suggested by S. N. Sokolova; they provide data for general birth rate and "useless" births for 1939, 1954, 1955, 1958, 1959, 1966, 1967, 1968, 1969, 1970. We used values – provided by Karryyev and Strygin – in an equation suggested by Sokolova in an earlier article: Rb=(Ro×Cd)/1,000, where Ro=general birth rate; Rb=useless births; and Cd=infant mortality. See N. S. Sokolova, "On the Influence of Infant Mortality on Birthrate Dynamics," *Sovetskoye zdravookhraneniye*, No. 8, 1967, pp. 33–37. Infant mortality estimated through these calculations reflect rounding error; for example,the calculated rate for 1970 is 31.3, the reported rate is 32.4 (about a 4 per cent difference). Nonetheless, the estimated rates provide a reliable portrait of general mortality trends in Ashkhabad.

12 *Naseleniye SSSR. 1973*, 1975, p. 141.
13 Khromov and Sveshnikov, 1969, p. 185.
14 N. A. Fetisova, "Analysis of the Dynamics of Lowering Infant Mortality in Voronezh," *Zdravookhraneniye rossiyskoy federatsii*, No. 2, 1970, pp. 26–27.
15 V. A. Nesterov and B. Kh. Bukrinskaya, "The Decline of Infant Mortality in Cities of Krasnodar Kray," *Sovetskoye zdrovookhraneniye*, No. 6, 1958, pp. 38–40.
16 Karyyev and Strygin, 1971.
17 Jones and Grupp, 1983.
18 Ansley J. Coale, Barbara A. Anderson, and Erna Harm, *Human Fertility in Russia Since the Nineteenth Century* (Princeton, New Jersey: Princeton University Press, 1979), p. 240.
19 Rasma Karklens, "A Note on 'Nationality' and 'Native Tongue' as Census Categories in 1979," *Soviet Studies*, Vol. 32, No. 3, July 1980, pp. 415–22.
20 P. G. Pod'yachikh, "Program and Basic Methodological Questions for the 1970 All Union Population Census," in G. M. Maksimov (ed.), *Vsesoyuzanaya perepis' naseleniya 1970 goda* (Moscow: Statistika, 1976), pp. 9–48. The strengths and weaknesses of the census questions, and the appropriate interpretation of the results derived from them, are carefully scrutinized by Soviet statistical and demographic officials. See, for example, the discussion and recommendations regarding the social and ethnic questions on the 1979 census at the 1977 All-union Convention of Statisticians. *Sovershenstvovaniye gosudarstvennoy statistiki na sovremennom etape*. *Materialy vsesoyuznogo soveshchaniya statistikov* (Moscow: Statistika, 1979), pp. 185–96, 214. See also I. Zinchenke, "Questions on Nationality and Language in the Program for the All-Union Population Census of 1979," *Vestnik statistiki*, No. 11, 1978, pp. 49–53.
21 *Vestnik statistiki*, No. 5, 1978, pp. 34–35.
22 "Polozheniye o passportnoy sistema v SSSR," 28 August 1974, *Sobraniye postanovleniyi SSSR*, No. 19, 1974, pp. 388–98. The relevant section is article 3. See also V. A. Gracheva, *Registratsiya aktov grazhdanskogo sostoyaniya ispolkomami poselkovykh, selskikh sovetov* (Moscow: Yuridicheskaya

Literatura, 1980), p. 34. This survey of passport procedure casts some doubt on the extent to which the comments made to Karklens by Soviet German refugees should be generalized to the rest of the population. Karklens' informants claimed, for example, that nationality changes are made "by those who want to get ahead and are hindered by their nationality." (Karklens, 1980.) Once nationality is recorded in the first passport, a change can be made legally only in the case of an error and establishing the error requires a court decision. Probably the easiest time to "change" nationality was during and immediately after World War II; the destruction of records would provide an opportunity for an ethnic German, for example, to claim Russian ethnicity. Illegal changes of nationality can also be made through bribes of court officials, but given the stringency of controls set up to limit passport changes, this is probably a relatively infrequent occurrence. On legal procedures for passport changes, see *Sobraniye postanovleniy pravitel'stva SSSR*, No. 2, 1977, pp. 18–29.

23 These figures were computed from data provided in *Itogi*, 1970, Vol. 7, pp. 272–73; and *Chislennost' i sostav naseleniya SSSR. Po dannym vsesoyuznoy perepisi naseleniya 1979 g.* (Moscow: Finansy i Statistika, 1984), pp. 284–85.

24 L. N. Terenteva, "Determination of National Identity Among Children of Interethnic Families," *Sovetskaya etnografiya*, No. 3, 1969, pp. 20–30.

25 A. M. Reshetov, "Ethnoconsolidating Processes in Soviet Central Asia and Kazakhstan," in *Etnograficheskiye aspekty izucheniya sovremennosti* (Leningrad: Nauka, 1980), pp. 74–84; and O. A. Gantskaya and L. N. Terenteva, "Interethnic Marriages and their Role in Ethnic Processes," in Yu. V. Bromley (ed.), *Sovremennyye etnicheskiye protsesy v SSSR* (Moscow: Nauka, 1977), pp. 460–83.

26 Yu. A. Yestigneyev, "Interethnic Marriages in the Several Cities of Northern Kazakhstan," *Vestnik moskovsogo universiteta*, No. 6, 1972, pp. 73–82.

27 Gantskaya and Terenteva, 1977.

28 Yu. V. Arutyunyan (ed.), *Opyt etnosotsiologicheskogo issledovaniya obraza zhizni. (Po materialam moldavskoy SSR)* (Moscow: Nauka, 1980), p. 82; and V. S. Zelenchuk and V. V. Chobanu, "Nationally-Mixed Marriages and the Development of the Rural Family in Moldavia," *Izvestiya akademii nauk moldavskoy SSR : Seriya obshchestvennykh nauk*. No. 2, 1980, pp. 53–59.

29 Terenteva, 1969.

30 Arutyunyan, 1980, p. 82.

31 Terenteva, 1969.

32 Ya. S. Smirnova, *Sem'ya i semeynyy byt narodov severnogo kavkaza* (Moscow: Nauka, 1983), pp. 244–45.

33 Gantskaya and Terenteva, 1977.

34 G. A. Sergeyeva and Ya. S. Smirnova, "To the Question of National Identity of Urban Youth," *Sovetskaya etnografiya*, No. 4, 1971, pp. 86–92; and Yu. A. Yestigneyev, "Interethnic Marriages in Makhachkale," *Sovetskaya etnografiya*, No. 4, 1971, pp. 80–85. A similar preference for Dagestani nationality among children of Dagestani–Russian parents was found in a study in Buynakske (Dagestan). P. B. Madiyeva, "On Several

Particulars of Bilingualism and Multilingualism in Dagestan," *Sotsial'no-etnicheskoye i kul'turnoye razvitiye gorodskogo naseleniya dagestana* (Makhach-kala: Dagestanskiy Filial AN SSSR, 1978), pp. 67–84.

35 Sergeyeva and Smirnova, 1971.

36 Rudolf Benninger, *Die sowjetische Gesetzgebung zur rechtlichen Stellung des nichtehelichen Kindes* (Berlin, 1977), pp. 88–89.

37 *Literaturnaya gazeta*, 7 January 1970, p. 12.

38 M. Bednyy, "The Illegitimate Child," *Meditsinskaya gazeta*, 9 September 1983, p. 4.

39 D. M. Chechot, *Brak, sem'ya, zakon: sotial'no-pravovyye ocherki* (Leningrad: Izdatel'stvo Leningradskogo Universiteta, 1984), p. 64.

40 Bednyy, 1983.

41 S. I. Golod, *Stabil'nost' sem'i: sostiologicheskiy i demograficheskiy aspekty* (Leningrad: Nauka, 1984), pp. 6–7.

42 K. K. Bazdyrev, *Yedinstvennyy rebenko* (Moscow: Finansy i Statistika, 1983), pp. 80, 82.

43 Bednyy, 1983.

44 Benninger, 1977.

45 V. Perevedenstev, "The Family: Yesterday, Today, Tomorrow," *Nash sovremennik*, No. 6, 1975, pp. 118–31. The data on Novosibirsk are on p. 127. The illegitimacy rate varies by age of the mother; 9 per cent of the births in 1966 to women 20–24-years-old in Perm were illegitimate, compared to 31 per cent for women aged 40 to 44. See M. Tolts, "Characteristics of Several Components of Birth Rate in Large Cities," in D. I. Valentey, *et al.* (eds.), *Demograficheskiy analiz rozhdayemosti* (Moscow, 1974), pp. 45–55. The Perm data do not include cases where parents register the marriage after the birth of the child. M. S. Bednyy, *Demograficheskoye faktory zdorov'ya* (Moscow: Finansy i Statistika, 1984), pp. 88–89.

46 N. A. Shneyderman, "Social-hygienic Factors of Fertility and Formation of Ablebodied Population in RSFSR," *Zdravookhraneniye rossiysky federatsii*, No. 1, 1982, pp. 25–28.

47 I. S. Kon, "On a Sociological Interpretation of Sexual Behavior," *Sotsiologicheskiye issledovaniye*, No. 2, 1982, pp. 113–22.

48 Bednyy, 1983.

49 Shneyderman, 1982.

50 Bednyy, 1983.

Index